Lillian's Diaries

Whispers from Galena's Past

edited by

Sheryl Trudgian Jones

ISBN: 1-4392-1235-X
ISBN-13: 9781439212356

Visit www.booksurge.com to order additional copies.

For my father
Lowell Donald Trudgian
12-2-1919 ~ 5-26-2008
Lillian's second cousin once removed

Introduction

In 1852 Joseph Trudgian and his second wife, Mary Thomas Pellymounter (my great-great grandparents) arrived in Illinois from St. Austell, Cornwall, England, with their children Joseph, Nicholas and Samuel. Two other children from Joseph's first marriage, Eliza (who later married William Tresidder) and William (who died in the Civil War in 1864) also made the journey to America.

The family purchased 160 acres from William and Phillippa Fiddick for the sum of six hundred and fifty-five dollars on what is now known as Stagecoach Trail just outside of the city of Galena, Illinois in Guilford Township. A barn was soon erected after their arrival - a landmark which is still standing and has been photographed and sketched by numerous enthusiasts of yesterday's rural structures such as the artist Carl Johnson. It is also rumored to be recorded in the Smithsonian Institute as an example of historical barns of America.

The family lived in that barn while their two story brick home was built. Soon two more children were added to the family; Thomas [my great grandfather] in 1855 and Charles, [Lillian's father] in 1856. On June 3, 1857, Joseph, the children's father, was struck by a tree while cutting it down and died. With the help of her sons, Mary was able to remain farming on the property until her death on September 3,1887. As Lillian began writing her first diary in 1913, her father, Charles Trudgian, was the only remaining child of Joseph and Mary who still lived on the 88 acres that remained of the original Trudgian property.

As a growing river port supported by a booming lead mining industry, Galena thrived. Originally named La Point, residents changed the town's name in 1826 to reflect its new status as a place of importance in the state of Illinois. In 1913 Lillian was sixteen, and Galena offered everything a family needed to live a comfortable life, including: churches, schools, a post office, railroads, merchants, doctors, dentists, parks, and an important American landmark – U.S. President Grant's home.

Her diaries offer a fascinating glimpse into this exciting period of time, detailing not only the "goings-on" of both the Trudgian and Dittmar families and their neighbors, but also highlighting many important historical events, including the beginning of prohibition and the start of World War I.

Lillian's diaries paint a word picture of what was happening in Galena area in the mid nineteen hundreds. She had a distinct personality and it is easy to identify with her sadness when her basket was the last chosen at a school social or to feel her joy when driving an automobile for the first time.

This edition of *Lillian's Diaries* represents the first seven years of Lillian's diaries. They are written exactly as she has written them with **her** spellings, punctuation and terminology. As a result my research there have been changes made to correct the spelling of surnames of some people and some towns. Tucked here and there among these diary pages are recipes, found in a series of little handwritten books in Lillian's kitchen. Some are handwritten on the backs of old calendar pages and scraps of paper, others are clipped from newspapers of days gone by. The handwritten jottings throughout the cookbooks are from the Sachs, Stauss and Trudgian families with the earliest dated 1880.

Lillian's People

For readers who are into genealogy, or those who just like to keep "who's who" straight as you read, below are the relatives and close neighbors mentioned in the diaries during the years 1913 thru 1919. The relationships indicated are correct as far as it has been possible to verify through searching multiple census, cemetery records and family history material. The relationship listed is that between Lillian and the particular person. While there are many more surnames mentioned throughout Lillian's diaries, these are the ones that are found over and over and that have a special relationship with Lillian.

Albert=Albert Weis[neighbor], Joseph & Mary Weis' 2nd son

Agnes=Agnes Tresidder[cousin-in-law], John Tresidder's wife

Alice=Alice Trudgian[cousin], Joseph Trudgian's daughter

Alvin=Alvin Trudgian[cousin], Thomas & Rachel Trudgian's 2nd son, Nancy[Hansen] Trudgian's husband

Anna=Anna Trudgian[cousin], Wilbur & Olive Trudgian's daughter, Wilbur & Alvin Trudgian's sister

Aunt Annie=Anna[Dittmar]Tippet, Amelia's Trudgian's sister, Edd Tippet's wife

Aunt Dora=Dora Dittmar, Ben Dittmar's wife

Aunt Lizzie=Elizabeth Dittmar, George Dittmar's wife

Aunt Lizzie T.=Elizabeth Trudgian, Nick Trudgian's wife

Aunt Lue=Louisa C. Dittmar, Henry Dittmar's wife

Aunt Maggie=Magaret Dittmar, Amelia Trudgian's sister

Aunt Rachel=Regina [Atz]C. Dittmar, Joseph Dittmar's wife

Aunt Rachel=Rachel[Kloth]Trudgian, Thomas Trudgian's wife

Aunt Tillie=Tillie Dittmar, Amelia Trudgian's sister

Bert=Bert Weis[neighbor]

Blanche=Blanche Tresidder[2nd cousin], John & Agnes Tresidder's daughter

Ethel=Ethel[Falconer]Tippet, Johnnie Tippet's wife

Evelyn=Evelyn Bastian[neighbor], Wilbur & Sarah Bastian's daughter

Father/Papa=Charles Trudgian, Amelia [Dittmar]Trudgian's husband

Fiedlers=Charles & Dorothy Fielder[neighbors]

Geraldine=Geraldine Trudgian[2nd cousin], Alvin & Nancy Trudgian's 1st daughter

Grandma=Mary[Winter]Dittmar, Amelia Trudgian's mother

Grandpa=John Dittmar, Amelia Trudgian's father

Helen=Helen Weis[neighbor], Joseph & Mary Weis' 2nd daughter [or niece]

John=John Tresidder[cousin] Agnes Tresidder's husband

John=John Weis[neighbor] Elizabeth Weis' husband

Johnnie=John Tippett [cousin-in-law], Uncle Edd Tippet's son from his 1st marriage

Josie=Josie Weis[neighbor], Joseph & Mary Weis' 1st daughter

L.S.=Leonard Stauss[future brother-in-law]

Martha=Martha[Westaby]Tippet, Win Tippet's wife

Mary=Mary Fiedler[neighbor], Charles & Dorothy Fiedler's daughter

Mayme=Mayme Weis [neighbor], Joseph& Mary Weis' daughter

Mother=Amelia[Dittmar]Trudgian, Charles Trudgian's wife

Milton=Milton Tresidder[2nd cousin], John & Agnes Tresidder's son

Nancy=Nancy[Hansen]Trudgian,[cousin-in-law], Alvin Trudgian's wife

Naomi=Naomi Dittmar [cousin] George & Elizabeth Dittmar's 4th daughter

Nick=Nick Weis[neighbor], John & Elizabeth Weis' son

Olive=Olive[Harrison]Trudgian,[cousin-in-law], Wilbur Trudgian's wife

Pearl=Pearl Dittmar {cousin] George & Elizabeth Dittmar's 2nd daughter

Ruby=Ora Ruby Trudgian, Lillian's older sister

Sadie=Sadie Dittmar {cousin] George & Elizabeth Dittmar's 3rd daughter

Uncle Ben=Ben Dittmar, Amelia Trudgian's brother, Dora Dittmar's husband

Uncle Dan=Daniel Dittmar, Amelia Trudgian's brother,

Uncle Erhard=Erhard Dittmar

Uncle Edd= Edward Tippet, Annie Tippet's husband

Uncle George=George Dittmar, Amelia Trudgian's brother, Elizabeth Dittmar's husband

Uncle Henry=Henry Winter

Uncle Henry=Henry Dittmar, Amelia Trudgian's brother, Louisa C. Dittmar's husband

Uncle Herman=Herman Dittmar, Amelia Trudgian's brother

Uncle Joe=Joseph Dittmar, Amelia Trudgian's brother, Regina Dittmar's husband

Uncle Joe T.=Joseph Trudgian, Charles Trudgian's brother, Alice Trudgian's father

Uncle Nick=Nicholas Trudgian. Charles Trudgian's brother, Lizzie Trudgian's husband

Uncle Thomas=Thomas Trudgian, Charles Trudgian's brother, Rachel Trudgian's husband

Vada=Vada Dittmar [cousin], Ben & Dora Dittmar's daughter

Wardie=Wardie Dittmar [cousin], Ben & Dora Dittmar's son

Wayne =Wayne Harrison Trudgian[2nd cousin], Wilbur & Olive Trudgian's 1st son

Weis=John & Mary Weis[neighbors]

Wesley=Wesley Dittmar[cousin] George & Elizabeth Dittmar's 1st son

Wilbur=Wilbur Trudgian[cousin], Thomas & Rachel Trudgian's 1st son, Olive
   Trudgian's husband

Willy=William Fiedler[neighbor], Charles & Dorothy Fiedler's 1st son

Win=Win Tippet, Martha Tippet's husband

Win=Win Tresidder

1913

Lillian Trudgian, circa early 1898

January

Wed 1: Papa, Mamma, Ruby & I went over to Tippets to the Ladies Aid Society. They had a very large crowd. There were one hundred and three or four there. The dinner consisted of three courses. They made thirty one dollars.

Thu 2: In the evening Ruby & I went down to Joseph A Weis' to a linen shower in honor of Clara. We went with Bert, Josie, & Helen Weis and Ida Bastian.

It was a regular dance. I was asked to dance but refused because I did not know how. A Shulty boy asked me. We gave her a pair of embroidered pillow cases that I embroidered. Clara got a pair of under drawers from Allie Genshirt. We got home at ten minutes after two in the morning. We came up from Weis' alone.

Fri 3:   It is a very nice day today.

Sat 4:   We did not go to town today. Several automobiles went along. I think it is rather late in the season for automobiles.

Sun 5:   It is snowing today. Ruby & Mamma went to church there was nobody there but Martha Tippet. They came home right away again.

Mon 6:   It is still snowing today. The kitchen chimney caught fire. We put it out in a short time.

Tue 7:   Well today is Jack Shulty's and Clara Weis' weding. It is snowing, Just awful. And all day too. Joe Shulty and Tillie Weis was groomsman and bridesmaid. They had a quiet wedding.

Wed 8:   Papa and Ruby went to Galena. Mama and I went as far as Aunt Annie's. Took my brown dress along to sew on it.

Thu 9: Papa went over to Shulty's and got two roosters this
afternoon. Papa is gone to the telephone meeting down
at Fattie Weis' this evening. Ruby is setting together
a nine patch quilt that we pieced when we were kids this
evening.

Fri 10: Papa went over to Virtue's to help kill a cow this forenoon.
This afternoon Papa went over to Bastian's and got a rooster.
We heard that Nick Weis and Annie Isbell are to be
married in about a week. A week from tonight will be
the basket sociable over to Miner's school. I hope that
we can get to go.

Sat 11: This morning papa went over to Arthur Bastian's
and got three roosters. We did not go to town today.
Well it will be preaching tomorrow in the forenoon. I
wonder if we will have any company tomorrow. I forgot
to mention before that parcel post went into effect Jan
1. We can now send parcels through the mail weighing
as high as eleven pounds.

Sun 12: Papa, Mamma, Ruby and I went to church this
morning. Mr. Collier said there would be quartly
meetings two weeks from today we will have preaching
in the morning afternoon and evening quite a day of
worship the elder is to be there afternoon and evening.
The preacher wants to have a sociable the Saturday

night before the quartly meeting after church we all went up to Uncle Edd's for dinner. My first ride on the sleigh this winter.

Mon 13: Papa went to town and got a load of corn. I was talking with Helen this evening she said they were going to have a sociable but did not know when. I hope we can get to go over to Miner's. I started to make my basket this evening.

Tue 14: We got a letter from Uncle Thomas this morning. Papa got a load of corn from town today.

Wed 15: It is warmer today. Mamma finished my brown dress today. Edd & Nick Weis got three roosters from us today. Today August Shultz and Bertha Genshirt are to married they are going to Charles City Iowa on their wedding trip.

Thu 16: It is warm and foggy today. It seemed just like spring. The snow about all melted today. Tomorrow night will be the basket sociable at Miners School. Wish I could go.

Fri 17: Well today we all went to Galena. The roads were awfully muddy. Mamma bought a new coat it is black. Ruby bought some goods for a dress. Would like to have it made for the church sociable if we have it. I was wishing I could go to the Miner's School sociable tonight but thought I could not go. Papa saw John

Tresidder in town he said we could go with them. So we bought a few things put in our baskets if we should go. We decided to go and we went down to John's. John was ready to go but Ida wasn't thinking to go but she got ready and went with us. She told Ruby she would have to let her eat with her. Ruby said she would. They had a fine programe. Will Weis bought Ruby's basket for sixty cents. Ida set aside until the last with another basket. After the rest was sold they were put up again. The other one was Miss Hart's basket it brought a quarter mine was put up last. Ehner Young bid a quarter and nobody else would bid so he got my basket. I had a good time. Ida, Will, Ruby & I came home together we came up from Weis' alone. We got home at twenty minutes after eleven. It was a very beautiful evening. Beautiful moon light.

Sat 18: Uncle Edd phoned down this forenoon and asked one of us to come up and stay with Aunt Annie today she isn't feeling very well. Ruby went up there and did her Saturday work. Mamma and I went to meet her in the evening. Johnnie brought her half way.

Sun 19: This forenoon Mamma went up to Aunt Annie's to get dinner because Byron Spencer was up there. Papa Ruby & I went to church there were twenty-five there without the preacher. They gave it up about having the sociable Saturday night but may have it some other

time. Mama staid up at Aunt Annie's so Uncle Edd
could go to church.

Mon 20: This morning I went up to Aunt Annie's. Old Mrs.
Tippet was up there to. In the afternoon Ida Bastian
and Clara Lenor came up there. In the evening Ida,
Agnes, Mrs. Eliza Bastian and Mrs. Will Lenor
came up here. There has been much talk latly of the
Illinois Central Railroad building a double track and
they expect to change the Route they expect to come
closer over this way than they are to make it straighter
from Scales Mound to Galena. They have been around
surveying. Today is Alvin Trudgian's birthday.

Tue 21: Well today Ruby went up to Aunt Annie's.

Wed 22: This morning Johnnie Tippet went out to Grandpa's to
get Aunt Maggie. Mama went up to Aunt Annie's
awhile this forenoon. Martha was there. This afternoon
mamma sewed on Ruby's dress. Ruby & I went up
church to get some lamps to fill and clean for Sunday
evening. When we got there Laura Bastian was there
she had swept the church. Ruby went over to Bastian's
and got some more water and then we washed all the
seats and most all the floor the church looks quite clean
now. I got a letter today from Pearl Dittmar of Idana
Kansas. Yesterday evening Helen said that they were
going to have their sociable the fourteenth of February.

Thu 23:   Last night it snowed this morning every thing was white it looked awfully pretty but it was so warm that quite a bit of it melted. Papa & Ruby went to town but they went in the back some people took sleighs. This afternoon I made some cookies. I saw Helen this evening she brought a dialogue along that they want me to be in I am to be Mrs. Marshall and Helen and Bernetta & Thelma are servants. I do not know if I will take it or not. She also brought a letter for me from Jeannette Werner she wants to visit the school tomorrow afternoon and she wants me to come up there to. She is better now. Only she said she was weak.

Fri 24:   I baked a cake this forenoon for Sunday. This afternoon Ruby and I went up to visit the school. When we got up near Fiedler's I heard a noise like an automobile I thought there would not be any automobiles when there was sleighing but turned around to look and sure enough there was one coming with one man in it he asked us to ride so we rode. They were surprised to see us come in an automobile. Jeannette was there she looks pretty well now but she looks pale. She looks about as fat in the face as she ever did but looks thiner on her body. They practiced their pieces a little while in the afternoon. I told her I would take the dialogue. When it was time to go home Mr. Werner brought up the sleigh to bring Jeannette home. She asked her father if he wouldn't leave Leo drive and they could bring us home he said yes so Jeanette, Leo, Walter & Raymond came along. They brought Helen, Vera, Ruby & I home.

Sat 25: There is not any news today we are baking tomorrow.

Sun 26: This morning Papa, Ruby, & I went to church in the sleigh. There wasn't many there. No body came home with us we was asked to dinner but did not go. In the afternoon Papa, Mamma, Ruby, & I went again. There wasn't many there this afternoon. Nobody from Council Hill or the Station. In the evening we all walked. It was the first time I never went to church here in the evening. There wasn't many there.

Mon 27: Mamma & I went up to Aunt Annie's this afternoon. Aunt Annie wasn't feeling very well yet.

Tue 28: We all went up to Scales Mound in the sleigh. We took a coop of chickens we did not have much room to sit. We heard the other day that John & Arthur Trudgian was back on a visit. Mamma & Papa went about the chickens and Ruby & I went up to Uncle Nick's. We met Arthur and Charles on the street I guess they wondered where we were coming from. Uncle Nick, Aunt Lizzie, & John were surprised to. They did not know if they would come down before they went home or not. John has sold out

all his stock and things and expects to go to Montana.
He is going to get married to a girl out in Dakota.
She is a german and is a catholic. We called to see
Mrs. Wilbur Tresidder. The oldest girl was sick. We
had supper at Uncle Nick's and then we came home.
When we went up to Scales Mound we could see where
they had surveyed for the rail road. It runs all along up
on the ridge from Pemperly's down as far as Walter
Combellick's woods.

Wed 29: This morning before Ruby & I were up the eye glass
man came. So Ruby & I had to stay in bed for a long
time. Mamma bought a pair of glasses for two dollars.
I talked with Helen but she did not know any news. We
said our dialogue over together. I am to go up school
Friday at about three oclock to practice our dialogue.

Thu 30: There isn't any news today. We got a letter from Uncle
Thomas. The stock sale is in Galena today and a lot of
teams went along. Papa went to town for a load of corn.

Fri 31: This afternoon I went up school to practice my dialogue.
We practiced it three times. We all know it pretty
good. Two weeks from tonight will be the sociable. I
wonder who will get my basket. They were going to
practice the play over to Amos Ford's tonight. It has
been awful cold today.

February

Sat 1: Papa went to town today he started out walking but got a ride. He sold the hogs for Monday. There is to be a play in Galena tonight called Madam Z. I would like to have went.

Sun 2: This afternoon we all went to church Ruby has a awful bad cold. It was awful cold today. We didn't have any company.

Mon 3: This morning Papa & John Tresidder took our hogs away. Ruby went up to Fiedler's awhile this afternoon.

Tue 4: It is quite cold today. Today is Nick Weis and Anna Isbell's wedding day they are to be married at nine oclock this morning. Will Weis and Bessie Allan are to be groomsman and Bridesmaid. Just the relatives are invited. Nick bought Rows Woods and they are going to live in Popp's house.

Wed 5: Well today is Ash Wednesday or the beginning of lent. It is just awful cold today. Uncle Edd, Aunt Annie, Mattie Tippet & Mrs. Win Tippet went over to James Spencer's to the Ladies Aid Society. Aunt Maggie came down here and stayed until they came back.

Thu 6: Papa took a load of oats up to Scales Mound to be ground. He didn't go up to Uncle Nick's. He heard that Arthur & John had gone back.

Fri 7: Papa & Ruby went to town today. Ruby had her tooth filled. Ruby brought me some red paper and some hearts to make my basket with. I made it this evening it is a square box covered with white crepe paper. I cut out small hearts and put on the edge of the lid. I put two hearts on each side of the basket and one large heart on the lid. The sociable is to be on Valentine's Day. Just think a week from tonight. I wonder who will get my basket.

Sat 8: I've got a awful bad cold. It is a lovely day today. I baked a cake. Tomorrow we will have forenoon preaching. I wonder if we will have any company.

Sun 9: Papa & Ruby went to church. I had to bad a cold to go. I have such a bad cough. Mama had an awful headache so she could not go. Uncle Edd, Aunt Annie & Aunt Maggie came down here to dinner.

Mon 10: It is cloudy today. Papa went to town to get a load of corn.

Tue 11: Today Uncle Edds hauled there hogs away. Papa did not help. In the afternoon Aunt Maggie called up

Weis and us and told us there was a run away team coming. She was down to Tippet's. They though it was either Will Weis' or John Tresidder's team because it was a white and dark horse. We saw it come down the hill but they came fast but they slowed down, down by Weis'. They started over the other side of Tippet's he had a seat high on the hog rack and he went to put on the brake he did that the seat came unhooked and he just about lost his balance and left the lines drop. The horses gave a jump and threw Will out. They then ran away. He did not get hurt. I made some of Ruby's basket tonight. It is white covered all over the sides with small red hearts that are all joined together.

Wed 12: Mamma went over to see Mrs. Irish Rob Virtue and little Pat this afternoon. I went up school to practice. They have practiced the play Fri night Mon night & Tue night but they are not going to tonight. Will and Josie Weis Warren Spencer Flossie Ford & Miss Garrity. The pop man brought out the pop and candy and peanuts. Just think day after tomorrow night.

Thu 13: Well today we are quite busy. ~~I baked two cakes.~~ I saw Helen this evening she said that they were going to put up the curtains this evening. Bessie Allan came out to Weis' ~~this evening~~ today. This evening they practiced the play.

Fri 14:   Well today we are quite busy. I baked two cakes. Papa, Mamma, Ruby and I went about a quarter after seven to the sociable there were quite a few there when we got there but a great many came afterwards. It was an awful big crowd. A lot of them had to stand. The bus came when the program was about through it was nice and quiet before they came but after they came you could hardly hear yourself think. They just about yelled their heads off. They started with the music at eight oclock. It was the Council Hill Orchestra which consisted of Minnie Merrifield, Paul Merrifield, Albert Williams & Fred Spencer. They had Werner's organ. It was good music. At half past eight they started with the speaking. The first dialogue was the Borrowing Piece by the whole school. Mertie Ford read the name of the pieces and by whom they were. She also helped to dress them for the dialogues. Our Servant Piece came off alright we did not make any mistakes. I wasn't so very scared. Thelma had on a Negro false face. We had it over again for them that came from Galena but they did not listen to it. Flossie sang a song alone. Miss Garrity played the organ. Albert Williams, Fred Spencer, & Flossie Ford sang several songs. Jeanette read kind of a rhyme that the teacher made up about all of the school children and Mertie and I. They had the play after the rest of the program. It was so noisy you could hardly hear what they were saying but they acted it just fine. Mr. Spencer sold the baskets. There was thirty-nine baskets. Mostly all of them had hearts on. The baskets did not go very high the highest was two dollars and I don't think any went below fifty cents. They wanted to buy an organ for the money. They thoughed they cleared about twenty-five dollars. ~~Archie White~~ Schoenhard got Ruby's basket. Lonnie Allan got mine. He is a brother to Bessie Allan. He drove out from Galena. He missed the bus. ~~Bob White~~ Keenan got Miss Lorraine Garrity's. ~~He was a brother to Ruby's fellow~~. The teacher's basket did not go any higher than anybody else's. Alvin Davis Jr. got Jeannette Werner's. Leo Werner got Mertie's. Walter Werner got Helen's. Raymond Spencer got Bernetta's. Charlie Ford got Ida Bastian's. Everybody had a hard time getting a seat some set with Mrs. Temperly and hold Dorine Davis' feet. He had to set on the desk. It was about one oclock or after when we got home we came home with Weis'.

Sat 15: I slept quite late this morning we all went to town. Mattie Tippet called up this morning and said we would not have any ~~chu~~ preaching tomorrow because the minister was sick. Aunt Annie is thinking to have the Ladies Aid Society Tuesday.

Sun 16: We did not know where to go today. So at last we decide we would go over to Popp's we did not know if they would be home or not but they were. Old Mrs. Young was there and Mr. & Mrs. John Wachter and little boy. We staid to supper.

Mon 17: I went up to Aunt Annie's this forenoon to help get ready for the Aid Society. She is going to have a supper. Mamma made the rolls & a cake, Mattie made two cakes & we made three cakes.

Tue 18: Mamma & Ruby went up to Aunt Annie's this forenoon I stayed home until this afternoon. It was awful muddy walking. When I stared to up the hill, Wilbur, Laura & Clifford Bastian came along in the buggy. They would have me ride. It was quite a load. It is awful warm just like spring. There were thirty-two there to supper. Papa, John Tresidder, Mr. Virtue and Vera came after they had done their chores. They staid for evening then. Mamie & Tillie Weis came up after supper. They made six dollars and seventy-five cents.

Wed 19: It is warm today and just awful muddy. We heard yesterday that Jesse Ford sold his farm to a fellow by the name of Trevethan.

Thu 20: Not much news today. We sent a letter to Uncle Thomas this morning.

Fri 21: It is snowing today. It is just awful windy. The stove pipe in the dining room caught fire we put it out right away I was scared to death.

Sat 22: It is still a snowing today. It is not quite so windy as yesterday. Today is Washington's birthday. No mail. It is to be a booster day in Galena today. But there is not many teams on the road today.

Sun 23: We all got ready to go to church, we hitched up in the sleigh. When we got between here and Weis' the runner came off of the sleigh and Papa had to come back again. The rest of us walked to church. We came home for dinner. In the afternoon I went sleigh riding I did not know what else to do with myself. I could go on the crust of the snow. In the evening we went down to John Tresidder's. Uncle Edd, Aunt Annie and Aunt Maggie was down there.

Mon 24: We washed today. We got a letter from Uncle Thomas today.

Tue 25: We butchered two hogs today. Uncle Edds butchered too.

Wed 26: John and Milton Tresidder was up here this afternoon. Not much news today.

Thu 27: Papa went to town today. Ruby and I went over to Irish Rob Virtue's. The baby's name is Elmer Benjamin. Mamma made the sausage today we have not done anything with the lard yet. Uncle Edds got through with their meat today.

Fri 28: This forenoon Papa went for a load of tailings at Dinsdale's mine. Mamma is grinding and rendering lard today. I baked some cookies but most of them got a failure.

March

Sat 1: We did not go to town today. Papa got another load of tailings this forenoon. This afternoon it stormed. It was just awful windy and snowing. We were afraid to have any fire. Mamma had some bread to bake, but thought she would wait until the sun went down to see if the wind would go down but it didn't it became worse. Mama put in the bread but it did not get baked very much. She left the coffee cake and saffron biscuits until tomorrow morning.

Sun 2: Mama bake the things this morning they got pretty good she put the bread in to bake some more but I guess it isn't fit to eat. Papa, Ruby & I went to church this afternoon. We walked there were twelve there without the minister. I wish somebody would come tonight.

Mon 3: Today Ruby & I went up to Aunt Annie's just for a visit. Mamma is frying down sausage today.

Tue 4: This forenoon Aunt Maggie came down. Aunt Annie came down this afternoon. Johnnie brought her down. They walked home this evening. Uncle Edd is thinking to take Aunt Maggie home tomorrow. They asked Mamma to go along. I don't know if she will go or not.

Wed 5: Uncle Edd & Aunt Annie, Aunt Maggie, & Mamma went out to grandpa's. Mama does not know if she will come home with Uncle Edds again or not. She took all her clothes along if she wanted to stay.

Thu 6: We got ready to go up to Scales Mound to the horse sale. It is just awful cold today. We got so much mail and we did not have much time to read it. In the Gazette in the Apple River items it said that grandpa had sold his farm to Uncle Joe. Papa & Ruby & I went up to Scales Mound we just about froze before we got there. Stella Graham and Elvin & Mamie Monnier and the two boy were there. It was Aunt Lizzie's birthday and it was kind of a surprise on her that so many came. Papa did not buy a horse. They all went high for what they were. It was about half past seven when we got home. Ruby called up Johnnie and asked if the folks got home yet. He said that they had called up and said that they would not be home until tomorrow.

Fri 7: I went down to John Tresidder's to get a pound of butter this afternoon. This evening Uncle Edd and Aunt Annie came home. Mamma did not come along. They said that she said that she might stay until next Wednesday. Uncle Edd said that Uncle Joe paid eighty-three dollars per acre for grandpa's farm. Uncle Joe bought all of the live stock and farm machinery. I suppose Uncle Joe will be getting married now. Grandpas don't know where they will go to live. Aunt Maggie & Aunt Tillie won't go to live up at Apple River. They have a house up at Apple River.

Sat 8:   Martha Tippet got sick this morning with palpatation of the heart. They had the doctor. She had an awful bad cold before. Johnnie Tippet went out to Westaby's to get Mary this afternoon they won't come home until tomorrow. Papa, Ruby and I went to town this afternoon. It is warm today and the snow all melted. When we started the creeks was quite high we were afraid the river would be high but it wasn't. There was a big crowd in town today.

Sun 9:   We went to church today this morning. There were not very many to church only ten without the minister. The minister taught Sunday school. We came home to dinner. We stayed home the rest of the day and nobody came to see us.

Mon 10:   There is not much new around here lately. We stayed home today.

Tue 11:   Ruby & I went up to Aunt Annie's this afternoon. Then Aunt Annie went over with us to Martha's she is quite weak. Mary Westaby was washing. Papa also

took the buck sheep to town. He sold him to Kasner.
He got four cents a pound or five dollars and thirty-two
cents. About seventy-five cents less and he paid for it.

Wed 12: Mamma called up this forenoon from Apple River
saying she was coming home on the noon train. She
said we could come to meet her to help carry the suit case.
Ruby and I went up on the hill we thought that when
we saw her coming we would go down over the hill we
took two cats ~~went~~ along with us. We waited for a awful
long time. We walked all over the ridge at last we saw
Mamma coming over by Young's. Mamma was down to
Woodbine and Elizabeth. Grandpas expect to move up
to Apple River Uncle Herman is going to work for Uncle
Joe.

Thu 13: Well today is the Ladies Aid Society over to Virtue's.
We washed this morning it is just awful muddy and looks
like rain sometimes. We hard time getting through the
mud. There were nineteen there. Mrs. Irish Rob &
Elmer Benjamin was over there. Everybody walked.
I guess it was to muddy to take a train out. When we
went home it started to rain. It rained just awful hard
in the night.

Fri 14: This morning quite a few of the clothes blew off and
got all muddy. Mamma had to wash again. I ironed
today. The mail carrier said the roads was just awful.

He did not go any farther than Fatty Weis'. I did not see any other teams than the mail carrier on the road today.

Sat 15: *It is colder today the roads are a little froze but the mail carrier did not go. It snowed some today.*

Sun 16: *It was a fine morning, but about noon it started to snow and storm like everything but we got ready to go to church anyway. In a little while it cleared up fine again. We all went to church. Their was not very many there. Sadie Young played the organ because there was no one else there to play. She wasn't ~~yous~~ use to the organ and couldn't make it go very good. Mr. & Mrs. Walter Combellick came to church it was the first time since they were married. I had not seen her before. I hope there will be more there next time they come. Uncle Edd asked Mamma to go up home with him from church. Aunt Annie wasn't feeling very well. Papa, Ruby & I went up in the evening. It is quite cold this evening.*

Mon 17: *This evening Helen brought me a letter from Jeannette she said that she was going to have a friend visit her this week by the name of Luella Brickner from out near Schapville and if I would be home Wednesday she and her friend would come down. I wrote a reply and will send it with Helen tomorrow morning. It is Saint*

Patrick's day we did not think of it until this evening. It is Josie Weis' birthday today.

Tue 18: It is just like spring today. We got fourty eggs today the most we got yet this year. I weighed today I weigh one hundred and thirty one pounds. The last time I weighed I weighed about one hundred and twenty six or seven pounds.

Wed 19: This afternoon noon Jeannette and Miss Brickner came over. They staid for supper. Jeannette had been visiting out to Brickner's and Smith's and they each gave a party in her honor. Jeannette said she had a fine time. It is very nice and warm today.

~~Thu 20:~~ This evening at eight oclock George Stauss and Sarah Ginn are to be married.

Thu 20: It is colder today. We got fifty eggs this evening.

Fri 21: Well today is the first day of spring but you wouldn't think so. When we got up this morning the ground was all white with snow. Papa & Mamma went to town the roads are quite bad. It is awful windy today. The snow was all drifted in places. Papa and Mamma had a hard time getting through some places, especially up by Uncle Edd's. Next Sunday is Easter. Today is Good Friday.

Sat 22:   Very few people went to town today. Uncle Edd had to shovel snow today. Up by his place and going up church way. We got a card saying that our freight is in Galena from Sears and Roebuck. Papa did not go after it. I don't know when the roads will be fit for him to go to get it. Ruby & I each got a postal card from Mamie Dittmar. I got one from Pearl Dittmar of Idana Kansas too. The preacher said last Sunday something about coming over this way and going over to Irish Rob Virtue's to christen the baby (Elmer Benjamin) we dressed up this afternoon we thought he might call in but Clayton Combellick came down to John Tresidder's after the mail and the preacher was along. Clayton took him over.

Sun 23:   Well today is Easter It is very early this year. I heard it is the earliest in 70 years. It is rainy this morning. It is to be forenoon preaching today. But it rained so much we did not go. I guess a great many people were disappointed because they could not go or wear their new things. Ruby & I went up to John Weis' hill to see if anybody was to church. We did not see anybody, but we saw a horse and buggy come up past Bastian and go past the church I guess it was Irish Rob I suppose he tool the preacher over or past way to the station. It rained all afternoon and about five oclock it thundered and lightening several times it would pass over and then another storm would come. When we were going to go to bed we look out doors. It was so dark that you could not see your hand if you put it right before your face. After we were in bed awhile it got lighter. It aught to have been real light because last night was full moon. Between twelve and one oclock I was awakened by the roar of an awful wind. It was just terrible. I thought any minute the house would tumble down. It was thundering and lightening too. It lightning seemed just awful, but the thunder wasn't so bad. But I never seen the wind so bad it was a regular cyclone. In just a few minutes the wind gradually went down. It rained awfully heavy too. It did not storm anymore that night but it rained.

Mon 24: This morning people were calling up each other to see if they were all right after the storm. We could hear a lot of cross talk. Everybody said it was an awful storm. John Weis' wind mill wheel got broke. Our mail carrier did not go today the river was so high. Nick & Anna Weis and Will Weis was in town and they could not come home. Nick & Anna came home in the afternoon but they had to come through by Hurbard Bastian's. The water was up to the Main Street in Galena. They got the mail out of the post office with skiffs. The water was up over the I.C. tracks and up to Marson's Gate. We heard they a cyclone in Omaha, Neb and other towns around and there is a great many killed and wounded. They also had it awfully bad in Chicago.

Tue 25: The mail carrier went today. In the paper it says they had a bad storm in Omaha about two hundred killed they think and a great many wounded. Some houses were blown down in Chicago two. We are quilting today the quilt grandma gave Mamma several year's ago. It is still cloudy today. I hope it will clear up soon. Ruby got a card from Wilbur with his and Chick's picture on it. I suppose they had it taken when Chick went out to South Dakota.

Wed 26: We are still quilting today. Papa went to town after our freight. The roads are awfully rough. Mrs. Seck's sale is today. Papa did not go. We got through quilting this evening.

Thu 27: There is a great flood in Ohio and Indiana we washed today.

Fri 28: We ironed today not much news today.

Sat 29: We did not go to town today. Ruby & I went up to Aunt Annie's this afternoon. Ruby went over to Martha's she took a coffee cake that Aunt Annie baked for her. We called in down to John Tresidder's for a pound of butter. We got a letter today from Uncle Thomas, Aunt Rachel & Anna. Aunt Rachel said she got a card from Mrs. Young saying that she was going to have the Aid Society this week. But I suppose as it was bad weather last week she will have it next Wednesday.

Sun 30: Uncle Edd & Aunt Annie came down to dinner today. This afternoon we all went to church. There were quite a few there today. There were twenty four without the preacher. Edd Young was there. He came back from Colorado to stay this summer. Sadie Young said they were going to have the Aid Society Wednesday. She asked Ruby to ask Mrs. John Weis and Anna. The preacher gave out today that Mr. & Mrs. Robert S. Virtue was taken in to the church Mr. by letter and Mrs. on faith. He also stated that he baptized the baby Sunday before and that because it was christened it was also taken in the church. (In that case we are members to.)

Mon 31: Well today is the last day of March. Mamma cut out and made a everyday skirt for Ruby. She also cut me out a drawers and I sewed it up. This afternoon Ruby & I went over to John Weis to see Anna Weis and tell them about the Aid Society. Josie came a little while after we came. Anna & Nick are going to move up in the Popp house soon. She sent for her wall paper today. The wanted us to stay for supper but we didn't.

April

Tue 1: Well today is April Fool's Day. I did not get fooled and did not try to fool anyone. Papa, Ruby, & I went to Galena. Papa wanted to get the plow. It is election day today. So there was quite a few in town today. I bought a new white waist today for a dollar sixty nine. It is pretty. It is teachers institute this week. Just as we got in by Stowe's Pearl Dittmar was standing there. She was just going to the institute we just talked a few minutes and Pearl had to go because it was getting late. We though maybe we would see her again after she got out but we didn't. It was just a beautiful day today.

Wed 2: Well today is Young's Aid Society. It isn't very nice weather this forenoon. But it looked better about noon. Mamma, Ruby and I went. There was quite a crowd there. There was about forty or more there. But some didn't go because it looked like rain. Mertie Ford was there ~~and her Mother, Lucille and I~~. She said Jeannette went down to the factory to pick out her piano today. It rained a little this afternoon just as they started to eat supper. But it cleared up again.

Thu 3: This afternoon Mrs. Fiedler, Mary & Raymond came down. Willie went to town with Mr. Fiedler. It has been kind of showery today. April showers bring May flowers.

Fri 4: It snowed a little today. But it melted as soon as it hit the ground. There's no news today. Ruby went down to John's and got two pounds of butter. It cleared up this evening.

Sat 5: It is a fine day today. We did not go to town. A few teams went along today. Helen & Bernetta were to take their central examination's today. They were to take them before but they were both sick and could not so Birkbeck put it off until today. It will be morning preaching tomorrow. I am writing this ten minutes to nine Sat evening. I guess I will have to go to bed now so I can get up to so I can go to church. "good night."

Sun 6: It is a lovely day today. Papa, Ruby & I went to church this forenoon. Mamma did not go because Mr. Irish Rob said last Sunday if it would have been a nice day Mrs. would come over here and stay. We thought maybe she would come today. When I was going to church I just about stepped on a snake. It was up in our woods. It is the second snake that I saw this season. There were quite a few to church today. There were twenty eight with the preacher. Mrs. Irish Rob and the baby were there. Tippets got stuck between the church and John Weis. John did not come to church he had to get out of the mud hole. Uncle Edds and Virtues drove around it. Mr. and Mrs. Robert S. Virtue and baby came down came down here to dinner. They staid to supper to. That is all the company we had today.

Mon 7: It is cloudy today. Mamma went up to Aunt Annie's & Martha's this afternoon. A pram went up past here I guess it is Jeannette's because she had botten one. She got a sheller. She bought it from Mrs. Jackson.

Tue 8: It is not a very nice day today. Uncle Ben came in to Uncle Edd's this morning. And then he and Uncle Edd went to Galena. Uncle Ben wanted to see Sup. Birkbeck some thing about the school. He got a petition to go into the Woodbine district and the people of Welsh hollow district is trying to keep him from it. He took Uncle Edd's team to go to town with. He told Aunt Annie that he was going home again today so we thought he would not come here. About half past three or so this afternoon I was playing on the organ and singing when I heard somebody come in the door. I looked and saw Uncle Ben standing there it scared me so. I could not say anything for a few minutes. He only stayed just a few minutes because he had to get home to do his chores. Aunt Annie phoned down and told us that Uncle Edd heard in town that the Jeweler House (the large hotel) over Dubuque had burned down and the block that the Jeweler was on was all burned. Helen brough a letter for me from Jeannette this evening she wants Ruby & I to come up there tomorrow afternoon because she got her new piano and two friends of her's are up there. Helen said they were Lizzie Smith & her sister. I have met Lizzie Smith before. We told Helen we would go if it was a nice day.

Wed 9:   It is raining today. Ruby & I did not go to Jeannette's it looked to much like rain. Helen did not even go to school. We wanted to wash every day this week but it has been such bad weather we didn't. I hope it will be nice tomorrow.

Thu 10:   It is still ~~raining~~ cloudy today.

Fri 11:   It is still cloudy today.

Sat 12:   Today we all went to town. The road are awful muddy. It turned out to be a fine day. There were lots of people in town today. I bought a new spring coat today it is kind of a tan. It is about three quarter length. I paid eleven dollars and a quarter for it. Ruby could not find any hat to suit her so she bought a cheap hat and some flowers and is going to trim it herself. The hats are all small this year and are all trimmed in red and blue. They look just horrible.

Sun 13: Well we all went to church this afternoon. There were not a great many there. Mrs. Fritz & Berdie were up there. It was the first time they were up to preaching. I wore my new coat today and my summer hat. We did not have any company today. It is just a beautiful day today. It is so warm I found some anemones today but there is only a few out yet.

Mon 14. Today we washed had a awfully large washing. I raked a piece of the lawn. Ruby took up some of the yellow rose bushes out here in the lawn and put them out by the back house and along the fence.

Tue 15: We ironed today. It is just a beautiful day today. But a little to hot. Papa is hauling manure today.

Wed 16: It is a nice day today. We cleaned the spare bed room up stairs today.

Thu 17: Papa & Ruby went to town today. We started to clean Ruby's room today.

Fri 18: We finished Ruby's rooms today. Papa is disking for oats today.

Sat 19: We finished with the oats today. Papa sewed and Ruby harrowed. This evening is school election. Joe Weis' time is out. He has had it for twenty-one years. They elected Alvin Davis for school director. Papa's time will be out next year. He will have had it fifteen years then Amos Ford had it eighteen years until last year.

Sun 20:   We all went to church this morning. We did not go any where to dinner and nobody did not come here. This afternoon Ruby & I went up to Jeannette's. They had company Miss Lily Brickner & Tony Gruby. They are going together. She is a sister to Luella Brickner. I like Jeanette's new piano. When we came home Jeannette came along as far as Spencer's hill to pick flowers. The anemones and blood roots are out.

Mon 21:   We made garden today we had made some before. Our line is crossed with the Bastian line and we get all their rings. Ruby & I got a letter from Anna today. The last letter she wrote something about going to the theater with Walter. When I wrote I asked what Walter's other name was and where he was from. She wrote today and said his name was Trash and that he weighs 235 pounds and is six feet tall. That he is a manager of an ice company and that he owns a motor boat. I would not like to go motoring with him for fear he sink the boat. I don't believe she means all she says.

Tue 22:   There isn't much news today.

Wed 23: It is ~~a nice day today~~ cloudy today. This evening Mamma Ruby & I sent up to Uncle Edd's

Thu 24: We are busy reading today because the Gazette came today. Well today is Papa and Mamma's silver wedding anniversary. They ought to have celebrated but there would be so many to invite, would not know where to begin or end.

Fri 25: Ruby & I put in a ~~some~~ few early potatoes today. It is a nice day today.

Sat 26: Well today it is Grant's birthday celebration. His birthday is on the 27 though. Quite a few teams went along. We all went in the carriage. There was an awful large crowd there. Former Senator Bailey of Texas gave a speech in Turner Hall we just went in to hear him a minute.

Sun 27: Today is quarterly meeting over at Council Hill today. We wanted to go but we were afraid we could not get up there with old Prince. We all went up to Uncle Edd for dinner. Mr. and Mrs. Robert Samuel Virtue and baby was there. Mattie & Mary Tippet was there to dinner to.

Mon 28: We cleaned the bed room down stairs today. Papa started to break sod. Uncle Jo was in Galena today to get his marriage license today Win Tippet saw him.

And he told Win what he was in there for. He said he was going to be married Wednesday. That is all we know.

Tue 29: We cleaned the parlor today. I started to cut the lawn today. It is quite hot today.

Wed 30: Well today is Uncle Joe's wedding day. I wonder when and where he got married. I guess it must have been a quiet affair. Miss Bernice Trevarthan was to marry a man by the name of Andrews from Hazel Green this evening. All of Frank Trevarthan went along here this evening. I was talking with Helen and Vera this evening. They said they were going to have a picnic up here last day. Helen showed me a violet that she had picked on the way home. I did not know that they were out yet. It has been a lovely day today. We washed today. Ruby has got the pink eye today. She started to get it in one eye yesterday. Papa is plowing sod today with Prince, Violet and the Big honey. I suppose grandpas will be moving up to Apple River soon. Well today is the last of April.

May

Thu 1: It is May Day and ascension day today. Some Catholics went to church. The rag peddler came around today. Mamma told him that she did not have the things ready. He said he would be around again tomorrow or next week.

Fri 2: It is quite warm today. An eye glass man called here today. I heard that Josie Weis went over to Dubuque today to pick out a piano. We got a letter from Uncle Thomas & Aunt Rachel today. The telephone line was out of order this forenoon. But is fixed again. Mamma churned a little butter today. The first of the season. It took a long time to churn. The plum trees & apple trees are out now. The apples are mostly in buds yet. I think about every tree in the orchard have blossoms but one small tree. Some seem to have so many on. Mamma baked bread and coffee cake today.

Sat 3: Papa and Mamma went to town today. Ruby & I went picking violets. Mrs. Collins called and got six dozen eggs for sitting.

" *Coffee Cake* " – handwritten in red ink & appears to be
by Miss Sophia Sachs born October 22, 1892

" 1 Cup Shurgar

1 Cup Maleses

1 Cup Butter

1 Cup Coffee

1 Cup Raisins

2 Eggs

2 teaspune Salartus

1 tea Simainans

1 Clove

1 Nutmak "

Sun 4:   It was raining this morning, but it stopped raining about time to go to church. Mamma and Ruby went. Ruby rode the pony horse back. She did not think there would be anybody there. But there were a few there. Papa and I stayed home. It rained about all afternoon. We had lettuce for dinner today. Mamma bought it yesterday.

Mon 5:   It rained about all day today. There's not much news.

Tue 6: We got a card from Chicago today it is from Uncle Joe. He said he and Regina were loyally entertained by friends. They went there on their wedding trip. I suppose they are seeing the wonderful sights. Aunt Annie got a card to. Edd Tressel died today noon. He is Fattie Weis' sister's husband. He had a cancer on his face every body was afraid of him. Laura Bastian is going to have the aid tomorrow.

Wed 7:
continued   Mamma, Ruby & I went to the Aid Society this afternoon. There were quite a few there. And there were quite a few that were not there. We had a pretty good time. Lottie Hocking was taken in as a member of the Aid Society.

Thu 8: I finished cutting the lawn today although that which I cut first is about ready to cut again. It says in the Gazette that Uncle Joe & Rachel were married up to Apple River at Uncle George's. And that they went to Chicago on the noon train. Mamma & Ruby cleaned the cellar today. They white washed it.

continued
Wed   As I forgot some I will start here again. Josie Weis was to the Aid Society today. They got a piano last Saturday. They went over to Dubuque and bought it Friday and Saturday they brought it over. It is a _____ . Josie said Miss. Garrity was coming down this evening and she asked Ruby & I to come down this evening to see the piano and as Miss Garrity

is a good player to hear it to. So Ruby and I went down. I think the piano is very pretty and has a pretty sound. Miss Garrity played for us. Miss Garrity, Josie, and Helen came up with us as far as the lawn. We had a fine time. Miss Garrity invited us to come to the school picnic. The last day is next Tuesday, but as it is on the thirteenth she did not if she would have it Tuesday or Wednesday.

Fri 9: There isn't much news today.

Sat 10: This afternoon Papa & Ruby & I went to Galena. There were quite a few people on town today. Mrs. Frank Trevarthan got a bunch of the women together that go to church up here. There were some cushions for church seats in a second hand store and she thought they would be nice for our church. They all went to look at them and as the door was locked they all had to look in the window. It must have been a picture.

Sun 11: Well this afternoon we all went to church. There was quite a crowd there. It is Mother's Day today there were quite a few flowers in the church. We heard at church that Tom Sheean was drown last night about six o'clock. They were over near Millbrig fishing. We heard that he slipped in or went in to get a fish and got in deep water. We heard that Mr. & Mrs. Shaneheart and a Mrs. Tom Sheean & Harry & Joe Trevarthan I do not know if Mrs. Joe Trevarthan was there or not. It seems awful sad. It is just two years ago in April that Dave was drown in the same river. And it has not been very long since Mr. Sheean died I think he died in September. Uncle Edd & Aunt Annie came down here after church. We saw the ambulance go down this evening. They took Tom over to Mary because it was pretty close. And they took him home today. Tom has not been married very long I guess not six months.

Mon 12: We heard that the funeral is to be Tuesday at ten oclock. We did not hear I the services are to be at the house or the church. We got a telephone message today the central had to talk she said that Miss Trudgian from Pennsylvania would be at our place tomorrow. We knew then it was Mrs. Barnum we had the dining room all torn up. She was about the last person in earth that I expected to come. We wanted to know if she really was coming so Mamma called up Uncle Nicks. It was them that had called us. She said that Mrs. Barnum was coming up to their place tomorrow on the two oclock train. She was not coming here then tomorrow. I was talking with Helen & Vera tonight. She said they put their picnic off until Wednesday on account of the funeral. She said that Tom was alive yet when they got him out of the water and that they sent for the Scales Mound doctor and that he did not get there for five hours. They say Mrs. Tom Sheean is in hysterics.

Tue 13:   Well we were all ready to go to the funeral but it rained and stormed so we could not go. I was awfully disappointed I would have liked to went so bad. The carriages all went along in the rain. This afternoon it looked brighter and Papa was bound that he would go to the Mound to see Mrs. Barnum so we started out. It was something to three when we left. We did our chores we thought we could stay until pretty late and come home by moon light. When we got a little way it got darker again. It rained some on the way up. We met quite a few of the carriages. They had stopped up the Mound for dinner. When we got up to Uncle Nick's, Ida was not there. She did not come on the two oclock train. She was going to stop off at Chicago. Aunt Lizzie read us the letter Ida had wrote her. It said that she was coming on the Great Western to Galena on the two oclock train and then to Scales Mound on the next train. Aunt Lizzie though she meant that she was coming at 2 oclock on the I.C. She went down to meet that train. Uncle Nick & Papa went down to meet the five oclock train. She and the baby came on that. Aunt Lizzie did not expect her on that train. The baby is nine months old and it name is Robert Trudgian Barnum. It is a great, great, great grand child of Daniel Boon. She said she though she would stay around until the second of June and then she is going to Colorado. Papa had not seen Ida for 25 years. So Ruby and I had not seen her before. Tom Sheean was brough to Scales Mound to the church Uncle Nicks did not go.

Wed 14: Well it is cold and cloudy today not a very good ~~time~~ day for the picnic. Ruby and I went. All the pupils were there but Alvin Davis and the outsiders were Mrs. Spencer, Flossie Ford, Pearl Ford, Jeanette Werner & Josie Weis Ruby & I. They had a nice dinner. I think there were nineteen there. We had a good time. The teacher came down here to get her order and Flossie Ford came along. After they were hear awhile it began to look like a storm but they did not notice it until it was nearly here. So we asked them to stay all night if it did not stop storming in a short time. So they said they would stay. They though that it might pass off and they could go home yet but it didn't. There were some awful flashes of lightning. Miss Garrity got awfully scared. It got lighter about ten oclock but it stormed quite a bit in the night.

Thu 15: This morning Papa took Miss Garrity & Flossie up as far as the school house. We washed today. I cut some lawn. We tore some paper off of the pantry. It is also reading day.

Fri 16: Mamma & I papered the ceiling of the pantry and seven strips on the side. Ruby & I cut quite a bit of the lawn today. Ruby also ironed. Papa went to town today to get some freight. It is a box of five hundred bee section boxes and some foundation comb also a brussel stair carpet and a rug for Uncle Joe for a wedding present. They are both quite pretty. The rug is to pretty to give away.

Sat 17:   We are awfully busy today. Mamma & I finished papering the pantry we wanted to get the carpet down in the dining room but we could not make we were so tired and had so many things to do. Ruby baked I finished cutting the lawn today. John Tresidder was up this evening to get his two hundred and fifty honey sections.

Sun 18:   Well this morning we all went to church. There were thirty there quite a crowd for up here. We had the new cushions to sit on today. Some are too long and some to short. The preacher wants to have a choir up here. He said we were to talk about it during the week. I am quite ancious to see it and I wonder who will be in it. Mrs. Virtue asked them that maybe we would come over in the afternoon. So we went quite a few people went visiting this afternoon. Mr. and Mrs. Irish Rob staid down to John's and Fiedlers went down there in the afternoon. Sadie Young was down there also. Josie and Helen Weis went down to Fattie's this afternoon.

Mon 19:   Mamma put down the dining room carpet today. Well we are all through house cleaning now. I am so glad. It rained this afternoon. We had four small radishes for dinner today our first we have been having green onions several times.

Tue 20:   It stormed awfully early this morning. It stormed for so long. There were such bad lightning and thunder I thought sure something would get struck yet. This afternoon Mamma ~~and~~ went up to Aunt Annie's. About five oclock it grew so dark it was dark enough to light a lamp. I thought it either was going to be an awful wind storm or hail. It was a windy for awhile. It rained awfully hard. It grew lighter after awhile. The creek was quite high. Mamma had to stay up to Aunt Annie's until after the storm. Aunt Annie said that they sheveried Uncle Joe last Friday night. Win Tippet went out to get Martha & Mrs. Westaby and he told them. It say in the Chicago Daily Journal in the state items that Thomas Sheean was downed in the Galena River while fishing.

Wed 21:   It has been cloudy all day today. Nick Weis stopped here and got a sitting of eggs today.

Thu 22:   Well it has been cloudy all day again. I hope it will be cleared up tomorrow ~~morn~~ We want to go to town but it looked so much like rain today. We washed some today.

I have been playing some with Boot today. Our little yellow kitten. It is to cute for anything. It is as good as a circus. We have quite a few cats just now seven old ones and Boots & three other kittens and some in under the porch. I do not know how many. If we could get at these that are under the porch we would drown them. Mamma has drown three sets of them already this year. And one of our black cats disappeared. It had been sick.

Fri 23: Well we all went to town today. Ruby got a new hat today. It is a plain hat with a plume on one side. The plume is white shaded light blue. The whole hat cost five and a half dollars. I had my hat fixed over. They lowered the crown and put some light blue and yellow ribbon on it. I got a new corset. It is a new style corset it is laced down the front and clasps down the side it is low busted. Ruby got the sick headache. We got an invitation to Anna's graduation today.

Sat 24: Well we were busy doing our Saturdays work today. We got postal card from Aunt Rachel this morning.

Sun 25: It is afternoon preaching today. Mr. Collier gave a sermon on "The World in Chicago." There is a great doings going on in Chicago and the preacher told us about it. The preacher's school is out and he isn't going back to Chicago this week. There were thirty-five out to church. It is quite a crowd. They had a choir today. It was composed of Laura Bastian as mucian. Martha Tippet, Lottie Bastian, Sadie Young and Alta Combellick. It rained quite hard this evening.

Mon 26: Well this morning it started out raining but this afternoon it cleared off. Papa took three calves over the station this morning. He got eight cents a pd for the calves or fifty-one dollars and twenty cents. It is Jeannette Werner's birthday today. She is seventeen years old.

Tue 27: This forenoon one of our hives of bees swarmed they lit on a plum tree and before papa could hive them they came back and went in the same hive that they came out of and before they had hardly went in the other hive swarmed. And lit on the plum about they same place that the other did. Papa sawed off the limb and put it before the hive and before they went it the other swarm came out again and went on the same bunch with the others. Most all of them went in again. About half past twelve or so we saw a man come walking across the field. We could not think who it was. Ruby and I ran in the hall. I was not dressed very good and I though if it was a stranger I would stay in there or else put on a different dress. Mamma hollered to us that it was Al. We came out pretty quick. He had walked over from the station. He surprised us all so. He isn't very well. He worked too long in the theater. He said he could not eat nor sleep anymore until he quit. He is looking thin.

Wed 28: Well Papa has been working all day with the bees and making supers. One of those swarms of bees came out of the hive again. Papa put them in another hive. A medicine man called here today Mr. Bowden. There was on here yesterday also. Al, Ruby & I weighed today. Ruby weighs one hundred and thirty-two. Al weighs one hundred and thirty and I weigh one hundred and twenty-five. There is not much difference between us three.

Thu 29: It is reading day today. This forenoon Al went away some where we did not know where. This evening Aunt Annie called down and said Al was up there he had been to town and over to Virtue's for dinner. He is going to stay up there all night.

Fri 30: It is decoration day today. We stared to plant corn today. We were to call up Uncle Nick's today to see if Ida's baby was better they would come down tomorrow but the telephone line is out of order. I went up the road and down but could not find it.

Sat 31: Mama went over the telephone line and found it tangled over by John Weis'. Papa went up after them this afternoon. It was about seven oclock when they got here. They went in up to Fiedler's. Ida wanted to see the old place. Uncle Nick and Aunt Lizzie came along.

June

Sun 1: John Agnes & Milton came up here before we had our breakfast. Then they went to church this forenoon. Ruby & I went to. Uncle Nick & Ida took a walk up in the woods with us. The rest did not go to church because they thought that they could not get ready to go to Galena in time. Ida was to go about three oclock. Uncle Nicks were going home on the ~~three~~ five oclock. Ida went down to the junction and then went on that train to Colorado. Uncle Edd & Aunt Annie came down after church to dinner. There were quite a few to church today twenty-eight I think.

Mon 2: Well today Ruby & I are packing up our clothes to go to Waterloo. We sent a letter to Uncle Thomas saying we were coming on the evening train. ~~It gets out there~~

Tue 3: Papa & Mamma took us to Galena to this morning we went on the something after two train. Ruby and I copied from a book written in Waterloo on our way to Waterloo. It is a beautiful day. Our train is a long one. We started from Galena on the two fourty-five train. There was not very many in our coach until we got to Dubuque. We saw Epworth Seminary. We got out here all right. It was a quarter after seven. It was the right time. Uncle Thomas and Wilbur were to the depot to meet us. Walter Trask was here this evening (Anna's fellow) he is six feet tall and weighs two hundred and thirty-five pounds. Anna was not in the play tonight so none of us went.

Wed 4: This afternoon Uncle Thomas took us downtown. We went into the ten cent store and into the Lyric Theater where Al worked. We also rode around the Loop on the street car. It is a long way around. This evening Anna, Ruby & I went walking in a park beside the Cedar River. It is Lafayette Park and from there we walked through a grave yard.

Thu 5: This morning Uncle Thomas and I went over to Hursts right across the street. I saw a big cat over there that I wanted to see. It is a Persian cat and is awfully large and has a large bushy tail. Its fur is quite long. This forenoon Uncle Thomas took us over the town. We saw some very fine houses. The High School that Anna goes to. We saw and walked around the Catholic hospital it is very large. It cost a half million dollars. When we came back Ruby and I went into a library. Uncle Thomas bought and gave me a beautiful little pocket book with a chain to put around my neck. It is just about exactly like one Anna got for a graduation present. This evening we went to the graduation. Smith came so Ruby & Smith went

together and I and Wilbur. Fourty one graduated.
There was quite a crowd there.

Fri 6:   This morning Anna went with us downtown. I bought
a dress and Ruby bought a white waist for Mamma.
Ruby saw a pretty silk under skirt there that she liked.
But did not buy it. Afterward Anna went down again
and bought it and gave it to Ruby. This afternoon
Mrs. Corey came and brought Anna a present of a
bar pin. She only staid a few minutes.

Sat 7:   Ruby & I went down to the market with Uncle
Thomas this morning. This afternoon Anna, Ruby
& I went over to the west side. We rode on the street
car. We went to the Pres. Hospital and was shown
through it. Then we walked to Mrs. Corey's. Mrs.
Corey showed us through her house. It is a fine house.
I fell down a part of the stairs. Margery would not
rest she must take our picture. So Anna Ruby &
I had our picture taken. We walked home we went
through Washington Park. This evening Wilbur went
downtown. Aunt Rachel wanted him & Smith to
take us to the Majestic (theater) this evening. Wilbur
said he did not know if he would come up any more
or not. It got pretty late and they wanted us to go
down town on Saturday night so Uncle Thomas took
us down. There were lots of people down town. We
went in several large stores. We got home after nine

oclock. They said that Wilbur & Smith was up just a short time ago to take us to the theater and that they had gone down again thinking they would probably see us. They would have come up sooner but Smith did not get there until late.

Sun 8: This morning before some of us had breakfast Smith came. Wilbur & Smith went fishing. The rest of us went to church. We went to the Grace Methodist church. It was children's day. When we got home Wilbur was cleaning fish. In the afternoon Uncle Thomas and Ruby & I went to Lafayette park and through the grave yard. When we got home Mrs. Corey & daughter was there. They staid to supper. Smith also came to supper. We tried to get Wilbur & Smith to go to church but would not. Smith said he would go but had to get a pass to go to Laport where he is working. Mr. Trask came and went to church with us.

Mon 9: Ruby & I went down town this morning. This afternoon Anna, Ruby & I went to the Majestic. They had a lot of trained birds there which was very nice. This evening Wilbur took Anna, Ruby & I to electric park. There was a large crowd there. We went to the theater first. Just before we went home Wilbur gave us a ride on the roller coaster. Oh I was never so scared in my life. I nearly fainted. We sat in the hind car. Anna & Ruby in the front seat and Wilbur and

I in the back seat. ~~We rode as far as~~ It takes fourty-five seconds to go around the thing. You go straight up and then just drop down and then go up again and down again and all so fast you can hardly catch your breath. We rode as far as we could home on the street car. We rode on the first seat on the last trailer. We got home at five to ten.

Tue 10: We got up some where around five oclock and got ready to go home on the seven oclock train. Uncle Thomas & Anna went down to the depot with us. It did not seem so long to me coming home as going out. But it seemed a long way from Dubuque to Galena. Ruby sent a letter to Pa and Ma yesterday so they would only get it today a few hours before we got home. There was nobody at the depot to meet us. We did not expect anyone. We got to Galena at about half past eleven. ~~We hardly expected any on~~ We carried our truck up to Stauss' we tried to phone home. But the line was out of order. After awhile Ruby & I stated to walk home. When we got over by Seck's Joe Weis & Bert came along and gave us a ride. They thought at home that we wasn't coming until evening because we did not phone out. Papa was just going to start to get ready to go after us.

Wed 11: The strawberries and cherries are starting to get ripe.

Tue 12: Al went out on the telephone line today. We washed today.

Fri 13: Papa & Al went out to work roads today. We ironed today.

Sat 14: Papa & Al went to town today. Al went up to Scales Mound. Papa brought home the seperator Uncle Thomas' Ours is wore out. Aunt Annie & Uncle Edd went out to Uncle Ben's today.

Sun 15: We all went to church this morning. There was not so many there as usual. We did not go anywhere nor did anybody come here for dinner. This afternoon Agnes, Ida & Milton came up & staid to supper.

Mon 16: We picked and put up cherries today. They are working roads near here today. This evening Mamma, Ruby & I went up to Aunt Annie's.

Tue. 17: We put up the rest of the cherries today. We put up ten and one-half quarts all together. They are working roads near here again today. They had a case of beer today.

Wed 18: This morning Mamma & I and Aunt Annie went to Dubuque. Johnnie took us to Galena. We went something after nine. We rode from the E Dubuque depot to Rasheck's store in the automobile bus.

Aunt Annie bought a hat & dress, Mamma bought a hat & dress and. I bought a dress and one for Ruby. They are just alike color. We paid four dollars and ninety-eight cents apiece for them. There was a fire there while we were over there. We saw the fire engines going. We walked over to East Dubuque and came home on the train that starts from over there at four fifteen. Mattie & Grace Tippet were to come this evening too. So they wanted to wait until they came to meet them. They came on the flyer. Byron Spencer got off on that to so rode home with us. Johnnie brought us all the way home.

Thu 19: We are washing today and it is also reading day. This evening Papa & Ruby went up to Council Hill to church. They are having meetings up there. They took the ponies in the buggy.

Fri 20: It is ironing day today. Papa & Ruby went to town today.

Sat 21: I am fixing our dresses today. There is not much news around here lately.

Sun 22: This afternoon we all went to church. Mr. Clark preached today while Mr. Collier went to preach at his charge. Some where up in Wisconsin. His wife was along to. There was quite a crowd there. There was thirty-one.

Mon 23: Al came home this evening he walked out from Galena.

Tue 24: Al started to paint the cow house. Papa is plowing corn.

Wed 25: Mamma, Ruby & I went to the Aid Society over to Mrs. Joseph Dower's. They had quite a large crowd. They have a nice new house. They had strawberries for supper.

Thu 26: This afternoon Papa took Mamma to town to go to Apple River. Aunt Annie went too. Mattie & Grace Tippet went to Apple River to. It is the last night of the meetings up to Council Hill. I would like to have gone. But could not. They are going to have choir practice up church tonight also. So women in Ill. can vote now. Today Gov. Dunne signed the women suffrage bill. Oh joy, votes for women.

Fri 27: Papa & Al are working on the shed today. Are getting some posts put up. It is just awful hot today. Ruby & I are quite busy. Are cutting lawn today.

Sat 28: We did not go to town today. Mamma came home with Uncle Edd & Aunt Annie. Mamma, Aunt Lizzie, & Aunt Maggie went out to see Mrs. Wilbur Tresidder while she was out there. It is awfully hot today.

Sun 29: This morning Mamma Ruby & I went to church. Papa did not go because he did not feel very good because it was so hot. We tried to get Al to go to church but he would not. He took his baseball glove and went up the road. There were twenty-six to church today. Irish Rob Virtue asked us to come over to dinner. Mrs. staid home to get dinner but she thought it was to hot to bring the baby anyway. So Mamma rode over with him and Ruby & I came home and got Papa and then went over. Al did not come home until tonight he had been down to John's to supper and he had been up to Engle's and over to Gillford playing ball.

Mon 30: Papa & Al are still working at the shed. Mamma and Ruby went up in the wood this forenoon and picked raspberries. It was enough for supper tonight and a quart and a half. It stormed and rained this afternoon. It was a fine rain. We needed it.

July

Tue 1: Well today is the first of July. Papa took two dozen hens to town today. They are buying in there today. Al painted the cow house and hay shed the second time today. This evening Agnes, Ida & Milton came up they took home poor no name and her four poor little kittens. Poor old cat.

Wed 2: Al finished painting the cow house and hay shed and did almost one side of the barn. It is all of the paint now so he can't paint anymore until dad gets some more. This after the minister called. He is talking about having a Sunday school picnic for all three charges. But haven't decided on the time yet. He also was after Mamma, Ruby & I to join the church.

Thu 3: Well it is getting very near the fourth. Probably Papa and I will go to Apple River. Al went to Galena this afternoon. From there he is going up to Scales Mound. He is to play ball up the Mound and had to be there at nine oclock. He said that he may go down to Apple River from there on the train and take in both celebrations. Mamma went ~~Uncle~~ up to Aunt Annie's to help clean house. I wonder what I will be doing tomorrow at this time (about five minutes to three). The way it looks today I am afraid it will rain tomorrow at least I hope not.

Fri 4:   Well this morning we decide to go to Apple River. Papa & I Uncle Edd and Aunt Annie are going to. Johnnie took us over we went through by Young's. There was quite a crowd over the station to go on the train. Almost all went to Apple River. Some of those that went from the station were Mr. and Mrs. Arthur Bastian and son Laura Bastian. Ben Young, Elmer Young & Lottie Bastian, Paul Merrifield, Minnie Merrifield and a lot of them that I didn't know. The train was a little late. The band was at the depot to meet the train. Grandpa & Aunt Tillie were there to meet us. We all had dinner down to Grandpa's after dinner we all went up to the park. There was a large crowd at Apple River. There were so many people their that I knew. I met quite a few people. Uncle Herman and Uncle Joe came up. Aunt Rachel did not come. She wanted to stay home & do the chores. We were to Grandpa's for supper. Uncle Edd staid at Uncle George's, Ada Grebner & Mrs. Schlichting and the two girls were at Grandpa's to supper. After supper I went up town with the Schlichting girls and Ada Grebner. It was the first time that I met the Schlichting girls. The youngest Schlichting girl and I went walking about all over town. We found the other girls and went around with them for awhile. They met two fellows and they then walked around with us. The oldest Schlichting girl and I and a fellow & the youngest Schlichting girl and Ada Grebner. The didn't give me no introducing to them. I did not want to go around with them because I did not know who they were after awhile. Ada Grebner & the youngest Schlichting girl went off and us two girls were left with the two fellows. I did not want to go around alone with a fellow I did not know. So when we met Aunt Annie and some of the rest I went with them then. Aunt Tillie said one was the Schlichting girl's cousin but she did not know who the other was. We then went up the park & saw the fire works rode on the merry-go-round and staid up there until quite late. We then went down the store for awhile. Oh I forgot something. On our way down we went into the hall to watch them dance. I did not see her but Aunt Tillie said Alto Combellick was dancing. Combellicks and Grebners drove out. Ada Grebner & Hannah Wenzel rode home with Uncle Herman. I met Mr. Bunker (Pearl's beau) out at the park tonight. Al came from Scales Mound on the five oclock & went to Galena again on the half-past nine. Aunt Tillie & I slept together.

Sat 5: At about three oclock this morning there was a storm we all got up for awhile. All but Papa. Uncle Edd &

Aunt Annie staid all night at Uncle George's. At This forenoon Papa & I went up to Uncle George's. We then went up the stores. Papa & I staid at Uncle George's for dinner. We all came home on the two oclock. Papa got off at the station the rest of us went to Galena. Mr. and Mrs. Ray Stevens and baby got on at Scales Mound and went to the station. Effie asked us to come over. I rode out with Uncle Edd's got home at twenty minutes to eight.

(What happened at home while we were gone)
At three oclock this morning just after the storm, Mamma & Ruby were awakened by a man hollering right down under their windows. They did not answer him. They thought that he might be drunk. He yelled Hello there and whistled for a long time and he then went around a shook the screen door. They had it hooked and he shook it until it come unhooked. He wanted to wake somebody up. At last he went away. He had a lantern. Mamma & Ruby watched him he went up the road and went into Fiedler's and then after awhile he went up the school house hill. Mamma & Ruby did not sleep anymore. After it got day light they went down the road and saw his tracks going up the road. They thought that he may have had a rig or that there may have been some more. But there was just his tracks. Mamma called up Mrs. Fiedler she said it was

a man that his horse had got away and wanted a horse to ride. We heard afterwards that it was a Breed that works up near the Mound. He was sleeping and let the lines drop & his horse ran away. If it went up past here it must have went before the rain. I don't know if he was drunk or not, but I suppose so. He got a lantern and a umbrella from Weis. At five oclock this morning Mamma went to the end of the porch and saw a ballon coming over by John Weis' little mound. It was a little cloudy and at time they could not see it because it went under the clouds. They could see a man in it. They said it looked like a birds. He looked so small. It came over and went over our woods going northeast. One came over Henry Hinkman's and they had a rope dragging along it caught in the telephone line and tore it up and caught in the fence and tore out a corner post that was braced on both sides. It went over Galena. I don't know if it were the same one that went over her or not. I heard some one say that they thought it circled around and that maybe it was the same one. In the today paper it said that nine was to start from Kansas City. So this were them. Youngs saw the one that went over here. They said that there were two men in it.

Sun 6:   Well today is afternoon preaching we hitched up to the carriage and went. There was quite a few there. After church we drove over the grave yard. Al came home this evening. He was in to Horning's. He brought him out in the automobile.

forgot Mon.

Tue 8:   Papa went to town this afternoon. It came to a storm about six oclock. Papa was not home yet. He went into Tippet's. Then again later in the night there was another bad storm.

Mon 7:   This forenoon I heard something on the porch and looked out and Willie Fiedler was out there. He had come down by him self for the first time. He staid until about half past ten. Mamma went up the road to look for some raspberries. Mr. & Mrs. Fiedler were haying on the field that joins us. They hollered and asked Mamma if Willie was down here. They did not know where he was. In the afternoon Mamma & I went up to the wood to pick raspberries & gooseberries and I came home before mother. I heard some hollering going on down here. It was Willie & Mary Fiedler. We thought maybe that they run away. They had been here quite awhile so Ruby told them that they had better go home so took them down the road and started them home. In a little while they were down here again. After awhile Mrs. Fiedler phoned down and wanted to know if they were here. They had run away. and told me to send them home. I sent them home.

Wed 9: We washed today. Papa started to cut hay today. He cut the little patch down the bottom and a little in the hay field.

Thu 10: Well today is a fine day. Had applesauce for the first time today. Papa & Al hauled two loads of hay in late this afternoon. The telephone line is out of order so don't know much news.

Fri 11: We hauled in four loads of hay this forenoon. I led the horse. Had carrots for dinner the first time this season. Al went down to John's to help haul hay this afternoon. I was up looking at the bees when one came around and got tangled in my hair. I grabbed the bee in my apron and killed it. It stung me. Ouch but it hurt for awhile. It rained this after.

Sat 12: We did not go to town today. They cut off a big piece of hay today. My forehead and the bridge of my nose is swelled. I look horrid. Hope it will be better for tomorrow.

Sun 13: My nose & forehead is still swollen. I did not go to church this forenoon. Papa Ruby & Mama went to church. I staid home alone. Al went off. Laura

Bastian came down from church to dinner & staid to supper. We did not have any other company.

Mon 14: This afternoon John Tresidder came up to help hay. We hauled with two teams. I led the horses. We got twelve load in the shed now all together. Willie Fiedler was down this forenoon and afternoon. Had to send him home.

Tue 15: Ruby got a birthday post card from Jeannette Werner this morning. Papa & Ruby went to Galena. Al cut hay this morning. This afternoon went down to John's. Papa went down after he came home from town.

Wed 16: Not much news around here lately. Helen called me up and said she had the girls to the club either today or tomorrow. But they did not come today. We hauled hay today.

Thu 17: Well today is reading day. The girls did not go down to Weis' today. I guess they are to busy. Ruby & I went up to Aunt Annie's this afternoon. But there was no one at home. We went over to Martha's and she wasn't home so we had to come home.

Fri 18: We hauled hay again today. This evening Aunt Annie phoned down and said that mamma should go down the road that there was an automobile coming. That it was Louie Weis and Mrs. Margaret and five children and they are going out to Uncle George's. They came from Independence, Iowa today. Mama talked with them for a little while.

Sat 19: Papa, Mamma, Ruby, Al & I went to Galena this afternoon for a half holiday. There were quite a few people in town today. Al staid in.

Sun 20: This afternoon we all went to church. They put it to a vote about a picnic. They all seemed to want it. The preacher and Martha Westaby Tippet wants it to. There were quite a few to church today. About twenty-seven or twenty-eight. Uncle Edd and Aunt Anne came down here to supper. Al did not get home until tonight at after ten.

Mon 21: Mamma, Ruby & I went picking blackberries. Got about a bucket full. We put up seven quarts and made a little jelly. This was the first picking ~~unless~~ but enough for a couple of pies. This afternoon Ruby & I went over to Ford's to see Elfie Stephens. She was at home. They were quite busy. She & her husband & baby went up to Scales Mound on the five train so she was busy getting ready.

Tue 22: This ~~Today~~ forenoon we hauled hay. We had just got through with a load and Al got off the wagon to pick up some hay when the horses (Violet & the big pony) backed up and turned out toward the field. We had opened a place to drive out off right back off the hay shed because it was hard to back out. We all hollered ho but they went up into the field as far as the fence and then turned around and came down and came in the stock yard and out the gate that comes over this way they caught in the gate post and pulled it out and pulled the gate down and then come over by the tank we though they were going to stop here but they didn't, the mower was standing out here by the gate they turned and caught in that and tipped it over and ran right through a bunch of cattle and went through the bar that goes into the field out here. And caught the rack into the fence and the horses tore loose from the wagon with the two front wheels and ran up the field into the little woods and ran against a tree and stood there until papa got there. It tore the rack all the pieces and broke the hind axle and the reach. The big pony hurt her hind foot. This afternoon Al went down to help John.

Wed 23:   We are ironing today. They are cutting hay today.

Thu 24:   We are hauling hay today. John is helping today. It is reading day today

Fri 25:   We finished haying today. Got the hay shed full and a small stack. This forenoon Louie Weis, Mrs. Miguet and four children and Aunt Lizzie & Naomi came in the automobile. They went up to Aunt Annie's.

Sat 26: This forenoon Uncle Edd brough them down Louie Weis went on home this morning. Papa & Al went to Galena today. Al staid in. This afternoon Mrs. Miquet & Mamma & I picked some blackberries for Aunt Lizzie.

Sun 27: This morning Ruby & I and Caroline Miquet the oldest that was here, (the oldest one staid at Apple River) went to Sunday school. We did not have any preaching up here today. There is quarterly meeting at the Station. There were ten at Sunday School. We practiced singing some songs. After Sunday school. Aunt Annie & Wesley came down for dinner. This afternoon Mamma & Papa took them all over the Station for the six oclock train. Johnnie came down after Aunt Annie & Wesley. Uncle Edd is in town. Mary has an awful sore foot she run a rusty nail in it. They are going to operate on it today. She is staying at Eustice's in town.

Mon 28: This morning at about half past six Al came home. Al helped John with his grass today. Aunt Annie said that Mary Tippet had symptoms of lock jaw yesterday.

Tue 29: Papa & Al are working on the shed today. This afternoon Uncle Edd Aunt Annie & Wesley came down to pick blackberries. Ruby & I picked to. Uncle Edd said that he saw more blackberries today than ever before. They all staid to supper. Mary is getting better.

Wed 30: Papa & Al are working on the shed today. We washed today had an awful big washing. Al went up to Fiedler's tonight.

Thu 31: We had a little shower of rain this morning. This afternoon, Papa and Al went to Galena. Al is going ~~away~~ home today. He thought maybe on the nine oclock tonight. It was to late to go on the two and there was no other until nine. He said before he went that he may stay in Galena until tomorrow morning and go on the morning train. Al got a card from Wilbur today. He and Anna had been up to Ft. Dodge Sunday. Wilbur went to see his girl I guess (Olive Harrison). He told Al he had better come home. That he might have to stand up. I suppose he was just fooling.

August

Fri 1: Today Ruby, Mama & I picked some blackberries and picked them over.

Sat 2: We did not go to town today. An awful lot of automobiles went along today. We are awful busy today. We are making jelly & jam. We got a letter from Uncle Thomas & Aunt Rachel they said Al got home all right. He got home about two oclock in the night.

Sun 3: This afternoon Mama, Ruby & I went to church. There was not a very big crowd there today. I played the organ from Sunday school the first time. Ruby & I went up in the choir today it also was the first time. The others in the choir were Sadie Young, Martha Tippet and Laura Bastian (organist). They are thinking to have a Sunday school picnic the twentieth of August.

Mon 4: We went up to Uncle Edd's this evening. There isn't much news today. Papa helped John Tresidder stack grain today. We had our first sweet corn today for dinner. The field corn isn't fit yet.

Tue 5:   We are washing today. It has been cloudy today and sprinkling a little. I hope we will have a good rain we need it awfully bad. We hear that Mr. & Mrs. Popp have a little girl.

Wed 6:   Papa and Mamma went to town today. Aunt Annie came down this forenoon. This afternoon Aunt Annie, Ruby & I picked a few blackberries for Aunt Annie. We ironed today. It ~~sprinkled~~ rained a little today.

Thu 7:   It is reading day today. This evening we had quite a storm. After the storm we heard over the telephone that one of Young's hay stacks was burning over on the Erby place. Papa went up on John Weis' mound to see it. Then Ruby & I went up. It was quite a fire.

Fri 8:   Early this morning there was another storm. Today the Chantaqua begins. We did not go. I would like to have went.

Sat 9:   Papa, Ruby & I went to town today. Ruby & I went to the Chantaqua. It was pretty good. There was a bunch of Pueblo Indians. A little papoose ten months old.

Sun 10:   It rained this morning. Papa, Mama, Ruby & I went to church. There wasn't many there twelve without the minister. I had to play the organ because Laura wasn't there. Made an awful lot of mistakes. We had no company today.

Mon 11:   Gloomy today. Mama, Ruby & I picked a few blackberries this afternoon. Papa working on the shed. No news.

Tue 12:   It rained today. It is good for the corn and things.

Wed 13:   Today we all went to Galena. We all went to the Chantaqua. He heard Mrs. Mamie Curtis speak. Music was furnished by the "Lyrics" Orchestra.

Thu 14:   It is wash day and reading day today.

Fri 15:   We ironed today and baked.

Sat 16:   Today Mamma & I went with Uncle Edd & Aunt Annie out to Uncle Joseph's. A Mr. Funk is going to preach at the Pres. Church at Shapville tomorrow. Mamma & Aunt Annie use to know him when they were children so they wanted to go out to hear him. I went along. We got out there somewhere around five oclock. Uncle Joe was gone up to Apple River. Aunt Tillie and Edward came along down with him. Uncle Joe has a little puppy he is just awful cute. Edward is awful scared of him but likes him awful well to. Aunt Tillie & I slept together we slept in what use to be the girls' room Uncle Edd & Aunt Annie slept down stairs. Rachel & Mamma slept in what use to be the spare bed room Uncle Joe & Hurman slept together. Edward slept on the floor. This is the first time we were out to Uncle Joe's since he was married.

Sun 17:   Got up at half past five this morning. started for church about half past eight. just as we were ready to go Uncle George, Aunt Lizzie, Naomi, Grandpa & Mr Funk came along. We all procede to church. They had mission fast at the Lutheran Church. Lot of people there. Quite a few at Pres. Church. They got a student from Dubuque preaching there. Is pretty good looking. Aunt Tillie gave me an introduction to him. Uncle Ben & Vada were there. Vada & Lester got a little pony. They had the Lord's supper and baptized a baby at church they had it because the student could not do it. We saw Fiedlers pass the church they came out to the mission feast. We did not stay. We had dinner at Uncle Joe's. There was quite a bad storm in the after noon. In the evening it looked a little better. So we started to go home. Uncle Georges started to. It kept getting to look worse. we had a notion to go in to Adam Dittmar's and stay all night. But kept on when we got up on the ridge it came pretty close. we saw John Hammon's gate there so turned around and went in. It led down a steep hill and we had never been down that road before. It got so dark we could not hardly see the road anymore. We got there all right. They were surprised. After awhile it rained and stormed just awful. And kept it up until eleven oclock or after. We had to stay all night. I slept with the little girl in a little room about 3 by 4 feet. Mamma & Aunt Annie slept in the same room with Old Lady Pulco. Uncle Edd slept in the parlor on the couch. There were thirteen there. All together that night.

Mon 18: After breakfast this morning we came home. When we got near Gill's Uncle Edd found that he had left his coat out to Pulco. had a notion to go back after it. tried to phone from Gill's to them to tell them to send it by parcel post. But line was out of order. So wrote what he wanted said on a piece of paper and gave to Gill to phone when line got fixed. When we got past Glick's we met our assistant mail carrier he said that Fiedlers had five milk cows killed by lightning last night in the yard. When we got up by Fiedler's we saw then the lightning struck the big cotton wood tree. The cows were right around the tree. He said it was his best cows. There were thirteen in the yard. He has two hundred dollars insurance on them. This afternoon all the neighbors went and helped him skin and bury them. He buried them in the bottom.

Tue 19:   I got a letter from Jeannette today. Papa & Ruby went to town. Ruby is going out to Apple River from there she intends to go to camp meeting maybe tomorrow if Aunt Maggie or some one will go with her then she is coming back to Apple River again. I don't know how long she will stay. Aunt Annie heard from Aunt Tillie today she said they just got home before the rain. It thundered and lightened before they got home. She said they had quite a time with Edward he was scared.

Wed 20:   Well I guess Ruby will go to camp meeting today. No news today.

Thu 21:   Today John Tresidder thrashed I went down to help. They had them for dinner Lottie Hocking was down there helping too. Mamma ironed some today. They thrashed up at John Weis' this afternoon.

Fri 22:   This morning Ruby walked home from the station was down to camp meeting Wednesday. Joe Weis & Fiedlers thrashed today. We made some plum and crabapple jelly today. We are awfully busy today. Cut most of the lawn.

Sat 23:   Mama went up to help Aunt Annie. Papa went to help but came home again because there were a plenty hands. I baked a cake and drop cookies this forenoon.

Sun 24: We all went to church this morning. Instead of our preacher preaching Rev. Odgers preached. He is grandson of the Clarks that lived down here in Weis' house. He asked Mr. Collier if he could preach. The Clarks use to go to church up here. Joe Virtue and his mother from Woodbine were up here. I guess they came for Sunday School I guess. But everybody was so late we did not have it. There were twenty-eight there. We did not go anywhere or have anybody for dinner. Rev Odgers said he might call this afternoon. He and Laura Bastian (they are old friends of Bastians) drove over. He wanted to go down to Jo Weis. So we all went along. There was nobody at home only Bert. He look around a little. Just as we were going away Josie & Helen came down off the mound. They would have us come in a little while. So Mama, Ruby, & I went in a little while.

Mon 25: We washed today. Mama sent for a 25 lb sack of sugar with Uncle Edds. we went up after it this evening.

Tue 26: Today we are quite busy baking and getting ready for the picnic.

Wed 27:   We all went to the picnic. Uncle Edd, Win & Martha and us eat together. Sadie Grundry and the children eat with us and Mr. Collier and the new preacher. Mr. Atkinson. The new preacher is beyond discription. There was quite a crowd there. Reverend Wilson of Galena spoke, the music was by the Scales Mound band. They had several ball games. They left the races until so late we had to go home before they had many. The men's race was won by Wesley (Dittmar) he won third in another race. Then they had two jumping races. Ruby & I went around most all afternoon with Josie Weis & Berdie Fritz. Helen Weis & Bernetta & Thelma Davis were with us some of the time. I had a pretty good time. This evening Mr. Collier and the new preacher came over and stayed all night.

Thu 28:   The preachers went to Galena. They took a can of cream for us and bought some coffee and vinegar for us. We had lots of fun about it. It is reading day today. The preachers stayed all night again tonight.

Fri 29:   Well today is my birthday. Got pinched. I am sweet sixteen. I am good looking and tall (about 5 ft 9 ½ in) and slender weighing about one hundred and twenty-eight or thirty pounds. I have brown eyes and long black eyelashes and medium brown curly hair (Ha, Ha) I made some fudge for my birthday. The two preachers staid here again tonight. I got a card from Anna today.

Sat 30: We did not go to town today. It is a fine day. I have quite a bad cold. The preacher went over the Station today coming back to Tippet's to stay all night.

Sun 31: Papa is sick today he was sick all night. I had an awful bad cold today. Mama, Ruby & I went to church this morning. Mamma and Ruby and Martha Tippet joined the church. The preacher wanted to take them into the church before he went away. There were quite a few to church today. Mr. Atkinson preached. Mr. Collier is going to preach his farewell sermon at the station tonight. We did not go anywhere or have any company this afternoon.

September

Mon 1: Well today is Labor Day. No ~~more~~ mail today. Papa got up today. Is feeling a little better. They are having a celebration in town today baseball and horse racing. Quite a few people went along.

Tue 2: We washed today. This afternoon Sadie Young and Lottie Hocking came over and asked us to go over to Mrs. Irish Rob's with them. Ruby & I went. May was helping Mrs. Virtue get dinner for the thrashers. She came a few minutes after we got there. Minnie (Rob's sister) is over there she isn't very well so she was there. May would have us stay to supper. School started today. Helen is going to take first year high school up here. Lorraine Garrity is going to teach again this year. Milton Tresidder went to school for the first time today. He was just crazy to go. Mr. Collier was to start from Galena this morning at three oclock for Colorado and will get there sometime this evening.

Wed 3: This morning Mama and I went up to help clean the church. Papa and Ruby went to town this forenoon. There were ten women up there to help clean the church. We washed the windows and washed lamp and lamp chimneys blackened the stoves and stove pipes. We blackened one length of pipe up and took the other down and put it up again. We washed all the pews took up the carpet and matting and the cushions did not fit so they cut some and sewed them on the other to make fit. Lottie and I examined and put a new strap on the organ. I would have cleaned out the things that make the sound in the organ but could not find nothing to take them out with until it was time to go home. They made out to paint the floor of the church and get a new carpet. They also made out that they were going to have a picnic Aid Society over to Mrs. R. S. Virtue's next week. Every body is to bring something. The most of us took over dinner along and ate it up there. We did not get home until about four oclock.

Thu 4: Well today is Shapville picnic would like to have went awfully well. But no way to go. It is reading and ironing day today. This evening Ruby & I went to look for some hickory nuts. We found a few.

Fri 5: It is awfully hot today. It is awful dry again I wish it would rain a nice shower. Milton Tresidder went again to school today. It is his second day. Helen was sick one day and didn't go so he could not go. And yesterday morning it looked like rain so I suppose that is why he did not go then. I got some hickory nuts from the tree over between us and Fiedlers.

Sat 6: We did not go to town today. There is no news around here.

Sun 7: This afternoon we all went to church. There wasn't very many there. It is awfully hot today. Rev. Atkinson said be thankful you got a preacher you might have got a grease spot. The men are going to begin about the cement platform. Uncle Edd & Aunt Annie came down to supper.

Mon 8: Papa went up church to help this morning. This forenoon I went picking up hickory nuts while I was up the wood they rang the bell for me to come home. Uncle Herman brought Mamma's Uncle George Dittmar and his two daughters. Mrs. Woodside and Mrs. Robinson and little daughter Aunt Annie came down late this afternoon and Uncle Edd came down this evening. The folks are going to stay here all night. Mrs. Woodside made some beads for us out of two tablespoons salt heated until it cracks and into that put one tablespoon cornstarch and mix some coloring in water and throw on salt and starch then stir and knead with hands then roll out in long strips and cut in small pieces and roll round when they get hard on the outside make holes through with a needle and leave stand until hard then string them. we heard that Rob S. Virtue was going to move tomorrow. He had a fallen out with

Rob R. Virtue. I don't know where he is going to move. Or if he will tomorrow or not. If they do was is to become of our picnic.

Tue 9: This morning the folks went up to Aunt Annie's. They went home this afternoon they are going to stay at Adam D. They are going back to Kansas Thursday. Mamma went up to Aunt Annie's this morning to. Papa helped about the platform this afternoon did not get through with it yet. They have the steps to make yet. I don't know if Rob S. Virtue move or not. Nice weather today. Quite cool.

Wed 10: Well today is the picnic at Rob S. Virtue's. This afternoon mamma, Ruby & I went there were quite a few there. We had a good time. They served a lap supper out on the porch and on the steps. Robs are not going to move until next Tuesday.

Thu 11: Well it is reading day today. Is raining today. We washed this afternoon. We couldn't this morning because it is raining.

Fri 12: Papa & Mamma went to town today. Ruby & I staid home. They are quilting an Aid Society quilt over at Tippet's today. But we did not go. Grandpa & Grandma came to Galena today. Grandpa Tippet went in after them. Pa & Ma had a big load. Irish Rob asked Papa to haul a load for them out to Westaby's next Tuesday.

Sat 13: Quite a few went to town today. It is just a lovely day today. Rob S. Virtue is helping Papa with the shed today so Papa can help him move.

Sun 14: We went to church ~~today~~ this forenoon. Mr. & Mrs. Rob S. Virtue and son and Minnie came down to dinner this afternoon. Fiedlers came down. Robs had to go home right after dinner because Mr. Virtue called up and asked if we knew where Rob S was. He said that Rob S. had company.

Mon 15: This morning Johnnie brought down Grandpa & Grandma. We put up nine quarts of peaches today.

Tue 16: This morning Papa went to haul Rob V a load. It rained about all day.

Wed 17: This morning Johnnie came down and got Grandpa & Grandma. They are going to take them to town this afternoon. They are going to Woodbine on the train to see their new grandson. We washed today. Papa got home this evening. He staid at Uncle Henry's all night and staid at Uncle Joe's for dinner today. I got a card from Colorado today from a Bastian.

Thu 18: Well it is reading day today and ironing day and fruit putting up day. A week from today is the great Galena Fair. Hope it is a nice day and suitable to my clothes. It is a fine day today.

Fri 19: No news today.

Sat 20: Rained all day today. We wanted to go to town awfully bad but could not.

Sun 21: Laura called up and said we would not have any church this afternoon because the paint wasn't fit to walk on. Ruby & I went up to Aunt Annie's this afternoon. It is just awful cold today.

Mon 22: It is a nice day today only rather cold. We all went to town today. Lots of people in town today. I got a new hat it is of navy blue plush with two light blue plumes sticking up the back with a band of light blue velvet across the front.

Tue 23: We are awful busy today trying to fix up my velvet dress. A red velvet dress and a blue hat will never do. But it will have to do. Papa & Ruby are cutting corn today.

Wed 24: Nice day today. It is nice and warm today. We are awful busy. We are baking today.

Thu 25: Oh it is raining today. I am so sorry quite a few want for this weather. But we did not go. It rains about all afternoon. I wanted to go so bad. I want to go tomorrow if it is nice.

Fri 26: It is fine weather today. Quite a lot of teams and automobiles went along. We all went we left our horses way out up over the hill from the smelter. There were quite a crowd in there. We seen a man jump from a very high ladder into a tank of water. I went around for awhile late in the afternoon with Jeannette, Mertie, and Mary Carson. Some more gathered to our crowd later on. I had a pretty good time. I suppose it will be Mertie's last Fair while she is living around here for they are going to move to Kansas next spring. We heard today that Jim Spencer sold out to lately. Spensley (Grace Bastian's husband) bought it. On our way coming home from the fair on Ehler's Hill a auto came down so fast and stopped right before our horses and scared them so they backed and cramed the carriages and broke the under part of the carriage. John Heer jumped out and left his horse stand to help get our horses by. The auto man helped to. Mr. & Mrs. Wallace Ford were behind. Mrs. Ford jumped out and went way up on the bank. She was awfully scared. Just awfully lot of autos went by tonight.

Sat 27: Papa and Mamma are cutting corn today. We had a late dinner and just as we were eating Mr. Rev. Atkinson called we looked a fright we had a dirty table cloth on. Potatoes with the skins a big dish of squash. The salt package was on the table and the pickle bottle hardly any bread and not much else. ~~On~~ My plate was first a big pile of potatoes on that I had a great big pile of squash. It was a mountain. I was so ashamed. My hair was down my back.

Sun 28: This forenoon we all went to church there were thirty-two there. The floor look fine now that it is painted. This afternoon we took a walk down to John's but they were not at home so we came home again. This evening Mr. and Mrs. Joe Weis Josie & Helen came up.

Mon 29: Papa, Mama, & Ruby cut corn this afternoon. I picked up hickory nuts. I got about a peach basket full.

Tue 30: Papa went to town today. Mamma, Ruby & I went along up to Aunt Annie's got some red crabs.

October

Wed 1:   We washed today. Ruby sent for a hat to Philisborn today. It is a poke bonnet.

Thu 2:   We ironed today. Reading day today.

Fri 3:   Mamma & Ruby went up church and took up the new church carpet and put it down this forenoon.

Sat 4:   Quite a few people went to town today. Papa cut the little patch of clover across the road this afternoon. It rained this evening.

Sun 5:   This afternoon we all went to church. There were twenty-two there. Mrs. Amos Ford and Flossie was there. This evening we went down to John Tresidder's but they weren't at home so we came home again.

Mon 6:   It was foggy all forenoon. Late this afternoon it cleared up a little. Papa went up church this forenoon to help make the porch steps. We pickled crabs and put up pears and picked a tree of bell flower apples this afternoon. This afternoon Jim Spencer went along he hollered to told Papa that Ruby & I were invited to a party Thursday evening at their place. I suppose it is for Warren's birthday. I do hope we can go.

Tue 7: Ruby & I picked apples this forenoon. This afternoon Ruby & I went up the wood and picked fall grapes. It was cloudy and rained a little today but it cleared and it is just a beautiful evening tonight.

Wed 8: We washed today. Ruby & I picked some apples. Well it is twenty minutes to eight. I suppose of nothing happens we will be on our way to Spencer's to the party. I hope so anyway.

Thu 9: Well we ironed today. This evening Helen brought me a letter from Jeannette. She asked us to come up there before dark and go with her and then stay the rest of the night there if we had no other way to go. Helen said they were invited but did not think they would go.

Fri 10: Well Papa and Mamma took us up past the school house last night we called for Jeannette Alvie & Bernetta Davis were their and we all went over together it was a surprise on Warren for his eighteenth birthday. We thought there wasn't nobody there so we went into the machine shed until some more came it was Albert Williams with his automobile. John Tippet and Ethel Falancer and Tom Pooley. We all flocked there together. As soon as Warren seen the automobile come in he said Oh I know what it is and and took about two steps up the stairs. Miss Garrity said. He was quite surprised. There were fifteen girls and fourteen boys not counting Vera Pooley and Mr. & Mrs. Pooley and Mr. & Mrs. Spencer. We had a fine time. My partner for supper was Edd Young. Ruby's was Elmer Young and Bernetta Davis had Ben Young. Mertie & Jeannette some way did not get any partners. Weis was not there. When we went we went home with Jeannette it was just awful dark. It was cloudy and was lightning. It was either twenty minutes to two or twenty after two. I don't know which now when we got over to Werner's. All three of us slept together in a bed. A little while after we got there it rained and rained awful hard most all the rest of the night. In the forenoon Mrs. Werner hitched up and brought us home. She thought it to wet for us to walked home. It was about ten oclock when we got home. This afternoon it stormed and rained awful hard.

Sat   Oh I forgot Thursday in the Gazette we read that a license was issued to Mr. Wilbur Bastian and Miss Sarah Young. In the afternoon I heard by cross talk that they had been married the night before (Wed Oct 8) at her home. We heard that they had relatives and a few others.

Sat 11:   We all went to town today. Mamma bought a new hat. It is black velvet with two thin plumes sticking up in the side.

Sun 12: This forenoon we all went to church. The bride and groom were there. They did not go on a wedding trip we heard that they thought they may go after awhile when Wilbur gets some one to do his chores. Laura is either in town or out at Ella's. Mr. & Mrs. Bastian or over there yet but wasn't at church they are thinking to move to Galena tomorrow. We went up to Uncle Edd's to dinner.

Mon 13: It is a beautiful day today. Papa raked clover today. (Papa took the bull over the Station today.)

Tue 14: Today Papa, Mamma and Ruby stacked all the clover. We got one little stack.

Wed 15: This afternoon Papa took a coop of chickens over the station to ship. Ruby and I dug a few potatoes this afternoon.

Thu 16: It rained all day today. It is a reading day. We sewed a little today. It has turned pretty cold this evening. I am afraid that it will freeze. I hope not.

Fri 17: We washed today. It is rather late in the week but it rained before went we were going to so we did not get at it. It is kind of gloomy today.

Sat 18:   Papa & Mamma went to town today. Ruby & I staid home. They heard in town today that Phillipa Trevarthan died this morning.

Sun 19:   This afternoon we all went to church. There were twenty-five there. Martha plays the organ. Lottie, Sadie & I were in the choir but I'm sort of an ornament because I can't sing. Next Sunday we are going to have Sunday school convention up here. In the morning Mr. Atkinson and Mr. Bray are to speak. In the afternoon Mr. Green from Galena and Mr. Joseph Virtue are to speak. We went down to John Tresidder's this evening.

Mon 20:   It looked like Christmas this morning the ground and trees were all white. The first snow of the season. It is awful cold also. This afternoon Papa, Mamma & Ruby dug potatoes this afternoon.

Tue 21:   This morning it was awful cold. This forenoon Papa went over the grave yard to Phil Trevarthen's funeral. There weren't many there only the relatives. They had the funeral at Apple River yesterday. I ironed this afternoon. I talked with Aunt Tillie this afternoon. She was talking from Warren.

Wed 22:   We washed today. Ruby & I husked six shocks of corn today.

Thu 23: It is reading day today. This forenoon Mamma was up at Aunt Annie's. She heard that Johnnie & Ethel Falancer are to be married on Thanksgiving day. Only the relatives are to be invited. They are going to be married at noon. They are going to live in with Uncle Edd and Aunt Annie this winter. They are going to leave them have three rooms. It is a beautiful day today.

Fri 24: Today Jo Weis, John Weis and us hulled clover. Fiedlers hulled one stack and have one to hull tomorrow. We got seven bushels. I was talking with Helen tonight. She said that Jack Malloy and Maggie Cleary were married at Galena yesterday and are out at Werner's now. Their wedding trip I suppose.

Sat 25: We did not go to town today. Quite a few teams and automobiles went along today. It is a nice day today. I hope it will be nice tomorrow for the big doings. I baked two cakes today.

Sun 26: It rained all day today. We did not go to church. It is to bad that it rained. I think maybe they will have the convention some other Sunday.

Mon 27: We husked corn today. I husked three this forenoon and four this afternoon.

Tue 28:   We husked and hauled in some corn today.

Wed 29:   It is snowy and rainy today but Papa & Ruby went to town this afternoon.

Thu 30:   Gloomy weather today. Today is Mrs. Tom Sheean's sale. Papa went but did not buy anything. It was quite a large sale.

Fri 31:   It is a nice day today. It is Halloween today. I talked to Helen this evening but she did not know much news.

❧

November

Sat 1: It is a fine day today. We did not go to town. I should like to have went. I want to get a new coat. I would like to have it for tomorrow for the convention.

Sun 2: Papa, Ruby & I went to church this forenoon. Joe Virtue and Edd Bray spoke and Mrs. Sincox and her son of Veta Grand sang a solo. The was quite a crowd up there forenoon. The middle row was full and a few in the side seats. Joe Virtue and his sister (Miss Virtue) Mrs. Collin and little boy and the preacher came here to dinner. We all went this afternoon there were a lot more there this afternoon than forenoon. I think there were about ninety are over. The Sincox sang another solo. Mrs. read a reading. Albert Williams and Flossie Ford sang a solo. Eliza Vincent, Miss Laird and a Mr. Redfern sang a trio. Mr. Bray spoke a part of the afternoon, and the other part Mr. Miller from Warren. They elected new Sunday school officers. Edd Young for Pres. Mrs. P Smart V. Pres. Mrs Williams Treas. Mrs. Redfern Sec.

Mon 3: Papa working on the shed roof today. We brought in the carrots, cabbage, and beets and things today. We haven't much cabbage this year.

Tue 4:   We washed today.

Wed 5:   We husked corn this forenoon. We got a letter from Anna & Aunt Rachel today. This afternoon we ironed and churned. Papa almost finished putting the roof on the shed today. This evening Uncle Edd and Aunt Annie came down.

Thu 6:   We husked corn this forenoon. This afternoon we hauled in a load and husked some standing corn.

Fri 7:   It is awful gloomy day today. Awful windy this afternoon and evening. Ruby & I husked standing corn alone. This forenoon and this afternoon.

Sat 8:   Papa, Mamma and I went to town today. Ruby cleaned up and then went up to Aunt Annie's. I bought a new black ostrichs cloth coat. Cost $16.00 I had a terrible time to get any. It is awful cold. I just about froze.

Sun 9:   We haven't any church today. It is quarterly meeting at Council Hill. This afternoon Ruby & I started out for a walk when we got up on the ridge we saw a buggy down by the house so we came home again. It was Jeannette and Leo Werner. They came down in the buggy. Jeannette wanted to go down to Weis' to see their piano. So this evening Jeannette, Leo, Ruby

& I went down to Weis'. They had a horse hitched up that was afraid of automobiles. They thought that there wouldn't be any today because the roads weren't very good but one went down tonight. Leo got pretty nervous he was wishing that they had one of the old horses hitched up. I guess they didn't meet any.

Mon 10: It is awful cold today. We husked standing corn this afternoon. Mrs. Joseph A Weis told us in town Sat. that Mamie and John Tobin are to be married November 26. They are going to Chicago on a wedding trip.

Tue 11: This morning Papa took two lambs and an old sheep of Ruby's and a sheep of mine. We got three and one half cents per pound for the old sheep and five and one half for the lambs. The lambs averaged not quite four dollars a piece. The sheep six dollars and twenty-one cents apiece. We husked corn today. Uncle Edd was to go to Chicago with steers today but the car did not come. This evening Helen, Vera & Milton brought us six or seven tiny chickens from down the road. The old hen had been run over I guess by an auto. We gave them to a hen that has one little chicken. She took them.

Wed 12: We husked and hauled in corn today. It is nice and warm today.

Thu 13: Husking shock corn again today.

Fri 14: We hauled and hauled in corn today. Mamma washed this afternoon, rather late in the week.

Sat 15: This forenoon everything was topsy-turvy and dirty. Uncle Joe & Aunt Rachel came after dinner they went to town going to stay at Uncle Edd's tonight. This morning I got a card saying that I and my sister are invited to attend a novelty shower Fri evening Nov 21st at the home of Joseph A. Weis in honor of their daughter Mayme's approaching marriage. I should like to go if it's not to be a dance. Today is Mertie Ford's sixteenth birthday. I sent her a card yesterday.

Sun 16: This afternoon we all went to church. There wasn't many there. Sixteen I believe. Uncle Joe & Aunt Rachel staid up at Uncle Edd's all night and went to church this afternoon. They and Uncle Edd came down for supper. They went home this evening. Aunt Annie is going to have the Aid Society Wed for dinner.

Mon 17: We husked corn today. Awful foggy this forenoon.

Tue 18: Mamma went up to Aunt Annie's to help get ready for the Aid Society. We husked nineteen shocks today we have twenty-one left and some standing yet. It has been awful foggy all day today. Helen brought me a letter from Jeannette this evening. Helen left it outside on the window we were up in the field. She said that she and Leo were over to Mount Morley social Fri. had lots of fun. Her basket brought two dollars and seventy-five cents. A Jorne got her basket. She said that they expect to have a social up here Dec. 5.

Wed 19: Last night it rained and thundered and lightning a little. Mamma staid all night up at Aunt Annie's. There were thirty-four at the Society for dinner. They presented Sadie Young Bastian with a quilt for a wedding present. Ethel Falancer was out to the Aid Society. helped to work. It is awfully warm today.

Thu 20: We husked corn today finished the shock corn this afternoon. It is warm today. It is Papa's
~~Fri. 2~~ birthday today. He is fifty-seven years old.

Fri 21: We finished husking corn at noon today. Hauled all the corn in this afternoon. Well the novelty shower dance is this evening we did not go. I guess it is to be a big affair.

Sat 22: Ruby, Papa & I went to town today. We bought a set of cream pitcher and sugar bowl for Mayme Weis. I don't know how we will get it down to her.

Sun 23: We all went to church this forenoon. This afternoon Win Tippet & Martha & Mary came down stayed to supper. Mamma rode along up to Uncle Edd's with them we went up after we had done the chores. Aunt Annie isn't feeling very well.

Mon 24: It is a fine day today talked with Helen tonight. They don't know when they will have their sociable. Helen said they had a fine time down to the shower Fri night. She said they counted eighty-two there.

Tue 25: Papa & Ruby hauled fodder today. I have an awful sore throat today. Today is Miss Jessie Woodrow Wilson's wedding day. She is going to marry Francis Sayre. A great doings at the White House. I sent for a dress to Bella Hess and Co. New York City NY. It is to be Copenhagen blue serge. It cost $5.98. I hope it will be a nice and pretty one.

Wed 26: It is a dark damp day today. Papa & Ruby finished hauling fodder today. We washed an awful, awful big washing today. It is Mayme Weis and John Tobin's wedding day today. I suppose they were married some time this forenoon. I didn't hear what time it was to be. I heard Edith was to be bridesmaid. I suppose one of the Tobin boys was best man. Tomorrow is

Thanksgiving and John Tippet's & Ethel Falancer's wedding.

Thu 27: Well today is Thanksgiving day. It isn't nice weather dark and gloomy. We had nothing extra to eat today. At noon today John L Tippet & Ethel Falancer were married by Mr. Warren of the first Pres. Church of Galena. They went on the afternoon train to Omaha. I'm not feeling very well today had an awful ear ache last night. Have an awful cold in my head.

Fri 28: It is reading day today. We ironed today. It is awful bad weather. We got a letter from Uncle Thomas today. It is a bad day again today.

Sat 29: It is awful warm and cloudy and rainy and foggy again today. Received an after card announcing Johnnie's & Ethel's marriage.

Sun 30: It rained all afternoon so we did not go to church or anywhere else today. Kind of lonesome.

December

Mon 1: It is cloudy and warm again today. Papa is hanging some of the doors on the shed. I have been patching things. Ruby made an undershirt. Mamma doing all sorts of things.

Tue 2: Dark and gloomy again today. Haven't seen the sun since a week Monday. We finished the shed today. We put in the heaper, the rake, the mower and the hack. I guess we will have to put the rest in some other time. Helen said tonight that they weren't going to have the social until after Xmas. About Jan. 16. She said Spencers were going to have their sale Jan 14 and Jesse Ford's Jan 21st.

Wed 3: Cloudy again today. We finished putting the machinery and rigs into the shed today. No news lately.

Thu 4: Reading day today. Horrah it is a nice beautiful day today. I'm so glad. I thought sure my dress would come that I sent for but it didn't. We washed today. This afternoon Uncle Edd and Aunt Annie came down Uncle Edd then went over to John Weis' something about the road. He then came back and called here awhile.

Fri 5:   My dress came today. It is a little to big around the waist and hips. It is kind of pretty.

Sat 6:   Well today we all went to Galena. It started to rain before we got quite in there and rained about all day. There was quite a few in town today. We expected Aunt Tillie to come on the afternoon train today. But she did not come I guess it was too rainy.

Sun 7:   It is awful cold and windy today. Sometimes it is snowing a little then again the sun is shining. We all went to church this forenoon. There wasn't many there only Jack Combellick's the preacher and Mr. & Mrs. Wilbur Bastian and us. We just had a little Sunday school. Fielders came down this afternoon.

Mon 8:   Papa took a load of hogs over the station for Fiedlers. Then Papa had to go up to the parsonage to a meeting about renting it. Aunt Tillie came on the nine train to the station and waited until Papa came home. The roads are so rough Aunt Tillie had to walk over from Werner's. They did not get here until three oclock or after. Then we got them some dinner.

Tue 9:   Beautiful day today. Papa took a coop of chicken over the station this afternoon to ship. This evening we all went with Aunt Tillie up to Uncle Edd's. I hope we can go over to the station tomorrow evening to the Bazaar. I got a card from Al today.

Wed 10:   It is a lovely day today. This evening Papa, Ruby & I went over the station to the Bazaar. There was a big crowd there. The church was full. Aunt Lizzie Trudgian was there. Quite a few from Galena and Scales Mound. We had to stand most of the evening. We paid twenty-five cents for supper. But did not get very much. Mamma staid home alone. We got home about eleven oclock. It was just a beautiful moon light evening.

Thu 11:   Beautiful day today. We washed today.

Fri 12:   Beautiful day today. We ironed today. Baked cookies, spice cake, bread & coffee cake. No news lately.

Sat 13:   Well today we all went to town. Lots of people there. Pearl & Sadie were in there shopping. They did not come out. Lots of Christmas things. Ruby & I were going to have our picture taken but we could not find any card that we wanted so we did not have it taken. We are going to have the Aid Society here Wed for dinner. We invited some people today. When we came home Uncle Bens was up at Uncle Edd's. They weren't home yet. And had been down to our place and we weren't home either so they came down again. John & Ethel came home Fri. from their wedding trip and came out to Uncle Edd's this evening.

Sun 14: This forenoon Mamma went with Uncle Bens up to Uncle Edd's. This afternoon we were all to church there were twenty-six there. Aunt Annie & Aunt Tillie came here after church and Uncle Edd came down in time for supper.

Mon 15: We are busy today I baked a cake and mama and I churned and did lots of other things. Tomorrow we will be quite busy.

Tue 16: Well today we were quite busy. Papa helped saw wood for Uncle Edd this forenoon. This afternoon he and Ruby went over to Jim Spencer's. Jim Spencer sent papa a letter saying Mr. Spencer would be over the at two oclock today. He has a horse to sell and that Papa should come over to see it. But they did not buy it. It was to small and looked old. He wanted fourty-five dollars for it. Aunt Tillie came down with Papa after dinner. I baked one cake yesterday and three today. They got pretty good.

Wed 17: It is lovely day today. There were twenty-three here for dinner. We sent out seven dinners or suppers. Had a pretty good time. Mrs. John Combellick brought Ruby & I a letter inviting us to a party at Walter Combellick's Friday evening (Dec 19). Some one phone today that Sianna's Aunt Catherine and Mr. Pingel were coming here tomorrow. Aunt Tillie stayed down here.

Thu 18: This forenoon Mr. & Mrs. Drink brought Aunt Catherine and Mr. Pingel down. ~~about~~ while we were eating our dinner a knock came at the door and it was Uncle Hurman. This evening our ring went and I answered it, it was Uncle Dan phoning from Galena. He came on this evening flyer. Mama asked him to come out. He said he would come some other time.

Fri 19: This forenoon I saw a man coming down the bottom it was Uncle Dan he changed his mind about coming here. He walked over from the Station. After dinner they all went up to Aunt Annie's. Tonight is the party.

Sat 20: Well last night we did not know how to get to the party. So Mamma went with us. It was cloudy and not moonlight either but we got over there all right. There were thirty or thirty-one over there all together. We had a nice time we played "Buzz" "Deacon" "Clap in and clap out" "Wink um" They left the boys to choose there partners for supper. Some was to bashful so not all of them had partners Ruby nor I did not have any partners. I baked a white cake and took it. It was just fine tasted like angel food. We got home at twenty minutes after one. We were the first one's to go. We did not want Mama to stay up so late. Flossie & Alta got it up. Today Papa & Mamma went to town. There were just piles of people in there today.

Sun 21: We all went to church this forenoon. We came home to dinner. Aunt Tillie & Annie Uncle Dan & Hurman went in to Wilbur Bastian's to dinner the preacher went in to. Ben Young came there to dinner also. Ruby & I went for a walk this afternoon. Mama went down to John's. Uncles & Aunts came over here to supper. Uncle Edd came down this evening. Dan & Hurman stayed all night.

Mon 22: Papa helped haul a load of hogs for Mr. Virtue. Dan & Herman went up to Aunt Annie's this forenoon. Mamma went up to Aunt Annie's and over to Martha's. She ordered some roosters from Martha. She took a half dozen cups and saucers up for John & Ethel for their wedding presents. They are about settled. Tonight John & Wilbur Tresidder came up. Wilbur walked down to John's this afternoon he came and bought two horse from John a gray colt and a grey mare (Minnie) we were thinking to buy old Minnie for us folks to drive and here he just snatched her away from us. Wilbur stayed here all night.

Tue 23: We washed today. Expected Uncle Dan & Herman for dinner but did not come. Martha Tippet went out with Uncle Hurman.

Wed 24: Uncle Dan, Aunt Tillie & Annie went on the noon train to Apple River. We were going to town but as we were getting ready Roy & Mabel Tresidder came. They came to buy our steers. He bought them Papa went to help drive them (after dinner). Ruby and I thought that we might go on the five train to Apple River to the Xmas tree tonight. But I guess we won't go maybe tomorrow.

Thu 25: Mama & I walked over the Station and went on the noon train to Apple River. Papa & Ruby staid home. It was after one oclock when we got out there we had to wait near low siding for a freight train that was stalled. Some of them were at the depot to meet us. There were just Mama and I Aunt Annie and Uncle Herman besides themselves there for dinner. Uncle

Georges came down in the afternoon. The presents I got were an embroidery scissors, a calendar, fifty cents and three hankerchiefs. Mamma and I went up to Uncle George's to stay all night. Grandpas had a goose for dinner.

Fri 26: Mamma went down to Grandpa's to dinner I stay at Uncle George's to dinner. I went down after dinner had supper at Grandpa's. After supper all but grandpa went up to Uncle George. Miss Sulton was there too. They popped pop corn, made two kinds of candy we pulled candy. We staid all night at Grandpa's.

Sat 27: Mamma & I came to the station on the afternoon train we walked over. Papa & Ruby went to town. We got a letter from Uncle Thomas today a sent us two pictures that Mrs. Corey gave them to send us. They are the ones that Margery took of us sitting on their porch (Anna, Ruby & I).

Sun 28: We all went to church this afternoon not many there. Did not have any visitors today. Ida Bastian was at church just got home from Col Fri. morning.

Mon 29: It is cloudy today looks like snow. Papa took poor old Betsy (cow) over the Station this morning poor Betsy. Papa sold the pigs for tomorrow.

Tue 30:   This morning Papa took our hogs over the Station. Robert Virtue and John Tippet helped haul. They weren't very heavy got Seven fifteen for them. Papa went out on the telephone line this afternoon. Papa heard that Robert Virtue bought a farm down New Rodden and they are going to move this spring. So many are going to move away. Robert Virtues Jim Spencer, Jesse Ford.

Wed 31:   They put in a new telephone pole out in our yard today. We had Uncle Edd & Fatty Weis for dinner. It has been cloudy all day today. It is awfully frosty. Everything is white. Mrs. Tippet is going to have Aid Society tomorrow. Well I guess this is the last that I will write in this book this year. Poor old nineteen thirteen is all gone.

Farewell, Farewell 1913.

December 31, 1913. Ten minutes to eight p.m. just about four hours more for 1913.

Good-bye.

1914

January

Thu 1: Happy New Year.
This forenoon Papa, Mamma, Ruby & I went over to Tippet's to the Ladies Aid Society. There were seventy-seven there. Had a nice time. They made $29.40. Edd Young and his bride were there. They just came home from Denver this week. They had a reception last night for them. I suppose they just had relatives invited. Some of Mrs. Young's relatives came over with them. It has been cloudy all day and snow flurries this afternoon and evening.

Fri 2: Cloudy all day today. This afternoon Mamma & Ruby went up to Martha Tippet's and got three roosters. I made some fudge this afternoon. Well a week from tonight is the sociable at our school. I wonder who will get my basket. I haven't it made yet. I hope it will get pretty.

Sat 3: Cloudy all day today. We did not go to town today. Nothing new.

Sun 4: This forenoon Mamma, Ruby & I went to church. Papa staid home. There were twenty-four there.

Mamma, Ruby & I went up to Aunt Annie's from there. Papa came up there then to dinner. Mattie was there too. Cloudy all day today. Birdie Fritz played the organ today and last Sunday. Was awful nervous last Sunday. Better today. (Lottie, Sadie & I in choir.)

Mon 5: It has been a lovely day today. Ruby made a black velvet hood for mamma. I finished making my basket tonight it is the same box that has served me four times before three times last winter and one the winter before. The box is red with a white cover with five American beauty's and one white rose well down with a red tissue paper bow.

Tue 6: Not a very nice day today. Uncle Edd and Aunt Annie went out to Uncle Henry's and Uncle Joe's this afternoon.

Wed 7: Helen said this evening that she was going to bring me a piece this evening but she forgot it. I told her I thought that it was to late now anyway. It was for Leo & I.

Thu 8: Well it is just awful foggy and misty today. But Papa & I went to town. This evening Helen brought the piece they want me to learn it yet. I am trying to learn it.

Fri 9: Well this afternoon I went up school to try to practice the piece. Byron Spencer, Jeannette and Miss Mary Carson was up there to. Jeannette and Byron came up to practice. They & Helen & Raymond are in a piece. Leo & I could not get it our piece very well. But they want us to have it. Berdie Fritz came this evening to go out with us.

Sat 10: Well last night we all went to the social but Mamma she had a bad a cold. There was quite a crowd there but not near so many as last year. They had a nice program. They all done fine. Leo & I did not have our piece. Leo didn't want it nor I either. They had lots of baskets (34) mine was ~~sold~~ the fourth one sold it brought seventy cents. Walter Werner bought it. He knew who it was. Ruby wasn't going to take any until the last minute then she wrapped up a box in a sheet of red paper and tied it with ribbon. Will Weis bought Ruby's basket first. He got three or four. Then Bert bought it from Will. It sold for sixty or sixty-five cents. Young George Trevarthan got Birdie's, Byron Spencer got Miss Garriety's. Raymond Spencer got Mertie's. Leo Werner got Helen's. Charlie Ehler got Thelma's. Ben Young got Josie Weis'. Edd Weis got Ida Redfern's. Bert Weis got Ruby's. _____ got Jeannette he is from out near where Mary Carson lives. Werner got Mary

Carson's. Will Weis got Bessie Allan's of course.
Jim Spencer was auctioneer. They took in something
in the twenty dollars. They also sold pop, cigars, and
gum. Walter took home my basket. Mrs. Werner
ate with us too. Had a fine time. Birdie went home
with Fullers. Josie, Helen Ruby & I came home
together. The bus did not come out from town but some
of that crowd came out in I guess a three seated surry.
They did not make so much noise this year. Clayton
and Alton came in from out near Schapville where
they have lately moved on a farm. Nice day today.

Sun 11: This after noon we all went to church there was twenty
three there. Mamma went down to John's from church.
It is just awful windy today.

Mon 12: It is just a beautiful day only awful cold. Up at the
sociable Mrs. Amos Ford told Papa that we folks
were invited to a surprise party at Wallace Ford's for
Jim Spencer and Jesse Ford that that we were bring
to cake, rolls, or chicken. I guess it is to be a big affair.
I counted up what I suppose will be invited. It was
over a hundred.

Tue 13: Today Papa & Mamma went up the Mound with
a coop of chickens. Papa went down to Fatty Weis'
to a telephone meeting tonight. A nice day today.

A medicine man called here today but did not buy anything.

Wed 14: Well today is Jim Spencer's sale. Papa went this forenoon. Ruby & I went this afternoon. It was a pretty big sale. They did not have any school this afternoon so Miss Garrity, Helen Weis and Lucille Ford was there. So was Alta Combellick and Flossie Ford. Jeannette and Miss Carson came there late in the afternoon and their was lots of other women there. Some of their horses did not bring very much. After we had left Mr. Spensley offered that horse to Papa again. So Papa bought it for thirty-dollars. It is bay and it looks quite old. I hope it is alright for us to drive. Mamma washed today.

Thu 15: We all went to town today. Mamma bought a new navy blue serge dress trimmed with green braid. Ruby also bought a Copenhagen blue ratine dress. They are for the party.

Fri 16: Well today is a nice day. Mamma is cooking a chicken to take tonight. We are busy getting our clothes fixed for tonight. (See tomorrow about the party).

Sat 17: We had a fine time last night there were sixty-eight there. We got over there about the first ones. Spencers were all looking out the window when we went past there. Spencers ~~were~~ came there after awhile. They were surprised. Mrs. Spencer was feeling bad that she wasn't dressed as she wanted to be. Mr. Spencer wasn't shaved. Byron did not come right away. He went down to the Station first and when he met people coming he knew what was up I guess he went home again and dressed. Jesse Fords come all dressed up I guess they thought what was up. They presented Mr. Ford and Mr. Spencer each with a envelope of money. They took up a collection they gave a quarter a piece. The Station Aid Society presented Mrs. Ford and Mrs. Spencer each with a rug. Mr. Atkinson gave a little speech and did the presenting. The orchestra played. Mrs. Edd Young sang a solo and Miss Bail sang a solo and so did Flossie. And ~~they sang~~ Albert Williams, Wallace Ford, Fred Spencer & Sherman Lipton sang two quartet and some others together sang. They served supper at about mid night they brought a plate with a roll a piece of chicken a pickle and a doughnut on a plate. (coffee then cake was passed. They did not partner up supper much only a few. I was setting near Byron so I guess he was my partner for supper. They did not play many games. They had a cord and stretched it all around the room and put two rings on it. They had two hunting for the rings. ~~Just b~~ after supper they took all the boys out in one room and left us girls in the other they lined us up and set one chair before us. We were numbered as we were lined up. They then brought in Cleo Swift and set him in the chair and blind folded him then ~~asked him who~~ told him the girls were numbered and he was to choose a number, He chose the number that Miss Bixtin had she had to stand up behind his chair and then Clifford Bastian kissed him then they took the hankerchief off his eyes and then he thought Miss Bixtin kissed him until afterward. Then they brought in Walter Combellick. I had to stand up behind his chair. Mrs. Amos Ford kissed him. They brough in two others. They had lots of fun over it. Miss Garrity played the piano and Flossie, Mable Muller, Fred Spencer and Jack Combellick danced a little just for fun. We got home at ten minutes to two. (none of Werners were there I don't know why). Ruby & I rode the horse horseback today a little.

Sun 18: We did not go to church this morning because it was snowing to much. Uncle Dan came out with Uncle Edds yesterday from town. He came down late this afternoon. Papa & I hitched up the horse in the buggy and drove up as far as Sheean's gate and back again she went all right.

Mon 19: Papa & Mamma drove the horse up to Uncle Edd's and then over to Virtue's. Papa went over to see if

Mr. Virtue had any oats to sell and Mamma wanted to go to see Mrs. Virtue.

Tue 20:   Well we sawed wood today. Had them for dinner Aunt Annie came down to.

Wed 21:   Well today is Jesse Ford's sale. Papa went this morning. Uncle Dan went over this afternoon. I wanted to go but still I didn't so I didn't go. Papa said that Mertie was there and Flossie, Jeannette and Alta Combellick and lots of other women. They sold quite a bit of house furnisher. They sold the organ for about twenty dollars.

Thu 22:   This afternoon Ruby and I got ready and went over to see Sadie Bastian but they wasn't home so we went down to Annie's and Lottie's for awhile.

Fri 23:   This evening just before we were going to set down to supper a knock came at the door and it was Uncle Henry. He asked if we would keep a tramp. It was Uncle Henry, Aunt Lue, Elma, Loretta, Olive & Clifford. Aunt Maggie is out there so they thought they would come while she was there. This evening the chimney caught fire out in the dining room. Throwed water in up stairs and put it out.

Sat 24: This morning Uncle Henrys went up to Aunt Annie's. Papa & Uncle Henry went to town. Mama went up to Aunt Annie's. Uncle Dan rode with Uncle Edd over to the station he is going home from there.

Sun 25: This morning Uncle Henrys went home want to get out to Schapville to church. Well today is quarterly meeting. Papa, Mamma & I went. Ruby staid home to get dinner. Uncle Edd & Aunt Annie, Johnnie & Ethel and the preacher (Atkinson) came here to dinner. There was about twenty-four there this afternoon. We all went this afternoon but it was snowing all afternoon. Youngs came in the sleigh. But there was very little snow on the ground. Birdie Fritz played today. There was twenty-four there again this afternoon.

Mon 26: Not much doing today. We are making a gingham dress for me. Cloudy and kind of stormy today.

Tue 27: This afternoon we hitched up our horse and Ruby & I drove up the school house. One of the teacher's schedules was missing and Papa wanted to find out if she had sent it down or where it was. We then drove down the ridge and came around the first time that we had driven her much. She went fine. We washed this forenoon and afternoon.

Wed 28:   It is cloudy and warm today. We got a letter from Uncle Thomas today. Will Ritter's sale is today. Papa did not go.

Thu 29:   Awful cold and cloudy today. Reading day today.

Fri 30:   Cold this morning. But it is beautiful. This afternoon Ruby & I hitched up Dolly and drove up to Aunt Annie's. We called at Ethel's also. It is kind of rough and muddy.[th]

Sat 31:   Today Papa and Mamma went to town. Ruby and I staid home. Early this afternoon we heard Aunt Annie & Mattie say three loads of furniture went by there. I guess it is Jesse Ford's. They said that Charley Ford and Raymond Spencer came on behind in a rig. Later this afternoon Jack Combellick went by in a carriage with a buggy tied in behind. I guess it was Jesse Ford's carriage. Papa & Mamma went over and called on Henry Bastians a little while. Laura asked Mamma if we were to the party over to Young's Wed night. She said it was to be a farewell party. But they aren't going very far. Now I don't know who got it up or who was there. I'm put out because we weren't invited.

February

Sun 1:   We all went to church this morning. No many there I believe seventeen. Martha played the organ. Sadie Bastian, Mrs. Edd Young & I were in the choir. We came home for dinner. This afternoon Ruby & I hitched up Molly and drove up to Werner's but they weren't home so we went back and went over the Guilford road we thought we would call at Nick & Anna Weis but it looked as if they wasn't home so we did not go in so we came around and up by Fattie's. The horse went fine.

Mon 2:   It was snowing this forenoon. Papa wanted to go up the Mound and out to Robert's to get some roosters. It stopped snowing after dinner so Papa drove the horse up there. He thought that he might stay all night if it got to late. Helen said that Mrs. J. Williams is dead.

Tue 3:   Papa stayed all night up at Roy Tresidder's. He came home about eleven o'clock this morning. He wanted to go to Ortcheid's sale today so he ate a lunch and hitched Prince and Violet up in the hack and went. At about twenty minutes after one, Papa called up and said that Prince was dead. He died over the other side of Tippet's near where Uncle Edd goes into the Miller place. He could hardly go and Papa had been stopping but he drove on a little way and was going to turn around to come home again but he looked as if he wanted to get down. He fell down as Papa was unhitching him. Poor old Printie. Poor Prince. Papa got a single tree at Tippet's and Violet pulled him into Uncle Edd's out of the way. He then rode Violet home. He harnessed Molly up with Violet (but they are strange yet and she don't like Violet) and drove over and got the hack. I guess Prince died of heart trouble. He could hardly go Saturday when they came home from town. We bawled some this afternoon. Helen said this evening that Mrs. Williams is going to be buried tomorrow at ten oclock. She said that Jim Spencers were going to move tomorrow. But I think that maybe they moved their things today and are going to Epworth tomorrow. She said that Jesse Ford & Cleo Swift went to Kansas with goods yesterday and that the rest are going Thu. I would like to see Mertie before she goes. Who know when I will see her again. I hope before very long. The last time I saw her was at the farewell party. Prince died Feb. 3 at one oclock. Age about 13 or 14 years.

Wed 4: We got a little letter from Vada D. this morning and two pictures postal card of her on her pony when she was going home to town. One is for Aunt Annie. Papa went this forenoon over and they pulled poor old Prince in a hole. Papa went to town this afternoon. Uncle Edd rode to town with him. Nice day today but cold.

Thu 5: Reading day today. Papa went over to Ortcheid's after ten bushels of barley today. I guess Jim Spencers went today. Ruby and I are sewing wool carpet rags for some rugs. I heard that Mrs. J. Ford & Mertie, Charlie, Lucille, & Pearl were to go to Kansas today.

Fri 6: Snowing about all day today. Mamma was down to John's this afternoon. I wonder if it will be sleighing.

Sat 7: We did not go to town today.

Sun 8: It is just awful cold today. Mamma said this morning (but not very early) that it was nine below zero. Aunt Annie said that Johnnie said that it was twenty below. It was to be preaching this afternoon but we did not go. It being to cold. And the snow was to deep to walk.

Mon 9:   Papa took our sleigh up to Uncle Edd's and hitched Uncle Edd's team to it and hauled a load of hogs for Uncle Edd. Erhart Dittmar came out to Aunt Annie's from Galena yesterday. He came down with Papa this afternoon. Nice day.

Tue 10:   This forenoon Erhart Dittmar went over to Wachter's. I got a Valentine post card from Jeannette today. We got a beautiful pink hyacinths out in bloom quite a few sleighs and cutters going along today.

Wed 11:   Well today Papa butchered two hogs. Aunt Annie came down this forenoon. This evening Uncle Edd & John & Ethel came down in the sleigh.

Thu 12:   Well today is Lincoln's birthday. Reading day Papa cut up the hogs. We ironed not much news.

Fri 13:   No news. Cold.

Sat 14:   Well today is St. Valentine's Day. A year ago tonight was the basket social at our school. I did not get any valentines today. Papa, Ruby & I went to town in the sleigh with Molly and Violet. Lots of people in town today. Saw Ora Pooley and her mother in town. It is the first time I saw her to speak to since they moved away.

"Sweetheart cookies" - handwritten on a piece of
tablet paper - author unknown

"1 cup sugar

½ " " butter

1 well beaten egg.

½ cup Sweet milk

3 or 3 ½ cup flour

3 level teaspoon cream tarter

1 ½ teaspoon of soda. Put both in with the flour.
1 teaspoon vanilla

Roll dough very thin

(Filling for cookies)

1 cup chopped dates

½ cup walnut meats

½ cup water

3 level teaspoon Flour

cook until creamy

- - - - "

Sun 15:   Well we were to have preaching this forenoon but it was awful cold and snowing. Mamma, Ruby & I got ready and even started out but came back again. Uncle Edds went but there wasn't any body there and no fire so they went home again. It cleared up late this afternoon.

Mon 16:   Well Papa took six and a fraction bushels of clover seed to town today. He got seven fifty per bushel. I got a Valentine post card from Wilbur today. Mattie Tippet and Aunt Annie called up Mamma today about having a surprise party of Virtue before they move. But could not make out when they wanted it. Or to have it afternoon or eve. It would be a funny and crazy thing to have it in the afternoon so I suppose there's nothing doing.

Tue 17:   This evening we all went up to Win Tippet. Mrs. Westaby is up there and Morris Roberts had been in on the jury and he was excused. Papa and I fixed the Cutter today.

Wed 18:   Today Papa hitched up Molly in the cutter and went up to Heuberger's sale. But he did not buy a horse. Aunt Annie got a letter from Aunt Tillie today saying that they were going to have it Saturday instead of

Monday but their anniversary is Sunday. They want Aunt Annie and one of us to come out before. Aunt Annie is going tomorrow on the eleven oclock.

Thu 19: Ruby and Aunt Annie went over the Station to go to Apple River with the men folks as they go to John Lupton's sale. Papa also went along.

Fri 20: Papa went with John Tresidder to Berryman's sale but did not buy anything. Well I guess today was the last day that Vera will go to school up here.

Sat 21: Well we got up early and done the chores. Papa, Mamma & I went over the Station in the cutter we drove Molly. We left her in Paul Merrifield's stable. We went on the eleven twenty-nine train to Apple River. Uncle Edd went to Galena and went from there. Every body else was there. Just before dinner Rev. Machurkin gave a speech. Those present besides children and grandchildren and in laws were Rev and Mrs. Machurkin and two daughters, Mr. Hammer and Mrs. Hammer's son. And Uncle Erhard and Aunt Lizzie Dittmar and Ella, Lennis and Donald. They had two tables at one they seated Grandpa and Grandma and all their children seated acording to age. Uncle George seated beside Grandpa and Uncle Herman beside Grandma. Aunt Lizzie, Aunt Lue,

Pearl, Ruby, Sadie and I acted as waitresses. ~~The d~~ The decorations were of yellow roses. There were forty-six present. Grandpa and Grandma were given many gifts a gold clock by the children a set of butter knife and sugar shell from Mamie, Pearl Wesley and Sadie. The bowl of the spoon and the knife were gold plated the handles were of silver. A two and a half dollar gold piece from Mr. Hammer, a set of pepper and salt shakers from Aunt Catherine Winter with gold tops. All the children, grandchildren, son in laws and daughters in law were there but Aunt Rachel. All stayed to supper but Uncle Henrys and Bens. Papa & Mamma went home on the nine oclock train and Ruby & I stayed we went to a George Washington program given by the school in the evening, at the opera house. It was fine going home Sadie fell and sprained her wrist. We staid at Uncle George's all night. It snowed.

Sun 22:   Ruby & I went to Sunday school and church with the girls. Heard Griswold preach. We stayed at Uncle George's for dinner. Mamie, Ruby & I spent the afternoon at Grandpa's. We all went to the Methodist church again this evening. Annie White preached. Griswold went to Warren. Called at Uncle George's after church. Staid all night at Grandpa's.

Mon 23: Ruby & I went on the morning train to Scales Mound and went up to Uncle Nick's. Arthur and Liddie were at Rittwager's. Aunt Lizzie got word to them to come to the depot to see us for the afternoon train. Arthur went along to Galena. Uncle Edd & Aunt Annie came that train from Apple River. John & Ethel were in to get us. John Collins told Fiedler to invite the neighbors to a surprise party at Virtue's. Fiedler told Papa Sunday morning we went this evening there were twenty-five there. Fiedlers, us, Mr. & Mrs. Jo Weis, Josie & Helen, John Tresidder, Ida & Milton Mr & Mrs. J.A. Weis & Catherine, Mr. Collins & Mr. Wachter. A little before midnight refreshments were served. We took a cake we all rode home with Fiedler. Papa & John Tresidder went to Balbach's sale today. Didn't buy anything.

Tue 24: Papa got twenty-five bu of oats from Virtue today. Mamma went along. She helped to pack.

Wed 25: Well Virtues moved today. Mamma went over to help them load. Those that help haul were Joseph A Weis, Edd Tippet, Will Wachter, John Tresidder Will Weis & Edd Weis. Lovely day today.

Thu 26: Reading day today. Also washing day. Papa helped Virtue drive cattle part way down this afternoon. I talked with Helen this evening. They are going over to

Guilford school to a spelling match. Thelma Davis & Jeremiah Thick are to spell. Tomorrow afternoon.

Fri 27: Snow is about all gone today. Ironing day today.

Sat 28: Well today is the last of Feb. Papa, Ruby & I went to town today drove Dela and Molly first time we drove them together besides Papa trying them the other day. They went fine only rather slow. Quite a few people in town today. It thawed a great deal today and when we came home from town the river was quite high just about ready to over run the banks. It was a beautiful day when we went to town but when we started from town it was blowing and snowing just awful and then it would clear up then storm again all the way home and turned awful cold.

March

Sun 1: Mamma, Ruby and I went to church this morning not many there to cold I guess. We came home and then went up to Aunt Annie's to dinner yet. Fred Rodgers of Michigan was there. Ida Bastian came up there in the afternoon.

Mon 2: Nothing much doing today. Helen said tonight that Thelma won in the spelling contest. Jerry came in fourth. Sheean's farm is to be sold at auction at the court house tomorrow I wonder who will buy it.

Tue 3: Cloudy today. J.A. Weis dehorned our cow this forenoon. Poor things. Made some candy this afternoon.

Wed 4: Well Papa started out ~~this forenoon~~ today to buy a horse. This evening he bought a black horse horse he got it from Menzemer. I don't know what it is like it is pretty. Nick and Anna Weis moved over to John Weis' yesterday and today. I suppose they are going to live with them.

Thu 5: Reading day today. We tried the new horse but do not like it very well. We think it is kind of scary and slow.

Fri 6:   Papa and Ruby tried the horse again today. But don't like it very well yet. Violet get just awful nervous.

Sat 7:   Papa & Mamma went to town today. They paid for the horse. One hundred and fifty-five dollars. The horses name is Niger and is five year coming six. Today about twelve oclock Cora Roberts came here. Some Berryman brought her this far. We wasn't going to have any dinner and everything was so up side down and dirty. We had to got to work and get some kind of a dinner. Papa & Mamma brought home some freight from Montgomery Ward. It is a couch (mission style) and some rice (25 lb.) and 25 lb sugar and 100 of gritt for chickens and ten yard of calico.

Sun 8:   Well this morning Mamma was called down to John Tresidder's. This evening she called up and said there was a little girl down there and that she wasn't coming home tonight. I suppose she will have to stay down there for weeks now. It makes me mad. Papa, Ruby & I went to church today (afternoon) sixteen there today. Lottie played the organ because there was no one else there to play it.

Mon 9:   Mamma came home this forenoon. A beautiful day today. I have an awful cold.

Tue 10: It isn't such nice weather today as it was yesterday. One of Ruby's sheep (Amy) had a lamb this morning. We have six lambs now. Ruby four and I two. Uncle Edd took clover seed up to the Mound today ~~with~~ and Aunt Annie came down here.

Wed 11: We washed today. Nice day. This evening just before we went to bed there was an eclipse of the moon it was almost total. There was just a little left yet. Papa is hauling manure today.

Thu 12: Well today is a lovely day. It is reading day and ironing day. I made a little round pin cushion of red silk and stuffed it with rice and gathered lace around the edge. It looks cute. I got a card today from Jeannette. She wrote that she had learned to dance this winter and had been to one at Guilford Hall. Mamma was down to John's this afternoon. Wilbur Tresidders have a young son.

Fri 13: A lovely day today. I bake a cake today. Everything went alright even if it was Fri 13.

Sat 14: Papa & I went to town today. The roads are awful bad. Lot of people in town today. We saw Jim Spencer he is back from Epworth came back for Mr. Warmouth's funeral today. I had my picture taken on a postal card into Bartell's today. He took it twice.

I ordered three for seventy five cents. I am standing up and have my hat on. I am afraid that they will be awful. But I hope that they will be good.

Sun 15: We all went to church this forenoon. Mrs. Walter Combellick played the organ. Mrs. Edd Young and Mrs. Walter Combellick sang a duet it was fine. Ida played for them. Mr. and Mrs. Popp and children and Uncle Edd and Aunt Annie came down from church to dinner. There were 23 at church today. This evening we went up to Fiedler's.

Mon 16: We got a lot of mail this morning. Mary Potter's picture. A letter from Lloyd he would like to come and work for us. He said the he was a greenhorn. We got a letter from Uncle Thomas. Uncle Thomas is thinking something of coming back this spring. And we got the proofs of my pictures. They are ugly my skirt looks so awful it just looks like bloomers. And I thought that I was better looking.

Tue 17: Not much doing now day. Quite windy. St. Patrick's day today.

Wed 18: Lovely day today only cold. Papa & Ruby hauled manure today with Violet and Niger. It is the first time they were hauled any thing with them. This afternoon we hitched up Fannie and Mamma and I went to

Aunt Annie's. Took up some truck to send out with Uncle Edd and Aunt Annie to Uncle Thomas' tomorrow. Mr. & Mrs. Tippet are going along. They are going to stay all night at Uncle Thomas' and then going to Tom Tippet's. Aunt Annie had a letter from Aunt Tillie today. She said that Uncle Joe's have a young son born Sat or Sun. We got thirty-two eggs today. The most that we have got yet this year. A year ago today we got fourty.

Thu 19: Uncle Edds went to Waterloo today. They took Grandpa & Grandma Tippet along they are going to Rockford, Ia.

Fri 20: I baked cookies today. It is a fine day today.

Sat 21: Well we got a card from Aunt Tillie today she said that Uncle Joe's baby was dead. Died yesterday and is going to be buried this afternoon. They aren't going to have any services because they haven't any preacher out there. We got a card from Aunt Rachel. Thanking for the stuff we sent. Papa & Ruby went to town today. It snowed a little all day today. It is the first day of spring.

Sun 22: Well we all went to church this afternoon. There were sixteen there. Mrs Walter Combellick played the organ again today. Mrs. Edd Young sang a solo accompied on the organ by Iola. Mrs. Walter Combellick, Mrs. Edd Young, Mrs. Win Tippet, Iola & I were in the choir today. Mr. Atkinson is going to sing a solo next Sun.

Mon 23: It is a fine day today. No news. We washed today. A year ago today was Easter and a year ago tonight we had that awful tornado here and a still worse one in Omaha, Neb.

Tue 24: Not much news. We ironed today. I baked a cake.

Wed 25: It is just awful windy today. This afternoon the preacher called here. He went up to Martha's. This afternoon an automobile came along and stopped out here. It was four drunken men. One came in for some water for the automobile. He was so drunk he couldn't find the bucket or the well. Uncle Edds came home from Iowa this evening.

Thu 26: Awful warm today. This forenoon Aunt Annie came in. She rode down with Uncle Edd and Rev. Atkinson. Uncle Edd took him over to Popp's. Uncle Edds came back here to dinner. Aunt Anne told us about their trip. They staid all night at Uncle Thomas' night before last and when they went out. I got my pictures today.

Fri 27:   Well it is booster day in Galena today. But we did not
           go and did not see many going.

Sat 28:   It is a ugly day today and just awful muddy. Saw one
           other team besides the mail carrier. I baked a hickory
           nut cake today.

Sun 29:   Well we were to have services this forenoon but it was
           raining this morning and looked a great deal like rain.
           We did not go. This afternoon it looked a little better
           so Ruby & I went over to Sadie Bastian's. Ben
           Young was there. We staid for supper. Sadie has
           everything fixed up quite nicely. They said that there
           was no church this forenoon.

Mon 30:   Cloudy all day today. No news today. Papa & Ruby
           hauled some posts this afternoon. Uncle George D.
           called up Aunt Annie from Galena this morning. He
           came in with Pearl. It is teachers' institute this week.
           Tomorrow is the last of March.

Tue 31:   It rained again today. Nothing new. Good bye
           March.

April

Wed 1: Well today is April Fools day. But did not do much fooling. It has been cloudy all day. This afternoon Mamma, Ruby & I went up to Aunt Annie's. John & Ethel were cleaning up the yard. The roads are awful bad and have been that way for quite awhile. There is quite an excitement over the country about the liquor question where it is to be voted on April 7. Galena is very much excited.

Thu 2: It is reading day today. It is a nice clear day today but is quite windy. I wrote a letter to Uncle Thomas this evening.

Fri 3: I raked some lawn today. No news. Tonight there is to be a debate between the "wets" and "dry" in Galena. I would have like to have went.

Sat 4: Well today Papa and Ruby went to town and got a supply of stuff. They took in thirty seven dozen eggs. They got fifteen cents a dozen.

Sun 5: Well it is Palm Sunday. We all went to church this afternoon. There was a quite a crowd there. Thirty I believe. Rev. Atkinson sang a solo. Lottie Hocking said that she was going to sing one next Sunday. It was a beautiful day today. Only windy.

Mon 6: Well this afternoon took the school election notices up school for Thelma to take home for her father to sign. I staid a few minutes. Miss Garrity sent for a new blackboard and it has come but is down the Station yet. Miss Garrity isn't going to have school tomorrow afternoon for she is going to town to vote and to vote for the "drys" she said. Tomorrow is election. Tomorrow night at this time (twenty minutes after nine) we ought to know if Galena went "wet" or "dry".

Tue 7: Well today is election day. Papa went to vote. It was this afternoon and there hadn't been a woman to vote there yet. It's a shame. We washed today. This evening Papa went over to Orlando Bastian's to see Billy about putting up the new blackboard at school. Well tonight we heard that ~~Gal~~ East Galena went "dry" by a majority of fifty-seven and West Galena by a majority of four hundred. It's a disgrace about West Galena. I heard by cross talk that Freeport and Rockford went dry.

Wed 8: Well we read in the Chicago Tribune what territory went wet and what went dry. E. Galena went dry by 57. The woman vote was 293 drys 84 wet. W. Galena went wet by 633. Woman vote: 421 dry 59 wet. Men's vote 269 dry, 207 wet. (disgrace) Apple River went dry by 50. Woodbine dry 127. Warren dry by 222. Nora dry by 120. Elizabeth dry by 173. Stockton dry by 214. There was some good work done anyhow. It was awful cold today. We ironed today.

Thu 9:   It has been a clear day today. But windy and a little cold. Mamma & I went up and swept the church this afternoon. Ruby washed the single harness. Papa started to plow the sheep pasture or the piece of ground right out here.

Fri 10:   Nothing doing today.

Sat 11:   Papa and I went to town today. Just lots of people in town. I had to buy some for my room today some paint.

Sun 12:   Well it is Easter today. We all went to church this forenoon. There was quite a few three. Lottie Hocking sang a solo ("On the Cross") and Mrs. Edd Young sang ("Face to Face"). There is to be ~~quior~~ choir practice at Lottie's Fri night. She asked us to come over. We all went up to Aunt Annie's to dinner. In the afternoon Papa, Uncle Edd, Ruby & I went down to the Miller house. Aunt Annie and Mamma went down and called on Mrs. Jo Dower.

Mon 13:   Ruby and I cleaned lawn today. Mamma fried down some meat. There's a big Easter Ball in town tonight. A automobile and three buggies went along this evening.

Tue 14: Ruby & I took the things out of my bedroom and took up the carpet and tore off the paper. I washed the woodwork and Ruby washed up the floor. It is ready to paint now. It was quite warm today.

Wed 15: We washed today and baked bread and Ruby painted my room. Papa finished plowing the sheep pasture tonight. It is just awful hot today.

Thu 16: It is reading day and ironing day. Ruby gave my room the second coat of paint. Papa plowed the garden today. Mamma planted some potatoes we all planted some other stuff for we did not have much seed. We got sixty-one eggs tonight the most that we got yet this year.

Fri 17: Well today we took the top off the buggy and Ruby & Mamma drove Fannie to town. It is the first time we drove her single to town and the first time any of us women folks ever ~~went~~ drove to town by ourselves. Coming home they met an automobile in a nice wide place they said Fannie did not look at it. Papa hauled brush and manure. Well this evening was singing practice at Lottie's. Mamma, Ruby & I went Wilbur and Sadie Bastian and Mr. & Mrs. Walter Combellick and Ida and Miss Tailor of Galena was there. Youngs didn't come because Mrs. Edd Young has been sick this week.

Sat 18: It has been April showery today. Sometimes awful windy. We put up the Dorothy Perkins rose bush today. Also planted some onions, cabbage, califlower, tomatoes. Well tonight is school election and it is Papa's time out. Hurrah he got out he has serve for over fifteen years. There was two directors to put in this year. One for Jim Spencer's place. They put Mr. Werner in for three years and Mr. Fiedler in for one year. Alvin Davis was put in last year. All greenhorns now.

Sun 19: Well it was afternoon preaching. We all went Aunt Maggie came in yesterday and was at church today. We got ninety-six eggs tonight. It was awful cold today. I wore my winter coat.

Mon 20: We washed today, finished raking the lawn of which I am very glad and finished making garden. It is warmer today.

Tue 21: Well today we were going to paper. But Aunt Annie and Maggie came down this forenoon and stayed to supper. Towards evening Mr. Werner called to get the school truck. I am so glad that it is gone. This evening Papa drove Fannie down to John Huilman's to take down some old after election stuff. He has just been elected school (I don't know what you call it).

Wed 22: Well Mamma and I papered the ceiling today and put on five pieces of sides. Well I must tell that there is quite an excitement about war between United States and Mexico. They have not really declared war yet but think there will be war. It says in the paper today that U.S. took the city of Vera Cruz. Men are inlisting all over the country. I hope that they may make peace immediately.

Thu 23: Mamma and I papered today. We are short of paper. So will not be able to finish it until we get some more. John Tresidder came up this ~~afternoon~~ evening to get our yesterday's paper. He wants to read about the war. He said the malitia of Galena had orders to be ready. He said that he heard that they wanted the Young boys to join and that Mrs. Young was about wild over it.

Fri 24: Well today Papa and I went to town. I bought another roll of for we did not have enough. I went in to look at the hats but did not get any. They are all so flat. Aunt Maggie came down here this afternoon. Had a hard rain this evening.

Sat 25: Well Mamma & I finished papering my room today. I got a card from Jeannette this morning. She said that she was going along here this evening about five oclock and that she would leave those books that she borrowed of us in the mailbox. I was watching for her. She and a young man went down in a buggy with a grey horse hitched up. I don't know who he was. I'm crazy to know. Aunt Maggie wants me to say that we had dandelions for supper the first we had this season. We also picked yellow dock. I guess we will have that tomorrow.

Sun 26: There is no services at Union today. There is quarterly meeting at the station. This afternoon we all started out for a walk. We went over and picked some flowers and then walked the ridge up to the school house. We saw an awful big snake lying beside the road. Papa killed it. It must have been seven feet long. It was a rattle snake pilot. We went on a few feet and there was another big dead one lying in the road. We saw a water snake above Fiedler's so that was three. We went in the school house and looked around We did not have any company today. Three years ago today Dave Sheean was buried.

Mon 27: Well today is Grant's birthday. Aunt Maggie went up to Uncle Edd's this morning and is going to town with them. Papa, Ruby & I went to town. I bought a new hat for four dollars and a quarter. We heard part of the speech by Charles Pickett of Waterloo, Ia. We expected Uncle Thomas to come today but he didn't. Aunt Maggie went home today. There was quit a crowd in town today.

Tue 28: Well it is showery today. A person can almost see things grow. We got an invitation this morning by mail to a surprise party. Friday evening May 1st for Mrs. John Tippet's birthday. We straightened up my room today and tore up Ruby's room. Took three calves away today are milking five cows now.

Wed 29: Straightened up Ruby's room today.

Thu 30: Reading day today and washing day. Ruby tore up the down stairs bedroom.

May

Fri 1:   Straightened up the down stairs bed room today. We are going to Ethel's birthday surprise party tonight but her birthday was yesterday.

Sat 2:   Well we were at the surprise party last night had a fine time. She was not very much surprised. I wore my old white all over embroidery dress. Ruby wore her white dress to. Those that were there were John & Ethel Tippet, Uncle Edd and Aunt Annie, Mrs. Falancer and Stella & Irma. Old lady Burton. Mr Eustice, John Heer, Marie & Martha, Blanch Ritter, Mr & Mrs. Win Tippet, Mr. & Mrs. Earl Ritter, Mr. & Mrs. Thomas Dower. John and Milton Tresidder, Ida Bastian, Tillie & Edith Weis, Mr. and Mrs. Walter Falancer and three children. We got home about half past one. Papa went to town this forenoon. Uncle George called up this forenoon and said that they were coming in early tomorrow morning. So we are awful busy today. ~~The~~ A chicken buyer called here today and as Mamma was talking to him there came a banty hen walking along. Mamma asked him if he brought it, he said he didn't. We were quite astonished. I called up Weis and asked if any of their's were going. She said the man had dinner at their place and we think it got in the buggy maybe. They did not come to get it or say it is theirs or not. It went to roost in the chicken house to night. It just made itself at home.

Sun 3: Well this forenoon all of Uncle Georges came in a three seater. Uncle Edd and Aunt Annie also came down this forenoon. They all had dinner here. Edward and Naomi were tickled over the lambs little calves and pigs and the cats. This afternoon Uncle George, Uncle Edd and Papa went to church. And Wesley hitched up and took us all up to Aunt Annie's. It came up to a storm about five oclock. It rained and hailed. It kept on storming for quite awhile after awhile it stopped a little and Papa went home. Then Mamma & Ruby they had to borrow overshoes and things they though I could come down with Uncle Georges when they went home. It stormed again and it rained just awful. It kept on until about nine oclock when it showed signs of clearing up. They all thought that they would have to stay all night and I to but they thought they would go then. Aunt Lizzie, Edward & Naomi stayed and will go home tomorrow. I rode down with them. It did not storm anymore.

Mon 4: We heard this morning that one of the Studier boys was badly hurt and that there was a tornado down there last night and that he got hurt. Mrs. Studier and one of the girls was up to Fiedler's she got awful badly scared and started right out to walk home. She did not know where to go she was so worked up. Sigerman and

Win Tippet went down and caught up with her and took her home. Fiedlers went down to. They said the boy's leg was broken and that he was quite bad and it was hard to tell if he would live. A piece of the barn fell on him the barn flew down and other buildings. Mr. Studier is hurt some to. One of the other boys was blew about 100 ft and hit against a building and is hurt some to. The girls was in the house and wanted to get out when they saw things going but could not open the doors. It had blew the house all crooked. They said it took other people's buildings and tore down fences and lots of trees. Helen took home her bantie hen tonight.

Tue 5:   Papa, Mamma & Ruby extended a fence out in the pasture for the sheep today. It was quite hot today. Mamma churned today.

Wed 6:   We tore up Papa's and Mamma's room today. We heard this evening that the Studier boys is dead. Papa is plowing for corn today.

Thu 7:   Reading day washing day today. The Studier boys is going to be buried tomorrow and are going to start at the house at eleven oclock. He is going to be buried up on the ridge. Helen told me we could bring Potatoe salad to the picnic Sat. It will be last day. They are going to have it on Sat instead of ~~starting~~ having it on Monday. Today is Miss William's and Mr. Madoo's wedding day. He

is fifty and she is twenty-four. It is also Ester Stauss'
wedding day is was to marry a Mr. Sanderson.

Fri 8:   We did not go to the funeral today. Papa was to busy.
I ironed today. It is a nice day today.

Sat 9:   Well it is the school picnic today. Ruby & I went.
We took potatoe salad there was about 28 there.
We had a fine time. We had ice cream. Papa &
Mamma went to town today. Uncle Thomas came
out from Galena. He came to Galena Thursday
we got a letter this morning for Uncle Thomas so
we thought he was coming. It stormed this evening.
~~I heard~~ Helen told me that Jeannette's fellow
was Fillie Altfilich. They was teasing her a lot
today.

Sun 10: We all went to church this forenoon. There were 27
there. Lottie sang a solo today. Uncle Edd and Aunt
Annie came down from church and Ida. After dinner
Agnes Milton and the baby came up.

Mon 11: It stormed last night it is stormy and rainy and just
awful cold and windy today. Papa got a little hay from
Uncle Edd's today.

Tue 12: Cool and cloudy today. Papa has a fellon on his left
thum and it pains him an awful lot. I cut the lawn
today. Uncle Thomas is fixing fence.

Wed 13: Papa and Ruby went to town this forenoon with old Fannie. Papa went to the doctor about his thumb. The doctor cut it open and took the matter out. Papa has to go in again tomorrow. His hand is all bundled up. Uncle Thomas plowed after they came home. It was a nice day today. I ironed and baked a batch of cookies today.

Thu 14: This morning Papa and I went to town. We got along all right the doctor dressed his hand. He has to go in again tomorrow. Uncle Thomas plowed today. Nice day today.

Fri 15: Ruby and Papa went to town today. The Doctor (Dr. Miller) said his thumb was getting along nicely. They got home about one oclock. Papa harrowed this afternoon. He drove with one hand. Uncle Thomas went over the grave yard and visited around. He is going to stay all night down at John's. Nice day today.

Sat 16: Well Papa and I went to town today. Not many in town before we left. Old Fannie got a balky spell when we turned around to come home. she got in a little ditch and we couldn't make her go any more. Two men had to help us. She went all right the rest of the way home. Uncle Thomas went to town with John Tresidder this afternoon. He is going to stay in all night. The doctor talked as if papa might have to have the bone taken out of his thumb. I hope that he won't have to.

Sun 17: Well Papa and Ruby went to town this morning. Fannie went all right today. Ruby & I went to church this afternoon. There was only fourteen there. Fiedlers came here just before Ruby & I went to church when we got home Raymond was awful sick. He had a spasm and they thought that he would die. They thought that he was dead once. Mamma had to phone for Dr. Bench. Mamma got Mrs. Joe Weis to come up. The doctor did not come until about an hour after we came home. He got to look better as soon as the doctor treated him. They went home then.

Mon 18: Papa and Ruby went to town today. The doctor said Papa's thumb was getting along fine. He won't have to go to town any more until Fri if his finger gets along all right. We started to plant corn this afternoon.

Tue 19: A nice day today. Papa, Ruby & Uncle Thomas are planting corn today. We had a few little radishes today the first of the season. Just a year from today we had our first too. This evening Johnnie, Ethel, and Stella Falancer came down this evening. They came after the curtain stretchers.

Wed 20:   Planted the little piece of corn out here today. We got through this evening planting corn. Not much news lately.

Thu 21:   Well this morning Ruby took Uncle Thomas part way up to Scales Mound with Old Fannie. Uncle Thomas wants to go home Saturday. Jim Spencer went along in his auto this forenoon with four other men and he and another man went back again this afternoon. It came up to a storm this afternoon. It got awful windy. Leo and Raymond Werner came in here. They had rode out from town with Weis. They are going to school in town. The Catholic school I guess. It cleared up again until this evening we had a big rain. I took a bath tonight.

Fri 22:   Ruby and Papa went to town this forenoon and phoned out that the doctor wanted to dress it again at seven this evening. They said that the doctor thought it was blood poison and that it was worse. Uncle Thomas came to Galena from S.M. and came out this afternoon and stopped in along the way. It was quite late when Papa and Ruby came home. Papa is awful worried about his hand. Uncle Thomas is going home tomorrow.

Sat 23:   Papa & Ruby went tot town about eight oclock this morning. Mamma wants to go in today about his hand so Uncle Thomas when down to John's to go to town with them and Mamma & I got ready and was going to try to chance it in. We saw an automobile coming so we started to walk. It was a Cording boy and his mother with an empty seat. They asked us to ride so we did. Had a fine ride. It was Mother first ride in an automobile. The doctor said that it wasn't blood poison today. But it looked all blue. The doctor got awful mad at Ruby. Papa was just awful worried today. We ~~though~~ did not know if we should go to another doctor or not or if another doctor would be any better or what one to go to. I rode out with Johns. Mamma stayed in until after Papa had his hand dressed. She rode home with Cordings again. Aunt Annie and some of the Tippets went over to Dubuque today. Uncle Thomas went home this afternoon.

Sun 24: Papa and Ruby went to town this morning. We did not have anytime to go to church this forenoon. Ruby went to church in town. Ruby came home alone this afternoon. Papa stayed in he is going to stay at Stauss'. The doctor wants to dress his hand twice a day. Uncle Edd and Aunt Annie came down this evening.

Mon 25: Awful hot day today. Uncle Edd and Johnnie came down to plant our potatoes today. Aunt Annie came along down. Papa phoned out that the doctor wants to lance his hand this afternoon and Papa wanted Mamma to come in. So she went in this afternoon with Johnnie & Ethel. Uncle Edd sheared our sheep for us this afternoon. Uncle Edd brought Mama down and got Aunt Annie. Papa's hand was some better this afternoon so they did not lance it. It stormed in the night (Mon night). We are having an awful lot of radishes lately they grow so fast and are so large.

Tue 26:   It has been just awful hot today. Just about sweat to death. We got a letter from Uncle Thomas this morning. Papa phoned out he said his hand was looking better this morning but was some worse this afternoon. It is Jeannette's (Werner) eighteenth birthday today.

Wed 27:   Papa thinks his hand is some better today. Awful hot today.

Thu 28:   Papa phoned out and said his finger was worse and he wanted to know if Mama could come in. Aunt Annie said Johnnie was going in this afternoon and Mamma could go along. So she went. Aunt Annie went to town to. Papa wanted Mama to go over to East Dubuque to a lady that he heard so much about that could cure fellows. She went over on the two oclock and came back on the five. The woman was not home but her daughter was they She said they cured a man that had been in the hospital two weeks. The doctor thought his hand was some better this evening. Ruby and I went up to Uncle Edd's and stayed until they came home and a while longer. We showed Ethel how to make salt and cornstarch beads.

Fri 29: Papa called up several times today. He isn't feeling very well and his hand is some worse today and if it isn't better by morning the doctor thought he would have to pinch off the cords farther down. I do hope it will get better now. Rained some this forenoon but cleared off fine. Nice and cool today.

Sat 30: Ruby and I drove to town this forenoon. Mama rode in with John Tresidder. Papa's hand was hurting him awful and he is awful nervous and worried. The doctor took out at piece of the bone and pinched off the cords this morning. We had a notion for Papa and Mamma to go to Waterloo on the afternoon train in but they didn't go. Then they thought some thing about go to Chicago maybe. Mama staid in all night. Ida came up to stay all night with us.

Sun 31: Mamma called out this morning, but I hardly knew how it is. Ruby & I went to church this afternoon. It came up to a thunder Shower but stopped raining so we could come home. Mama called up this evening and said she wasn't coming home today. So Ida came up to stay all night with us again.

June

Mon 1: Well Papa called out this evening and said that they were going away. Ruby asked east or west and he said east. I suppose he went to Freeport. Ida came up and stayed with us again tonight.

Tue 2: This morning Nick Weis came to plow our corn. Ruby & I was wondering if mamma would come on this afternoon train. So we went up on the hill and watched. We saw her coming. She called in to Bastian's so we had to come home again. She came after we got home. Papa went to Dr. Stalegy but his assistant tended to it. They rented a room near his office. It think Papa will feel better satisfied with another doctor. Well Will Weis and Bessie Allan were married today don't know much particulars.

Wed 3: Washed today. Nick stayed to dinner today. This evening Uncle Edd and Aunt Annie came down to see how we were getting along. There is to be a barn dance up at Cording's tonight. Quite a few people went along tonight.

Thu 4: Reading day and ~~washing~~ ironing day today. We got three letters and a postal card from Papa today. One written eve of 2 another Wed morn. and another Wed eve. He said there was another deseased bone in his finger. They thought that they may have to take it out. They took and exray photo of his thumb. It says in the Gazette that Mr. & Mrs. Jesse Ford have a baby boy. It is storming tonight. We had our first strawberries today.

Fri 5: Got letters from Papa. He thinks his thumb is some better. Mama white washed the dining room ceiling today. John came up this afternoon and put two supers on our hive of bees. Milton came along. We went up in the woods late this afternoon and picked and ate a lot of wild strawberries.

Sat 6: We sent our can of cream with Mr. Fiedler this morning. Mama rode to town with Uncle Edd and took the eggs. Ruby and I stayed home had lots of work to do.

Sun 7: This forenoon Mama, Ruby & I went to church. There wasn't many there. After church Mama rode to Aunt Annie's with Uncle Edd. Aunt Annie is sick. Ruby & I came home to see if everything was all right. Then went up to dinner yet. Awfully hot today.

Mon 8: Hot today. We got two letters from Papa today. He don't think his thumb is getting better very fast. I am cutting lawn today. The cherries are starting to get ripe.

Tue 9: Hot today. Nick Weis fixed the fence between the corn field and the orchard today. We brought the pigs over this evening. We got a letter from Papa but it seem as if his thumb isn't getting better very fast. I cut some lawn today.

Wed 10: We washed today. Had a cherry cream pie the first and had a strawberry cream pie also. Lazy feeling today. No news.

Thu 11: We got a letter from Papa this morning. It doesn't seem as if his thumb is getting better very fast. Some one called up from Apple River this forenoon and said that Uncle Dan was coming to Galena and wanted to now if we could meet him but we don't like to drive old Fannie so we told him to try to get a chance out. So he got a chance out with Engels. I picked a bucket of cherries today and put up four quarts of stoned ones.

Fri 12: Papa was wondering if Ruby & I could come down tomorrow and stay over Sun. Just to get a little outing. I guess some of us will go. Nick plowed corn for us today. Ruby & Uncle Dan fixed the barnyard fence and I picked two buckets of cherries. Dan and Ruby picked some too. One tree is just awfully loaded.

Sat 13: Well it rained all day so we did not go to Freeport. Mr. Fiedler took our cream to town and we sent the eggs up to Uncle Edds for them to take.

Sun 14: This forenoon Mama got ready and went to Freeport she walked over the station. Uncle Dan went along and carried her suit case. Her face was all swelled up a bee stung her yesterday on the fore head. Ruby, Dan & I went to church this afternoon not many there. There is to be Sunday school convention down the Station next Sunday forenoon and afternoon.

Mon 15: We got a letter from Papa this morning. He said Mamma got down there all right. Nick plowing corn for us this afternoon. Ruby and I went over about as far as Bastian's to meet her. She doesn't think that Papa's thumb has improved very much. I picked cherries today. This evening Uncle Edd & Aunt Annie came down. John Tresidder came up also.

Tue 16: We are washing today. Dan & Ruby hitched up Fannie and drove to town to get some bran. Dan wanted to try Fannie. He thought maybe the harness hurt her back so he got a piece of felt boot and padded it and moved the piece back a little. He bought some pads in town today. They say she went fine.

Wed 17: We got a letter from Papa this morning. He thought his thumb was improving a little. Dan is fixing fence. Had old Fannie hitched up to haul wire around with. She went fine Dan was talking with Nick Weis. Nick said that Spensley said that Fannie never balked when he had her. Said he drove her every which way and everywhere and his wife drove her and that she went all right. We put up four quarts of cherries today we have twenty-one and one-half quarts now. I don't know if we will get anymore or not.

Thu 18: Well Ruby drove Uncle Dan over the station to go to Apple River. Fannie went all right. Reading day today. It is Soldiers' reunion at Elizabeth. Uncle Edd & Aunt Annie went yesterday they are going down to Uncle Ben's to. Grandpa & Grandma was going down to and is going to visit here on their way home.

Fri 19: Got a letter from Papa, he is feeling awful discouraged. It doesn't seem to get better. Not much doing around here. Uncle Edds came home today.

Sat 20: We sent our cream in with Mr. Fiedler this morning. None of us went to town today. Uncle Edd & Aunt Annie brought Grandpa & Grandma down this afternoon. They are thinking to take them up to Scales Mound to church for afternoon. There is to be Sunday school convention at the Station church tomorrow.

Sun 21: Well it looked stormy this morning so they did not go up the Mound. This afternoon Fiedlers came down. Ruby & I wanted to go to the Sunday school convention but it looked like rain and the grass was wet.

Mon 22: We did not get any letter from Papa today. So we thought he must be coming home. This afternoon he called up from Apple River. He is going to stay there all night and wanted us to come up to Scales Mound after him tomorrow forenoon. Uncle Edd came down after grandpa & grandma this morning they then went home this afternoon. Uncle Edd took them to town. This morning we got a letter all edged in black. It was an announcement of Clara (Trudgian) Duggan's death June 4th.

Tue 23: Well Ruby went to Scales Mound after Papa. Papa called up this morning from Scales Mound. He said his thumb was getting better. Dr. Tyrell is going to dress it. That is the fifth doctor. Ruby & Papa got home all right. Papa walked all over the farm. He has been away four weeks. Mama & I stretched the curtains today.

Wed 24: Well Ruby and Papa went to Scales Mound again this afternoon. They brought home five cents worth of ice. Papa's thumb is worse today. A lot of matter came out today. The Dr. did not squeeze it yesterday. The Dr. said that maybe Papa would have to have his thumb taken off yet. I hope not I thought it was getting better.

Thu 25:   Papa and Ruby went up to Scales Mound this afternoon. The Doctor said Papa's thumb was some better. He doesn't have to go tomorrow. We are to tend it. We made some ice cream this morning. Papa & Ruby brought five cents worth of ice from Scales Mound yesterday. The telephone line is out of order, it must be tangled somewhere.

Fri 26:   Well it has been storming and raining every little while today. Mamma & I went picking raspberries this forenoon. It came up to a storm and we had to come home. I ran right into a swarm of bees but I took to my heels and ran out again. We got about two quarts of raspberries and some for supper and I made some more ice cream and put in some mashed berries it made it sort of a pink it was pretty good. We wanted to pick some more this afternoon but it stormed, so we couldn't. There is lots of berries and lots of ripe ones and nice and large.

Sat 27:   This forenoon Mamma, Ruby & I went picking raspberries. We put up five quarts and one before.

This afternoon Papa and Ruby went up the Mound again. They called on Uncle Erhard's.

Sun 28: It is cloudy and just awful cold today. I nearly froze. Mamma wore her winter dress to church and the most of the people wore coats. We all went to church this afternoon quite a few there.

Mon 29: Nick plowed corn here today. We picked berries this forenoon put up six and one half quarts and one quarts thin jelly and had a pie. Banked some potatoes this afternoon. Next Sat is the fourth of July. They are going to celebrate in Galena. I wish I could go. Hope I can get a chance to go.

Tue 30: Papa and Ruby went to Scales Mound this afternoon. The hole is growing shut and they want the doctor to open it up. The doctor cut it a little down farther. He said it would have broke anyway. Mamma and I banked some potatoes this afternoon. Cut some lawn today. It is getting quite big.

July

Wed 1: The first of July today. Mamma, Ruby & I picked raspberries this forenoon. We put up eight quarts and made a little jelly. We have twenty quarts now. I cut some lawn today. My but the Dorothy Perkins rose bush is pretty now. Papa is trying to fix things up for haying. Most people are making hay now.

Thu 2: Washed today. I cut some lawn and some more to cut tomorrow. Quite warm today. Papa went up to Uncle Edd's tonight. He got a ride in an automobile.

Fri 3: Mamma and Ruby picked five quarts of raspberries. That makes twenty-five. Aunt Annie asked Ruby & I to go to Galena to the fourth of July tomorrow. They want to go at eight oclock.

Sat 4: Ruby and I went in town with Uncle Edd and Aunt Annie at eight oclock this forenoon. We went down to meet the morning train it was just awful crowded but did not see any of the folks from Apple River. But when we got up town again Uncle Dan was up there. He said Aunt Tillie and Mamie was coming in on the afternoon train. Wesley came on the morning train to. About noon Uncle Herman came and Papa came to town with him. Aunt Tillie and Mamie came on the afternoon train. There was just an awful big crowd in town. A person could hardly crowd along the side walk. There was lots of drunks. We rode home with Uncle Edds again. Mamie rode out with Uncle Herman. Uncle Herman came here for supper and then home. Early this morning there was a team and rig on Tippet's hill with out any driver so Win took it home. The sheriff called up Tippets and asked if they saw anything of it. He then came out and got it. It had been stolen from the depot last night a man had tied it up to meet the train. They think somebody wanted to get away and took the horses and drove out this way.

Sun 5: Papa went up the Mound this morning. Mamma Ruby and I went to church not a very big crowd. Mrs. Walter Combellick taught Sunday school. Uncle Edd, Aunt Annie, Aunt Tillie and Mamie came down for dinner also stayed for supper.

Mon 6: Mamma & I picked some raspberries. Papa cut the piece of hay across the road.

Tue 7: Well Papa, Mamma & Ruby went to town this forenoon. I staid up to Aunt Annies. They had to take two wagon wheels to town to have them set before we could haul hay. We also had cream and eggs. They drove Fannie and Della. They when fine going to town but Fannie had some spells again coming home.

Mamma was going to walk home from Aunt Annie's we was just ready to come home when we saw two ladies coming walking up the road. We could not think who it was. Aunt Tillie said its "May and Maggie Winter" and sure enough it was they walked over from the Station and we wasn't at home so they came up there.

Wed 8:   Well this forenoon Aunts Annie & Tillie & Maggie Mamie and Maggie Winter came down. In the afternoon Ruby took the two Maggies part way over the station. Aunt Tillie and Mamie is going to stay all night. They picked gooseberries late this after. Papa raked and they hauled two loads of hay across the road. Papa also cut the other little patch.

Thu 9:   Tillie and Mamie went up to Aunt Annie's this morning. They hauled hay today.

Fri 10:   Mamie went home today. She got a chance to town. I baked a batch of cookies. Haying again today.

Sat 11:   Awful busy. I baked some. Mamma washed and Ruby cleaned then after we hauled in hay. It is just awful hot I heard somebody say one hundred and two in the shade. It is just awful.

Sun 12:   Quite warm again today. We all went to church this afternoon. Not many there. Just Annie Bastian

& Lottie Uncle Edd, Aunt Annie and Tillie and Martha and the preacher. Nice evening.

Mon 13: We hauled two loads of hay this afternoon. It is cooler today. I picked our first cucumber today. This afternoon Aunt Tillie called on us. She and Aunt Annie were picking dewberries along the road. Jake Stauss came along in their auto so Aunt Tillie rode down. She went back again in a little while.

Tue 14: Well we hauled in five loads of hay this afternoon. We have twenty-one in now. I sent for a dress and a pair of Mary Jane pumps this morning.

Wed 15: Well we hauled in four loads of hay this afternoon. So that makes twenty-five. We are awful tired this evening.

Thu 16: Well it is Ruby's twenty first birthday today. Almost an old maid. And no show of being anything else. Well she will be able to vote now. She will have to go to vote this fall. Well this morning it came up to a storm so we got in only a little jag of hay. Some that was left over from yesterday. It kind of brightened to towards noon so Papa and Ruby went to town. Mamma washed today.

Fri 17: Well it has been a very nice day today only quite windy to haul hay. We hauled in four loads this afternoon making twenty-nine loads. Well us women folks went picking blackberries this morning put up seven quarts and some over. They were pretty nice. I was expecting my dress and pumps today but they didn't come. I hope they well fit all right. I sent for size bust thirty six for dress. ~~Also~~ And no. five pumps the rest thing that they will be to small. I hope not and I hope that they will come by parcel tomorrow.

Sat 18: Awful busy today. Hauling hay and Sat. work.

Sun 19: Well this forenoon we all went to church. Rev. Holliday from Hazel Green preached and our preacher went to Hazel Green. There was quite a crowd there. About 35. Papa went along up to Uncle Edd's but we came home. We stayed home all the rest of the day.

Mon 20: We hauled hay again. Are busy as usual well this afternoon five fellows came along on motorcycles. They stopped and got a drink and asked if they were on the right road to Galena. They also sat down on the lawn and rested. They said that they were from Chicago. And was going to camp down the river below Galena.

Tue 21: Busy again as usual haying. Most people are cutting grain. My dress and pumps did not come yet. No news.

Wed 22: Aunt Annie and Tillie came down this forenoon. Aunt Annie went with us picking blackberries. Aunt

Tillie staid here and got a little of the dinner. Awfully warm today we hauled some hay this afternoon. Aunt Tillie is going to stay down.

Thu 23: Hurrah we got through haying this afternoon. We got about fourty-five or six loads. My but it is just awful hot today. It was just awful hot last night. Hardly slept any. Well my pumps came today they are pretty nice fit all right only tight across the toes.

Fri 24: It rained a little this forenoon. My dress came this morning. It is pretty and fits pretty good if any-thing a little big. Aunt Tillie went up to Aunt Annie's this morning. This morning we got a card from Uncle Thomas saying that Anna was is coming to Galena tomorrow on the five oclock. Papa's thumb has been hurting him quite a bit lately. We could see a piece of bone just stick out. Ruby tried to pull it out but could not get it. So Papa though he would go up the Mound to the doctor to have it taken out but before he got ready they tried to get the bone out again they squeezed it out. It was quite a piece. Papa went up the Mound anyway but not to the doctor we wanted some flour and pigs feed. He went to the doctor and got a little medicine for it. The doctor said he though it would heal up now. Mamma washed today. An awful big and dirty washing.

Sat 25: Papa, Ruby & I went to town this afternoon. Anna came on the flyer. We had to bring something from town for Aunt Annie and Martha and Mary Tippet. Quite a colection. We saw Miss Garrity she just came off the train her and her mother and sister and little brother they just came from away out west. They got home sick and so they came back. Anna says Wilbur's wedding is to come off the sixteenth of September.

Sun 26: We all went to church this afternoon from church Anna went up to Uncle Edd's and we came home and done our chores and then we went up. Awful hot today. Not many at church. Lots of automobiles today. Last night about twelve or after Albert Pooley came in and woke us up there was another man along who was broken down with an automobile down the road. He wanted a lantern to see if he could fix his auto. He asked if he could bring his wife up here to lie down if he could not fix it. Kept us up for long time at last they went along with their auto.

Mon 27: This morning Ruby, Anna and I picked blackberries. Mamma put up nine and one half quarts. It makes nineteen and one half now. Papa took four lambs and a small last year's sheep over the station this morning. We got twenty six dollars and sixty cents.

Tue 28: We picked berries again this morning. Mamma put up ten quarts which makes twenty-nine quarts. This afternoon Anna, Ruby and I went down to Weis' and then down to John's. Staid down to John's for supper.

Wed 29: Nice day today. We picked berries again this forenoon. Got a little bucket full and we were going to send them by parcel post but they thought the mail carrier was gone so Anna is going to take it over the Station this evening. Ruby took drove her over to Ford's and then she wants to go with them down to the ice cream social this evening and then she wants to go to Freeport tomorrow forenoon. I wish we could go to the sociable this evening. Papa want to take us but he isn't feeling very well and I don't want him to bother.

Thu 30: Well it is reading day and washing day quite a big washing. I wonder what kind of a time they had at the social last night. There is going to be a Sunday school picnic in Parkin's Grove Aug the fourth or next Tuesday.

Fri 31: Well this is the last day of July. My but the time flies. We ironed an awfully big ironing and churned. And went over the blackberry patch but did not find so very many. The Chautauqua is going to be the eighth to the thirteenth of August.

August

Sat 1:   Mamma and Ruby went to town with Uncle Edds. Ruby wanted to go in to get a new dress and Papa isn't feeling very well so we though that he hadn't better go. They heard in town that the Sunday school picnic isn't going to be until the fourteenth. Ruby bought a new dress. It is pink and white stripe. I guess ratine.

Sun 2:   Well there isn't any church today. We hitched up Fannie and Papa and Mama went out for a little ride. After dinner Ruby and I drove her up to Werner's. They were at home. They had company from Apple River. Mr. and Mrs. Anchute and two children. We staid to supper. Jeannette's fellow wasn't there but I guess he was going to come in the evening. Papa and Mamma went down to John's a little while this evening.

Mon 3:   Well we picked a few blackberries and some choke berries this afternoon. We drove up in the wood. It was the first time we ever hitched Niger up in the hack he went all right. I do hope that Niger won't be afraid of autos or train or any thing when he gets out on the road. Anna telephone this evening from Scales Mound. She wanted to know if we could go and get her tomorrow. We said that we would try and get her tomorrow.

Tue 4:   Well we went up to Scales Mound today. Anna had
          come down to Uncle Nick's this morning from Willie's
          Uncle Nicks had been out there to. While we were there
          there an old agent came and wanted to give Uncle Nick
          a treatment for his ears and sell him a phone so he
          could here. They gave him twelve dollars. I'm afraid
          he is nothing but a swindler. ~~We we came ho~~ Just
          before we came home we called Uncle Eheart's to see
          Willie an Eheart. When we came home Anna and
          I stopped off at Fiedler's. Anna wanted to see the
          place. We stayed quite awhile. Fiedlers went over to
          the picnic today. They did not that it isn't to be until
          the fourteenth.

Wed 5:   I have been sick all day today. I guess I ate to many
          bananas before I went to be last night. I believe I
          ate three. This afternoon Ruby and Anna went up
          to Aunt Annie's. Anna is going to stay up there
          all night tonight then Papa is to take her to town
          tomorrow. This afternoon an awful lot of autos past
          here some all dressed in white caps and some with white
          caps and yellow coats. They looked like sailors. They
          were advertising the Great White Fair Darlington
          Wisconsin.

Thu 6:   Well Papa and Ruby went to town took Anna in.
          Anna is going to stay at Henry Bastian's all night.
          There is great excitement the last few days about war.

Almost all of Europe is waring against each other. But I don't know what for. There has been thousands killed already.

Fri 7: Well we put up peaches today. Papa and Ruby brought home a box yesterday. They cost a dollar. We put up nine quarts and eat quite a few. They were very fine peaches. I counted our fruit that we got put up this evening we got just seventy quarts now without the jelly and jam. And we have eaten a lot. We need rain awfully bad the grass is all dried up and I'm afraid the corn won't amount to anything.

Sat 8: Well we got a card from Anna this morning. She said she got home alright. The card is a picture of their house. Well today is the first day of Chantaqua but we did not go. It was so hot and dusty. Aunt Anne said this evening that tomorrow is going to be free. That they can't charge anything on Sunday. Ruby and I had old Fannie hitched up in the buggy and hauled some limbs for the sheep and hauled away some brush.

Sun 9: Well we hitched up the carriage to got to church the first time since it was broken last fall. There was a medium size crowd at church today. Aunt Annie came down from church Uncle Edd went home to do his chores and came down to supper.

Mon 10: Well Mamma washed today an awful big washing. Today is Mrs. Woodrow Wilson's the president's wife funeral services. I believe she is to be buried tomorrow.

Tue 11: Well we all went to town today we went to the Chantaqua. The lecture was good. The subject was "Winning the Nation's Greatest Fight." by Dr. E. L. Eaton. It would have been just the thing for the saloon and brewery people to hear if they would only have been there.

Wed 12: Ruby and I ironed today. It kept us busy.

Thu 13: Well we are busy getting ready for the picnic tomorrow. I bake filled cookies and a cake Mamma bake bread and rolls and cooked some ham. Mamma churned also. My but it is so dry I'm afraid the corn and potatoes won't amount to anything. The grass is all burned. The cotton wood trees leaves have ~~about all fell~~ been falling all day and I guess they will all fall off. I do hope that it will rain Saturday.

Fri 14: Well today we all went to the picnic drove Della and Fannie in the carriage. We got along fine with the horses. We took our dinner. We ate our dinner alone. Uncle Edds had dinner before they left. We had lunch again awhile before we came home. There was quite a crowd there. Just an awful lot of autos and teams. They had a parade headed by two girls on horseback. One was Birdie White and the other Reba Ritter. Then came four ragamuffins, three women and one man. One was Mrs. Sherman Lipton. Then came a hayrack full of Council Hill Sunday school young people. Then came a lot of Council Hill women marching. Then came an automobile with Rev. Atkinson and Rev. Hyingia the speaker. And in between some where was the Masonic band. And George Smart carrying a big flag. America was sung by all. Flossie sang a solo. Flossie, Hattie Bail, Albert Williams and a red headed Redfern sang several pieces. Ruby & I went around awhile with Mayme Tobin. But most of the time alone. Jeannette wasn't there she said when we were up there that she was going to stay at home and rest that day because she was going home with Spencers. They all went along about eleven oclock this forenoon in the Ford car. Weis wasn't there either. They had a few races before we left. I wanted to see the rest but it was getting time to go home.

Sat 15:   Papa and Ruby went to town today. They wanted to get some chicken and hog feed.

Sun 16:   We all had a dandy rain early this morning. It rained some this forenoon so we did not go to church. It cleared up a little by this afternoon so we were getting ready to go up to Aunt Annie's. But John Tresidder came. So Papa and Mamma went up about four oclock. Ruby and I done the chores and then went up.

Mon 17: ~~We~~ I got a card from Anna this morning. Mamma got a letter from Annie Curley. She wants Mamma to put up so plumbs for her and send them to her. She send a check along to help pay for them. We put up three half gallon bottles of cucumber pickles and two half gallons of mixed pickles of cucumbers, green tomatoes and caulaflowers. Uncle Edd was going to take a calf over the Station this morning. He said he would that our sheep along. So he took four lambs and my old sheep. Papa went along. We got twenty-eight dollars and thirty-five cents.

Tue 18: We washed today.

Wed 19: We ironed today.

Thu 20: Today we all went to town. Ruby went to have a tooth fixed at Dr. Kittoe's she said it didn't hurt. Jeannette was in town today. I went around with her some.

Fri 21: Today we got a letter from Uncle Thomas Aunt Rachel and Wilbur. Wilbur said he supposed we heard that he is going to be married. He said it is so. He said he is going to be married September sixteenth at four oclock.

He said they were going to take the nine something train for Chicago and that possibly they might stop off a day. They are thrashing at Will Weis' and on the Ivey place today.

Sat 22:   *They are thrashing at Joe Weis' this forenoon and at John's and they thrashed Fiedler's this afternoon and then they moved over to John Weis. Papa took Mamma over the Station to go to Apple River on the five oclock train. She is going to stay until Monday. Papa said Pearl and Sadie was on the train coming home from Iowa. Quite a few teams and autos went along today.*

Sun 23:   *We this afternoon at about time to go to church it clouded up and rained at about half past two it started to clear up. We went up on John Weis' hill we could see the preacher down at the church so Papa went down. Popps went along to but they went down to Young's. We came home again. Then Papa went down to John's he staid to supper.*

Mon 24:   *Well this afternoon Mamma is coming home so Ruby & I hitched up old Fannie and drove over for Mamma. Edward came along with Mamma so we were rather crowded coming home. Ruby stood on the back of the buggy part of the way. We got home alright Fanny went fine.*

Tue 25:   We washed today. Papa is painting the barn. Nothing
much doing.

Wed 26:   Papa & Ruby went to town this afternoon. Ruby
had a tooth filled. Mamma and I pealed tomatoes
for preserves. And fixed something for mixed pickles.
Edward is busy hauling leaves and wood. Uncle Edds
are going to thrash tomorrow we are all invited up.
Mamma picked and sent by parcel post a market basket
full of wild grapes to Uncle Thomas. It cost thirteen
cents to send.

Thu 27:   Well today we all went thrashing. Mrs. Falancer was
there to and Martha. They had two tables one in Ethel's
apartment and one in Uncle Edd's. They got through
at about two oclock. Then they went down to Tippet's.

Fri 28:   Well we ironed today. Edward is still busy draying.
We put up some grapes awful cold today. Not much
doing now days.

Sat 29:   Well today is my seventeenth birthday. I got a card
from Anna a week or more ago. We got a letter from
Uncle Thomas today. He said they mistook the date.
It has been a nice day today. Papa and Ruby hauled
a load of manure and some other things. Edward was
to go home today but we did not go to town. And he
would rather stay awhile longer.

Sun 30: Well we all went to church this forenoon. We rode in the carriage. I don't know if this is Rev. Atkinson's last Sunday or not. He said it would be if Rev. Holliday would come for next Sun. but if he wouldn't he would preach again next Sunday. Jessie Williams and a young man and a little girl cousins of hers were up here to church. We did not go any where from church. This afternoon Papa, Ruby, Edward and I walked up as far as the school house and then ~~by~~ walked back but the ridge way. On the way up we met Mr. and Mrs. A. Hathaway, Mrs. Ivey, and who use to be Lula Hathaway and her daughter. We talked with them awhile.

Mon 31: Well Ruby & Papa went to town today. They went in to get some roofing paint. Billy Bastian is coming to paint our barn, hay shed and cow house roofs. We washed today.

September

Tue 1: Papa & Ruby drove over to Independence School house with the big horses to get Billy Bastian's ladder this forenoon. It stormed last night all the first part of the night. It rained awfully hard. This afternoon Mamma and Ruby took Edward over the station to go home. They said our school started today. They were talking with Miss Garrity. This is Lorraine's third year. We have been thinking lately something about going out to the Presbyterian Mission feast tomorrow. Uncle Edd & Aunt Annie are going.

Wed 2: Well we got up early this morning and tried to get ready early to go to the Mission feast but it got ten minutes to ten before we got started. It was a fine ride it was so clear and nice. Only the roads was badly washed in some places. We got out there a little to twelve. Church was out when we were there a few minutes. There was lots of people there Grandpa, Grandma and Tillie were there. Uncle George, Aunt Lizzie and Naomi. My but the things they had to eat. The table we sat on was mostly Dittmars. They were all relation any way. There was about twenty five or thirty at the table. They had another long table. At the afternoon they had two sermons one German and one English. Mrs. Wilson sang a solo. After church they served supper.

We had supper. Ruby & I was thinking something about staying out but came home with Uncle Edd tomorrow ~~but the~~ because Aunt Annie is going to stay out but they had only one horse. And ~~Gran~~ we could not decide which one should stay. They wanted one of us to stay. And there was so many to stay all night. We was thinking about going down to Uncle Ben's with them if they were up but they were up in the buggy. Vada and Lester went to school. They were feeling sorry that they didn't have the carriage. It was something to eight I believe when we got home. We came home in about two hours.

Thu 3:   Billy Bastian came to paint the roofs today. It has been a lovely day again today. Saturday is to be the Schapville picnic. We are wondering if we could go. I wish we could go.

Fri 4:   Billy Bastian here this forenoon painting roofs. Helen (Weis) called up at noon said she was going to visit the school this afternoon. She asked me if I wanted to go along. I wanted to bake this afternoon there was so much to do but I wanted to go to. I decided to go. Helen said that she is going to school Monday. She is going up to Madison to sort of a catholic school. She said it is a term of ten months. It is to be out the seventeenth of June. She is going to have two weeks vacation Christmas time. She isn't to write but one letter a week home and very little to anybody else. Loraine walked to town this evening. Milton came in here he said Ida was in her. She wasn't here when we got home but she came in a few minutes. Milton left two sweaters at school. So Ida went up to get them. Milton stayed here. Milton said he was going to stay here to supper. He told Ida supper would be ready when she came back but Ida wouldn't stay to supper. Mamma tried to give him something to eat she offered him some jelly roll but he wouldn't take that. She then offered him some little cakes made out of oatmeal he said he didn't want that but he wanted something else. Then Mamma asked him if he wanted bread and jelly he said yes so Mamma opened some jelly. He asked what kind of jelly it was before he would take it. He slaped, pinched Ida and I don't know what else. I bake two cakes yet after I came home.

Sat 5: Last night when we went to bed it was just as clear and fine as it ever could be. But just as it was getting day light a storm came up. Then I knew the Schapville picnic was all off for me. It cleared up quite nice this forenoon. Quite a few autos went along about eleven oclock and after. A carriage went along while Mamma was down near the corner digging potatoes but they did not see her. They said look at the plums. Go in and get some. A young fellow climed in a give the tree a vigorous shake to shake ripe green and all off. Mamma said that's not allowed, I guess he was scared. He said I can have a few can't I and Mamma said yes. But he got out pretty quick. It clouded up again this afternoon. A lot of autos went back early. About eight oclock it started to storm and is storming yet. Twenty minutes to ten.

Sun 6: We all went to church today. Not many there only us Martha, Win and Mr. Tippet and Anne Bastian and Lottie. Mr. Atkinson preached again this evening we all went over to John Weis'. Nick and Anna did not come home until we were there quite awhile.

Mon 7: Cold and rainy today we were going to wash but because it rained we did not wash it all. Well Helen W. was going up to Madison this morning to a Sacred Heart Academy.

Tue 8: Awful cold. We finished washing today. I picked up to buckets full of plumbs. We picked over and cooked a kettle full or one bucket full. Papa cleaned out the chicken house and hauled it away. Papa and Ruby hauled one load of manure. I made my gingham dress longer.

Wed 9: It is a pretty nice day today only cold. I rode Fannie horse back this afternoon. I rode up past Fiedler's just for fun. When I came back we put on the saddle. I was afraid Fannie wouldn't like the saddle but she went all right. Ironed today. Picked over a kettle of plums to make jam out of.

Thu 10: It is rainy and awful cold. It rained all day. We put up five quarts of peeled plums and five quarts of plums without sugar. I've have been fixing my last winter's Copenhagen blue dress today. I hope it will be a nicer day tomorrow and warmer.

Fri 11: We all went to town this afternoon. We had lots of shopping to do. But we did not get it all done. Quite a few people in town today for an every day. We sent Uncle Thomas a market basket full of plums. We sent them by express. I don't know if it would have been cheaper by parcel post or not. It cost thirty-nine cents.

Sat 12: Well today there is going to be some horse buyer in town today. Dad had it in his head to take the old pony in to them. He wanted to hitch it up single or hitch up Della and Fannie and lead it behind but we wouldn't let him. None of us would not go with him. We wanted him to leave it at home. It looks so awful I was so ashamed for people to see it. Dad put the saddle on it and rode it to town. I was so ashamed but we thought maybe they would take it. But here about half past one or two he came home riding it again. It nearly killed me to think he met so many people. I suppose all our neighbors. The horse buyers wouldn't take it. I suppose Dad didn't like to part with it by that time.

He thinks a lot of it. I nearly bawled my head off. This afternoon at about four or five oclock or somewhere around there. I heard central ring. I rubbered. It was a man's strange voice. He said it was Harold Monnier. He asked for Dr. Logan. He asked if the Dr was in he said he was at John Tresidder's and that he had found a woman that was thrown out of a rig and was unconscious. She said the doctor wasn't in so Ida then called Dr. Bench and that he should come out quick. She said its Mrs. Trevarthen. We thought right away it was Mary Trevarthen and so it was. Charlie Berryman called up somebody up the Mound and got them to tell Emma Schoenhard and to tell her to come down. At about seven oclock Ida called up Mamma and told her about it and asked if she would come down. Because Joe Trevarthan wanted to go home to do some chores and he wanted John to go along with him and Ida & Agnes did not want to stay there alone with her. So Mamma & I went down. Mary was lying on the couch. She slept about all the time. She did not seem to know much. Joe & Mary were both drunk they said He said Mary was driving and he was holding the baby. They were driving awfully fast. The line kind of slipped out of her hand she stopped to get it and she fell out over the dash board back of the horses. The horses stopped. They though she was dead for awhile. There was lots of teams there. They hauled her into John's in the back of Arthur Bastian's hack. They said he just screamed with pain. Her arm and shoulder and leg and the side of her face was bruised but there was no wounds. The baby was so good with us. I was holding her when Emma Schoenhard & her husband came. She seemed to know her voice right away. She jumped down off my lap and ran for her. Emma gave it to Joe she said I've been expecting this for a ling time. You both will have to mind your ways or you'll both get killed. He always said he wasn't to blame. They thought she would have to stay there all night. We have been awful busy today put up three quarts of peaches three quarts of peeled plums and seven of plums without sugar. And our Saturday's work we got a letter from Uncle Thomas this morning. He said that Wilbur and his bride intend to come up to Uncle Nick's Sat morning then come down here Sat afternoon and spend Sunday here.

Sun 13: This morning Dr. Tyrell came down in an auto and got Mary Trevarthan and Emma. They thought last night they would take her up to Emma's. We all went to church this morning. Very few there. It looked like rain. Today is Mr. Atkinson's last Sunday. He said he did not know if he would get over her visiting or not before he went. He is going up to Minnesota. We stay home all afternoon. This evening we all went up to Fiedler's.

Mon 14: It has been raining and storming all day. We had terrible floods this afternoon the creeks were like tearing rivers. It rained just awful hard. A lot of water got in the cellar. It rained more today. I believe than I ever saw it rain in one day before.

Tue 15: Every body thinks the storm and flood was terrible. I hear that the Galena River was awful high and is awful high. The mail man did not come out. Nobody and cross it. All of Marsdens and other people's shock corn in gone. The water came up to Marsden's porch. They say the water came up to the main street. Tippets went to Scales Mound today because they could not go to Galena. The plums are getting ripe so quick we sent a box (one we got peaches in) full of plums over to Tippet's. To help pay for the potatoes they gave us last spring. Martha was to have some of them. We sent a peach basket full down to John's. Papa gave Joe Weis a market basket full.

Wed 16: Wilbur's Wedding Day. Wilbur was to be married this afternoon at four oclock at Ft. Dodge Iowa to Olive Harrison at the home of her sister. Wilbur said we shouldn't feel bad because that we wasn't invited because they wasn't going to have a wedding. Al was to be groomsman and one of Olive's girl friend's was to be bridesmaid. Uncle Thomas Aunt Rachel and Anna was going up there to. Uncle Thomas wrote "Poor boy I hate to give him up." Well I guess the giving up is over with by this time. And maybe the bawling to. It is ten minutes after nine. And they are going to start nine something for Chicago. They think they will come to Uncle Nick's Sat morning and come down her Sat afternoon. Mrs. Joe Weis called her this afternoon wanted to pay us for the plums wouldn't take anything. She said when they had something we didn't have they would give us some. We washed today had an awful big washing. Papa went up to Uncle Edd's and got the sheep buck today.

Thu 17: We ironed today. I baked a batch of cookies. Ruby went down to John's T. to borrow some yeast cakes. I wonder what Wilbur and his bride is doing in Chicago. Aunt Annie came home from her long visit today.

Fri 18: Papa & Ruby went to town this morning and got home again about noon. They bought a half dozen of silver knives and forks as the wedding present. They are the Wm A Rodgers. They cost three dollars and a half. We have been quite busy cleaning and baking today.

Sat 19: We were expecting a card from Wilbur today to tell us to come up to Scales Mound after them but we didn't get any. We can't get central so we couldn't call up

Uncle Nicks. We didn't know if we should go after them or not. So Ruby got ready and went up to Werner's to telephone and Papa hitched up in the carriage and started but he met Ruby met him between here and Fiedler's. She said Aunt Lizzie said that they had just left for Galena on this afternoon train. Wilbur had tried to get us but couldn't. So then Papa and Ruby started for Galena. They met Wilbur and his wife riding out with John Tresidder between Falancers and Marsdens. Wilbur's wife isn't very good looking but seems very nice. They were married at six oclock Wednesday. We have been awfully busy all day.

Sun 20:   Wilbur and Olive didn't get up very early this morning. Uncle Edd & Aunt Annie came down this forenoon. This afternoon Wilbur, Olive, Papa, Ruby & I went walking we went up on John Weis' hill and walked around and came down William Bastian's hill. Aunt Annie stay to supper but Uncle Edd went home we didn't have any more company today. Lots of autos and teams on the road today.

Mon 21:   Wilbur & Olive was going home today. So they went up to Aunt Annie's to dinner. I went along with them. We called at Tresidder's we went in and called at Johnnie & Ethel's after dinner until Papa came. Wilbur wanted to get shaved so Olive and I went into Kloth's. I guess she was scared. My but it was awful.

When Wilbur got back it was getting pretty close to train time. So we had a walk pretty fast to the depot. All three Kloths had to kiss Olive and Wilbur when they came and when they went. I told Wilbur I was sorry for him. We just got to the depot and Wilbur got the tickets and then the train came. Olive kissed me and Wilbur kissed. I was the most honored by the groom than anyone else besides the Kloths. I got a new winter hat today. And got it all by my self. It is a black velvet sailor with a white thing sticking up in the front. It is like three head of wheat or barley. This morning a whole gang of gypsies went along and when we went to town they were camping on Ehrler's hill.

Tue 22: Papa & Ruby cutting corn today. Mamma and I washed.

Wed 23: Well today is entry day at the fair I guess. We may got to the fair tomorrow. I rode Fannie horse back up to Aunt Annie's to get some peppers from Ethel this forenoon. Fannie went fine. I didn't meet any automobiles. I met Ben Young with a load of hay. We got a card from Aunt Rachel today she said that they got home from Ft. Dodge and that Wilbur and Olive got home all right. Aunt Annie got a card from Aunt Tillie. She said Grandpa & Grandma were come to the fair tomorrow and was coming out. She did not know if she would come or not.

Thu 24: Papa, Ruby and I went to the fair. Uncle Herman came in and went with us. There was quite a crowd there but nothing compared to other years on Thursday. Grandpa, Grandma & Aunt Tillie was in there. They came out with Uncle Edd's. Aunt Tillie and I had a rooster ride on the merry-go-round. Uncle Herman stayed up to Uncle Edd's all night. We got home about dark. Mamma didn't want to go to the fair. Aunt Tillie found a broach and ten cents at the fair. She found fifteen cents at the Warren Fair.

Fri 25: A beautiful day. Uncle Herman went home this forenoon. My but the teams and automobiles that went along today was just awful. It just about killed me to stay home. They wanted to cut corn. And Ma & Ruby didn't want to go. This afternoon Uncle Edd and Aunt Annie brought Grandpas down this evening Uncle Joe & Aunt Rachel came in. They staid here all night. I counted the teams and automobiles going home tonight. I counted until half past six. There were thirty-five automobiles and twenty teams and I guess I missed some. a beautiful day.

Sat 26: Quite a few people went along again today. They said there was quite a crowd there again today. But yesterday was the big day. Uncle Dan had a new horse and buggy he went along about eight oclock this morning. He went up to Aunt Annie's to breakfast.

Joe & Rachel went to town and fair today. Grandpa & Aunt Tillie went in town with Uncle Edds. I wanted to go again today but couldn't. It quite cold today. A beautiful day.

Sun 27: Uncle Edd came down and got Grandpas they went to Galena to a mission feast at the German Pres. Church. Uncle Dan came down this morning and staid to dinner then went up the Mound to church. There was to be Sunday school up here this forenoon. Mrs. Walter Combellick was to lead. We did not go. I didn't feel much like it. This afternoon we hitched up to go for a ride we called at Popp's. We staid for supper. It was dark before we got home. A beautiful day.

Mon 28: A nice day today. Papa & Ruby cutting corn. I'm feeling kind of bum today. No news.

Tue 29: Ruby & I each got a post card from Olive and Wilbur. Written by Olive. Cutting corn today.

Wed 30: Today we were going to wash but Aunt Annie said Ethel and she were coming down so we didn't wash. They came down this afternoon. Aunt Annie said they were going up to Minnesota. Them and Old Mr. and Mrs. Tippet.

October

When the frost is on the pumpkin

Thu 1:   Today is wash day and reading day. It is a nice day today. Nothin' doing'.

Fri 2:   We all went to town today. Didn't get any new clothes or anything of the kind. Papa went to Dr. Dolamore about his stomach.

Sat 3:   Uncle Edd & Aunt Annie and Mr. Tippet went on this afternoon train to Waterloo they are going to stay there all night then they are going to Tom Tippet's. Mrs. Tippet is out to Tom's from there they are going up to Minnesota to Ben Tippet's. Papa and Ruby hauled some wood here then they hauled some corn.

Sun 4:   There was to be Sunday school at Union this forenoon. We did not go. We were going up the Scales Mound to church. But Fannie got quite lame. So we came home again when we got up by Engle's gate. We stayed home this afternoon. My but the hunters are awfully thick today. This evening we all went up to John & Ethel's. Stella Falancer was up there.

Mon 5:   Mr. Fuller brought us about thirty buckets of oats. He stayed to dinner. I picked up walnuts and stepped on them today.

Tue 6:   Put up tomatoes today. Nothing new we got a letter from Uncle Thomas today. He said he was busy trying to find a house for Wilbur and Olive. He said they thought they had one but wasn't sure.

Wed 7:   I sent a post card to Olive today. It rained today. We washed today.

Thu 8:   Reading day today. We husked six shocks of corn today. We hauled it in, in sacks in the one horse shoe with Old Fannie.

Fri 9:   Ironed today. Mamma got a post card of the capital building St. Paul Minnesota from Aunt Annie they were at Minneapolis they were going to stay there all night before they go to Ben's. I bake a double batch of oatmeal cakes this afternoon. Dad eat about half of them for supper. A year ago this evening we were to Warren Spencer's surprise party. He is nineteen years old.

Sat 10: Papa, Ruby and I went to town today. It rained like everything on the way in but was all cleared up by the time we came home. Quite a few people in town today.

Sun 11:   A beautiful clear day today. We got ready and drove up to Scales Mound to church this afternoon. At the Presbyterian church. They have English in the afternoon. After church Papa wanted to go up to see Uncle Nick a little bit so the rest of us went up to Uncle Ehert's. Uncle Nicks wasn't at home so Papa came back to Uncle Erhardt's. They would have us stay to supper. It was dark before we got home. This evening when Ruby and I were coming in from milking I was carrying the can and a bucket I stumbled or slipped and fell in the creek and all the milk went in the creek. I thought sure my leg was broken but it wasn't.

Mon 12:   It is awfully rainy today. Nothing much doing today.

Tue 13:   Awfully rainy and cold today. It rained about all day. It was so dark today. No mail today. I believe it is Columbus Day. I baked a batch of cookies this forenoon.

Wed 14:   Cloudy and rainy again today. Uncle Edd and Aunt Annie came down this forenoon staid for dinner told us about their travels. They came home yesterday.

Thu 15:   Cloudy and rainy all day today. We haven't seen the sun shine since Saturday. This afternoon Roy Tresidder called here. He came from John's. He came from the station on the morning train and walked over the station again for the five oclock. Ruby dug some potatoes today.

Fri 16: It is rainy and cloudy all day again today. ~~There has~~ We have not see sun, moon or star since Sunday evening and not one sign of it clearing up yet. It's raining some now I believe.

Sat 17: Cloudy all day today until this evening it was cleared up fine. I guess it was due to Ruby taking two umbrellas to town. Papa and Ruby went to town today.

Sun 18: We were getting ready to go to church this forenoon when Aunt Annie phoned down and asked us up to dinner. She said that there wasn't going to be any church. Uncle Edd saw the new preacher in town yesterday. He told him he didn't think that anybody would come out that weather. We went up to Uncle Edd's. John Tresidders came up in the afternoon and Mattie and Mary also came up there. A nice day today. Quite warm.

Mon 19: Well it is a lovely day today. We dug potatoes today. Worked awful hard.

Tue 20: Nice day today. We dug potatoes again today. Nothing doing around here.

Wed 21: Dug and hauled in potatoes again today. We got them all in now except a few along the edge of the little corn field. This evening Papa and I took the buck up to Uncle Edd's. We sold three steers to Jo Weis today. We got seven and a quarter cents or one hundred and seventy-one dollars and ninety-five cents all together.

Thu 22: Reading day and an awful big washing day. We had eleven pairs stockings seven sheets and the others are to numerous to mention.

Fri 23: A nice day today quite hot. We ironed. I baked a cake this forenoon. Mamma bake a batch of cookies this afternoon. Papa & Ruby hauled in a load of corn the first load of the season.

Sat 24: We all went to town today. Ruby bought a new hat. It is small black velvet trimmed with a peacock feather and yellow ribbon. Lots of people in town today.

Sun 25: We all went to church this afternoon. We heard the new preacher Rev. Freeman. He is a young man yet. There was a medium size crowd there. Mrs. Fritz and Berdie was there. We did not go any where this evening and didn't have any company. It has been a very beautiful day today.

Mon 26: We started to husk corn in earnest today. We husked twenty-six shocks. I husked seven three this forenoon and four this after. But I didn't get out very early this forenoon.

Tue 27: We husked and hauled corn today. I husked five shocks today. Uncle Edd & Aunt Annie came down this evening.

Wed 28: Papa, Mamma & Ruby hauled and stacked the fodder on this little piece today. I husked four shocks of corn this afternoon.

Thu 29: A nice day today. I husked five shocks of corn this forenoon and five this afternoon. Nothing new.

Fri 30: ~~Well it is Halloween today~~. A very beautiful day and evening. I husked five shocks of corn this forenoon. I churned this afternoon. Papa & Ruby hauled corn. Mamma washed. I wish I could have gone to some entertainment tonight. I said it was Halloween today but it isn't until tomorrow.

Sat 31: Halloween today. A very nice day. We all went to Galena today. I tried to find a dress today but couldn't find anything at the price that I thought I could pay to suit. I haven't seen any spooks yet. Uncle Edds drove out to Apple River today.

November

Sun 1: We all went to church this forenoon. A nice crowd there. This afternoon John Tresidders came up. Lottie & Annie Bastian came over. A very beautiful evening tonight.

Mon 2: I husked seven shocks of corn this forenoon and two this afternoon. Papa & Ruby hauled in the corn. We husked twenty-one shocks all together today. We got Mr. Potter's picture today.

Tue 3: Husking corn today. Well today is election day. Mr. Popp told Papa Sun. that Cordings would come around in their auto after him. This afternoon he went up with a load. So Papa thought that they might not come. So he, John Weis & Fiedler waited up the school house and had a ride over and back. We went up to Uncle Edd's this evening.

Wed 4: Husking standing corn today a beautiful day. Well he heard some of the election news. John Bardell got elected as sheriff. Mr. Birkbeck got in for County Sup of schools.

Thu 5: We husk standing corn again today. We finished up the standing. There is a Ladies Aid Bazaar at Council Hill tonight. I would like to have gone.

Fri 6: We washed today. Papa & Ruby husked and hauled in some corn.

Sat 7: Papa & Ruby went to town this afternoon. They brought home a barrel of apples. They are New York Balwins.

Sun 8: Papa & Mamma went with John & Agnes down to Robert Virtue's to Rodden. John hitched his team on to our carriage. Ruby & I drove Old Fannie to church this afternoon. We had quite a time turning around. Papa & Mamma came home about half past six.

Mon 9: A nice day today we husked fourteen shocks. And hauled it in. We are thinking something about going to Dubuque tomorrow. I hope it will be a nice day.

Tue 10: Well we got up early this morning and got ready and went to Dubuque. Aunt Annie went along all of us went. It was a lovely day. We walked over to Dubuque from E. Dubuque and back again. I bought a dress at Stanfer's it cost eleven dollars and a quarter with fifty five cents off. It is a basque concern. A long loose waist tunic of accordian pleated and lower portion of ~~black silk or~~ messoline and a black messaline girdle. It is navy blue. Ruby got a navy blue serge suit. We got home at seven oclock. We had dinner at the Y.W.C.A.

Wed 11: We husked eight shocks of corn this forenoon. We didn't husk this afternoon. We got one hundred and nineteen yet. We got a letter from Uncle Thomas and Aunt Rachel.

Thu 12: We husked some corn this afternoon.

Fri 13: Papa & Ruby husked corn today. I sent a letter to Uncle Thomas this morning.

Sat 14: Papa & I went to town today. A gloomy day. I bought a pair of shoes and rubbers. Uncle Ben came in about noon went up to Uncle Edd's. Uncle Ben & Vada & Lester drove one of Uncle Edd's horses to town this afternoon but we did not see them in there. Papa sold the old sows and the old pig today for Monday got six seventy five for them. Well tomorrow is quarterly meeting.

Sun 15: Uncle Bens came down this forenoon So we did not go to church. Uncle Edds didn't either. It was kind of snowy anyway. Uncle Bens went home right after dinner. It cleared off a little. Just as we were ready to go to church a buggy came down the road. It was Jeannette and Les they were coming here. but because we were going away they would not come in. Jeannette promised to come some other time. I was so sorry that they had to go back again. There was quite a nice crowd at church this afternoon but no preacher came. There wasn't anybody to church this morning some said the preacher was there. I suppose he must have got mad or something. Any way we sung several songs. Uncle Edd took up a collection. Quite early or late this evening I picked some lilac buds off one bush.

Mon 16: It is just awfully cold today. I got the tooth ache today. Papa got along alright taking the hogs away. I'm mending today. Ruby mended mits and gloves.

Tue 17: We washed and churned today. Papa & Ruby husked eight shocks of corn but it is so bad husking.

Wed 18: We husked fourteen shocks of corn today. We had to stop husking it was so windy and dry. I made some ice cream for supper.

Thu 19: Just awfully cold today. I believe six above zero. We did not husk any corn today. We had a junk man here for dinner today. We heard today that Mr. Griswold is dead. He died Sunday night. Funeral service at Apple River Wednesday. He was to be buried today at Oregon Ill. I baked a batch of oatmeal cookies this afternoon.

Fri 20: Well today is Papa's birthday. He is fifty eight years old. I made some candy today. Mamma & Ruby took up the dining room carpet this afternoon.

Sat 21:   Well we husked corn this forenoon. We husked eight shocks. Papa, Ruby & I went to town this afternoon. Old Mr. Tippet rode out from the Ore Mill with us.

Sun 22:   A lovely day today. So nice and clear. We all went to church this afternoon. A nice little crowd there. We are going to have afternoon preaching again next Sunday afternoon. ~~as is goin~~ On account of having some meetings at Council Hill. We went up to Uncle Edd's this evening.

Mon 23:   We husked eight shocks this morning. But it was awful dry. I bake a batch of cookies. Ma made butter. Pa & Ruby brought in the corn and did some other hauling. I started to crochet a handbag this evening.

Tue 24:   We husked corn this forenoon two shocks this afternoon. There is forty ~~eight~~ six shocks yet. A lovely day and evening.

Wed 25:   Well this is the day before Thanksgiving. We are not preparing anything extra. It will be just like any other day to us. I wish we could have some body come here or else go somewhere. But everybody is like dead around here. I do wish they would come to life and have something doing. We husked this forenoon and five shocks and hauled it in this afternoon. We have twenty-seven shocks left. I suppose we will have to spend our Thanksgiving husking corn.

Thu 26:   Thanksgiving day. It was just a beautiful day today. Clear and warm. We spend the day in husking corn. We husked fifteen shocks. We have twelve left yet. We had no very extra dinner. I made some like a filling for ~~poultr~~ chickens or turkeys or any other kind of poultry and baked it. And Ruby claimed it made her sick. We had no meat of any kind. I did not hear of anybody having any big dinner or anything of the kind around here. A lot of automobiles went along today.

Fri 27:   Well we finished husking corn today. This forenoon. We did not get much done because we had so much reading to do. This evening Uncle Dan drove in. But did not stop long. He went up to Uncle Edd's. It was just a lovely day again today. A great many automobiles on the road. I husked ninety-two shocks this year.

Sat 28:   This afternoon we celebrated being through with the corn by going to town. A big crowd in town. Ruby had a wisdom tooth pulled by Dr. Kittoe. She says it didn't hurt. I guess I will have to go and have some pulled some day. This evening Uncle Dan came down. This afternoon Uncle Edd & Aunt Annie went up to Scales Mound. They are going to stay all night. Tomorrow afternoon they are going to dedicate the Pres. Parsonage.

Sun 29: Cloudy and foggy & misty today. This afternoon we all went to church. But did not expect anyone else there. But the preacher and the five singer came. I had to play. The singer sang a solo it was fine. The preacher preached just as if the church had been full. Aunt Annie called up this evening. She said they had a fine time up at Scales Mound. A large crowd there.

Mon 30: Uncle Dan went up to Uncle Edd's this morning. Dan said that they were going to move today. Mamma & I went up to help them move today. They did not move much, no furniture. Mattie was up there. Mattie & Mamma put down to carpets. Aunt Annie & I carried over all the good dishes. I guess they will move the furniture tomorrow. I finished crocheting my hand bag tonight.

December

Tue 1: It has been cloudy and foggy and rainy today. We washed an awful big washing. Uncle Edds are moving today.

Wed 2: Papa, Mamma and Ruby hauled fodder today. We got a letter from Uncle Thomas today. He said he was coming back tomorrow. This afternoon I went up to help Aunt Annie. We fix the dishes in the pantry. Aunt Tillie came in this afternoon. Uncle Dan went to town to get her. Papa, Mamma & Ruby went up to Uncle Edd's tonight.

Thu 3: Papa went to town and got Uncle Thomas today. He brought us our Christmas presents. I got a little box for trinkets. And a fancy hair pin. Ruby got a sovenior spoon.

Fri 4: Papa & Uncle Thomas hauled fodder today. Hauled all but one shock. I baked a batch of filled cookies and washed my hair this afternoon.

Sat 5: We did not go to town today. Uncle Thomas started out this forenoon to visit folks and I guess the most of them went to town. He was going down to John's and up to Uncle Edd's and probably down to Tippet's.

Sun 6:   Awfully rainy and snowy today all day. ~~There was~~ We did not go to church this afternoon. ~~We have bee~~ It is awfully lonesome here today. Papa went down to John's awhile this afternoon.

Mon 7:   Papa hauled a load of hogs for Mr. Fiedler this forenoon. It is awfully rainy again today. This forenoon Ruby went up to Aunt Annie's to see a silk waist that Aunt Annie bought over to Dubuque. And to see if she had any patterns to make her pink waist. She brought the waist down. I suppose she will keep it.

Tue 8:   Oh my but this morning it was beautiful. There was quite a bit of snow on the ground and all the trees were just loaded in snow. The evergreens looked as beautiful as you could imagine anything. But by this evening the snow was just about gone. Mr. Barnes was here today and bought the big red cow. Poor old thing and never even got a name in her life besides "the" big red cow. He also bought the calf. We lumped them off forty dollars for the calf and fifty dollars for the cow. Ninety dollars in all. Papa wants to take them over to the cross roads and then drive them along with some cattle of Glick's. Mr. Fiedler is going to help Dad drive them we washed today.

Wed 9:   Well today they took the big red cow and the calf to town. Mamma and Ruby went along as far as the cross roads. They took some of the other cattle along and then brought them back. Papa came home this afternoon. It has been cloudy all day today.

Thu 10: Papa went out working on the telephone line today. They were putting in new telephone poles out there by our place. Uncle Dan & John Tippet were out on the line they came in to dinner. Uncle Thomas came out from Galena this evening he came from Scales Mound and rode out as far as the crossroads and walked the rest of the way.

Fri 11: Well this morning Uncle Thomas killed the Poor Old Pony (Bella). Papa led her up in the wood and Uncle Thomas killed her with the axe. I hope she died easy the poor old thing. ~~Papa, Ruby & I~~ Papa, Ruby & I took Uncle Thomas to town to go home on the two fourty-two train. It was a nice day today only quite cold.

Sat 12: Papa went to Galena again today he chanced it in. He wanted to see if he could sell the heifers today. Berryman said they were down a quarter so he did not sell. I guess we will have to keep them over winter now. An awful lot of teams went home from town this evening.

Sun 13: Well it is a beautiful day only cold. We all went to church this afternoon. Nobody else there only the preacher, Uncle Edd & Aunt Annie, Uncle Dan & Aunt Tillie and us. Aunt Tillie played the organ. Aunt Tillie came down from church. Is going to stay all night.

Mon 14: Awful cold today. But it is a nice clear day. Aunt Tillie went up to Aunt Annie's this afternoon. Mamma and Aunt Tillie is sewing on Ruby's pink silk waist. Papa isn't feeling a bit well.

Tue 15: Awful cold today. This afternoon Mama went up to Aunt Annie's, she called in at John Tresidder's on her way up. Aunt Annie sent a dollar down with her. Fifty cents for Ruby and fifty cents for me for Christmas for which we are to buy something for ourselves. That makes a dollar in money already for Christmas. I've got more now than I expected for Christmas. Papa and Ruby was trying to clean out the old tool house then I believe they are going to use it for chickens. I heard Josie Weis and Agnes talking. Flossie Ford is teaching school this week. I guess Lorraine must be sick. She had an awful bad cold.

Wed 16: A nice day only cold. We washed today. This evening Papa, Mamma & Ruby caught up some chicken. Maybe they will take them to the Station tomorrow. Mr. Hicks is going to buy over the station. I made fondant this evening then dipped them in chocolate made beautiful looking chocolates. I guess I will make them for Christmas presents. I wonder when there will ever be any parties or sociables around here. I hope there will be some soon.

Thu 17: Well this afternoon Papa and Ruby took the chickens over the station. They took twenty four of all kinds. Got fourteen dollars and fifty-nine cents. We are expecting Uncle Herman and Raymond, Leon & Helmer to come in tomorrow.

Fri 18: A cloudy day today. We got a letter from Uncle Thomas & Aunt Rachel today. This evening a little after six Uncle Herman and the three boys came. We had a fire in the parlor this evening.

Sat 19: Well it is a beautiful day. We were thinking of going to town today. But Uncle Herman did not care to go and we wanted them to stay here and have a visit and them some thought it would be to busy to buy anything today anyway. The boys had a fine time. Sleigh riding and trycicle riding. Raymond was riding the trycicle. They all went up to Aunt Annie's this afternoon.

Sun 20: Well Papa, Ruby & I went to church this morning. Uncle Herman & the boys staid and went up here to church. There were fifteen at church. Mamma staid home to get dinner. Uncle Edd, Aunt Annie, Aunt

Tillie Uncle Herman & the boys were here to dinner. Uncle Herman & the boys went home right after dinner. Uncle Dan went to town to church came here this afternoon started to snow this afternoon. And has snowed quite a bit. Aunt Tillie is going to stay here all night.

Mon 21: Well it was a beautiful morning only cold. The sleigh went along here quite thick today. We all went to town in the sleigh today. Aunt Tillie & Annie went along. Bought Christmas presents today. Quite late when we got home. This morning before we started Pete MacDonald came here and wanted to warm. He stank Aunt Tillie and I almost out. Quite a few people in town today.

Tue 22: I am making fondant and then making it up into chocolates and bonbons. I am going to fill three one pound boxes, one for Aunts Annie, Maggie and Tillie and am going to make one for ourselves. Ruby was talking with Milton this evening. He said the teacher is staying at Werner's now. Quite a sleighs went along again today.

Wed 23: This afternoon I took the boxes of candy up to Aunt Annie's. Papa & Ruby hauled wood down from up near the woods this afternoon. I believe Helen Weis came home today on her Christmas vacation from

Madison. Mamma is making her Christmas bread, saffron bread and fruit cake today.

Thu 24: Well it is the day before Christmas. It is Christmas eve now. Five minutes after eight. This morning at nine oclock a young daughter was born to Mr. & Mrs. Wilbur Bastian. At twelve oclock a son was born to Mr. & Mrs. Wm. Studier. Christmas presents. One on each side of the hill. We also heard that Mr. & Mrs. Joseph Engel have another young son. Uncle Edd took Aunt Tillie out to Schapville this afternoon. There is going to be a Christmas tree at the Pres. Church this evening. Aunt Tillie expects to go with Uncle Herman up to Apple River tomorrow. I baked a cake today. And Mamma baked cookies. Ruby and I each got a card from Wilbur and Olive this morning. It will be sleighing and fine moon light for Christmas.

Fri 25: Christmas. Christmas dawned clear and cold. It has been a beautiful day all day only awfully cold. We got a postal card from Rob & May Virtue today. My Christmas presents are from Grandpa and Aunt Annie two fifty cent pieces, a pair of mittens from Papa a comb and flare collar from Mamma, a hair pin and box made of shells from Uncle Thomas. Ruby got a pair of mittens from Papa, a lace collar from Mamma, fifty cents from grandpa and grandma, fifty cents from Aunt Annie a silver solverin spoon from Uncle Thomas. Mamma got a pair of mittens from Papa, a hair back comb from Ruby and I, a glass dish from Aunt Tillie, a plate from Papa, an apron from grandma, a pair of rubbers from Uncle Thomas. Papa got a pair of mittens from Mamma, a pair of suspenders from me, a necktie from Ruby, a handkerchief from Grandpas, a pair of leather mittens from Uncle Thomas. Uncle Edds went down to Tippet's to dinner. I suppose Uncle Dan went there to. I asked this morning if he was coming down afterwards Aunt Annie said he wasn't coming down. Well we had the poor old duck for dinner. It was just awful fat. Ruby & I had an egg each. We had a can of peas, mashed potatoes, cold slaw and lots of other stuff. This afternoon Ruby & I went down to John Tresidder's. We took Milton a little box of writing paper and the baby a ball. Milton has a tree. He got a lot of presents. This evening Uncle Edd, Aunt Annie & Uncle Dan came down. Had a nice visit. Well Christmas is about over for this year. It is about half past ten. Quite a few teams went along today sleighs and cutters. Goodbye nineteen fourteen Christmas.

Sat 26:   I got a Christmas card from Jeannette this morning. I also got a package with some white goods and a bunch of lace. It said from the Curley kids. From Annie Curley of Montana. Papa chance it to town today. He wanted to go in on account of a tooth that is sore. But he didn't have anything done to it. It is just awful cold today. Twenty-six below zero in Galena this morning. I cleaned up this afternoon. We did not bake anything only Mamma baked some pies. Not very many people in town today.

Sun 27: A lovely day today. Warmer than yesterday. We drove to church this afternoon in the sleigh. There were eighteen to church. Mr. & Mrs. Temperly of Council Hill brought Rev and Mrs. Freeman in the sleigh. It is the first time we saw Mrs. Freeman. Nobody came this evening. This forenoon Mrs. Fiedler called up and asked if we were going to be home. Mamma said we were going to church. She said it was alright. They thought they would come down if we were going to be home. I thought maybe Helen would come up or call up some time today but she didn't.

Mon 28: A cloudy day today. Little flurries of snow. We washed an awful big washing today. I hope it will be a nice day tomorrow and that we may be able to go visiting in the afternoon. Maybe at Bessie Weis'. Nothing new.

Tue 29: Well all today and last night it has been snowing the snow is quite deep. The snow is awfully wet for it is quite warm for this time of year. My but the evergreens are just bending down with snow. And the telephone wire. I should think it would break. I called up Helen this forenoon. She said you don't know how fat I have gotten since I have been away. I think she said she had vacation until the eleventh that will be a week from next Mon. She said she would try and come up. We got a letter today from Uncle Thomas and Aunt Rachel. I mixed up the bread and saffron bread today. I am crocheting lace for a centerpiece. Well this book is nearly finished. I have a new one bougthen for nineteen-fifteen. I don't know if it will be large enough for two years or not.

Wed 30: Well it was just beautiful all day. It was so clear and the snow on the trees and everything. It has been quite cold. Nothing new. A few teams went along. The snow is awfully deep. We had to shovel paths everywhere that we wanted to go. Mamma has been sewing some on Ruby's pink silk waist. I have crochet some this afternoon. I have been trying to study some grammer and geography. I split a little wood this evening. Well tomorrow is the last day of nineteen fourteen. Poor old year.

Thu 31: Quite cold today. Well this afternoon Papa and Ruby drove the big horses Violet and Niger to town. The first time that we have ever driven him to town. Violet hasn't been on the road for nearly a year. They say they got along quite nicely. The did not see any trains close and did not see any automobiles. Niger shied some at Uncle Edd's pigs. They say the snow is awfully deep. Today is Milton Tresidder's birthday. He is eight years old. Tomorrow is Edward Dittmar's. I have been wondering if Ruby & I could go to Apple River tomorrow. Well tomorrow is New Year. The beginning of nineteen fifteen. Poor old Nineteen fourteen is nearly ended. It is ten minutes to two more hours of the old year. We aren't invited anywhere for tomorrow. Nor have we invited anybody here. I do wish someone would begin the New Year by having a party or something of the kind. If we could be invited and could get to go. Goodbye Old Year Farewell. This is the last I will write in this book. I hope we will have better luck in Nineteen fifteen.

ॐ

1915

January

Fri 1:   We did not go anywhere to dinner today. The reason we stayed at home was because we weren't invited out anywhere. We did not get up this morning until quite late. We had a very simple dinner. Ruby and I were thinking something of going to Apple River this afternoon but it seems as though they backed out or something. It was clear and cloudy in spells today. This evening we all walked up to Uncle Edd's. It was clear and beautiful when we came home. It was full moon this evening. Old Nineteen fourteen is a thing of the past.

Sat 2:   A nice day today. Well, we were surprised by getting some more Christmas presents in the mail today. They were from Anna. She said she did not get them made in time for Christmas. Ruby got a towel inserted with tatting. I got a Chamois with the back of it crochet in blue. It is very pretty. Mamma's is a handkerchief that Aunt Rachel made. Papa got a box of home made candy and a picture (small camera picture) each of Uncle Thomas, Aunt Rachel, Alvin and Anna. Anna got a camera for a Christmas present and these were the first pictures she took. No news.

Sun 3: We did not have any church this forenoon. We were thinking a little something about going to town to church this morning but it was snowing. Bishop Vincent was going to preach. We thought maybe Fiedlers would come down this afternoon but they didn't. This evening we were ready and were going down to John's when we heard some hollering. I went up stairs and listened it was a sleigh load of people. I heard Helen Weis say something I new then that she was coming up. We all got our things off quickly. It was Josie and Helen. My but Helen is so fat. I don't see how she could have gotten so fat in such a short time. She weighs one hundred and twenty lbs. We had a nice visit. She is going back to school a week from tomorrow.

Mon 4: I wanted to go to Woodbine today but didn't get there. I hope it will be a nice day tomorrow. And that we can get to go. I wrote a letter to Annie Curley this evening and one to Anna. Papa is writing one to Uncle Thomas.

Trip to Apple River copied from my trip book.

Tue 5: Well today we made up our minds to go to Apple River. So Papa took us over for the five o'clock train. We got out all right. They were surprised. Luie Weis came to Apple River on the same train that we did. Maggie, Tillie, Herman, Ruby & I went to meetings at Presbyterian church this evening.

Wed 6: Raining and snowing today we were up to Uncle George's store this afternoon. We went to the Pres. Meetings again this evening. We called at Uncle George's after church. Ruby talked with Mamma today.

Thu 7: Aunt Maggie and Uncle Herman went to Independence Iowa this afternoon. We went to depot with them. Then Tillie, Ruby and I went calling at Hammer's and Anchute's and then at Lena Fisher's. This evening we went to church again then Tillie and I went up the store awhile then called at Uncle George's. It cleared up today.

Fri 8: We talked with Mamma this forenoon. We had supper at Uncle George's. Pearl could not come home this evening. There was a wreck a freight train between here and Scales Mound. We all went to church again this evening. There was to be a returned missionary there this evening he was going to give an illustrated lecture this evening but he did not come on account of the wreck. After church we went up town awhile. Uncle Joe was up this afternoon. He brought hogs up. I guess we will go home tomorrow.

Sat 9: We went up to Uncle George's this forenoon had dinner there. Pearl came home this morning. Ruby and I came to Galena this afternoon. Papa and

Mamma was in Galena. Mamma was at the depot to meet us. An awful lot of people in town today. It is just dandy sleighing.

Sun 10: Uncle Dan and Aunt Annie came down to dinner today. Uncle Edd and Old Mrs. Tippet went out to Tom Tippet's yesterday. This afternoon we all went to church we rode with Uncle Dan and Aunt Annie. There were twenty-one there I believe. ~~Aunt Annie rode all~~ Mamma rode along up with Aunt Annie. It was dark and snowing this evening. So we did not go up. Mamma called up and said she would stay all night.

Mon 11: Well Papa took three hogs to town today. One old sow and two shotes. He got six sixty. One of the pigs broke it leg and he sold it to a butcher he had to throw off fifty lbs. He got fourty-four dollars for them.

Tue 12: We made up our minds to go over to Bessie Weis' and Mamma was going over to Studier's but as were just ready Mr. and Mrs. Walter Combellick came about some roosters. It took quite awhile to get them hunted up. Mrs. said we could ride along down with them but it got so late so Ruby and I went along. Had a nice visit with Bessie. Was treated with candy and oranges. Helen went up to Madison to school again yesterday. A nice afternoon. Mamma had to stay home.

Wed 13: A nice day today. It thawed quite a bit today. We washed today. I finished crocheting and sewed it on a handkerchief. I crochet on braid.

Thu 14: Well it has been quite a day today. It was beautiful weather. Aunt Annie came down this forenoon. She got a letter from Aunt Tillie this morning. She said that Grandma's leg had been awful bad. They had Dr. Gracist from Shellsburg. He said she had to be awful careful or she might loose her leg or might die from it. Uncle Herman took quite sick at Independence. It was heart trouble. He had the doctor several times. He and Aunt Maggie are coming home as soon as he is well enough. She also said that Uncle Henry was up to A.R. and said that Irish Rob had borrowed his cutter to come in this way. Agnes and the baby were going up to Aunt Annie's but because she was down here John brought them up here right after dinner. Uncle Dan drove down before dinner. They all went home towards evening. This afternoon May Virtue called up from Wachter's she said that Rob went to town with Mr. Wachter if they came home early they would come over this eve but if he did not they would not come over until morning. They did not come. This evening Nick and Anna Weis & Rawland came over today. It makes two babies that were here today. Today I read in the Gazette and in the Scales Mound items that Ford School is going to have a sociable Friday evening Jan. 22 that will be a week from tomorrow. I will have to be making my basket soon. I hope no little kids won't buy it. I got a correspondence card from Olive today.

Fri 15: Well Irish Robs came this forenoon. Little Elmer has got to be quite a boy. He can talk some. Quite warm today. This evening we all went up to Uncle Edd's.

Sat 16: Well it has been a very nasty day. It rained a lot. Irish Robs went over to Popp's in the rain this forenoon. They were afraid that the snow would all go away and that they would not be able to go home in the cutter. They thought if the weather wasn't so bad they would go home this afternoon. Been awful lazy feeling. It is awful windy tonight. Well tomorrow is forenoon preaching. Youngs have invited us to come over there to dinner tomorrow. I'm afraid it will be to icy or maybe bad weather yet.

Sun 17: Well it is just awful icy today. We did not want to hitch up. Mamma & Ruby went to church. Popps and Irish Robs were there. Robs staid all night there. Lottie and John Tresidder was there to I believe that was all besides the preacher. This afternoon Fiedlers were down and Uncle Edd and Aunt Annie walked down, they stayed until this evening. Fiedler said that

John Bardell is to auction on the baskets at the social Friday eve. They said that they wasn't going to have any speaking. They said she was going to have the Council Hill Orchestra.

Mon 18: A beautiful day but awful icy. I am trying to make my basket. I fixed it with a red box and green covers looks crazy. Who knows what color it will be before Friday eve.

Tue 19: Snowing some today. Well this evening I am fixing my basket some yet. And I made Ruby's. I gathered strips of white paper and sewed it along the bottom of the basket and on the edge of the lid the box is square. I made two buds and one rose of white paper and up on the top. Ruby's is a long box covered with green tissue with a red rose and two buds. We are Irish.

Wed 20: A lovely day today. It snowed some last night. It isn't so slippery now. Mamma and I washed. Papa and Ruby cleaned out the cow house, hauled some fodder and cleaned out the chicken house. Day after tomorrow evening is the social. I wonder who will get my basket.

Thu 21: Papa, Ruby & I went to town today. It is beautiful sleighing. I do hope it will stay nice for tomorrow evening. We got some truck to put our baskets. Well it is half past eight. I suppose we will be at the social tomorrow night at this time. But I don't suppose I will know who got my basket yet.

Fri 22:   We we have been quite busy today. I baked a cake and cookies. Mamma baked bread and saffron cake. We are all thinking of going this evening. It snowed a little this morning. It has been between clear and cloudy all day. It is quite cold. See tomorrow for tonight's description.

Sat 23:   Pshaw. I'm mad as a hornet. The old sociable was almost a failure to me. Papa and I rode up the school house with John and Milton. Mamma & Ruby wasn't ready yet. Bert and Josie Weis rode along up to. Not very many there when we got there. It was a very small crowd. The smallest I have ever seen up here. There were thirteen baskets and mine was the thirteenth to be sold. Unlucky number sure enough. Old Mr. Trevarthan got my basket. Darn it. I was so mad I could have bawled. Milton got Ruby's. She got the youngest that bought a basket and I got the oldest. Sheriff, auctioneer Bardell auctioned off the baskets and he got Bernetta's. Poor thing. Charlie Tobin got Josie's. Jack Combellick got Jeannette's. Clayton Combellick got Flossie's. Charlie Ehrler got Lorraine's. Walter got Thelma's. Alta Combellick and Geneveve Mrs. Fuller's sister had a double basket. Les and Jerry got them A Shulton got that Hazel

Pooley and another girl had a double basket Leo and Jerry got them. Mr. Werner got Mrs. Werner's. Mr. Davis got Mrs. Davis'. John Duerr got Fannie Trevarthen's. There were a lot of young men there that didn't but any baskets. I don't see what was the matter with them. Fiedlers Josie and Bert and us all rode home with John Tresidder we got home about half past ten. It is a beautiful day only just awful cold. Mamma went to town with Uncle Edds. From there Aunt Annie and Mamma went to Apple River. Papa got some oats at Fuller's this forenoon.

Sun 24: This morning one of the heifers had a calf. Had to bring it in the house to warm it up. This afternoon Papa, Ruby & I went to church in the cutter. There were ten there. A lovely day only cold. Did not have any company.

Mon 25: The cow stepped on the calf and broke its leg. We bandaged it all up. Papa took three hogs over the station this afternoon got six thirty. He got fourty-two dollars all together. Lorraine told Papa this evening that she was here yesterday afternoon and that we wasn't home. Mamma and Aunt Annie came home today. Uncle Dan got them from Galena. Uncle Herman was in bed all day today. And Grandma stays in bed so as to rest her leg. Grandpa isn't feeling very well either.

Tue 26:   It is just beautiful moonlight tonight. It would be nice for a sleigh riding party. I've got an awful sore toe. It was frozen I guess before Christmas. I am putting everything on it I can think of. Uncle Edds hauled their hogs over the station this forenoon. This afternoon Joe Weis took their over. They had eighty hogs. At midnight tonight fifteen counties in this state are to be quaranteened. Jo Davies included. It is on account of the foot and mouth disease. I guess people won't be able to have any sales. You can't even drive any cattle on the roads. Aunt Annie talked to Uncle George today. He said that Uncle Herman is worse. He was awful bad last night thought he was going to die. Grandpa is better.

Wed 27:   It has been just awful cold today. Papa wanted to butcher the hog but it was to cold. Mamma talked with Mamie today. She said Uncle Herman was feeling some better. There is going to be a supper at the Station church tomorrow evening.

Thu 28:   It is just awful cold today. Young's sale was to be today. Papa went over this afternoon but the sale had been called off. They thought that they hadn't better have it that they might get into some trouble on account of the quarantine. Papa heard that Mr. Young was home in bed. It looks to be just a lovely evening but so cold. I don't suppose that there will be many at the supper at the Station tonight. We couldn't talk with Uncle Georges today. The line was out of order.

Fri 29: Just a lovly day. But quite cold. Aunt Annie got a letter from Aunt Tillie this morning. Uncle Herman isn't any better. Ruby also talked with Mamie this afternoon. Uncle Dan brought the letter down for us to read. He and Papa then butchered the hog this afternoon. Oh, just a beautiful evening. I wish some one would get up a sleigh riding party or a party. And that we would be invited and could go.

Sat 30: Stormy day today. Windy and snowy. Papa went to town today. Aunt Annie talked with Mamie today. She said that Uncle Herman was feeling some easier. The other heifer had a calf this evening. I got a card from Jeannette today. She is visiting at Apple River. Said that she was coming down some time soon.

Sun 31: Awfully rainy today and windy we did not go to church today. Jack and Clayton Combellick went along this forenoon said their grandmother Combellick was dead. She died last night. Papa and I went down to John's this afternoon but they weren't at home. So we came home again. We didn't have any company today. Did not hear from Uncle Herman today.

February

Mon 1: Awfully stormy, snowy and windy. I guess all the roads are blocked. I thought the wind was going to blow the house down last night. Not much better all day. The mail carrier didn't go. No teams at all. The telephone line to Apple River is out of order.

Tue 2: It is Ground Hog's day today. It has been cloudy all day so he did not see his shadow. It hasn't been so windy today. It snowed a little this afternoon. We got a letter from Uncle Thomas and Aunt Rachel today. Papa, Ruby and I cleaned out the cow stable today.

Wed 3: Cloudy all day today. This forenoon Uncle Edd brought Aunt Annie down. He then took the mail around the other way. He came down after her again this evening. Aunt Annie and Mamma talked with Uncle George today. He called up from Galena. He and Johnnie Weis were in there. He said that Uncle Herman was quite a little better yesterday. They had doctor Snyder from Freeport. Dr. Brink doesn't know what is the matter with him. The Freeport doctor hasn't said yet what is the matter with him. Haven't seen the sun for five days.

Thu 4: Raining again today. I wonder when we shall see the sun again. We didn't hear anything from Uncle

Herman today. The line to Apple River is still out of order. Nothin doin.

Fri 5:   Cloudy again today. We washed today. Mamma got a letter from Aunt Tillie today. She said Uncle Herman is some better. The doctor said he had symptoms of typhoid but it may be perintontis.

Sat 6:   Well it cleared up today. Hooray! It had been a whole week that we did not see the sun. Papa & I went to town in the cutter today. Quite a few in town.

Sun 7:   Just a lovely day today. This afternoon we rode to church. Just eleven there with the preacher. George Lupton drove him over. There is going to be quartly meeting at the station next Sun. Mrs. Young invited us to come over there next Sunday. We went down to John's tonight. Uncle Edd and Aunt Annie were down there too.

Mon 8:   Papa wanted to go to town on business today so Mamma and I went along to see what I could have done to my teeth. Dr. Kittoe did not have any time to do anything on them today. But he looked at them. Said he thought he could crown the three old decayed ones. And the one front one. He thought he could fill the others. The back crown cost ten dollars a piece and eight for the front one. That makes thirty eight already. I'm going next Fri at half past two. Ruby rode along up with us and stayed at Aunt Annie's for a while. She came home before we did to do some of the chores awhile.

Tue 9:   A lovely day today. Mamma fried down the sausage today. Ruby & I ironed.

Wed 10:   Well today we all went up to Scales Mound to Uncle Nick's. Uncle Nick isn't very well. Aunt Lizzie sprained her wrist some time ago. Clifford Tresidder came in to Uncle Nick's he was helping Perrys move. There was to be a supper for the Catholic Church at the Mound tonight. We met all of Werners and Lorraine. I guess they were going up there. It was fine sleighing but it melted some this afternoon.

Thu 11:   Reading day today. I got a card (valentine) from Jeannette today. She said that she was down here twice Sun. afternoon and evening and that we weren't at home.

Fri 12:   Papa, Mamma & I went to town today. Ruby staid at home all alone. I had to go to the dentist. He filled two cavities in the two front teeth and cleaned some others out. I'm to go in again next Fri at two oclock. It hurt me some. The goods came from Montgomery was everything fine.

Sat 13: Well it is awfully icy. The snow is all melting today.
It is also cloudy and rainy awfully nasty. I fell down
right off the porch and nearly broke my back. It hurt
just awful and hurts yet.

Sun 14: Well it was cloudy all day today. And just awful icy but
Dad had it set in his head to go over to Young's today.
Uncle Edd and Aunt Annie walked over. We drove
we had an awful time to get there. The horses hasn't
any shoes on the hind feet. Mamma and I walked a
good part of the way. We wanted to turn around and
come home again but Dad wouldn't do it. When we
got there. Mrs. Young was lying on the lounge she
has to lie still or she gets the nose bleed so awful. Aunt
Annie and Elmer were getting the dinner any way.
Ben wasn't at home he went over to Sadie's. He and
Mrs. Young's sister came home just as we were going
away. Aunt Annie, Mamma & I walked most of
the way home. Papa, Ruby & Uncle Edd drove the
teams up through Miller's place and Joe Dower's and
came out up by Uncle Edd's. I was so glad when we
got home. Awful windy tonight.

Mon 15: Awful icy again today. It cleared up today. Uncle
Edd went over the station to the quartly Quanference
and then went on the noon train to Apple River and
then came back again in the afternoon. He said Uncle
Herman sits up several hours a day now. Uncle Edd

heard that Joe Gundry's at Warren has the foot and mouth disease. And that he has about eighty fat hogs.

Tue 16: Nice clear day. We are washing today. Dad is chopping in the woods.

Wed 17: A lovely day today. The snow is going away pretty fast. I baked bread today. It looks to be fine. It is made of the flour we got from Montgomery Ward. I am just learning to bake bread. I made some. Ruby is sewing up a shirt for herself. Aunt Annie talked with Uncle Ben over the telephone today. The first time for years. He said the baby had been sick.

Thu 18: Mamma went up to Aunt Annie's to help with the butchering. Papa, Ruby & I went up there for supper and to spend the evening. Nice day today.

Fri 19: Papa, Mamma and I went to town today in the hack. I went to the dentist. He filled one cavity and filled the roots of another. We are to go in again next Thursday at two oclock. Ruby staid up to Aunt Annie's but came home and done the chores.

Sat 20: Warm today. Lots of work to be done but all lazy. Managed to get it done. Mamma talked with Mamie Monnier this afternoon could hear her fine. About the first time we ever talked to them. Mama wanted to know if the foot and mouth disease was very close to them. She said it had been within a mile of them but that they were all killed. I'm wondering if Werners will come down tomorrow afternoon preaching tomorrow.

Sun 21: It is awfully rainy and bad today. This forenoon a Miss. Manual called from Galena. She said that they had lost a dog out here. So she came out to see. We are wondering who ever told her that. A man in a buggy staid down on the road. She said it was a friend. They came out here on purpose I guess. The dog has been advertised for in the Gazette it has been gone about six weeks. It is a fox terrier. Rev. Mr. Freeman called up Uncle Edd to know if they thought it of any use to come up to church because the weather was so bad. They told him it wasn't any use so we didn't have any church. Mamma talked with Agnes this afternoon she said they lost two calves with black leg. They were scared I guess thought that they might have the foot and mouth disease. Doc Evert vaccinated the others. A year ago today was Grandpa's and Grandma's Golden Wedding Anniversary celebration. Their anniversary was on the 22.

Mon 22: Washington's birthday today. No mail. We was looking for mail this morning and wondered why we did not see the mail man if he didn't leave us any mail. Aunt Annie told Ma this afternoon that he didn't go. Mamma and Ruby cleaned out horse stable and cow shed today. Papa didn't feel well today. Staid in bed till noon trying to make a wheel barrow this afternoon. I split wood this afternoon. A cloudy day today.

Tue 23: Awfully rainy all day today. I made two kitchen aprons today. Ruby finished one and made a big all over apron. Nothing new.

Wed 24: Cloudy all day today. We washed today. Uncle Dan came back to Uncle Edd's from Apple River today. He says Uncle Herman is quite poorly yet. He can't keep any thing on his stomach. He say grandma's leg is getting better but that the other one is starting now. Papa was chopping wood today. I am to go to the dentist tomorrow if we can. I hope the roads won't be so bad.

Thu 25: Papa, Ruby & I went to town. I had to go to the dentist had the nerve killed and then filled of one. Had two other cavities filled. I'm to go in again a week from tomorrow. The road were quite muddy coming home tonight. They were more frozen when we went to town. It cleared up today. Mamma was up to Aunt Annie's this afternoon. Anna Weis and Little Rawland was up there too.

Fri 26: A fine day today. This afternoon Ruby & I went up to Clara Engle's. First time we saw their new house.

Edward is quite a big boy. The baby is quite big to. Its name is Calzamine. I guess Clara was glad we got to come up once.

Sat 27: A nice day today. I baked a cake and a batch of filled cookies.

Sun 28: Just a lovly day today. So clear and nice we all went to church this forenoon. Only nine with the preacher there. Did not go anywhere this afternoon. Papa & I went walking on Joe Weiss' hill. This evening we all went up to Fiedler's.

Mon 29: Oh! I was going to make leap year out of this year I guess.

March

Mon 1: March certainly came in like a lamb. Just a beautiful day again today. Well Tippets are moving. Mattie and Mary went to town to stay today. The old people are going in a few days. Uncle Edd went out to Tom Tippet's again today. Aunt Annie was going to stay all night here and then go to Apple River tomorrow but she wanted to stay with Old Lady Tippet. Martha was going to come in today but didn't.

Tue 2: A lovely day today. This afternoon Mamma walked over the station and went to Apple River. Aunt Annie went to town and then went to Apple River.

Wed 3: Papa is chopping wood. Mamma came home from Apple River this afternoon. Ruby and I went part way over to meet her. Uncle Herman isn't very well yet. He seems to have a pain in his side something like he had when he had appentisidas. Aunt Tillie wasn't very well today either.

Thu 4: Reading day today. Cloudy all day and awfully windy. Mamma & I made an everyday dress for me today. Martha Tippet came back ~~today~~ yesterday. The old folks went to town today.

Fri 5:   Quite a bit of snow on the ground this morning. Awful windy all day. And cold. Mamma and I made another dress today for me.

Sat 6:   Snowy all day today. Quite a bit of snow on the ground now. I baked a batch of cookies today. We have six little lambs now from three sheep. But one of the sheep doesn't want to take one of the little lambs and I am afraid it may die. We have it in the house now.

Sun 7:   Papa drove up to Uncle Nick's this afternoon. Mamma, Ruby and I went up on the hill and looked down to see if any body came to church. Popps and Win Tippets came but went home again. The preacher did not come. It clear up fine this afternoon. Did not have any company and guess we won't ever have any more.

Mon 8:   Oh just a beautiful day today. The snow is going away awfully fast. Papa hauled fodder and wood today. Mamma & Ruby cleaned out the cow house, horse stable and cleaned something else out. I split some wood this evening.

Tue 9:   We washed today. A very nice day. Papa is hauling wood down from the woods.

Wed 10:   This afternoon Uncle Edd and Tom Tippet came down. He came back with Uncle Edd when he was out there. We got a letter from Uncle Thomas today. Aunt Rachel is sick a nervis breakdown the doc said. And if pnewmonia set in it would go hard with her as she is so weak. She has had the grippe. One more lamb today. That makes seven lambs. I'm to go in to the dentist tomorrow. I hope it won't hurt.

Thu 11: Papa, Mamma & I went to town today. The roads are awful bad. We got the goods from Montgomery Ward. The dentist crowned or screwed in a front tooth but I don't like it at all it doesn't match the one on the other side. He also filled one tooth.

Fri 12: A lovely day today. Nothing doing.

Sat 13: Busy day as Saturday usually are. The roads are awfully bad. Aunt Annie came home from Apple River today. Aunt Tillie is up and around now. But can't do anything yet. Uncle Herman is just about the same. Aunt Annie says he is getting awfully discouraged. Mayme Monnier called up today. She said that Stella is sick in bed. That she had been some better for a week but had a relapse. Aunt Lizzie told Papa, Sun., that she had pentisitis.

Sun 14: We all went to church this forenoon. There were ten there. Uncle Edd and Aunt Annie came down to dinner. John Agnes, Milton and Blanch came up this afternoon. Blanch is quite cute now. She can't walk yet by herself. It has been cloudy all day today. It is awfully muddy. I have not seen a team on the road today only Uncle Edd's.

Mon 15: A nasty day. Kind of snowing all day. It is just awful muddy. Mamma, Ruby & I cleaned out the cow house today. Ruby & I also cleaned out the horse stable and pig pen. Papa hauled and chopped wood today.

Tue 16: A lovely day today. Papa and Mr. Fiedler was out on the line today. Putting the wire on the new poles. Mr. Fiedler came in to dinner. We notted a comforter today. The top was for a quilt Aunt Tillie gave it to Mamma for their silver wedding anniversary. It is woolen. We put in lamb's wool that we sent for. I got a letter from Jeannette today. She said horse back riding is the craze with her lately. She rode to the Station several times and Leo & her rode up to Scales Mound to church Sunday. The roads are very quiet these days.

Wed 17: A nice day today. Aunt Annie came down this forenoon and we helped her put a quilt together. It is yellow and white. Today is St. Patrick's Day. Today is Frank Hart's sale. Papa did not go.

Thu 18: Snow flurries today. We washed today. Mamma went over to Sadie Bastian's this afternoon. Aunt Annie was talking with Uncle George this afternoon. He said that they had had a doctor from Shellsburg this forenoon. He said he had a elevated stomach that he had to have an operation.

Fri 19: I was to have gone to town today about my teeth but I wasn't feeling very well so Ruby went and took my time. She had some fixed. Aunt Annie had a letter from Aunt Tillie today. They haven't decided yet if Herman will have an operation yet or not. We got a card from Uncle Thomas. He said Aunt Rachel was some better. Papa went to help saw wood a little while this forenoon over to John Weis'.

Sat 20: Busy as usual on Saturdays. John Tresidder told Papa this evening that he heard in town that Mr. Popp got hurt today. Don't know exact particulars. He said he that Mr. Monnier told him that Estella Graham went to the hospital and had an operation. Aunt Annie thinks that Mamma ought to go out to Apple River. I suppose they will have a hard time deciding if he should have the operation or not.

Sun 21: Spring begins today. This morning Aunt Lizzie called up. Asked if we heard that Stella was at the hospital. She said that she had her operation yesterday and that she is awfully bad. We all went to church this afternoon. Mamma took a few clothes along in a bundle she thought she could bring them home again if she decided not to go. There were twenty at church today. Sadie Bastian was out with the baby. Mrs. Freeman came up with Mr. Mamma walked along down the station with Rev. Mr. and Mrs Freeman.

Mon 22: Ruby called up Galena and talked with Aunt Lizzie this morning. She said that Stella is getting along fine but isn't out of danger yet. Mamma called up this morning she got out all right. She said they were awfully glad that she came out. She said she called at Freeman's yesterday and that Mrs. came to the depot with her. Mamma said that they were about the same no better she said then that the doctor was coming there in a little while. Mama called up again about four. We were out Aunt Annie talked. They are going to operate on Uncle Herman Wednesday or Thursday. They are going to have a doctor come from Milwaukee and are going to have two nurses. Papa went over to help clean the grave yard this afternoon. They burned off the dead grass. Ruby cleaned out the sheep's house today. Ruby & I cleaned out the cow house this afternoon.

Tue 23: Well we sawed wood this forenoon. We had five men with papa for dinner. Edd Weis did not stay. Aunt Annie came down this morning she is going to stay down all night. Mamma called up this afternoon. Said Uncle Herman is going to have a operation not now any way. The doctor pumped out his stomach yesterday examined it said that he hasn't got what he thought he had. Mamma thinks she might come home tomorrow.

Wed 24: A lovly day today. Mamma came home this afternoon. Aunt Annie, Ruby and I went to meet her. She rode up from the station with Wilbur Bastian. Uncle Herman is about the same. They are thinking to take him up to Milwaukee hospital next week. They are not thinking to operate on him. The Doc. Thinks that it is growing together about the stomach. They are going to try to open it up by putting a tube in.

Thu 25: Cloudy all day. Mamma talked with Aunt Lizzie she said Stella isn't getting along as well as they would like her to.

Fri 26: A lovly day today. We are fixing over my crepe and ratine dress today. Uncle Edd came down this evening. Aunt Annie is here yet.

Sat 27: A lovly day but quite cool. Papa, Ruby and I went to town today. I had to go to the dentist he filled four teeth I believe did not hurt much today. Just an awful big crowd in town today. More like Grant's birthday or something like that. Masonic band played on the streets today. Aunt Annie went up home this afternoon.

Sun 28: Mamma, Ruby & I went to church this forenoon. There were sixteen to church I believe. Uncle Edd and Aunt Annie came down for dinner. This afternoon Uncle Edd and Papa went over the Station to go to Apple River to see Uncle Herman. I guess they will come back again on the half past nine. It was and is just a lovly afternoon and evening. Quite cold. I thought that Jeannette and Leo would come down today but they didn't. It is Palm Sunday today.

Mon 29: Papa and Uncle Edd got home last night about half past eleven. I guess they are about the same out there. A beautiful day but cold. We washed today. Mrs. Smart called up and wanted to know if Papa could come over the Station. That they were going to meet over there about putting a new roof on the parsonage. That they were going to meet at eleven oclock. Papa went over. Nothing doing.

Tue 30:   A lovly day today. Mamma went over the Station to go to Apple River on the noon train kept awfully busy al the time. Getting meals and doing dishes all the time is awful.

Wed 31:   A beautiful day again today. Mamma called up this forenoon said if we were getting along all right she wouldn't come home until tomorrow. She said that Uncle Herman went to the hospital this morning. Grandpa and Aunt Tillie went along. Uncle Edd came down this eve.

~~Wed 31:~~

෫෬

April

Thu 1: April fool's day. A Nice day today. Mamma came home from Apple River this forenoon. She didn't know anything very new. She thinks Uncle Herman looked a little better than he did when she was out before. Uncle Dan drove Mamma out to Irish Rob Virtue's last night for a little while.

Fri 2: We got a card ~~a card~~ from Aunt Tillie today. Aunt Annie got a letter Uncle Edd brought it down. The letter was written first. The Dr.'s say that medicine will not do him any good. They say his stomach is to far down and it lies on the intestines and that the tube leading into the stomach is to long and narrow from being stretched. Dr's say he will have to have an operation but that they will not promise anything. We got a letter from Uncle Thomas to. They have a automobile now. It is a Hudson. I believe Uncle Thomas Anna and Al been running it already. Helen Weis is home. She came Wednesday and is going back again Monday. We just heard this by rubbering.

Sat 3: Papa, Ruby & I went to town today. Just a beautiful day. A lot of people in town. Jeannette W was in. Jeannette Ruby & I walked the streets quite a bit. Mrs. Young's father was buried today. The funeral was at the undertaking rooms. Papa went to the funeral. Edd Young is back. A lot of beautiful flowers in town today. We got a Easter card from Uncle Thomas. We did not get any letter or card from Aunt Tillie. But Mamma talked with Mayme she said that Aunt Maggie had a letter. Hadn't decided yet if he would have the operation or not. But I guess he doesn't want any. They thought that they would come home tonight if they decided not to have it.

Sun 4:   Easter Sunday. Cloudy today. Rained a little. Quite windy. Aunt Annie is here yet. Uncle Edd came down this forenoon. Had lettice for dinner today and green onions. We all went to church this afternoon. There were twenty one there. Lottie and Mrs. Walter Combellick sang a duet. Iola played the organ. Billy Bastian was to church today. First time for a good many years I guess. Edd Young was to church to.

Mon 5:   Quite warm today. I raked lawn today. We got a letter from Aunt Tillie today. It was written Fri. Mamma called up Mayme she said that they came home Sat eve. She said that Uncle Herman has been wishing since he came home that he had staid and had an operation. A grand Easter ball in Galena tonight. Jeannette said Sat. that she was going. I suppose your that Helen went back to school today.

Tue 6:   Very warm today. I raked some lawn. We cleaned my room today. A start. Did not hear from Uncle

Herman today. Mamma got a card from Estella Graham she said she is getting along fine. I made some ice cream this eve.

Wed 7:   We walked today. A lovly day. This afternoon I went a long up home with Aunt Annie to spend the afternoon. She had been here over two weeks.

Thu 8:   Mamma staid in bed until nearly noon. She was quite sick last night sick to her stomach and dizzy. She is feeling better but not well yet. It is hot today. I ironed this afternoon. Papa & Ruby hauled manure this afternoon. Hauled five loads. First time the team been hitched up for a long time. Worked awful hard today trying to clean house and lawn too.

Fri 9:   Mamma fried down the meat today. Papa hauled manure. Ruby helped load up some. Ruby straightened out her room today. I cleaned a little lawn but it was to windy to do much.

Sat 10:   Papa and Mamma went to town today. I baked a cake and a batch of cream puffs today. Well Papa shaved off his whiskers this evening. But had to leave on his mustache yet. I trimmed up my last summer's hat today. Took the green velvet ribbon off Ruby's last summer's dress. It has streamers down the back. This evening we had a little tornado. Mamma & I was out in it, it blew the rack for the rose bushes all down and strewed things around.

Sun 11: We all went to church this forenoon. There were fifteen there. Papa & Mamma went up to Uncle Edd's from church. Ruby & I came home and fed the calf and lamb. Then went up there for dinner. John Tresidders came up to Uncle Edd's to this afternoon. Blanch is real cute now. A girl came past Uncle Edd's on horse back this after. Looked very much like Jeannette. There is horse tracks out before the door here. Guess it was Janet and I suppose she was going to stay here but did not find us home. Its awful.

Mon 12: Cold and cloudy this forenoon clear and warm this after. Papa plowed the garden this afternoon. Mamma planted one row potatoes. Ruby & I are thinking some of going to Apple River on the morning train and coming back on the two.

Tue 13: We got up at six this morning and started for the station at five after seven. The train goes at eight seventeen we were over there in plenty time. We found a lot of croq. on the way over. At Scales Mound Mr. Kinsler, Mrs. Shapp, Mrs. Winter and Mrs. Stadel got on the train. They went to Grandpa's. Uncle Herman looks awful bad. They say he cries so much. He gets up a little most every day but he did not get up while we were there. There is no hopes of him getting better the way he is doing now. He either aught to have an operation or try a rub doctor or something. Did not get to visit or hear much. They talked German most all the time on account of the old women. We came home on the two. Just a beautiful day today.

Wed 14: I had a card from Jeannette today saying that she was down here Sun. but as usual we weren't at home. Mamma & I put in a lot of garden today. We put in radishes a few onions and a row of potatoes last night. Papa and Ruby hauled manure and hauled some hay over from across the road. My but the grass is growing like everything.

Thu 15: We washed today, Ruby cleaned the rag room. Papa hauled manure. Jeannette rode past here on horse back today. Went to town to take music lesson I guess. The assessor was around today. I have to go to town to the dentist tomorrow.

Fri 16: Papa, Mamma & I went to town today. Aunt Annie rode in with us. She and Mamma went to Apple River this evening. I had two cavaties filled today. Did not have anything done to those three old teeth all the rest are fixed now. Got the bill today. It is thirty-six dollars. Mamma called up this evening said Uncle Herman is about the same. Mamma got a new hat today.

Sat 17:   A lovly day today. Quite a few people went along today. Mamma came home this afternoon. She thinks Uncle Herman won't live very ling any more. They coaxed him awfully today to have the rub doctor. The doctor from Galena goes out there twice a week but he did not want to have him. Uncle Edd was going out on the eve train and came back Aunt Annie too to Galena on the nine.

Sun 18:   This forenoon Ruby & I went for a horse back ride. Ruby on Della and I on Fannie. We rode up through the woods and went out the bars and then rode around by the church. Had a fine ride. The horses went together nice. This afternoon we all went to church. There were only twelve without the preacher. The flies bother us terribly the last few day can't hardly go out side the church. We staid at home this evening but as usual nobody came.

Mon 19:   A very warm day. Eighty-one degrees. Cleaned Papa's and Mamma's room all done up stairs but hall. Papa hauling manure.

Tue 20:   Awfully hot again today. But turned quite cold this evening. Ruby cleaning down stair bed room today. I ironed some and doing all kinds of odd jobs. Always busy. Nothing doing.

Wed 21:   Cleaning the parlor today but did not get it finished. Papa hauling manure yet. We turned Fannie and Della out to pasture today.

Thu 22: Washed today. Also got the parlor straightened out. A lovly day. Just awful dry. Need rain awfully bad. Our radishes and lettice are up.

Fri 23: Just awfully hot today. I ironed today. Mamma went up to Aunt Annie's this afternoon. Aunt Annie got a letter from Aunt Tillie today. I guess Uncle Herman is about the same. They always have so much company. Its awful.

Sat 24: Hot again today. We did not go to town today. Thought we would wait till Tuesday (Grant's birthday) an awful lot of automobiles went along today. I baked a batch of cookies and an angle food cake toady. The cake seems to be fine. The wild plum trees are out in blossom. The tame ones are not quite out yet. The cherries are out to.

Sun 25: Warm today. This forenoon we all went to church. Pretty good crowd there. We went out riding this afternoon. Went down the bottom and way over in Guilford then came back through Walter's and come out by Hacker's at Guilford saw lots of country I never saw before. This evening we went up to Uncle Edd's.

Mon 26: I cut some lawn today. The first cutting of the season. Cloudy but did not rain. Quite windy. Always busy. Aunt Annie was talking with Mamie today. Couldn't hear very well. Said Uncle Herman had made up his mind to have an operation but changed his mind again

Sat. She said the worried so much about it they was afraid he would go crazy.

Tue 27: Well today is Grant's birthday. Papa, Ruby & I went to Galena. There was quite a few in there. But I don't believe as many as sometimes on Grant's birthday. Was thinking to see Uncle Thomas in there today with their auto but did not see them. The road are beautiful, grand, magnificient. I have reason to believe that Joe Weis got an auto today. They and Hicks were going over to Dubuque to get one.

Wed 28: I cut some lawn today. Awful hot today. Had a few little showers of rain today but not enough to do any good. Joe Weis went up the road in their new auto this evening. It is a Ford. I sent for paper for the dining room this morning.

Thu 29: We washed today. A lovly clear and cool day. Ruby & I went up church this afternoon to see if we could get some asparagus. Did not find much. Guess it has been cut. Finished cutting the lawn today.

Fri 30: I ironed today. Mamma, Ruby and I went up to Aunt Annie this evening to get a twelve dozen egg case she bought in at Helm's for us. She gave us some asparagus. Quite cool this evening.

May

Sat 1:   May day today. Papa and Mamma went to town. Mamma went out to Apple River on the five train. Aunt Annie got a letter from Aunt Tillie this morning. She said they were looking for some one out. She says the rub doctor comes down every day from Warren. Aunt Tillie thinks Uncle Herman is getting some weaker. We received our dining room paper by parcel post this morning. It cost twenty cents postages. It is tan oatmeal paper (plain) with a cut out border of pinkish red roses. I think its nice. But won't know until it is on. An awful lot of autos on the road today. Papa say that J. L. Tippet bought a new auto.

Sun 2:   It rained last night and a good part of the day today. We needed it awfully bad. To rainy to go to church. Nobody on the road today. Only a fellow on horse back.

Mon 3:   Papa started to plow out here today. We tore up the dining room today. Mamma came home this afternoon. I guess Uncle Herman is about the same. Agnes is going to have the Aid Society Wed.

Tue 4:   Everything is growing fine. It is quite cold though. Tearing off paper in the dining room today. Mamma white washed the ceiling.

Wed 5:   Well this afternoon we went to the Aid Society. Quite a few there. Everybody about but Lottie and Annie. Martha wasn't there either but she resigned. Had a lap supper. Mrs. J. A. Weis, Bessie and Josie were the only catholics. They made a_____.

Thu 6:   Reading day. Aunt Annie came down this forenoon. Mamma & Ruby washed. Aunt Annie and I papered some. We baked to. I also baked a cake. Raining this eve.

Fri 7:   Nice day. Papa & Ruby went to town today. Ruby bought some oil cloth for the dining room. Mamma & I papered. We have some more side and the border and base board yet to put on. Aunt Annie got a letter from Aunt Tillie today. She says Uncle Herman is growing weaker all the time. The rub doctor give him up. Said he couldn't do anything for him.

Sat 8:   Awful cold today. Papa is plowing. Mamma & I finished papering the dining room. I expect a lot of company tomorrow because we did not bake much today. Forenoon preaching tomorrow. Mother's Day.

Sun 9:   Aunt Annie called up this morning said that there would not be any preaching up here today. That there is quarterly meeting at Council Hill. Uncle Edd and Aunt Annie went to Apple River today on the eleven

train and are coming back tonight. Papa, Ruby & I
to up to Council Hill to quartly meeting this afternoon.
When we got up in the woods near the school house
we met Jeannette. She was coming down. She didn't
want us to go back. She said she would go out for a
ride. Quite a few people at church. Just a beautiful
day but quite cool. Nice and clear. Home this evening
no company.

Mon 10:   A lovly day today. I cut some lawn today. Trying to
get some of the things back in the dining room today.
Papa killed a rattle snake pilot out by the board walk
today. We had a few green onions for dinner the first
of our own for the season. Ida Bastian came up this
evening to get some pie plants.

Tue 11:   Warm today. We had our first radishes today for dinner.
Papa and Ruby are planting corn on the little piece beside the
house. Mamma, Ruby and I went up to Uncle Edd's this
evening. They are building a kitchen and bedroom. Aunt
Annie say Uncle Herman looks awful. When we were
coming home there was an automobile coming up the hill it
was Johnnie and Ethel and Irma so we got in and rode as
far as their gate. First time I saw or rode in their car.

Wed 12:   Warm day. We washed today and planted some
early potatoes. Just piles and piles of autos came along
today.

Thu 13: Cut some lawn this forenoon. I went up to help Aunt Annie this afternoon. Cleaned out the pantry and the dishes. They are going to tear out the pantry and are going to tear out the boards along the wall and plaster it. John and Ethel and Irma went past here in their auto this evening. Lorraine G. sent a note down with Milton. She wants us to go up to the school picnic Sat.

Fri 14: Papa and Mamma started out for town. It came up to a storm they took ten dozen eggs over to Dower's. Then they came home. It was raining like everything before they came home. It then brightened up a little and they started out again. It was three oclock. They got home before dark. I am trying to cut some lawn.

Sat 15: This morning between eight and nine. Twelve automobiles full of men went toward Scales Mound. They are Grant Highway inspectors. They are to pick out the Grant Hiway route about all of them came back later. Ruby and I went to the picnic. We were to call for Willie and Mary but they had gone with Bessie and Josie. There was about twenty-five there. Had a nice time. Lots to eat and lots of ice cream. Jeannette said she would come down and go horse back riding with me tomorrow if it is a nice day.

Sun 16: Kind of rainy today. Jeannette didn't come to cold to ride horse back. We all went to church this afternoon.

Thirteen there with the preacher. Uncle Edd & Aunt Annie came down to supper.

Mon 17: Had lettice for dinner. First of our own for the season. Also had mushrooms for dinner. The first I ever ate I believe.

Tue 18: Awful cold today. We sold Win Tippet the spotted cow and calf this afternoon for seventy-six dollars and a quarter. He took them right away. Papa finished plowing today.

Wed 19: Awful cold and rainy again today. We washed today. Nothing doing.

Thu 20: Rainy all day. We ironed today. Mamma went up to Aunt Annie's this afternoon. She had a letter from Aunt Tillie she thinks Uncle Herman is just about the same.

Fri 21: Awful windy and cold & cloudy today. Papa and Ruby went to town today. I got a card from Wilbur and Olive today.

Sat 22: A nice day today. Busy with Sat. work I baked an angel food cake. Mamma another cake batch cookies, bread coffee cake cinnamon rolls and pies. I don't suppose we will have any company tomorrow. Morning services tomorrow.

Sun 23: We all went to church this morning. Twenty three there I believe. Papa and Mamma went down to John's to dinner. Ruby and I came home. Jeannette came this afternoon horse back. Jeannette and I went riding together. We went down as far as J. A. Weis talked with Tillie and Edith. Then we came back. Jeannette stayed for supper. Ruby went part way home with her horseback. Joe Weis was learning to run the auto today running it up and down the bottom.

Mon 24: We tore off the paper in the kitchen and put five pieces of ceiling on today. It says by the paper today that Italy has declared war. The war in Europe is just awful.

Tue 25: Rained awfully hard this morning. Been cloudy all day. We papered some.

Wed 26: We finished papering the kitchen today. Ruby went up to Aunt Annie's this afternoon. Rode Fannie horseback. Ida Bastian came up to get some pie plant this afternoon. Awful windy today. Cloudy about all day Jeannette is nineteen years old today. We're all getting old.

Thu 27: Papa and Ruby went to town today. Just awful, awful cold and rainy. Big cattle sale in Galena today. There is going to be a surprise party on Mr. & Mrs. J. A. Weis this evening for their silver wedding anniversary. We heard this evening that Fiedlers have a little girl. Fourth one now.

Fri 28: Weather a lot worse than yesterday. I don't know what tomorrow will be like. I bake a batch cookies and drop cakes today. Got a letter from Uncle Thomas and Aunt Rachel. Al & Anna wanted to come back Sat and stay till Sun but the road are to bad.

Sat 29: Not nice doing on the road today. It rained about all last night and a lot today. It is warmer than it has been tonight. John Tresidder came up a little while this afternoon. We made the curtains for the dining room today. Papa fixed our old clock yesterday. It is back in its old place working fine now. Mamma was talking with Mamie today. She said she thought Uncle Herman about the same.

Sun 30: Decoration day. A lovly day. Quite warm an awful lot different than it has been. We all went to church this afternoon. Aunt Annie and Mama went to Apple River this eve. Uncle Edd took them down the station from church. They are thinking to come home tomorrow afternoon.

Mon 31:   Papa took three calves up the mound this forenoon. One was Little Fannie the one that had its leg broken. Mamma walked over from the station this afternoon. She says Uncle Herman looks awful bad. I cut some lawn today.

June

Tue 1: A nice day. I cut some lawn. Mamma and Ruby washed an awful big washing twenty-two dish towels and about thirteen towels. This eve one of the cows that we just the calf away from wasn't here. Ruby went up and saw her in Bastian's pasture. We all had an awful time tramp all over till nine oclock. Didn't get her then. I hope she will be back by morning.

Wed 2: Papa and Ruby planting corn today. I went up to Aunt Annie's this afternoon. The house looks much different since the new doors and windows are in. The carpenters are building the front porch now. I staid for supper. I rode down with Uncle Edd and Aunt Annie. Uncle Edd got some seed corn. The preacher Rev. Mr. Freeman was here this afternoon.

Thu 3: A nice day. Papa and Ruby are planting corn. I washed my hair and head this afternoon. Mamma went up to see Mrs. Fiedler and the baby. Its name is Ida I believe. A week old today. Mrs. Fiedler's sister is up there. Cording's dance tonight.

Fri 4: Finished planting corn today. Mr. Werner got a bushel of seed corn here today. I ironed today. A nice day. There is going to be a circus in town the tenth of June. I wish I could go.

Sat 5:   Papa, Ruby & I went to town today. Quite a crowd in town. Ruby got a new hat a white one.

Sun 6:   Just a lovly day. We all went to church this forenoon. Only Lottie and the preacher there besides us. I don't know what was the matter with the people. Ruby and I went up to Fiedler's a little while this afternoon. Met Ida Studier. An awful lot of automobiles went by today. The roads are nice now. Our strawberries are getting ripe now. Had all we could eat for dinner.

Mon 7:   It rained last night and this morning but cleared off lovly this evening. We worked in the garden some today. Ruby & I went riding horse back this evening. I can ride fast now with out a saddle but I'm afraid I can't stick on very good with a saddle on account of the stirrups they are closed. Will have to learn I guess. Had a fine ride.

Tue 8:   I went up to Aunt Annie's this forenoon to help her she had a man there to put on the trim on the porches besides the carpenters. I didn't come home until after supper. Ethel was over there in the afternoon. We cut out and trimmed the borders of Aunt Annie's paper. Mamma and Ruby wants planted corn today. People say there was frost last night.

Wed 9:   A lovly day but quite cool. Washed and baked bread and a cake. Last night and tonight the class play is of

Galena. Tomorrow is the circus at Galena. Wish I could go tomorrow eve. Ruby and I rode horse back again tonight. Went as far as the bottom of the school house hill. I guess I can go quite fast now. Mamma got a letter from Aunt Tillie today. I guess Uncle Herman is about the same. Maybe a little worse.

Thu 10: Aunt Annie is sick today in bed. Mamma went up Uncle Edd came down after her. Didn't have any way of going to the circus. Just the same as all the other things I would like to go to. Have to stay home all the time.

Fri 11: We all went to town today. Mamma bought a new black skirt and a white waist. I bought goods for a new white dress. I hope we can make it. It is plain white voile. Ethel had to stay up to Aunt Annie's all day.

Sat 12: Uncle Edd came down and sheared our sheep this morning. We got fourty pounds from five sheep. Mamma went up with Uncle Edd. Edmond Levins brought Mamma and Aunt Annie down after dinner. Thought Aunt Annie couldn't stay up there alone.

Sun 13: A nice day today. Uncle Edd came down this forenoon. This afternoon John Agnes Milton and Blanch came up. Ida was to go away to Helena Montana this after. Aunt Annie is feeling some better today.

Mon 14:   We planted some potatoes. Couldn't plant any more because it rained. We picked and put up four quarts of cherries from the smallest tree. A quart of strawberries and a quart of pineapples from two pineapples. Aunt Annie is feeling worse today. Has awful bad pains. Called Uncle Edd to come down tonight.

Tue 15:   A lovly day. Johnnie came down after Aunt Annie and Mamma in the auto this morning. Papa & Ruby went to town took the cream and the wool and bought home a washing machine and one hundred bran. I staid home alone. Uncle Edd brought Aunt Annie and Mamma down again this evening. Aunt Annie has been worse today.

Wed 16:   Ruby and I picked about a bucket and a half of cherries today. Put up eight quarts got twelve quarts now. Also put up two and one half gooseberries. We got a letter from Uncle Thomas today and two pictures of Wilbur's house and their auto. They want to come back for the fourth. Aunt Annie is feeling some better today. Jeannette rode down Ruby's coat we lent her the Sun she was down here.

Thu 17:   Well we washed today with our new washing machine. We got through about a quarter after eleven. Ruby and I picked and picked over cherries we got ten quarts now. We also baked bread and Mamma churned. I wanted to cut lawn yet but didn't get at it. Lots to do *again tomorrow. Jeannette and Charlie Tobin went past they are going to the Knights of Columbus dance tonight. The way Jeanette talked last night she expected to go in the auto. But it seems she got left about that.*

Fri 18: Awful busy putting up cherries. It rained today.

Sat 19: Papa and Ruby went to town today. Ruby went to Apple River this evening.

Sun 20: Papa and Mamma went to church this forenoon there were four others there yet. Edd came down to dinner. We had our first peas for dinner today. Ruby came home this afternoon. Didn't have any company.

Mon 21: A lovly day today. Mamma went up with Aunt Annie this morning. I cut some lawn. Ruby and I picked some cherries. Papa took the fall pigs over the station this forenoon. Papa got the freight to, got the vacuum cleaner. I got a beautiful under skirt. They did not have what I send for so they sent me one that is one dollar higher in prices. A four dollar and a half skirt. I paid one ninety-nine. Papa plowing corn this afternoon.

Tue 22: A lovly day today. Ruby went up with Aunt Annie this morning to help her. This afternoon Mamma and I cut out my white dress. Aunt Annie didn't come down today.

Wed 23:   Cloudy today. We washed this forenoon. Mamma and I worked on my dress this afternoon. I got all the shirring done.

Thu 24:   A beautiful day. We ironed this forenoon. This afternoon we worked on my dress. Helen Weis is home now. Mr. and Mrs. and Bert and Helen went up the road in their auto.

Fri 25:   Papa and Ruby went to town this morning. Ruby bought herself dress goods for a white dress. She bought me goods for a corset cover. I made it this afternoon and evening. A tramp asked for something to eat this eve. Papa went over to the Station to get a roll of wire we sent for this afternoon.

Sat 26:   Quite warm today. An awful lot of automobiles went along this evening. We got my dress about all done. Papa caught a skunk in some traps last night. It had been taking our chickens. He shot it. Afternoon preaching tomorrow. We did not bake much extra things today. I wonder what fine company we will have tomorrow. I wish I could go to the circus at Dubuque Monday.

Sun 27:   Quite warm today. We all went to church this afternoon. About fifteen there. Mr. Young is quite poorly. Edd and his wife are back. Ben took the preacher over there. We went over to Orlando Bastian's this evening.

Frank Bastian is over there. Eliza Bastian was over there. Uncle Edd and Aunt Annie came down here to supper from church.

Mon 28: I put a band on my under skirt today. Mamma cut out Ruby's white dress today. It is rice cloth. I sewed up the skirt. I started to cut the lawn today. This week we have to wash and iron yet and make Ruby's dress and go up and help Aunt Annie straighten up the house one day and I have to cut the lawn and Papa has to plow corn. We have to bake and clean up to get ready for the third and fourth. I have to put a band on another under skirt. We also have to go to town one day and a few more things.

Tue 29: Mamma and Ruby went up to help Aunt Annie straighten up. I cut some lawn. Put a band on Ruby's underskirt. Working awful hard these days.

Wed 30: A lovly day today. Ada Kloth was to be married today. Anna was to be bridesmaid. Geneviere Clark was to be married also today. We washed this forenoon, sewed on Ruby's dress this after. I cut some lawn this is the f_____ time I cut it. The roads are fine now, hope they will be nice for the third, fourth and fifth. Our crimson rambler is out now. It is awful pretty. The Dorothy Perkins is out to hasn't so very many flowers because it all died off last winter.

July

Thu 1: Papa Ruby & I went to town this forenoon. Got home at nearly two. I bought a new hat paid three dollars for it. It is a white straw with two rows of black velvet running around the brim and a little bunch of white flowers on one side. When we came home we went in to see Aunt Annie's house since it is papered and some things straightened. It look like all together a different house.

Fri 2: Had a little shower this morning but turned out to be a fine day. I finished cutting the lawn today. I bake a cake, pattie cakes and a batch of cookies. I also mixed up bread and coffee cake. We finished Ruby's white dress today. The celebrations are tomorrow. We got a letter from Uncle Thomas said that they aren't coming back. I saw three big loads of beer go past here up to the slug today. I hope in a few years there will not be any liquor made in the whole United States.

Sat 3: Just a lovly morning out a little more cloudy in afternoon. Quite cool today. Some people wearing coats some winter ones. We all went to Galena there was just an awful big crowd in there. And an awful lot of autos in there. There was not so very many people that I knew. It was quite a rough looking crowd. Some quite a few drunk. Ruby & I wore our new white dresses. An awful lot of autos went along this evening. It rained about ten oclock or after. Uncle Edd and Aunt Annie went to Apple River this forenoon. Quite cold tonight.

Sun 4: Showery all day. And cold. Could hardly stand it to go out with out a coat. It did not have any preaching at Union because it was to wet for the minister to walk up. Quiet on the road today. Uncle Edds came home this afternoon. Edward came along. We went up there this evening. They say Uncle Herman is no better.

Mon 5: A lovly day. Papa took over lambs over the station. All but Bob. Seven of them. Got eight dollar all together and got just sixty dollars from five sheep the wool and lambs and a lamb over yet. Mamma Ruby & I picked gooseberries and three quarts raspberries and got gooseberries for jelly. Edward came down this afternoon. We had new potatoes for the first time today for dinner. They are nice. We have an awful lot of peas now having them almost every day.

Tue 6: We washed and ironed today. We also made a batch of gooseberry jelly and baked bread. Rainy this afternoon and evening. Edward went up to Aunt Annie's this forenoon. He was going over to Ethel's to dinner.

Wed 7:   It rained all day today. It stormed about all last night. Aunt Annie had a letter from Aunt Tillie. They had Dr. Hagie from Elizabeth for Uncle Herman. He wants to take him to some sanitarium. He doesn't want anybody to see him not even any of his folks.

Thu 8:   A lovly day. Papa and Ruby went to town. Mamma and I went up to Aunt Annie's. We helped wash an awful, awful big washing. Saw by the paper today that Werners are going to have a big dance in their new barn. Music by Harps Orchestra. Edward came along down with us this evening. Ruby and I went picking raspberries yet this evening. Got quite a few. A lot more up there. Will have to get up early tomorrow morning.

Fri 9:   Ruby and I went picking raspberries. Baked bread and used up all the flour. Mamma and Ruby drove Old Fannie up to Aunt Annies, borrowed some flour. Aunt Annie went along with them they drove down the Miller Place to get currants. They were all picked when they got down there. Tonight was Werner's dance. Just an awful lot of people went past here. I would kind have liked to have went to see what it is like when it was so near but didn't have any way of going. Dad offered to go with us but didn't want him to go. We saw some of Weis go up.

Sat 10:   I baked a big batch of cookies and a cake today. We had our first apple sauce today. Made of duchess apples. Papa cutting hay first we cut this season.

Sun 11:   We drove to church today. Twenty-one there. Edward went up to Aunt Annie's to get his good clothes after dinner. He came down from church with us again this evening we got ready and was going down to Weis. When we got nearly there Will and Bessie Bert and Mrs. Weis came out in their auto. We didn't say anything to them. Then we saw Aunt Annie, Agnes, Milton and the baby down the road they were coming up to Weis' to. We thought we would go in any way. Then they came back in the auto they had just taken them up to Fiedler's. Josie and Helen was all out ready to go for a ride so we wouldn't stay we then went down to Tresidder's. I guess Milton was tickled to have Edward come.

Mon 12:   Didn't haul any hay today for it wasn't dry enough. Ruby and I picked berries this forenoon. Got six quarts. Got seventeen and one half quarts of R. B. now. We put up seventy three and one half quarts of fruit this year without the jelly. Edward went up to Aunt Annie's from Tresidder's last night.

Tue 13:   An awful hot day. We hauled five loads of hay today. Did not get it all in a load or maybe two out yet. We also baked bread today. I'm afraid our hay will get wet looks like a storm.

Wed 14: It rained an awful lot last night and an awful lot today. Papa and Ruby went to town this afternoon in an awful hard rain. It cleared up this afternoon. Edward came down from Aunt Annie's with them when they came home.

Thu 15: We washed today. Ruby and I picked raspberries this afternoon. Got quite a few. It is raining again this evening.

Fri 16: Ruby's twenty-second birthday. Didn't have any celebration. Ironed today. I baked a batch of cookies and cut the piece of lawn north of house. Ruby got a card from Aunt Tillie she said Uncle Herman is no better. It cleared up nicely today. Hope it will stay nice for awhile.

Sat 17: A nice day today. We hauled hay today. Made a stack out side. We think it was about five loads. It would make ten loads in now. And ten load for this whole week. Papa cut some more this evening. I baked an angel food cake today. It is quartly meeting tomorrow. Edward went up to Aunt Annie's this evening.

" Angel Food Cake " – handwritten in black ink with
additions in pencil on a sheet of tablet paper folded in fourths.
Author unknown

" 1 Cup of egg Whites

1 ½ Cups of sugar

1 Cup of Flour

1 Teaspoon cream tartar

1 Vanilla or Almond

a pinch of salt

sift-flour cream Tartar. Sugar & salt-together 5
times

Then mix with the stiffly beaten Eggs . in beating
eggs, Just beat them till where you lift
up the beater they stand up in little peaks.
Measure flour after sifting. stir in sifted
mixture very lightly then beat

2 tabelSpoon Water

little Bakin powter "

Sun 18:   This morning at about four oclock it stormed and
rained a lot. Papa and Ruby got up and put the cover
on the stack. It looked so like rain. Didn't hardly
know if we should go to church or not. Papa and Ruby

went in the hack. Nobody else came to church but Wilbur Bastian so Rev. Mr. Madlock and Rev. Mr. Freeman came down here to dinner. It brightened up a little by afternoon. Papa Mama and the preachers rode. Ruby and I walked to church. There was only sixteen there. Papa and Ruby took the preachers over the station after church.

Mon 19: Cloudy part of today. Papa cut quite a bit of hay. Mamma and I picked raspberries this afternoon. They are about all gone now. The blackberries are turning red. We put up two quarts from what we picked today. Mamma wants to give them to Grandma. Had a few left and saved up enough for a pie. Nothing new.

Tue 20: Partly cloudy and partly clear today. We hauled in two loads of hay this afternoon. Aunt Annie got a letter from Aunt Tillie this morning. I guess they don't know what to do out there. She said he was worse in his mind.

Wed 21: Papa cut hay this morning. They got one load in this afternoon. Hardly got that unloaded. It stormed and rained like everything. It rained a lot. Couldn't do anything more much for the afternoon.

Thu 22: Papa and Ruby started to town at a little after seven this morning. Got home before dinner. Edward came along down with them. We were thinking to haul hay this afternoon if it was dry enough but before we got started it rained. Couldn't haul any today. It didn't rain any at all up to Aunt Annie's even John Weis' hay right over here wasn't wet.

Fri 23: We hauled hay today.

Sat 24: We got a card from Uncle Thomas this morning said Wilburs have a nine and one half pound boy. The card was signed Grandpa. He said it was born the twenty-second that was Thurs. Mamma got a card from Aunt Tillie. They are trying some kind of medicine for Uncle Herman now. They were going to take him to Rockford but the doctor said they could try the medicine for a week. We hauled two loads of hay this forenoon. All that there was cut. Papa cut this afternoon. I baked a cake and a batch of cream puffs this afternoon.

Sun 25: Cloudy all day but it didn't rain. This forenoon Ruby, Edward and I went up to Aunt Annie's this forenoon. Edward wanted to get his clothes down here. We staid to dinner. Then after dinner we brought his suit case down. Then we went to church from here. A medium sized crowd. Quite a few people on the road today. We didn't go anywhere this evening.

Mon 26: A ship (the Eastman) turned over in the Chicago River Sat. forenoon believed to be over one thousand drown. There was over two thousand on ship. I believe a terrible disaster. Worse than the Iroquois theater. The paper was full about today. We hauled five loads of hay today. Twenty-four loads up now.

Tue 27: It rained last night and today. Papa took Mamma and Edward over the station to go to Apple River this forenoon. We thought it would be a good chance for her to go now we can't do anything with the hay. Lots in the paper about the Eastman disaster. A terrible thing. I baked bread today.

Wed 28: I got a card from Jeannette today. It is a picture of her on horse back taken beside their house. Papa went up the Mound this afternoon. Mamma came as far as Scales Mound and came home with Papa. Mamma doesn't know if Uncle Herman is better or worse. She thinks that he has a little better appetite and his food stay down better. Mayme is going away to learn to be a nurse Saturday. She is going up somewhere in Wisconsin.

Thu 29: It rained again this morning. Aunt Annie came down this forenoon. Uncle Edd brought her down. Came down after her this evening. I cut some lawn today.

Fri 30:   Cloudy again today. Didn't haul any hay today. Rev.
          Mr. Freeman called here a few minutes this afternoon.
          We washed today.

Sat 31:   The last of July today. We hauled three loads of hay
          this afternoon. All we had out. It makes eight loads
          for this week or twenty-seven loads all together. Worked
          awful hard today. Awful hot today.

August

Sun 1:   Papa, Mamma & Ruby went to church this forenoon nobody else there but the preacher. Didn't have any services. We got ready and went to Galena to the Chautauqua this afternoon. The Chautauqua was good. The music was by the Craven Orchestra which consists of a man and his four daughters. They sang also. A minister spoke. It was just about a sermon. We called on Henry Bastian. A few minutes after Chautauqua. It looked like a storm. We had to go into Win Tippet's for awhile. There was a hard crack of thunder before we got in there. We had supper there. It rained again before we got home. It stormed quite a bit after we got home.

Mon 2:   Ruby and I picked blackberries this forenoon. We got quite a few. Papa cut some hay this forenoon. It rained this after and evening guess it won't clear up yet.

Tue 3:   It has rained all day. Don't know what the world is coming to. And cold! My I nearly froze. Had a fire in the house. I thought that it might snow yet. I crochet a little today. Papa and Mamma hoed a little in the potatoes.

Wed 4:   Rained ~~all~~ some today again and cold. Papa and Ruby went to town this afternoon.

Thu 5: Cleared up this morning but got cloudy again. Ruby and I picked quite a few blackberries this forenoon. Papa and Mamma hoed potatoes this afternoon. I picked over the blackberries and put up four quarts.

Fri 6: We washed this forenoon. Papa cut some hay. Ruby turned hay. We hauled two loads of hay this afternoon which makes twenty nine. A lovly day today first for a long long time.

Sat 7: We hauled four loads of hay today. It makes six loads for this week or thirty-three all together. The carrier broke to. I spilled by accident about all of this morning's cream. Quite a busy day for us. A nice day today.

Sun 8: Nice part of today. But after dinner it came to a storm. Rained like everything. Then it cleared up again. So I guess there was no church this afternoon. We didn't go anywhere and nobody came here today.

Mon 9: A lovly day. Mamma and I picked blackberries this forenoon. We got about a bucket a half full. We put up twelve quarts and a dish full left over. And a dish full raw. Papa cut some hay on the piece across the creek. We hauled one load of hay this afternoon. Cleaned the big field all out now.

Tue 10: A nice day again today. We hauled three loads of hay this afternoon. Had sweet corn for dinner. We had some cobs before.

Wed 11: We hauled one load of hay this forenoon and one this afternoon. Before we got that one in it rained quite a shower. We would have finished haying if it wouldn't have rained. I felt awful bad. I guess there is one load or a little more out yet. We did our chores early this evening. Then Ruby and I rode horse back up to Aunt Annie's. Didn't stay very long because it was getting dark. Had a fine ride.

Thu 12: Papa and Ruby went to town this afternoon. They brought home a bushel of peaches. Mamma and I washed this afternoon. After we got through washing we picked blackberries. Oh my but there is just piles of them. We didn't pick near half I don't think. I got nearly a bucket full and Mamma about a half. I don't know how we are ever going to get all the work done tomorrow. A two weeks' washing.

Fri 13: Awful, awful busy today. Well we got through haying today. Papa and Mamma and Ruby hauled two loads. We put up eight quarts of blackberries and ten and one half of peaches. Aunt Annie came down this forenoon. This afternoon she and I went picking blackberries. We each picked a big bucket full and Aunt Annie picked nearly a gallon bucket full to. My but I never saw such lovely berries. And so many. Aunt Annie nearly went wild over them. Uncle Edd came down after Aunt Annie this evening.

Sat 14: A nice day awful busy again today putting up peaches and blackberries and other work. I made a angel food cake today. We put up nineteen quarts of peaches from the bushel. Aunt Annie talked with Uncle George didn't think that they would come in tomorrow. Forenoon services at Union tomorrow.

Sun 15: We all went to church this forenoon. A common crowd there. We all went up to Uncle Edd's after church. Uncle Edd and Papa went over to see Mr. Young a little while this afternoon. Papa & Mamma stayed up to Uncle Edd's to supper. Ruby and I came home and done the chores. Papa and Mamma had a ride down from Uncle Edd with Mr. & Mrs. Wallace Williams in their auto. A lot of autos went by here today. The roads are quite nice now.

Mon 16: Mattie Tippet came out from town to pick berries here. Aunt Annie came down with her. After dinner we all went picking blackberries. Mattie thought that they were the nicest berries that she ever saw. We got quite a lot. I cut some lawn today. We also took out some of the onions. My but the lovliest onions. Biggest onions that we ever grew here ~~that~~ since I can remember. Mattie thought they were the biggest onions she ever saw. Thinks we ought to take them to the fair. Uncle Edd came down and got them this eve.

Tue 17:   I cut a lot of lawn today. Hope I can finish cutting tomorrow. We finished digging the onions today. We got about a bushel and one half. Mamma is busy all day putting up the berries.

Wed 18:   We picked berries this forenoon. I cut some lawn this afternoon also helped to pick over the berries. Mamma made jam and jelly out of the berries this afternoon. Mamma got a letter from Aunt Tillie this morning. I guess Uncle Herman is no better.

Thu 19:   A beautiful day. We all went to town today. Town was pretty quiet. Bought a new table cloth and set of napkins. I got a corset. Everybody very busy stacking.

Fri 20:   Washed today. I finished cutting the lawn. Mamma got a card from Aunt Tillie. The Dr. advised a wheel chair for Uncle Herman. Mamma was to see if Bastian's have one yet. She went over this afternoon. The one they had was only a rented one. Ruby picked some blackberries. Mama picked some to.

Sat 21:   A lovly day today. We were as busy as usual today. Just an awful lot of automobiles and teams went along today. The roads are nice now.

Sun 22:   A nice day. No preaching today. The minister was going to camp meeting. Ruby and I were going down to Weis' this afternoon. We went down that far. But they were not at home. They autoed up to Sinsinawa Mound Academy. One of Helen's friends that went up to Madison is up there and Helen wanted to see her before she went up to Madison again. She is going up there about the seventh. We talked with Mrs. Weis and Will. Asked us to come down this evening. Ruby & I then called at Tresidder's awhile. This evening we all went down to Weis'. John Tresidders were there to. Also Will and Bessie. Miss Astringer of Dubuque is down there. She is a music teacher. Had lots of playing and singing. Roads are full of autos today.

Mon 23: Ruby and I are thinking something of going down to Woodbine tomorrow. We may make the round of Uncles. But don't know if we will get started or not. I washed our silk gloves and a few other things today. A lovly moon light evening.

Tue 24: Cloudy today. Papa, Ruby & I went to town today. Mamma was going up as far as Aunt Annie's but Ethel said she was gone to Dubuque so Mamma had to go home. Ruby & I was going down to Woodbine. But we missed the train. We thought it wouldn't go till after three to five o'clock anyway. We didn't know the time. It was to go at two twenty. Awfully disappointed. Had to come home again. Our line was out of order we couldn't call up anybody to ask when the train went. It was tangled at the foot of Tresidder's hill. Papa went down and untangled it.

Wed 25:   A nice day. Mamma washed this afternoon. I hemmed some napkins. Ruby picked some blackberries. Aunt Annie went out to Apple River today. Lovly evening. Beautiful moon. We got a card, that is Papa & Mamma did from Anna from Salt Lake City. She just said she saw some beautiful cenery but expect to see better. It is a picture of the Mormon temple.

Thu 26:   Awful cold today. We got a letter from Uncle Thomas today. The baby's name is Wayne Harrison. They say Wilbur thinks he has the best baby there ever was. Olive has gone to Ft. Dodge for a visit. They said Anna was to Denver and Boulder. Was to her Aunt Carrie's and Edie's and was to see Willie and Leslie Trudgian and Mrs. Poundstone. She is now at Salt Lake then she is going to Cal. and she is going to Wash. to see Uncle Joes and then they are going to spend a week at Yellowstone Park. And she is going up in Canada and then to Minneapolis. Miss McLarnin went with her. Papa, Ruby & I went up to Scales Mound today. We went to the Chautauqua. It was pretty good. Clifford and Lucille Tresidder was there but didn't see Lucille.

Fri 27:   A nice day. I baked a batch of cookies this afternoon.
Aunt Annie called up from A. River today. Mamma
couldn't hear her very well. She said Uncle Georges
have a new car. They are going down to camp meeting
in it Sunday. I wrote a letter to Uncle Thomas this
evening.

Sat 28:   My but the autos are just a flying along. And an awful
lot of them. A lovly day and lovly roads. I've been
thinking for months to have my picture taken today,
but did not go to town. I baked a chocolate spice cake
today.

Sun 29:   My eighteenth birthday. But I don't realize it. It
doesn't seem like my birthday. It has been so cold
today. Had a fire in the house most of the day. I
looked at the thermometer once it was _____ had to
wears coats today. Some of us intended to go to camp
meeting today. Got up early and did the chores but
it looked so cloudy and it sprinkled rain a little so we
gave it up. It has been cloudy all day. But didn't rain
only drizzled a little. This afternoon Ruby and I rode
Fannie and I horseback. Went up to the school house
then down by the church. Had a lovly ride only it was
so cold. Didn't have any church today on account of
camp meeting. Didn't have any company nor did we
go to see any body. Oh, yes Dad did go down to

John's a little while this afternoon. Roy & Mable were down there.

Mon 30: A very beautiful day today. We had quite a hard frost last night. It froze the cucumber leaves and squash. It froze the tomatoe vines in the garden but not up in the field. Papa took the bull over the station this morning. Poor Deak. Got five cent a pound or fifty seven dollars all together I believe. Ruby drove Old Fannie over to meet Papa. She didn't get all the way over Papa was riding with Mr. Fiedler. Put up plums and cucumbers today. Aunt Annie came home from Apple River today. Did not talk with her yet.

Tue 31: A lovly day. Papa, Mamma and I went to Galena today. Ruby went up to Aunt Annie's. I had my picture taken today at Collier's. They are going to be five dollars a dozen or three dollars for half dozen. I do hope that they will be good. He said he would send the proofs tomorrow eve. So we would get them the next day. Just an awful lot of automobiles on the road today. Mamma stopped off at Aunt Annie's she wanted to hear the news from Apple River. Papa went part way to meet her tonight. Uncle George's auto is a Buick.

September

Wed 1: A nice day again today. We washed and baked bread today. Well tomorrow is the Schapville picnic. Undecided wether to go or not. I would like to go very bad. Don't like to ride out there in the old rigs and the carriage is to heavy.

Copied from my book of trips.
Trip to Schapville and Woodbine

Thu 2: Papa, Mamma, Ruby & I came out to the Schapville picnic a big crowd there. Papa & Mamma went home alone. Ruby & I came out to Uncle Joe's. Rode over this far with Uncle George's in the auto.

Fri 3: This forenoon we went up to Uncle Henry's stayed all night. We rode up with Raymond.

Sat 4: Uncle Dan went to Elizabeth today. Ruby & I went along. First time we were ever there. Had a fine time. Called at William's and at Ivy's. Helped Uncle Dan pick out a new suit, hat, tie, suspenders, and collar. Came back at Uncle Joe's at fifteen to eight. Staid here all night. Thinking of going down to Uncle Ben's tomorrow.

Sun 5: It looked like rain this morning. But it brightened up a little. Uncle Joes and Ruby & I went down to Uncle Ben's.

Joes went to church but we didn't. All of Uncle Georges but Pearl came down to Uncle Bens to for dinner. All of Uncle Bens had been sick but are feeling some better. It looked an awful lot like rain in the afternoon. So Uncle Georges went home. But it cleared off quite nice again without raining. Did not go to church any where today.

Mon 6: Uncle Ben took us to Woodbine this forenoon came home at fifteen to twelve. First time we ever rode on that train. The train from Galena Junction up was off the track or something. Had to ride up in a box car. A fine ride. Lots came up on it. I rode home with Mrs. Davis and Ruby with Mrs. Temperly. They had taken Bernetta and Thelma and Gordon Glasco in town to go to highschool tomorrow. Eddie Weis was going to bring out their new Overland car today. We saw Mr. Weis and Eddie in there.

Tue 7: Papa went to Galena today in the big wagon and brought home three new iron gates and a roll of wire. Paid fifteen dollar and a half for the three. One of the wagon wheels came off on the way home. Some men helped Papa put it on again. Some men and teams are working road right below our place. They are plowing the roads all up. Then I believe they are going to grade them after awhile.

Wed 8: I felt sick to my stomach this forenoon. Staid in bed about all forenoon. We washed today. Had just an awful big washing. It stormed and rained late this afternoon. Papa put up one of the new gates today down across the road. It looks quite fine.

Thu 9: ~~Ruby & I~~ We ironed today. Mamma went up to Aunt Annie's to get crabs.

Fri 10: It stormed and rained a lot today. Wanted to do such an awful lot of work but because it rained we did not get as much done as we would have. We finished ironing today. I bake a batch of cookies. Mamma churned. Mr. Pimperton the eye glass man called here this afternoon. Win Tippet thrashed some today but had to stop on account of the rain. Uncle Edds expect to thrash after Win. Our young Dorothy Perkins rambler is out in bloom now. The second time this year. It is only a few bunches. They are very, very pretty. The old one has a few buds too.

Sat 11: Misting about all day. Win Tippet finished thrashing today. Papa put up another gate today. Put in a gate post down by the road. The roads where they worked them are just awful bad. One auto a Ford nearly got stuck out here this afternoon. Wanted Papa to pull them up the hill but Glick came along. Fiedler said Glick pulled him up the hill. I suppose Fiedlers. We were expecting Uncle Georges tomorrow but I suppose that they will not come that the roads are muddy.

Sun 12:   Partly cloudy all day. But we had quite a storm tonight. An awful heavy rain. We all went to church this forenoon. Just us, Uncle Edd & Aunt Annie and John Tresidder and the preacher there. I don't know what is the matter with the people. Staid to home all the rest of the day. Not many people on the road today. John Weis were running their auto around in their field.

Mon 13:   It has been a lovly day but quite warm. Uncle Edds did not thrash today. I suppose they thought it to wet. Ruby and I hitched up Della and Fannie and took down and hauled away an old corn crib. We cleaned out the chicken house and hauled the many away. Dad worked on his fence or putting in posts.

Tue 14:   Uncle Edds thrashed today. We were all up. Aunt Annie had ten men to dinner. They got through about two oclock. They then to Heer's. Had a shower of rain just as they were through. Had an another shower tonight. We got a letter from Aunt Rachel today. They were to Ft. Dodge in their car this week Sun. and Mon. They expect Anna home by next Sun.

Wed 15:   Papa and Ruby went to town today. Mamma put up some pickled crabs. I made some chili sauce. Mamma got a card from Aunt Tillie today. She thinks Uncle Herman is getting a little stronger every day. He can walk quite a bit now!

Thu 16: Well today was the Mission Feast. We did not go because it was cloudy and rainy. It rained just awful several times in the night. We washed this afternoon. I tried to help Papa with the fence. Today is Wilbur's and Olive's first wedding anniversary.

Fri 17: It has been just a lovly day. And it a beautiful evening. Uncle Edd & Aunt Annie went to the Warren fair today. I baked a batch of cookies this afternoon. I also started to cut the lawn. I have an awful lot of work to do tomorrow. We got the wire fencing up today. Have the stakes to put in yet.

Sat 18: Just a beautiful day today. Aunt Annie said that Uncle Georges are not coming in tomorrow. The roads are to bad. Uncle George and Wesley were down to the Warren fair in their car. Uncle Edd & Aunt Annie rode to Apple River with them. Uncle Herman can walk quite a bit now. Grandpa and Aunt Tillie went down to the Mission Feast. They went with Mr. Hammer. I cut a lot of lawn today.

Sun 19: A lovly day. We all went to church this afternoon. I believe there were twenty there. Uncle Edd and Aunt Annie came down from church. We had just got home when Uncle Georges came. They had been up to Scales Mound to church. They all stayed here to supper. They went home again after supper. They got stuck up on the school house hill when they came. They were worried about getting back over it. They said if the roads were nice they may come in to Aunt Annie's next Sunday. A little late before we got through with our chores this evening.

Mon 20: It rained last night but a nice day again today. Mamma and Ruby dug some of the early potatoes this afternoon. I helped Papa put up some post up back of the little woods.

Tue 21: A very pretty day again. Papa & Mamma stretched the wire up between us and John Weis.

Wed 22: Just a manificient day today. Papa cut some clover for hay this afternoon and hauled some new wood. We got a card from Aunt Rachel said Anna got home early Sat. morning. Mamma baked bread today.

Thu 23: Papa, Ruby & I went to Galena today. Looked to see if we could find ourselves a hat but couldn't find anything. Mamma washed this afternoon. We sent a market basket of plums to Uncle Thomas today.

Fri 24: Cloudy today. Did all kinds of odd and end work. We got a letter from Uncle Thomas today. He said Anna had a wonderful trip. He said he thought they wouldn't come back to the fair this year.

Sat 25: Mamma and I went to Apple River today to the picnic. Papa took us over for the noon train. Uncle

Herman was sitting up to the table when we got there. He looks better and is getting stronger every day. Mamma staid at home with the rest and helped put up plums we took out. I went up the park with Sadie. I heard McKinzie speak. They had a merry-go-round but did not have any rides. Just when the speech was over it started to rain. It rained the rest of the afternoon. Sadie & I went to the movies in the eve. We went down to the depot to see the people off on the nine train. Rained just awful. The train was awful late. Stood out on the platform most of the time. Got wet. It rained I believe as hard as I ever saw it rained. I staid at Uncle George's all night. Slept with Pearl. It rained just awful hard all night.

Sun 26: The trains didn't run at all today washouts. One at Bowden. We were going home this afternoon but couldn't do it. I went to Sunday school and church at Methodist church this forenoon. Went down to Grandpa's to dinner. We took Uncle Herman out in the wheel chair a while this afternoon. Uncle Herman just started to walk without any one leading him today. Went to church at Methodist again this eve. Staid all night at Uncle George's again tonight. Mr. Bunker was there this evening.

Mon 27: Trains started to run again this morn. Mamma & I came home on the two train. Papa came over the station after us. They say Galena River was as high I guess Sun. as it has ever been known to be. Had to go to the post office in boats. Everything about the same as usual at home.

Tue 28: Busy getting plums ready. A bushel for Mrs. Potter and a box full for Mrs. Barnum. Papa took them over the station this afternoon. It took all day. An awful lot of bother for nothing. I fixed my hat today. Took the satin from bottom of my dress and made the brim wider shirred it around.

Wed 29: We washed today. I fixed my dress today. I made it longer. Aunt Annie came down this afternoon. Uncle Edd came down and got her about seven oclock. Quite a nice day today.

Thu 30: Ironed some today and did all kinds of odd jobs. I baked a batch of cookies and a cake. Mamma baked bread. We got a card from Uncle Thomas today. Said they got the plums all right. Said Wilbur and Olive had Wayne christened last Sunday in the Presbyterian church. I got a card from Mayme from Ano' Wis. Today. She was up on the hill ~~watchin~~ caring for a consumptive patient. They live in screen houses. This evening about five Uncle Dan drove in. He went up to Aunt Annie's to stay all night.

~~Fri 31~~

October

Fri
Oct 1: A lovly day today. Papa, Ruby & I went to the fair today. Mamma didn't want to go. We left our team and carriage up on the hill up from the smelter. A pretty good crowd there. Had a pretty good time. An awful lot of embroidery crochet and tatting work on exhibition. Quite a few autos and teams went along. We got home a little after six. Uncle Bens were here when we got home.

Sat
Oct 2: Uncle Bens went to the fair today. Aunt Annie went along with them. An awful lot of automobiles went along today. I wanted to go today but didn't have any way to go. Uncle Dan came down this eve. He was to the fair to today.

Sun
Oct 3: A nice day today. Uncle Bens, Uncle Dan and Uncle Edds were here to dinner today. Uncle Bens went home right after dinner. About two oclock. Uncle Georges came in. They went up to Aunt Annie's. Uncle Edds went home to. Mamma and I went up to Aunt Annie's to. Uncle Dan stayed here and had supper first then he went home. Nice and warm today.

Mon
Oct 4: Awful cold today and cloudy. Papa and Ruby went up Oct to Scales Mound today took up a bushel of plums for Mayme Monnier, a half bushel for Stella Graham, some for Aunt Lizzie and quite a few more. Some of the cows got in the corn this evening.

Tue 5: Ruby & I picked apples this forenoon and dug potatoes this afternoon. Mamma is busy putting up plums, cucumbers and such things.

Wed 6: Cold today. Papa cut some clover for hay this forenoon. Ruby & I dug some potatoes and then hitched up Old Fannie and hauled them in. It rained this afternoon. They thrashed at Willie Studier's this afternoon. Last job around here.

Thu 7: Awfully cold today. Ruby and I were digging potatoes today. Papa picked some apples. Mamma busy with plum jam, grape jelly, tomatoe preserves. A fellow here today selling pears. We did not buy any. Were selling them a dollar a bushel. We got a letter from Ida Barnum said she got the plums Sat. They were in good shape only a few spoiled. I hope it won't freeze tonight.

Fri 8: We dug potatoes today. Mamma washed today. It cleared up this afternoon. Awfully afraid it will freeze tonight.

Sat 9:   A terrible hard frost last night froze ice in a pan over a inch thick at the edge. The plums are frozen. Corn is all froze. Papa & Ruby went to town today. Quite a few autos went along today.

Sun 10:   A lovly day. An awful lot of automobiles went along today. We all went up to Uncle Edd's this afternoon. No other place to go. Nobody came to see us. Never have anybody come here only those that are relatives.

Mon 11:   We hauled some hay this forenoon. Ruby & I picked some apples also this forenoon. We cut corn this afternoon. Cut thirty two shocks. I cut twelve shocks. We have to cut as fast as we can now because the corn is all frozen and dry.

Tue 12:   Busy cutting corn today. I cut ten this forenoon and ten this afternoon. Making twenty today. We also picked a few apples this afternoon. This evening there is to be a dance in Young brothers' new barn. Cloudy and warm started to rain about ten oclock.

Wed 13:   It is rainy today. Couldn't do much outside today. Papa cut some corn towards evening. I finished making a pair pillow cases with fillit crochet inserting. Guess I will keep them for myself. About the first I crocheted. I have two pairs pillowcases now. One embroidered. Don't know any news.

Thu 14:   Papa and I cut corn today. Eighteen today making fifty all together for me. A lovly day. Mamma washed today.

Fri 15:   A nice day. Papa, Ruby & I cut corn. I cut eleven this forenoon and nineteen this afternoon making thirty today and eighty all together. Mamma baking bread, coffee cake and pattie cakes and ironing. Hope it will be a nice day tomorrow. We want to go to town.

Sat 16:   We all went to Galena today. Mamma bought a new hat. Got my pictures today. They are pretty good. Quite a few people in town today. Cloudy today. Wilbur Trudgian's birthday today twenty-seven years old.

Sun 17:   Mamma's birthday today. Forty-nine years old. We all went to church this afternoon. A new minister today. His name is Franklin. He is a young fellow. Quite tall. Red hair and dark eyes. I believe he is unmarried and that he came from Kentucky. A good singer. There was twelve there without the minister. Cloudy all day. It just poured down raining after we got home but I think it is all clear out now.

Mon 18:   Picked some apples this forenoon. Cut corn this after. I cut seventeen. Got a card from Aunt Rachel this morning. I don't know anything new.

Tue 19:   Papa went over to Evan Evan's and Ehrler's to see
if he to find a sheep buck. But couldn't get any. Aunt
Annie rode down with Papa. Papa had dinner up
there. Cut corn today. I cut ten this forenoon and fifteen
this after. Which makes one hundred twenty-two in
all.

Wed 20:   Cut corn again today. I cut twenty-five. It was just
a beautiful day. And it is a perfect evening. Mamma
washed and baked bread today.

Thu 21:   Another model day and evening. Mamma, Ruby &
I cut thirteen shocks each of corn this forenoon making
one hundred sixty all together for me. Papa picked
apples this afternoon. Ma & Ruby dug some potatoes
and I ironed some.

Fri 22:   A lovly day. Quite warm. Full moon tonight. An
awful log of autos going along today. We all cut corn
this forenoon. I cut thirteen. We have about another
forenoons cutting yet. Uncle Edd and Aunt Annie
went out to Uncle Henry's and Joe's this afternoon.

Sat 23:   We all cut corn this forenoon. We finished cutting
corn. I cut eight which makes one hundred eighty-
one all together for me this year. We got a card
from Mrs. Fiedler saying she was inviting a few
neighbors for this eve. for Charlie's birthday. We

also got a letter from Uncle Thomas. It contained a clipping that Miss Nancy Hansen had a towel shower in honor of her coming marriage to Mr. Alfred Trudgian next month. We went to the party tonight. Only us, Win Tippet and Herman Studier and Will Studier wife and baby from over the hill. A nice day.

Sun 24: A lovly day. Papa, Mamma and Ruby went to church but the minister did not come. Papa and Mamma went down to John's to dinner Ruby came home. I did not go. I did not feel well. This afternoon Willie Tresidders came down. Ruby phone for Papa and Mamma to come home. They staid till four oclock. I wasn't well enough to come down to see them. Uncle Nick and Aunt Lizzie are down to John's.

Mon 25: A beautiful day. Uncle Nick and Aunt Lizzie came up this afternoon.

Tue 26: Papa & Ruby went to Galena today. Uncle Nick, Aunt Lizzie and Mamma went to call on John and Joe Weis this afternoon. I staid home alone.

Wed 27: A lovly day. Papa went up to Scales Mound this forenoon. We washed this afternoon. Nothin doin.

Thu 28:   Ironed some today. Papa went over to Elmer Mayne's sale. Didn't get anything. Ruby & I husked a little corn. A lovly day.

Fri 29:   A lovly day again. Papa took Uncle Nick and Aunt Lizzie and Mamma up to Uncle Edd's this forenoon. He staid to dinner. Papa took the sheep up to Uncle Edd's this afternoon. Then he brought them home after supper. I baked drop cakes and bread this afternoon.

Sat 30:   A lovly day again. John Tresidder took Uncle Nick and Aunt Lizzie to Galena this forenoon. Quite busy doing Saturdays work and cleaning up.

Sun 31:   Well it is Halloween. But I guess Fri. and Sat. was celebrated. Another nice day. Ruby & I went up to Werner's but Jeannette and Leo were gone horse back riding. We staid a little while then we came home. Fiedlers were here this afternoon. They staid for supper. A good many autos going along today. Never one would ask us to have a ride.

November

Mon 1:   We husked corn this forenoon. We churned this afternoon.

Tue 2:   Annie Poundstone phoned out from Galena this forenoon said she came last night and was going up to Scales Mound today. She is going to see Ida Barnum. I suppose she will come down here.
We got a letter from Mr. Potter. He said Lloyd is married. Was married Sat. August 23, married Mary Margaret Sullivan at Buffalo N.Y. They are residing at Niagara Fall. He said she was stenographer. Very pretty and of Irish decent. We washed bed clothes this afternoon. A nice day.

Wed 3:   Cloudy today. Papa went over the station this morning to see a bull calf. Berryman said he had over there. He walked. He bought it and went over and got it this afternoon. It is a nice dark red one. Paid fourty dollar for it. We washed this afternoon. Ruby cleaned her room. Joe Weis are hulling clover today. Didn't get quite through. They have the stacks over here in the fields.

Thu 4:   I sent three of my pictures today one to Uncle Bens, one to Uncle Thomas and one to Uncle Joe Trudgian. Wesley, Sadie & Naomi and Grandpa and Grandma came in this afternoon in the car. Stopped here awhile. Grandpa and Grandma staid here the rest went up to Aunt Annie's to stay all night. Grandpa and Grandma were visiting at Henry Joes and Ben just got up to Apple River this morning. Uncle Herman and Maggie and Tillie are visiting around down there all over. They think they may come here before they go home. Ruby cleaned the downstairs bedroom today. Saw by the paper John Trudgian is at home. Came Sun.

Fri 5:   A nice day. This afternoon Wesley, Sadie, Naomi and Aunt Annie came down. Naomi had a fine time Wesley, Sadie, Naomi Ruby & I went up on John Weis' hill. Wesley took Grandpa and Ma and Aunt Annie up to Aunt Annie's then they went home something after four. They were going to take Pearl along home. Had watercress for dinner today. Also a few days ago. First we ever had of our own.

Sat 6:   We all went to town this afternoon. An awful lot of people in town. A nice day. Quite warm. Ruby bought a new hat. Grandpa and Grandma went home this evening.

Sun 7:   Awful windy today. No preaching at Union today. Wouldn't go anywhere else. Afraid to ride with Old Fannie afraid of her. She is getting worse every day. Home all day. A lot of automobile going along. This evening we went up to Uncle Edd's.

Mon 8: A lovly clear day but awful windy. Aunt Maggie, Aunt Tillie and Uncle Herman came to Galena today from Woodbine. Uncle Edd went in after them. We brought in our cabbage, beets and carrots today. Also the last of cauliflower. Pickling it this eve.

Tue 9: We husked corn this forenoon. Pretty nice husking. This afternoon Papa and Ruby hauled in the corn and hauled some rock. Papa is fixing the wall in the back end of the cow house. I baked a batch of cookies this afternoon. We got a letter from Anna today telling us all about her trip west. They slept in twenty different beds and rode on thirteen different railroads. Rode on the train thirteen days not counting nights. She said Al isn't married yet but that's all she said.

Wed 10: It rained a little today. Cloudy all day. Mamma & Ruby husked corn this afternoon. I ironed. No news. Nothing doing.

Thu 11: Didn't husk any corn today it was to windy. It was just awful. Aunts Annie Margaret and Matilda and Uncle Herman came down this afternoon. Uncle Herman looks very much better. Face is getting fat. Aunt Annie went home this eve. The kitchen chimney caught fire right after dinner. We washed today.

Fri 12: A lovly day. Aunt Tillie and Maggie went husking corn with us this forenoon. Uncle Herman helped a little. Mamma staid in. We husked twenty-eight. Aunt Annie came down again today. We ironed this afternoon. Mamma churned, Aunt Tillie and I wrote Mayme (the nurse) a letter this eve.

Sat 13: A lovly day. Aunts Margaret and Matilda and Uncle Herman went up to Aunt Annie's this morning. They went to town with Uncle Edds. Ruby & I husked twelve shocks this forenoon. Papa and Ruby hauled corn this afternoon.

Sun 14: Cold today. We haven't any services at Union yet. Uncle Edds and Aunts and Uncle went to Galena to church this forenoon. We would like to have gone some where to but afraid of Old Fannie. We went up to Uncle Edd's a while this afternoon.

Mon 15: Awful cold today all day. We husked fifteen shocks of corn this forenoon. Ruby cleaned Papa's and Mamma's room this afternoon. Nothing new.

Tue 16: Mamma and Ruby husked ten shocks this forenoon. Papa tied them up. I got dinner. Papa and Ruby went up to Scales Mound to get some grub. They were at Uncle Nick's a little while. We thought maybe Annie Poundstone would come along down but she was down to Graham's. Aunt Lizzie said at Annie Poundstone stove said Al is going to be married Thanksgiving day. That is the ~~fifteenth~~ twenty-fifth. He is going to live with Uncle Thomas. His fiancée is a orphant and has no home. Uncle Henry Dittmar and Raymond and Helmer drover to Galena this forenoon. Coming back they called at Uncle Edd's and drove in here but did not come in the house.

Wed 17: We husked twenty shocks this forenoon. We washed this afternoon. Aunt Maggie Aunt Tillie and Uncle Herman went home on this evening train. They went to Galena with Johnnie and Ethel. A bazzar at Council Hill tonight.

Thu 18: Cloudy today. We husked twenty shocks corn this forenoon. Papa and Ruby hauled all the corn in that was out. Mamma and I ironed. We got a letter from Uncle Thomas today said Al is going to be married Thanksgiving Day at noon. Will take the two train for Galena. Thinks they will stay at Galena over night. Will go to Kloth's. He thinks then Al will phone out for us to go in after them in the afternoon. Uncle Thomas wrote all this in confidence. Al wants to surprise us but Uncle Thomas thought we might not like it. I suppose we wouldn't be prepared if we didn't know. The wedding is going to be at Uncle Thomas'. They are going to invited her folks and Wilbur and Olive.

Fri 19: Awful windy and snowy all day. About the first snow of the season. Did not husk any corn today. Mamma churned this afternoon. Win Tippet and Herman Studier came over to get his cow this morning. The cow he bought of us last spring. Been over for a couple days. He bought our two yearling steers. Six and a quarter and two percent discount. Got ninety-one dollars and some cents. Uncle Edd's and Aunt Annie's wedding anniversary today.

Sat 20: It is Papa's birthday today. Fifty-nine years old. Between cloudy and clear today. Didn't husk any corn today. Busy with other outdoor and indoor work.

Sun 21: Between cloudy and clear today. This afternoon Mamma, Ruby and I went to church to hear our new minister. It was quite late before they got there. Mr. and Mrs. Haines I believe their name is. An awful big feeling fellow. We don't like him. Mrs. is very pretty. They bought a guitar or banjo or some such thing along. He played it and both sang. That was just fine only he sang to loud. Uncle Edd and Aunt Annie came down from church and spent the evening. Beautiful moon light. Full moon.

Mon 22: Snowing this afternoon and evening. Mamma and Ruby husked some corn this forenoon. And Ruby husked some this afternoon. Mamma and I cleaned the dining room. But couldn't clean the carpet. Will have that to put down another day.

Tue 23: I got a letter from Alice Trudgian this morning. Thanking me for my picture. Papa and Ruby husked some corn this afternoon.

Wed 24: Quite a nice day. We washed and ironed most this evening. Papa and Ruby husked twelve shocks today. I finished making tatting ends for dresser scarf this evening and sewed it on. I think it looks very pretty. We baked bread today. We got a letter from Aunt Lizzie Trudgian said Mrs. Poundstone had come up from Warren and that she is going away Sat. would like for us to come up some day. Just think the night before thanksgiving and just think the day before Al's wedding day. I just wonder what he is doing tonight. Oh, I would just love to see him married.

Thu 25: Alvin's wedding day. Cloudy all day and very warm. But rained like everything this evening. I suppose Al and his bride are in Galena now. Papa would go up the Mound this afternoon to see Mrs. Poundstone. We didn't want him to go. None of us wouldn't go along. Came home at a little after nine in all the rain. The new harness is just soaked. He had supper at the hall. Didn't go up to Uncle Nick's they were at the hall. I went down to Agnes' to get a few needle crafts this afternoon. My but the roads will be awful bad if we have to go in after the honeymooners tomorrow.

Fri 26: Raining nearly all day. Alvin called out this morning said they were in town. Wanted to know if Papa could come in after them. We didn't know what to do it was so rainy. Al called out again he said they didn't have much time to stay they would like to come out. Didn't hardly know if we could get through the mud or not. Papa and Ruby went in after them. Got home about half past five. Nancy is pretty good looking. Wears glasses. Has brown hair. Gray or blue eyes. Quite small. I believe weighs one hundred seventeen pounds. Papa asked Al how old she was. He said she was eighteen. So I suppose she must be somewhere my age. Al is twenty-four. It stopped raining towards evening. They were married yesterday at noon at Uncle Thomas' by the Methodist minister pastor of Grace Church.

Sat 27: The sun shined a little this forenoon. Al went hunting shot a rabbit to take home. Husked some corn. Nancy, Ruby and I went up on Wilbur Bastian's mound and came down on John Weis' Mound. Nancy said she like to walk around on the hills. Nancy has a Father one sister and five brothers. Al told dad they were Danes. She worked in a laundry. They are going to live with Uncle Thomas this winter. Al seems to think quite a bit of his little nephew. We all went down to John Tresidder's this evening. Quite muddy.

Sun 28:   Rained some last night. Cloudy and dark all day today. After dinner Papa and Ruby took Al and bride over the station to go home on the two train. They couldn't stay any longer. Al couldn't get off any longer. They thought it would be the best roads over the Station. So they didn't get to go up to Uncle Nick's. Mattie Tippet called up this after said they were down the depot Uncle Edds to when the train went through. She thinks Al's ~~fine~~ wife looks quite young. Mattie and Mary are going to leave tomorrow for New Mexico for Mary's health. Said she didn't know how long they would stay. She called up to day goodbye. It cleared up very nice this eve. and it is quite cold.

Mon 29:   Quite cold today. To cold to husk corn. Ruby went up to Aunt Annie's this afternoon. Papa went up towards evening and they drove our sheep home. They hadn't forgotten home yet. They knew just where to go. I made some ice cream this afternoon.

Tue 30:   Just think the last of November. Papa, Mamma and Ruby went out in the field about the corn this forenoon. I staid in to get dinner. This afternoon we all went out. We have one-hundred and one up in that field yet and one hundred eight out in the little field. A nice day.

December

Wed 1: A lovly day. Papa, Mamma and Ruby working in the corn field this forenoon. I got dinner. This afternoon Papa and Ruby hauled corn. Mamma and I packed a lot of corn out of the corn crib. It was quite poor. Wanted to put the other in. We got a letter from Uncle Thomas today. Said Al and his bride got home alright. A piece put in about the wedding. It said she was dressed in white silk chiffon. Her attendent wore lavendar messaline.

Thu 2: We husked corn this forenoon and some this afternoon. Papa and Ruby hauled in a load towards evening. Mamma washed today. We have seventy-two shocks left up in the field yet.

Fri 3: A lovly day today. We husked corn all day. We husked twenty-five shocks today. I sent for the Christian Herald and Modern Pricilla for two dollars this morning.

Sat 4: We husked seven shocks this forenoon. We now have fourty up in the field. We sent to town with Aunt Annie for a quarter's worth of bread and a stolo. We all went up this evening to get it.

Sun 5:   No preaching at Union today. Having kind of a dedication at Council Hill. They fixed up their church. A lovly day. Ruby and I went up to Werners today. Jeannette was at home. We stayed for supper. Just about as we got home. Papa gargled his throat with kerosene this forenoon. Some of it went in his windpipe or lungs. He nearly choked. Has been sick all the rest of the day.

Mon 6:   Papa has been sick all day. Has pain in his lungs. His head aches and eyes ache. Ruby and I husked and tied up ten shocks today. Agnes called up wanted to know if we wanted to go to Dubuque with them tomorrow. We don't know if we should go or not. I guess we can't if Papa isn't better. I hope he will be better by tomorrow.

Tue 7:   Papa was no better this morning so we couldn't go to Dubuque. John, Agnes and the baby went. Milton went to school. Quite cloudy this forenoon but cleared up fine this afternoon. This morning Ruby and I husked corn. Got six out of the way. Makes twenty-four left. I went up to Aunt Annie's this afternoon to borrow some flour. Papa has been in bed all day. Don't know if we should get a doctor or not. Uncle Edd and Aunt Annie came down this evening. Lorraine Garrity social at Guilford tonight. Oh, but how I should like to have gone.

Wed 8: Papa about the same. Maybe a little better moved down in bed room this forenoon. Been up and around some. Ruby and I husked two shocks corn this forenoon. It was so awful dry and windy we couldn't do anymore. I split some wood this afternoon. Ruby and I made a cat house. Ma & Ruby fixed pig pen and cleaned stables. Mamma and Ruby hauled the corn in with Old Fannie in the buggy.

Thu 9: Ruby and I husking corn. We husked tied and stacked up fourteen shocks today. Papa up a little today.

Fri 10: Ruby and I finished up the field of corn this forenoon. Eight shocks. It was awful dry. This afternoon we hauled in a load of corn. Papa went out and drove the horses. The big ones. Agnes called up said somebody could go to town with John tomorrow. And if we needed anything they could bring it out for us.

Sat 11: Mamma went to town with John and Milton this forenoon. Brought home some supplies. Fifty pounds flour. Ruby and I did the Saturday's work. Forenoon preaching tomorrow.

Sun 12: Kind of snowy this forenoon. Mamma and Ruby went to church. Dad and I staid at home. A few at church. I guess another hard sermon. Uncle Edd and Aunt Annie came down to dinner. John, Agnes,

Milton and Blanch came up this afternoon. Blanch is awful cute. It brightened up some this afternoon. Rev. Haines is going to start meetings at Council Hill this evening.

Mon 13:   A lovly day. Doing odd jobs today. Mamma and I husked three shocks of corn out here this afternoon. We were going along the road I looked over the bridge saw some kind of a bird looked much like a little dark duck swimming in the water. Mamma and I were laughing about it wondering were it hailed from. Bunny cat was around there all at once there was a jumb, a plung, a scramble. Bunny had jumped down after this object not thinking about getting wet I guess. The duck dived in under the ice and Bunny got out a quick as possible. Had to put him in the house to dry. The object is a great diver. We thought it a wild duck. One wing looked as if it might have been injured.

Tue 14:   This morning Ruby caught the object. She had on leather gloves. Brought it in the house. Has a long very pointed bill. And tried to pick nearly like a snake. It has short legs and large dark web feet. I believe three web body like a duck long neck. Don't know what it is. Wanted to put it in something and leave it in here to warm up. Ma wouldn't have it. Ruby put it down there again. Saw it several times today sitting down there. This eve we found it dead feet in air head turned back under. Papa and Ruby hauled two loads fodder this afternoon. Mamma and I washed.

Wed 15: I kept house today and made bread. Papa, Mamma and Ruby hauled fodder. Making a long stack in the stack yard.

Thu 16: Cloudy all day. Rained this afternoon and some this evening. Uncle Edd and John Tresidder came this morning to help stack fodder. Had Uncle Edd's team. Papa and Ruby hauled with our team. Finished at about three oclock. Made a stack up in the field. Aunt Annie came down also. Aunt Annie had a letter from Aunt Tillie today. Uncle Herman weighed one hundred twenty-four last time he weighed. They invited us all out there for Christmas. Tillie, Pearl, and Sadie have been to Dubuque one Saturday.

Fri 17: My but the rained froze made it just awful icy. Have to be very careful when you go out. Papa and Ruby wanted to go to town today but it was to icy. Been all day taking rack off wagon and putting box on and getting out sled if it should come to snow. And cleaning stables. I split some wood. Heard Helen Weis is going to come home tomorrow.

Sat 18:   Papa and Ruby went to town today. Didn't want to go on Sat. but wanted the horses shoed so bad. The roads are awful icy was afraid to have them go to town. They got along though. But couldn't get the horses shoed all the shops full. A very busy time for blacksmiths. They got a few things but not all. A sleigh went past today. First one for season.

Sun 19:   A beautiful day only mighty cold. Mamma, Ruby & I went to church this afternoon. A few there. Heard another hard sermon. Uncle Edd weren't there were in town. Didn't have any company today.

Mon 20:   Well this morning Dad took the old sows over the station in the sleigh. Got sixty dollar for three. Got six cent a pound. Hard pulling for the little horses. He got stuck several times. A man with a team pulled him up the hill. Couldn't go because it was so icy and they weren't shoed. Choring all day.

Tue 21:   Papa and Ruby went to Galena today to get the horses shoed. I haven't been to town for so long and don't know when I will get to go. Afraid of that Old Fannie. It's terrible to have to stay here and never get out to see any thing or go to anything doing. Its terrible.

Wed 22:   We washed today. Ruby cleaned out stables. We had the old eye glass man here for dinner. Wasn't expecting to have much of a dinner. Only a few fried potatoes. Didn't have any bread hardly. Mamma baked some biscuits quick. She had some sausage. He thought those biscuits just fine. He at four or five. Dad bought a pair of glasses for seventy-five cents and his dinner. Ten cents glasses I guess.

Thu 23: Awful windy today. Mamma cleaned out both chimneys today. Papa walked over to Gaber's to see if he could get some oats this forenoon. We can have ten sacks now will see if he will have anymore to spare after awhile. Papa went over after it this afternoon. Mamma, Ruby and I went up to Aunt Annie's this evening to take up Christmas presents. A dresser scarf with tatted edge for Aunt Annie and a pair of fine gloves for Uncle Edd from Ruby and I for keeping our sheep up there so long.

Fri 24: This is Christmas Eve. Santa Clause came this morning through the mail. A package from Uncle Thomas three handkerchiefs with Lillian on and a bar pin for me. A sofa pillow cover for Mamma and some darning needles. A crochet thimble case and a handkerchief for Ruby. A neck tie and three pairs black socks for Papa. We also got a card from Uncle Thomas. Said Wilbur has been sick with the grip. Mamma and Papa husked some corn. I made bread, Mamma saffron cake. I made a cake with figs between.

Ruby and I made a little candy this evening. Aunt Annie was going out to Apple River today. Some of us would have gone to but did not have anything to wear. Christmas trees at Apple River tonight. Hope we will have a Merry Christmas. I wish, I wish Santa Clause would bring us a horse one just like we want.

Sat 25: Christmas Day. I was sick all day. Nothing very merry for me today. Didn't eat any breakfast, dinner, or supper. Just a little lunch. The rest didn't have much of a dinner either. We got a picture of Wilbur, Olive and the baby. It is a nice picture. Wilbur is sitting down holding Wayne. Olive is standing up behind. Wayne looks to be quite pretty. Papa and Ruby went down to John's this eve. Milton wanted us to come down to see his Christmas tree so they went.

Sun 26: Papa, Mama, and Ruby went to church this forenoon. I staid home and got dinner. Nobody came home with them to dinner. Nobody came here today. Didn't go anywhere. Russell Ford was buried this afternoon at two oclock. He died Thursday of thyphoid pneumonia. He carried mail in Galena.

Mon 27: A nice day. Only quite cold. Papa took a load of hogs over the station this morning and one this afternoon. They average one hundred sixty about got five sixty.

Sold a little ruptured pig for four cents per pound. All the hogs are gone now. Only two to butcher and two sows. Got a card from Uncle Thomas said they got the parcel we sent them. Aunt Rachel thinks her present is handsome. Anna's is grand and so on and so forth. Got a Merry Christmas card from "The Barnums" also. I wrote a letter this eve to Uncle Thomas and a card to Wilbur and Olive. Heard today Helen Weis has the measles. Nice way to spend vacation.

Tue 28: Papa and Ruby took chicken up to Scales Mound. Got twelve cents for young roosters, eleven for hens, seven for old roosters. Took three old roosters they weighed nearly ten pounds a piece. Sold them to Will Hick's. He said they were the nicest coop of chicken he had taken in this year. Papa and Ruby called on Uncle Nicks. They went out to Gunnow's to look for roosters but they weren't at home. Mamma and I husked and tied up three shocks of corn this afternoon.

Wed 29: This afternoon Papa and Ruby drove over to Jim Ivey's to see some roosters. They bought four. Aunt Annie came down this afternoon. And Uncle Edd came down for supper and spent the evening. A nice day.

Thu 30: We husked twenty-seven shocks of corn today. It has been just a lovly day today. Nice and warm. We have fifty-six shocks left. We won't get through husking this year. Just think only one day more in nineteen hundred fifteen. Been for year's thinking we would take in the worlds fair this year. But didn't get to do it. Gazette day today.

Fri 31:   Not a nice day today. Misting and it has been rather dark all day. Papa, Mamma and Ruby husked nine shocks corn today. We have fourty-six or seven shocks yet. I don't we ever had that much corn to husk to start the New Year with. I baked a cake this afternoon. This evening I made chocolate candy. Fondant dipped in chocolate. They look lovly. It is the last day of nineteen-fifteen. The old clock is ticking off the minutes. It is half past ten. One and one half hours of the old year yet. May nineteen sixteen be a happy and prosperous year for us all. I will never write in this book anymore this year. I did not get it full.
Goodbye 1915.

Wilbur Trudgian
423 Vinton St. Waterloo, Ia.

Alvin Trudgian
219 Lafayette St. Waterloo, Ia.

Thomas Trudgian
64 Mulberry St.

Waterloo, Ia.

Anna Trudgian
1750 W. Congres St.
Chicago, Ill.

Thomas Trudgian
2174 Lafayette St., Waterloo, Ia.,

Private Charles Trudgian
348 Field Artillery
B. Battery.
America lake

        Wash.   nov.27

1916

The Trudgian home [circa 1854] on Stagecoach Trail,
Galena, Illinois

January

Sat 1: Rainy, foggy and dark. just awful windy tonight. We
have all been busy today. Baking and cleaning up.
I baked a batch of cookies this forenoon. I hope all
the days of nineteen sixteen won't be like today. There
maybe snow by morning. I washed my head this
afternoon. There was no mail today. I am starting
my third book today. two years in one book and one
year in last book. My fourth year to keep a diary.

Sun 2: A beautiful day today. Clear not a cloud in the sky all
day. no services to day at Union. Rev. Haines has the
grip. We all went up to Uncle Edd's for dinner.

Mon 3: Another beautiful day. We cleaned out the stables this forenoon. We husked corn today. We have twenty-eight shocks left. This evening Uncle Dan came in from Uncle Joe's He is going to stay here all night.

Tue 4: Well we got through husking corn this afternoon. We husked twenty-eight shocks today. Uncle Dan helped us. Uncle Dan is going to stay all night again. Uncle Edd and Aunt Annie are not at home. They are in to Tippet's. Old man isn't very well. It has been dark and gloomy all day. and warm for this time of year.

Wed 5: Awful windy all day today. Papa and Uncle Dan stacked the fodder from the little field today. We washed an awful big washing today. We also baked bread. John Tresidder came up to ask Dan if he would help him get up some wood. He said he would.

Thu 6: Uncle Dan went down to help John cut wood. We ironed some today.

Fri 7: Well we got up a little early. Hurried just awful. Papa took us to town. We nearly ran to depot. The train was about half hour late. we would have been late if train was on time. Papa staid in town all day. We bought Mamma a waist, I a black skirt. Ruby a dress. We rode to Dubuque from E.D. on the bus. My but it was so crowded we were nearly smashed. We walk back to E.D. Awful tired. Ruby sick. My shoes hurt so I could hardly stand it. Got home all right.

Sat 8: Got up late today. Ruby and I made up our minds to go to Apple River. Worked just terrible. Had to fix a skirt and sew button on things. We walked over the Station for the four fourty-two. Surprised Grandpa Dittmar. They were eating supper. Herman, Ruby and I went to the class play tonight lasted from eight to half past eleven. The name of the play was "The Prairie Rose" Sadie was in it. It was just fine. Aunt Tillie isn't very well.

Sun 9: Aunt Maggie, Uncle Herman Ruby & I went to Sunday school and church to the Pres. Church. Had dinner at Grandpa's. We went up to Uncle George's after dinner. Staid to supper. We then went to the Methodist church this evening. Mr. Bunker at Uncle George's to supper. Rained some. Walks very icy.

Mon 10: Clear up today. Awful cold and windy. This afternoon Herman, Maggie, Ruby and I walked out to Irish Rob Virtue's. staid to supper and a little after. Sadie and Naomi were down to Grandpa's this evening.

Tue 11: Were thinking to go home this morning but missed the train Came home this afternoon. It started to snow just before we left. snowing all the time We walked home from the Station. Milton told Mamma last night that Davis' house burned down Sun. Didn't hear any particulars. Ancious to know them.

Wed 12: Didn't get up until late this morning. Snowing and stormy and windy all day. I made a kitchen apron this afternoon and am tatting on a corset cover. First one I ever tatted. We got a letter from Uncle Thomas today.

Thu 13: Whew, but its cold today eighteen below zero here. Twenty-five below up at John Tippet's. Uncle Dan came up from John's this morning. To cold to cut wood. But had to go over to Studier's to saw wood this afternoon. I have been tatting most of the day. Davis' house burned down Sun. morning. Started from the chimney. Tried to put it out but the wind drove it on. They saved most things down stairs. They saved the summer kitchen.

Fri 14: Awfully cold again today. We made doughnuts this afternoon. fried in Crisco. Nice and clear today. Uncle Erhard Dittmars are celebrating their Golden wedding today. Grandpas are invited.

Sat 15: Uncle Dan came up here this morning. Papa and Uncle Dan went to town this forenoon with Uncle Dan's horse in the buggy. Quite a few sleighs going along. A cattle sale in Galena today. My throat is quite sore lately. I suppose its the grip.

Sun 16: Uncle Dan went to Galena to church this forenoon. Forgot to put on his collar and neck tie. Spent part of afternoon and evening at Uncle Edd's. Papa, Ruby and I went to to church this afternoon. Only Rev. and Mrs. Haines and Wilbur Bastian there besides us. Very cold today.

Mon 17: A very cold day again. Wanted to wash but its to cold. Ruby made a big apron. I tatted some.

Tue 18: Quite cold but as clear and beautiful as can be. We washed today, a very big washing. Papa and Dan went up in the woods chopping. My throat is sore yet. Have an awful cold too.

Wed 19: Snowing this afternoon. Some warmer. It snowed quite a lot this afternoon. It will be sleighing now if it don't snow to much. I hope it won't. Mamma went up to Aunt Annie's today. Joe Weis shipped a car of logs today. Will went with them.

Thu 20: Rainy and dark. Snow is melting. This afternoon Uncle Edd went out collecting for the church. Brought Aunt Annie down. Uncle Edd came back and spent the evening here. Very warm today

Fri 21:   The snow is all gone. Very warm. Had the door open some of the time and hardly any fire. I baked cookies this afternoon. We finished up the ironing. Heard the river was high.

Sat 22:   Dan went down to John's to saw wood for us. Papa and Ruby went to town to day. Very warm today. Just beautiful. Quite muddy.

Sun 23:   Another beautiful day. Dan went to Galena to church. Ma, Ruby and I went to church this forenoon. Quite a few there. We were kind of expecting Youngs down but they had to go home. They were expecting Popps over there. John Tresidders came up this afternoon.

Mon 24:   Another beautiful day. We washed and ironed today. Dan went up to Fiedler's to saw wood. Papa chopped wood.

Tue 25:   Ruby went up and helped Aunt Annie wash a very big washing today. Papa and Dan chopped some wood. Cloudy and very warm. Ruby and I each got a card from Nancy, our cousin in law.

Wed 26:   Rainy all day. Very warm and very muddy. Dan and Dad chopped some this afternoon. Ruby cleaned stables. I did some tatting.

Thu 27:   It got colder today. Froze up. The mail man didn't go today. I don't know if the river was to high or not but I don't think he could get through the mud. Papa and Dan chopped wood. I finished tatting the yoke for corset cover. Ruby made a dressing sache.

Fri 28:   Papa and Ruby hitched up the big horses and hauled down some wood. Dan was chopping. I baked a cake this after for supper. It is froze up today. Roads very rough.

Sat 29:   Cloudy, Rainy and dark today. Quite icy. Dan and Dad didn't chop any wood today. Our line and the other two lines are crossed. Amusing our selves by rubbering.

Sun 30:   Cloudy all day. Dan went up to Aunt Annie's this forenoon horseback. This afternoon we all went to church. Quite a few there. Uncle Edd and Dan walked. Mrs. John Combellick has been quite sick but is a little better today. There is going to be a meeting at the Station this week. Snowing.

Mon 31:   A very beautiful day, but cold. It snowed last night but not enough for sleighing on these rough roads. Dan cutting wood. Pa hauling wood. Our lines are still tangled.

February

Tue 1: Just a beautiful day only very cold. Ruby and I went up to Ethel Tippet's but she wasn't at home so we spent the afternoon at Aunt Annie's. Rode home from there to Tresidder's with John in the sleigh. Dan chopped today and Papa hauled wood.

Wed 2: Another beautiful day and also very cold. Ethel T. called up this morning. Asked if we wouldn't come up today. So Ruby and I went up and spent the afternoon. Had a nice time.

Thu 3: There was to be an eclipse of the sun this forenoon. I didn't see it but the sun didn't shine very bright for awhile. Quite cold today. Uncle Dan went up to Aunt Annie's this forenoon. I guess he will stay there for awhile. I did some crochet and tatting today. I finished crochet and sewing on a pillow case. It finished a pair for Mamma I started I guess over a year ago.

Fri 4: Papa and Ruby went to town today. Cloudy and snowing today. Will be sleighing for awhile after this. I baked a cake this afternoon. Had a beautiful supper tonight. Good raw fried potatoes. And green onions, and some celery. I sawed some wood today.

Sat 5:   Just beautiful today. Quite a few sleighs going along to town. Would like to have gone awfully well to. I baked a cake today. The rest cleaned out the stables.

Sun 6:   Papa, Mamma and Ruby drove to church this forenoon. I would re_____ so staid at home. Preacher had all kinds of things to say again. Not a soul came to see us and didn't go any where. Would awfully well have liked to go to the Station tonight. Having meetings. Quite a doings.

Mon 7:   A lovely day but very cold. We made aprons today. Made out an order to sent to Montgomery Ward and Co. tonight.

Tue 8:   We washed this afternoon. It looked to stormy this forenoon. Papa went over to Gaber's sale this afternoon. He drove over in the sleigh. He didn't buy anything but seven tin cup for a dime.

Wed 9:   A lovely day. This afternoon Mamma went over to see Mrs. John Combellick. She staid and had supper. Mrs. Combellick is a great deal better. Papa hitched Della up in the cutter this evening and drove over as far as the Baker's house and came home. said she went fine. Hope we will be able to drive her.

Thu 10:   We ironed today. Mamma, Ruby and I went down to John's this evening. Blanche isn't feeling very well.

Fri 11:   Baked bread and a cake today. Ma and Ruby cleaned the cow house today. Papa chopped wood.

Sat 12:   Lincoln's Birthday. Papa and I drove up to Uncle Edd's with Della in the cutter just to break her in. She went quite nice only the sleighing is getting very poor. Aunt Tillie and Uncle Herman came in today. Came out with John.

Sun 13:   A very beautiful day. We all went to church this forenoon. Uncle Edd and Aunt Annie, Aunt Tillie and Uncles Dan and Herman came down from church for dinner. We rode home with them. Ruby and I have been very anxious to go to the meetings at the Station. So Uncle Edd told Dan he could take us all some where to church. Couldn't make up minds where to go. Tillie wouldn't go over to the Station. She was nervous. Can't hardly stand his preaching. So Papa, Dan, Herman, Ruby and I went over the Station. Tillie rode over to Wilbur Bastian's. visited there until we came home. Mamma and Aunt Annie staid here at home. First great meetings Ruby and I ever were at. I'll never forget it. The minister went through such terrible manuverings. Took off his coat and collar and neck tie. There were twenty or over at the alter praying all at once. Scared people into going. Made terrible threats. A man went up crying with his little boy. His wife followed soon. Several more went up. We motioned to Dan to go out, that we wanted to go. So they went out then we went out. I guess we will get something terrible for going out. Such a racket when we went away. I don't think I want to go to another one. Mrs. Weis and Josie was up there tonight.

Mon 14: Didn't do much today but talk about meetings. Valentine's Day today. Not any of us got any Valentines.

Tue 15: Quite warm today. The snow going away quite fast. Papa butchered today. Did it alone with Mamma's help. Uncle Edd's butchered to.

Wed 16: Snow all going away very fast. Very warm. We got word by mail that the goods from Montgomery Ward was over the Station. Papa and Ruby went this forenoon in the sleigh after it. It seems to be all very satisfactory. We got a barrel of flour, 25 lb sugar, five pounds peanut butter, a gallon sorgum, six cans corn, six cans peas, 2 cans pineapple, goods for auto scarfs for mother, Ruby and I. One gray, one light blue, one green. And a few other things.

Thu 17: Very warm today. Mamma working at the meat. Ruby and I cleaned the cow stable this afternoon. Papa chopping willow wood. Victor Engel's sale today.

Papa didn't go. I would have gone if there had been a chance.

Fri 18:   Nothing much doing. I went up to Aunt Annie's this forenoon to get a frying pan for Ma to fry meat in. Hemmed two sheets this afternoon.

Sat 19:   Busy with Saturday work. Very warm. Water running every where. Quite a few teams went along today. Dan called up this evening and asked me if I wanted to go to Galena to church tomorrow. They are going in the hack and I can go along.

Sun 20:   Well I went up to Uncle Edd's and went to Galena to church with Aunt Tillie, Uncle Dan and Uncle Herman. We went to the First Presbyterian Church. Heard a missionary preach. Had dinner at Aunt Annie's. Got out there about two o'clock. Uncle Edd and Aunt Annie went up to Union. Mamma and Ruby also went to Union. Papa staid at home. They were invited up to Aunt Annie's to. But Mr. & Mrs. Young came down to dinner. I rode home from Aunt Annie's with Fiedlers. Uncle Georges sold their house. Got $4500 for it. Would like to sell their store to.

Mon 21:   Mamma frying down some meat. Ruby and I cleaned stables this afternoon. A nice day. Papa chopping wood.

Tue 22: Washington's Birthday. Also Grandpa's and Grandma's Dittmar fifty-second wedding anniversary. No mail today. We washed an awful big washing. Rained a lot this afternoon. Some say it thundered.

Wed 23: We ironed some this forenoon. Bessie Weis came over this afternoon. She called us up this forenoon. Had a nice visit. Had her stay to supper. A very nice day.

Thu 24: Reading day. Mamma went up to Aunt Annie's this afternoon. We finished the ironing. Papa, Ruby & I went up to Uncle Edd's this evening.

Fri 25: A very beautiful day. Ruby and I cleaned out chicken house and horse stable. Ma & Ruby cleaned out cow house. Sheriff and Auctioneer Bardell was accidentally shot last night. Shot through the liver. I guess it's quite serious. Took him to Dubuque hospital.

Sat 26: Papa and Ruby went to Galena today. Quite cold today. Bardell was accidentally shot by City Marshall Dwyer at Milbrig while trying to open a car door to capture a negro. They think there isn't much hope for him. Mrs. Bardell has been and is quite ill.

Sun 27: Dan asked if one of us wanted to go to Galena with them this morning. So Mamma went. There was no service at Union. Mrs. Haines is sick. Aunt Annie & Tillie stayed in town from yesterday. They all went to 1st Pres. Church. Then they went over to Tippet's for dinner. Then went up to Henry Bastian's in afternoon. Mamma got home about six o'clock. Bardell died at midnight last night. He leaves eight small children.

Mon 28: Well if this wasn't leap year it would be the last of February. Snowing a little today. Bardell's funeral tomorrow. Services at the house at nine and at the Court house at two in the afternoon. I think it will be an awful big funeral.

Tue 29: Well this is our extra day. We only have this day every four years. Oh, just a lovely day. Sky just a beautiful blue. An awful lot of people went along to the funeral today. Heard that there never was more people in Galena at Fair time that there was in to the funeral today.

March

Wed 1:   Well March coming in like a lion. Snowing quite a bit today. We sawed wood today. We had eight men for dinner. Uncle Herman came along down. He is staying here all night. Aunt Maggie came in today. Walked over from the Station to Uncle Edd's this forenoon. Aunt Annie is going to quilt tomorrow. Aunt Tillie talked to Uncle George today. Mayme was to come home today. Pearl is home. Has an awful bad cold. Sadie is teaching in her place.

Thu 2:   Well Papa took us all up to Aunt Annie's in the sleigh with the big horses. We quilted a white and yellow quilt partly. Ethel Weis and her grandmother and Martha were there to. Ruby came home to do chores. Then she and Dad came up there to spend the evening. Win came up to in the evening. Quite a party.

Fri 3:   A lovely day, but very cold and windy. We cleaned out the stables this forenoon. Mamma went up to Aunt Annie's to quilt again this afternoon.

Sat 4:   Papa and Ruby went to town today. Brought home three hundred bran. It is Uncle Thomas and Aunt Rachel's wedding anniversary today. thirtieth I believe. Dan called up again tonight. Asked one of us if we wanted to go along with them to town to church tomorrow morning.

Sun 5: Uncle Ben called up Uncle Edd's this forenoon. Said Mrs. Williams is dead. She is going to be buried tomorrow at one o'clock from the Methodist church at Elizabeth. She is going to buried at Welsh Hollow. I went up to Uncle Edd's and went in Galena to church with Uncle Dan & Herman & Aunt Tillie. She & I went to the 1st Pres and D & H went to the South. We came out to Aunt Annie's to dinner. They would have come down here but Maggie isn't well enough to go out. Ma & Ruby came up there towards evening. Ma and Dan are talking of driving to Elizabeth tomorrow. Can't make no connections with trains. Papa, Mamma & Ruby went to church at Union this forenoon.

Mon 6: Well Dan and Mamma went to Elizabeth. Went about quarter to nine. Ma called up something to twelve said they got down alright. They are staying all night down there somewhere I guess. Dark and foggy this forenoon. Rainy this afternoon and just terrible windy this evening. Papa & Uncle Edd sawed wood today.

Tue 7: This afternoon Aunts Margaret and Tillie came down here. Then Maggie went over the Station to go home. Ruby went all the way over with her. Tillie & I just went a little way. Ruby did a little shopping over the Station. This evening Ma called up from Aunt Annie's. She is going to stay up there all night. They missed the right road and they then crossed over through Ritter's and H. Weis'. They staid at Uncle Ben's all night last night then this morning they came back to Elizabeth. Had dinner at William's and then came home. Wardie has just got the measles. Vada and Lester is nearly over them. none of the children went to the funeral.

Wed 8: Just a beautiful Day. Mamma came home this morning. Tillie went up to Aunt Annie's this afternoon. I made a corset cover for the tatted yoke. I made it this afternoon. finished it all. We got a letter from Uncle Thomas & Aunt Rachel this morning.

Thu 9: Reading day. A very fine piece in the paper about the meetings at the Station. We washed today. Awful windy. Clothes got dry nearly as fast as we hung them out.

Fri 10: Ruby & I cleaned the cow stable. Ruby & Ma the horse stable. Agnes Tresidder called up today. Said the baby had pneumonia in one lung. Dr. was out yesterday & Today. Wanted to know if somebody could come down tomorrow afternoon to look after the baby while she do her work. Papa hauling manure today.

Sat 11:   A nice day. Mamma went down to John's this forenoon and she is going to stay all night. Said she didn't know how. she is having awful crying spells. Aunt Tillie and Uncle Herman went home today. Aunt Annie went along. Mayme has to go again Tuesday.

Sun 12:   Mamma came home from John's this morning. Blanche is getting better. There is no services at Union today. Heard the minister was called away. We were at home all day. no company. Just Ruby & I went walking on the hills. Just a beautiful day. Very warm.

Mon 13:   A nice day. Mamma went over the Station and went to Apple River on the evening train. Thought she could see Mayme yet. She called up this evening said she got out there all right.

Tue 14:   Quite cold today. Papa went over to help John Weis saw wood. Ma called up this after. Said she would come home tomorrow morning. We just heard this evening that Warren Spenser is dead. Old Mr. Tippet told Win. Said it was in the paper, said they were going to bring him back. We hope it is a mistake. Uncle Edd called us up and told us. Nobody had heard that he was sick.

Wed 15:   Well Warren is dead. Martha Tippet called up Mrs. Amos Ford. said he died last night at five o'clock.

They just got a telegram said they were going to bring him back today on the noon train to Galena. But this afternoon Mrs A. Ford called out said he is going to be brought back on the noon train tomorrow. Going to have services at Epworth in the forenoon and then a short service in at Grandma Ford's in the afternoon then he is going to be buried at Greenwood cemetery. Mamma came home this afternoon. Dan came along home with her. Mrs. Amos Ford was getting on the train as Mamma got off. She told Mamma that Warren is dead. She just said he had pneumonia and it developed into Bright's disease. We want to go to the funeral very bad. I sent Anna a postal card this morning to leave them know of Warrens' death. Warren is twenty years old. Would be twenty-one next October the ninth. Dan went up to Uncle Edd's this evening. Papa went to town today and got four sacks of shelled corn.

Thu 16: This forenoon, Papa, Ruby & I went in Galena to the funeral. The funeral came on the twelve to one train. We went down to the depot. Mr. & Mrs. Werner and Leo & Walter where there to. And a few others. Jeannette wouldn't go to the funeral. She staid at home. All that came from Epworth that I know of were, Mr. & Mrs. Spencer, Byron and Raymond, Mrs. Amos Ford & Wallace Ford.

And six young men for pallbearers. and I guess the minister. His coffin box was a white or light grey. made of some metal. His coffin was a sort of grey. He had a lot of boxes of flowers. We went up to the house about two or after. We saw Warren right away. It didn't look a bit like Warren we didn't think. Wouldn't have known it was him. The minister read, prayed and spoke a little. Very nice. That was all. He had a good many flowers. Mostly white. some light yellow and some pink ones. After the services Mr. & Mrs. and the boys took their last look at him and then it was closed up forever. They had five carriages. The only team that went out to the graveyard was Werners. Ruby & I would have like very much to have gone. Furlong was undertaker. There was quite a few to the funeral. as many as could get in the house comfortable I think. Mrs. Werner said Warren had be sick about a week. The minister said he was apparently in good health a week ago. Mr. Werner had been out to see him Sunday. he died Tuesday. None of Jesse Fords there. Cassie Lennor, Eliza Bastian's grandson from Canada, rode out with us. to the road going up church way. He seem a very friendly fellow. I read in the paper today that Harry Pierce is in the war. He & I were first reader classmates. Weather kind of chilly. rather cloudy. Fri. 17 St. Patrick's day today. Also Josephine Weis' birthday. Papa dehorned the calves today. Nasty job. We got thirteen eggs tonight.

Sat 18: Just a lovely day. Papa hauled manure. I bake a batch cookies, a cake and two pies. Mamma also made two pies. We cleaned out the cow house today. Aunt Annie wasn't well enough to come home today. Uncle Edd went out to Apple River.

Sun 19: No preaching again today I guess. I took a little horseback ride on Della this forenoon. Dan came down here to dinner. He asked Ruby & I if we wanted to go to Galena to church tonight. So we went. First time I had been to Galena at night for a good many years. We walked around awhile before we went to church. We went to the Methodist church. We got home about a quarter after ten. Mamma went up to Fiedler's awhile this after. Mary has been sick is some better.

Mon 20: Ma, Ruby & I each made our selves a skirt today. top or under. Papa hauling manure. Nick Weis is quite sick. He has pneumonia. Have a nurse.

Tue 21: This afternoon Uncle George called up said Grandma Dittmar was sick and all the rest was sick to. Wanted to know if Mamma wouldn't come out on the five o'clock train to take care of them. We didn't know what to do. Mamma is sick herself isn't able to do anything. but she went. Dad drove up to the end of the woods with her. she walked from then. She called up tonight said Grandma is pretty sick. Aunt Annie is worse. Tillie & Maggie is sick Grandpa Dittmar. Was storming so I didn't want to talk so long. Uncle Edd and Dan came down to supper. Had to go home early on account of storm.

Wed 22: Awfully funny weather. It storm all night. Terrible lightning and terrible cracks of thunder. And what do you suppose we found in the morning. Almost more snow than we had all winter. Melting fast. Roads are terrible. Mail man only came as far as Heer's. Nice and clear today. Didn't hear from Apple River today.

Thu 23: A lovely day. but muddy and sloppy. Ruby & I washed today. a two week wash. We got quite tired. I tried for Apple River, the line was out of order this morning. But afterward Mamma called up. Ruby talked. She said Grandma is very sick. Has pneumonia. The doctor was there three times today. They are going to get a nurse tonight. Said the rest wasn't very well. Ruby didn't ask how she was. I hope she is better. Nick Weis is getting along all right.

Fri 24: Very warm. Snow is all going. Creeks are very high. I made bread today. It got quite nice. I also baked a cake. This evening Mamma called up. Ruby talked. She said Grandma is very bad. We was to tell Dan. They got a nurse last night. Uncles Henry and Joe were up to see Grandma. She knew them. she knows them some times and sometimes she doesn't. Grandma took sick last Sunday. Mamma said Aunt Maggie has something the matter with her legs. she can't walk. Tillie is up and around. Aunt Annie felt some better but had been lying down again this after. Dan called up tonight said he was going out to Apple River tomorrow morning on eight o'clock .

Sat 25: Grandma Dittmar is dead. Uncle George called us up this morning at half past nine. Said she died at eight this morning. Said she is going to be buried Tuesday morning. Dan asked how the rest were. He said Maggie and Tillie were pretty bad. Oh I do hope they will get better. I feel so sorry for them. Dan went to Galena to go out to A. R. on the noon train. The weather is so bad. It rained so last night, thundered and lightninged. My guess the roads are terrible. I hope the weather and roads may improve. Uncle Edd came down this forenoon. Was here to dinner.

Sun 26: It rained an awful lot all night and It rained all day. The weather is awful. The Galena river is awful high. Haven't heard a single word from Apple River. Nearly worried to death. Don't know what the reason is unless Mamma is sick and they don't want us to know. Ruby called up Central this forenoon and asked if the line to Apple River was in order. She said they were in order. but didn't know if could hear or not.

Mon 27: Well this morning I called up George but could not hear him. I told them to tell Ma to call us up. So Mamma called this forenoon. The funeral is to be at half past eight and if we wanted to go we would have to go on the five train this evening. The morning train would be to late. Well John T. said he would do the work. but we did all the chores for evening. John is gong to do them in the morning. We got over the Station in good time. Walking was quite good. Dan, Uncle Henry Winters and Maggie Winter and some others were there to meet the train. Poor Aunt Maggie has to sit with her feet on a chair. Tillie is up and around. very thin. Uncle Edd , Mr & Mrs V Grebner went to A. R. on same train we went. Aunt Rachel T., Mr Winters & Maggie came at noon. Uncle Ben & Aunt Dora drove up there this afternoon. An awful lot of people came there this evening. We saw Grandma. She looks very nice. Every body says so. She has lots of flowers. Uncle Edd took a wreath out. its very pretty. The children got a pillow. A bunch of flowers of the church. another from some people in Apple River. a bunch from Uncle Thomas. a bunch of lovely roses from Mr & Mrs Johnnie Weis and Mr & Mrs. Magret. Lovly flowers. Most every body went to neighbors to sleep. Ruby & I went to Sutton's. Papa staid at Mr & Mrs. _____.

Tue 28:   We had breakfast at Sutton. The funeral was at
half past eight. All the Relatives were up stairs. Mr.
Eustice Read, Prayed and spoke a little. two girls sang
a song. It was all quite short. They took Grandma
down to Schapville on a long hack. Put the coffin in a
wooden box. Three carriages went and Uncle Bens in
their buggy. Uncles George, Dan & Herman and
Uncle Edd went. Mrs. Winter, Maggie & Lena
Winter. (She came on the midnight train.) Mr
Hammer went he took his team and the undertaker.
about all that went. Mamma, Aunt Rachel & Uncle
Henry Winter started out but came back. the roads
were to awful. We had dinner at Grandpa's. Neighbor
women getting meals and such things. People very
good. Papa, Ruby & I went to Scales Mound on
the one train. It doesn't stop at the Station. We went
up to Uncle Nick's for awhile. then we walked home.
we went through fields and came out over Temperley's
Mound. went along the road but inside of fields from
there on. Walked the road from Sheean's home. Got
along all right only my shoes hurt my toes just terrible.
had to take them off and go in my overshoes. We got
home at twenty minutes after five. left Glenn's store ten
after two. John & Milton were here doing chores. A
little calf & two little lambs since we have been gone.
and two more lambs tonight.

Wed 29: Another calf and two more lambs by this morning. Six lambs now. The mail man didn't go today. Mamma called up this forenoon. Said Grandpa got awful sick yesterday afternoon with Erysiplas. Had the doctor. a little better this morning. Uncle George, Uncle Edd and the undertaker came back to A. R. last night. drove till the horses were played out then walked the rest of way. The rest had not come back from Schapville yet. Uncle Edd came to Galena on this morning train. Mamma said there was an awful lot of people to the service at Schapville. They took Grandma in church. First person to be taken in that church. They had just put in a new door so they could take her in Monday. I don't know when Mamma will be able to come home.

Thu 30: Another calf and another lamb today. Quite warm today. I baked a pie this forenoon and a cake this afternoon. Mamma called up this afternoon. She said Grandpa is some better. If every thing is alright she said she might come home Sat. morning. Uncle Edd and John Tresidder came this evening. Uncle Edd said there was an awful big crowd at Schapville Tuesday.

Fri 31: Another calf. One every day. Five calves all together now. I bake bread and coffee cake today. My first attempt to make coffee cake alone. I've mixed it before. We got twenty-seven eggs today. Ma didn't call up today.

April

Sat 1:   Well Mamma came home this morning. Ruby & I went to meet her. Aunt Rachel came to Scales Mound this morning. Intends to go to Galena Monday. There was another calf today. And another lamb last night. All the lambs now I guess eight. A few people going to town. not many though. roads very bad in places yet I guess. Uncle Edd went out to Apple River on this evening train. Just a beautiful day.

Sun 2:   A very beautiful day. Mamma lying down quite a bit today. No services at Union today. John Tresidders came up this afternoon awhile Uncle Edd came home this afternoon. came down here to supper. spent the evening.

Mon 3:   Papa worked on telephone today. Everybody was out. Some worked up by Fiedler's putting poles in and so on. Uncle Edd was here to dinner. Ruby & I made a little garden today. in corner of garden. Don't expect it to grow. too awful wet. We put in a few onions & radishes & lettuce.

Tues 4:   Well it is election day. Papa went over to Guilford with Mr. Fiedler this afternoon. He didn't see any women over there. But I heard over the phone ten women came to vote a little to five. All Rep. got in but three. L. Werner road commissioner, Charles Tobin town clerk, Wallace Ford supervisor. Galena went wet. Aunt Rachel came out from Galena with John & Ethel Tippet. They brought her down.

Wed 5:　Aunt Rachel went down to John T.'s this forenoon. John came up with her this evening. Uncle Edd and Dan came down to supper this evening. Heard Apple River went dry again. Most or all towns around are dry now but E. Dubuque and Galena. Galena went wet by five hundred. one hundred less than a year ago. (four hundred sixty eight.)

Thu 6:　Mamma and Aunt Rachel went up to Fiedler a little while this forenoon. This afternoon Aunt Rachel, Ruby & I went up by Union Church. Then down to John Combellick's Aunt R. wanted to go see Mrs. C. because she is sick. Mrs. C is sitting up. but can't do any thing. her leg is swelled up again quite a bit. They would have us stay for supper. Clayton is going away tomorrow to LaCrosse. Is going to work on railroad. His uncle got him a job. We called at Wilbur B's. then called in at Annie's & Lottie's a few minutes. About dark when we got home.

Fri 7:　John Tresidder took Aunt R. to Galena this morning. She intends to go home Sat. I went down to John's to get some parsnips this after. Mamma talked with Uncle George D. said they aren't any better out there.

Sat 8: Well Papa and Ruby drove the big team up to Scales Mound today. In the wagon. Took up thirty dozen eggs. They didn't meet any autos or go near the trains. They got along fine they say. They say the road is fine now. Quite a few teams going along to Galena. We baked a cake, a jelly roll & coffee cake & bread today.

Sun 9: Well Mamma went out to Apple R. again this morning. Ruby & I went over the Station with her. Ruby went all the way. I went up on the hill and looked down to the Station. We made it over & back in two hours & ten minutes. Just a lovely day. Dan came down to dinner. We had lettuce for dinner. It was just grand.

Mon 10: A lovely day. Ruby & I raked lawn. we raked about half. Ruby cleaned out horse stable & helped Papa load manure. Papa hauled manure. I set two hens this evening. one on two goose eggs that Agnes gave us and six hen eggs & one on 4 eggs. Mama is thinking to come home in morning.

Tue 11: Well Ruby & I went to meet Mamma this morning. She says they are all getting some better out there.

Grandpa gets up now. Dan drove out to Apple River today. He is going to work for a Mr. Long. Very warm today.

Wed 12: Ruby & I rake some more lawn today. Ruby & I went up church this afternoon and swept and dusted. There is going to be Quarterly meeting next Sun. Another little calf today.

Thu 13: We washed today. And baked bread and took up the rose bushes. Aunt Annie came home from Apple River today. She has been gone over a month. Grandma's obituary is in today's Gazette. Raining this afternoon.

Fri 14: A beautiful day. We ironed, bake a cake & cookies. Papa was plowing. We got sixty eggs tonight. Well we had an old fashioned peddler here this afternoon. Bought some needles & a set of little pins. Uncle Henry D. have another little girl, ninth kid.

Sat 15: We got up early this morning. Mamma, Ruby & I walked over the Station and went to Galena on the train. And came home on the five oclock train. Had a good day of it. I got a new spring coat and hat. The coat's navy trimmed in lighter blue silk. the hat is black straw with black quill. Ruby's hat is black straw trimmed in blue ribbon. It is raining & storming this evening. Papa got through plowing this piece of ground out here today.

Sun 16: Rainy this morning. Didn't know if we should go to church or not. But we went. Fifteen there with the Elder & preacher. Blanche T. & Evelyn B. were to be christened at W. Bastian's after church. We went up to Aunt Annie's for dinner. It rained like everything but we went in Win T.'s machine house.

Mon 17: Papa & Ruby were going up the Mound this forenoon. Just as they were starting Old Black caught his bridle in V's harness & pulled it off. Then they ran around & run into the fence. They were half over then stopped and eat grass. Scared us all terrible. Didn't break anything. Then after dinner they drove Violet & Della up the Mound. Couldn't get alfalfa seed – mostly what they went for.

Tue 18: Papa harrowing today. Mamma frying down meat. It rained this afternoon and evening. We had greens for dinner and supper today. Dandelion and dock mixed. Fine.

Wed 19: Papa & Ruby went up the Mound this after to get the alfalfa seed. They got home just before it stormed. Storming this evening. Pa & Ruby were up to Uncle

Edd's this forenoon. Ruby moved all furniture from her room in mine. I took up the carpet and tore all the paper off. Ruby is going to paint the woodwork. They took old Della & Violet up the Mound.

Thu 20: Rainy again this evening. We washed today and cleaned cow house. It rained awfully last night. There is another little calf today. The ninth. We turned Della & Fannie out on grass.

Fri 21: Rainy again today. We ironed today. Ruby painted her room. We had water cress for dinner. Uncle George called up Aunt Annie and Tillie talked. She said Aunt Maggie's leg is worse. Had a doctor from Warren today. Wanted to know if Aunt Annie couldn't go out tomorrow. Good Friday today.

Sat 22: I baked mock angel cake this forenoon. A total failure. I made a devil's cake then. Busy with Saturday work as usual.

Sun 23: Well this is Easter. Ma, Ruby & I went up on the hill to see if any one came to church. Rev. & Mrs. Haines came but no one else so they didn't go down. (I didn't intend to go) They went home again then. I pick some anemones this forenoon. A lovely day so we all walked over the grave yard this after. They staid to supper. Sadie & Wilbur B were over there. Mr

Y. is up & around again. (Its so lonesome) Helen Weis has been home. Thought she might come up. but not a soul showed up.

Mon 24: Papa harrowing & seeding oats. Ruby & I cleaned the rag room today. A nice day.

Tue 25: Showery today at times. We washed today. We got our paper we sent for today. trimming that. Papa sowed alfalfa. first we ever planted. then harrowed. Then he plowed the garden.

Wed 26: Cloudy today. We ironed today. Mamma and I started to paper Ruby's room. Got most of ceiling on. Had hard times. too dark I guess. Papa hauling manure.

Thu 27: Well today is Grant's birthday. First time for a good long time I missed going. A few teams and some autos going along. Mr. Werner & Mr. Fiedler are plowing the roads all up. getting them ready for the grader. Ma & I finished papering ceiling & got about three fourths of sides done. Then late this afternoon we put in some early potatoes and some garden. Have some things to plant yet. We got a card from Aunt Tillie said Aunt Maggie is no better. Dr. says she has inflammitory rhumatism. She and Aunt Annie has to stay up with her at night.

Fri 28: We finished papering Ruby's room today. Then all three of us finished putting in garden. Papa went over the grave yard to help burn it off this after. Uncle Edd got a letter from Aunt Annie. she said Aunt Maggie is quite bad. She telephone this afternoon. said they got a nurse out on noon train. Ma wanted to go to A. R. on five train but couldn't make it very well.

Sat 29: Mamma went to A. R. on this morning train. Ruby walked over with her. took a basket of eggs and got a few grocerys. I baked an angel cake. and churned a little butter. Had been churning on it all last night before. Papa hauling manure. Quite a bit of travel on road today. Tillie Weis is sick. She has scarlet fever.

Sun 30: I was sick all day today. In bed. A steady rain all day.

May

Mon 1: Well this is May day. Didn't get much done today. Ruby took some of the things out of Papa & Mamma's room Ma called up this afternoon. Doesn't know when she will come home. Tue. or Wed. Aunt Maggie didn't rest very well last night but was resting easier.

Tue 2: Well Mamma came home this morning. Aunt Annie is thinking to stay till Sat. Then one of us have to go out again. Aunt Maggie is guess is about the same. Nurse is nice. Her name is Miss Gardner. We pull the paper off the room this after.

Wed 3: Papa & Ruby went up to Scales Mound took up forty three dozen. Drove Fannie & Della. Mamma and I washed this afternoon. Nice afternoon. We got a letter from Uncle Thomas. Al & Nancy went housekeeping last Thu. At 219 LaFayette St. three blocks farther downtown than they & three blocks from I. C. depot.

Thu 4: We ironed today. Mamma white washed their room today.

Fri 5: Mamma and I papered Papa's & Mamma's room today. pretty tired.

Sat 6: Couldn't make up our minds who was to go to Apple River. So I went, when we got up on the ridge it started to rain didn't know what to do. but it stopped so I went on. Ruby went as far as Ford's. This eve, I went walking with the nurse. She seems very nice. Then Aunt Tillie and I went up town. Had some ice cream. didn't get to bed until late.

Sun 7: Uncle Ben & Uncle Herman came up town. They, Grandpa, Dan & I went to Pres. church. They staid to Grandpa's to dinner. Some of Uncle Georges down this afternoon. Two Mr & Mrs. Hammers, Miss Gardner, Tillie & I went to Pres. church in evening.

Mon 8: Grandpa thought we hadn't better wash so they sent it out. So we started to clean the girl's bed room.

Tue Wed & Thu: I don't just remember what went on. Oh, yes. On Wed. eve. the Christian Endeavor met at Grandpa's. not many there. Aunt Maggie sits up a little while every day. Thu. eve. I went to the lecture coarse. went on their ticket.

Fri 12: The nurse went away at noon to Warren. I went to the depot with her. This evening. Pearl, Sadie, Mildred Sutton, Naomi and Wesley called for to take me out auto riding. I sat in front with Wesley and held Naomi.

We rode out about three miles toward Warren. A fine ride. Lovely moon light. My throat is quite sore.

Sat 13: Doing Sat. work.

Sun 14: Grandpa & I went to Pres. church this forenoon. Dan was there. Mother's day today. Dan there to dinner. Uncle Georges down in afternoon all but Wesley. Sadie staid to supper. Tillie went to church in eve. I & Sadie went to Methodist. quite a few there. Saw Wesley's girl, Hazel Winen.

Mon 15: Uncle Joe was up. Had dinner there. Cleaned spare room.

Tue 16: Put down matting of spare room.

Wed 17: Cleaned attic today. Uncle Henry & Clifford up town at Grandpa's for dinner. talked to Ruby today. Mamma went to Galena to Mrs. Fred Kloth's funeral yesterday came home today. Aunt Rachel was back but went home last night. Ma staid in Galena all night at Kloth's. I went up store this eve. Tillie went to Endeavor at Spear's. Forgot to call for me. So I staid at Uncle George's all night.

Thu 18: Grandpa & Mr Ewer went to Scales Mound. Going to install a minister there. I got home some time this forenoon. Ruby came to meet me. So many things look so different at home. I was gone nearly two weeks. just think. took all day to look around. The road is fixed very fine. graded. Pa & Ruby finished planting corn.

Fri 19:   We washed today. Aunt Annie came down this afternoon. Papa hauling brush in ditches. About four this after. I went down to Tresidder's and Milton & I went out picking asparagus. I got about enough for three meals.

Sat 20:   Awful busy. Sat. work and getting dining room carpet down and get straightened out. I have an awful cold and awful sore throat.

Sun 21:   Rainy today. We didn't go to church. We went up to Uncle Edd's this after. John Tresidders up there. We started out. It rained. We went in wagon shed at John Tippet. It stopped after a while. Then we came home.

Mon 22:   I have an awful sore throat yet. I didn't do much today. I cut a little lawn this evening.

Tue 23:   This forenoon Papa and Ruby went up to Scales Mound. They were up to Uncle Nick's a little while. I cut some lawn.

Wed 24:   Papa, Mama & Ruby planted potatoes this forenoon and some this afternoon. Papa plowed up a little patch up in the field by the oak tree for some potatoes. Milton came up this morning. brought some nice tomatoe plants.

Thu 25: Very warm today. We finished planting potatoes by noon today. Papa planted melons this afternoon. This eve. Ruby & I went up to Aunt Annie's a little while. She gave us some asparagus.

Fri 26: We ironed today. We did up two pairs of lace curtains but it was so windy and cloudy.

Sat 27: I was sick today. Couldn't do much. I had an awful headache and one side of my throat is sore and swollen. I thought it was the mumps. Papa hitched Della up in the buggy this afternoon and drove to Galena. First time she had been driven much alone. Papa said she went very nice. Ruby rode along and picked asparagus on Tresidder hill. They said we could. I went to bed several hours this afternoon. Lots of Autos going along today. Uncle Edd & Aunt Annie went down to Uncle Ben's today.

Sun 28: I couldn't sleep last night. I'm feeling better than yesterday. A beautiful day. Autos just whirrling along. Uncle Edds came home this afternoon. Aunt Annie came down here late this afternoon. Uncle Edd came down to supper. John Tippet called up Uncle

Edd. wanted to know if they wanted to go for a ride. He said they could come down here after them. But they didn't come. forgot about them. At nine oclock they came. Had trouble about getting their auto out. backed in a wet place. It took them all that time to get it out. They staid about an hour. Ruby went up on the hill this morning to see if any body came to church. Minister and wife came. no one else. They looked in church then went off.

Mon 29: Quite rainy this forenoon but cleared off this afternoon. We set out our plants today. Dad and Ruby made a trouth for flowers. I shortened my black skirt. Ma fixed Ruby's checked skirt and sewed on her black waist. We got an invitation to the commencement excersises of Apple River high school to be held on June sixth. From Sadie. We have radishes and lettuce and little onion fit to eat in our garden now.

Tue 30: This is decoration day. A nice day. We washed today. no rural delivery today.

Wed 31: Mamma and Ruby worked some in the garden this forenoon. They ironed this afternoon. I was in bed about all day

June

Thu 1: A nice day until toward evening. It rained. This afternoon Uncle Edd came down to shear our sheep. Aunt Annie and Ethel came along down. They had supper here. We haven't weighed our wool yet.

Fri 2: We thought something of going to town but we thought the roads would be muddy. We had quite a storm last night. It rained just awfully hard. The creeks got awfully high. It washed so. The cornfields are washed terrible and some things in the garden are washed over. Milton came up this morning. brought us some honey.

Sat 3: Well we all went to Galena today. Didn't like to go. Had so much to do in town. Nearly went crazy. Bought a pin for Sadie's graduation present. A handerchief for fifty cents for Beulah Potter. A very nice day.

Sun 4: Mamma and Ruby went to church this morning. Quite a few there. Home this afternoon. Nobody came near. This evening we went down to John's. Uncle Edd and Aunt Annie came down there to.

Mon 5: We washed today. And ironed nearly all. I cut some lawn. Ruby helping Dad replant corn. and other things. We got a letter from Aunt Rachel today. Oh, the awfullest biggest auto truck went past today. We think it was some people from Dubuque getting dead things. horses or cattle. I guess they make fertilizer out of them. Ruby and I are thinking of going to the graduation tomorrow. Don't know if we will get there or not.

Tue 6: We were very busy. Pa, Ma & Ruby working in the corn field this forenoon. Very cloudy all forenoon. About noon it started to rain. It rained very, very hard all afternoon. We had to give up the idea of going to Apple River. Quite disappointed. Aunt Annie & Martha wanted to go. had to give it up to. It has rained all evening. I don't see how any body can go to the graduation.

Wed 7: It has been raining all day. And it rained all last night. It is just awfully cold today. Mamma and I made myself a waist. have the collar and button and button holes to make yet and tatting to sew on. Beulah Adellah Potter was to graduate today.

Thu 8: It's rainy again today. Reading day. Dad is making gates.

Fri 9: I cut some lawn today. Mamma baked some cookies. Pa & Ruby transplanting corn.

Sat 10: Papa & Mamma made up their minds to go to Apple River on the five train. Ruby and I are going up to Aunt Annie's to stay all night. I picked quite a few strawberries for our supper. Quite a nice day.

Sun 11: We staid to breakfast at Aunt Annie's this morning. Got home at seven thirty. Went to church this forenoon. Quite a few there. A very queer preacher. We didn't have much dinner, a little lunch. About half past one, a tramp came wanted something to eat. Ruby gave him. two pieces of bread & butter and 3 cookies. He sat on the porch and ate. Kind of scared. We laid down a while this afternoon. Did chores. Went up to Aunt Annie's for supper. Rode part way with Will & Bessie W. in their auto. They promised to give us a longer ride some time when the roads get better. Win & Martha came up there awhile tonight. A very beautiful day.

Mon 12: Quite warm today. Ruby & I went up on the hill to meet Pa, & Ma. Dad plowed corn this afternoon. Class night in Galena tonight.

Tue 13: Papa plowed corn today. Ma, Ruby & I hoed some in the garden. Well tonight is Werner's barn dance. It came up to a storm this eve & rained. but it stopped. An auto went along nine or after. And some teams. When they were going home about three. It stormed and rained awfully hard. Aunt Margaret D's birthday.

Wed 14: Quite a nice day. But it rained again tonight. Papa went to Scales Mound today. We washed today. There is a Soldiers' reunion at Warren today. Uncle Edd and Aunt Annie went. Annie went to A. R.

Thu 15: We ironed today. Rainy again today. It hailed some today. I have an awful sore throat yet. Today is the day of the steamboat excursion to Clinton. I would kind have liked to have gone.

Fri 16: Papa and Ruby went to Galena today. Some kind of doings at the fairground this afternoon. Pagent I believe. Store were locked up. Rained this afternoon & this morning. Agnes said today they are going to Dub. tomorrow said a couple of us could go if we wanted to.

Sat 17: Rained again this afternoon. Well Mamma & Aunt Annie went to Dub. with Agnes & Milton & Blanche. John didn't go. Ma bought a black silk skirt. Aunt Annie got a black silk dress. Pa plowed corn today.

Sun 18: It has been a very beautiful day. Well Ma, & Ruby went to church this afternoon. The Haines are just like always. Didn't go anywhere this afternoon. This evening Dad hitched up Della, He & Ruby went up the road for a ride. When they got back Tresidders came down this evening. First time they ever were down at night. Heard today that Mr Young lost his mind today. Took him to Rockford today. Quite exciting.

Mon 19: Another beautiful day. Pa plowing corn. Ma, & Ruby hoed potatoes. & Ruby made some curtains for hall window. I cut lawn.

Tue 20: Rainy again this afternoon. Ma churned. Ruby made herself a pants. We also baked bread.

Wed 21: We washed today. And Ma & Ruby hoed potatoes.

Thu 22: First day of summer. Reading day today. We ironed today. We all took a walk up to Aunt Annie's tonight.

Fri 23: Dad went to Scales Mound today. I baked a big batch of cookies this afternoon.

Sat 24: I baked a marble cake, busy with Sat. work. A very beautiful day.

Sun 25: It has been a very beautiful day. This morning Uncle George called said they were coming in today and for church. They went up to Union. Pearl wasn't along she is off on her vacation. Naomi stayed here with Mamma. She staid at home to get dinner. Rev. Harris took the church with us on the platform. They all came back here to dinner. Uncle Edds too. This afternoon the men folks rode to Galena and way out toward Hazel Green. They staid here to supper went home so they would be in time for church.

Mon 26:   It stormed again last night. But has been a nice day. I dyed my old linen dress this afternoon. dyed it a tan.

Tue 27:   A very nice day. Dad and Ruby went to Galena today. got home at two o'clock. We washed today.

Wed 28:   I ironed today. Ma & Ruby hoed this forenoon. I helped hoe this afternoon. banking some early potatoes yet. Dad is plowing corn.

Thu 29:   Ruby & I hoed some corn this afternoon. Ma hoed in garden. It is just burning hot today.

Fri 30:   Mamma is quite sick today. and last night. terrible pain in back, and headache and sick to her stomach. Aunt Annie came down this afternoon. She fixed the hem of her black silk dress. We ironed the things today that we didn't get done the other day.

July

Sat 1:   Just think its July. Ma in bed all day again today. Not a great deal better. I baked cake & drop cakes this forenoon. This afternoon I was sick in bed all afternoon.

Sun 2:   Well Uncle Edd brought Aunt Annie down this morning then he and Pa went to church. Nearly surprised to death when about half past twelve Helen Weis called up wanted to know if Ruby & I wanted to go riding. We didn't have no dinner. We hurried awfully. We started twenty after one. Mr. Weis, Bert & Helen, and us. We went to Galena. It looked an awful lot like a storm all the time. Went out on the turnpike. went out several miles. it looked so much like rain, we turned back. First time I ever was on the pike. They wanted to go to Hazel Green or farther. We stopped at Cane's and had ice cream. Then rode around town awhile and came home. Mr. Weis got out at home. Helen run it up went up the road quite a way. and came back. Had a fine ride. John Tresidders were here to when we got home. Uncle Edds staid to supper. Mamma was up quite a bit today.

Mon 3:   It rained some this morning but not enough to make it muddy. It cleared up this afternoon. Pa & Ruby went to the Station got a barrel salt and 50 lb flour.

Ruby went up to Mrs. Southcott's and paid for some blinds for the parsonage. Ma is some better.

Tue 4:   Well it has been a lovely day. Ma wasn't well enough to go anywhere. or hardly to leave home alone. Anyway I wouldn't have gone anywhere with a balky horse. I felt kind of dissapointed all day. But this evening Josie Weis called up said they were going in town this evening just the three said Ruby & I could go along. So we went. We went down to Weis'. started at half past seven. Quite a crowd in town. We rode around town and sat in the auto. Then Josie, Helen Ruby & I went to Dreamland. The pictures were quite good. We got home just eleven. Had a fine time. Roads were just full of autos today.

Wed 5:   Lot of autos on road again today. W. W. Hicks came and showed Pa a Ford car this evening one he has been using. Gave him a little ride. We washed today. Ruby ironed all but those that are to be dampened. I cut some lawn.

Thu 6:   Well we hauled three loads of hay this afternoon. I am trying to get some lawn cut. Ma went to meet Aunt Annie this evening to get some kale plants.

Fri 7:   Quite hot today. We hauled four loads of hay this afternoon. Seven in now. pitched it all in. More down to haul tomorrow.

Sat 8: We hauled four loads of hay pitched it in the barn. I got quite tired by evening. It has been terrible hot today. I nearly finished cutting the lawn.

Sun 9: Ma, Ruby, & I went to church this forenoon. Five others there and Mr & Mrs Haines. They were talking to having bush meetings around here somewhere. Hope he don't. We all went up to Aunt Annie's for dinner & staid to supper. Ruby & I had a ride part way up with Mr & Mrs Temperly in auto. Just an awful lot of autos going along especially this eve. Ruby & I came home did the chores. Then Uncle Edd & Aunt Annie came down to 'Weis'. Pa & Ma went in to and called us up we then went down. Lovly day.

Mon 10: Fine clear day. We hauled what hay we had down. Two small loads called it one.

Tue 11: Another fine day. We hauled four loads this afternoon. Used a horse for putting it in. have sixteen loads in now.

Wed 12: This morning Uncle Georges phoned in said they were coming in. Mayme is home. came home yesterday. Ma & I went raspberry picking this morning. in Tresidder's lane. they said we could have them. got a gallon. Just got home a few minutes they came staid to dinner. All along but Uncle George. After dinner they went up to Aunt Annie's. They all went to Galena a little while this afternoon. They called us as they went home. Gave them some roses. Edward didn't stay. Some of them evidently intended to stay. Had two suitcases along. Aunt Tillie and Loretta and Olive came to Galena today. Uncle Edd went in after them this eve. We got in the hay this afternoon. Two loads makes eighteen. This evening we had an awful storm about ten o'clock. Terrible cracks. Thought sure once it struck the house. Terrible hot today.

Thu 13: Well, Pa & Ruby went to Galena today. Couldn't work at hay. My but the oats is flat. Lightening struck one of our evergreens. Second up from the road. Ma & I washed today. Awful hot again today.

Fri 14: We hauled four loads of hay this afternoon making twenty-two loads. Have been just terrible tired all day. Ma & I picked berries this forenoon. Got some over a gallon.

Sat 15: Hauled four loads today making twenty-six loads. Just awful hot. Ma churned. I cut a little lawn. Ruby did some ironing. Aunt Tillie, Olive & Loretta came down this evening.

Sun 16: Ma & Ruby went to church this forenoon. The rest of us staid at home. Aunt Annie came down to. Uncle Edd went to church. It was Fannie Crosby Sunday. It is Ruby's & Olive's birthday today. Ruby is twenty-three and Olive six. We gave Olive a blue hair ribbon. Aunt Annie gave Ruby a tie or bow. Uncle Edds went home after supper. This eve Ruby, Olive, Loretta & I went down to Tresidder's a little while.

Mon 17: We brought in three loads of hay today making twenty-nine. Ma & I went picking berries over in the lane this forenoon. Got about half gallon between us. Ruby went up in woods got half gallon. Tillie and children went up to Aunt Annie's this afternoon.

Tue 18: We hauled four loads of hay today which makes thirty-three. Ruby picked some gooseberries this forenoon. We baked bread today. I also made some drop cookies.

Wed 19: Hauled four loads this afternoon. Thirty-seven loads in now. It is storming tonight guess we won't haul any hay tomorrow. Dad finished cutting the big piece today. About three or four loads.

Thu 20: Well, Pa & Ma went up to Scales Mound today. Went up to Uncle Nick's awhile. Ruby & I washed. A big washing. This evening Aunt Tillie, Loretta & Olive came down this evening. They were down to Tresidder's.

Fri 21: Aunt Tillie and the girls went up to Aunt Annie's again this afternoon. We hauled four loads of hay today. And finished up the big field. which makes forty-one loads for this field. Dad cut down the piece across the road today.

Sat 22:   We finished haying today. We made a stack of the hay. About four loads. Making about forty-one loads. We baked a cake, pies, bread and coffee cake today. Been quite busy.

Sun 23:   This morning a auto stopped it was Uncle Joe and Aunt Rachel & baby with John Westaby and Miss Pratt. Just called a few minutes. Uncle Joes went up to Aunt Annie's and came down this afternoon late. Aunt Annie came to. Had supper. Then went so they could get out to S. M. for church. Pa & Ruby went to church this forenoon. An awful lot of auto going along today. Uncle Edd came down this eve.

Mon 24:   Ma and I went to look at the blackberries this morning. The blackberries are just starting to get ripe. We got enough blackberries & raspberries to make one quart. We heard yesterday that Mr. Popp is crazy. Today we heard they took him to Watertown today.

Tue 25:   Dad cut the grain here by the house with the mower. Ma bound some. I bundled some. Just awful hot today. We got a letter from Wilbur today.

Wed 26:   Awful hot today. We hauled some grain today. But can't work much.

Thu 27:   We hauled four loads today. Just terrible hot. Ninety-six here I believe. Our stack is getting quite high.

Fri 28: Mamma and I went to pick blackberries this morning. Didn't get many. Drying up so. We need rain very badly. Hauled part a load of hay to finish up the stack. We washed this afternoon. Ruby & I met Aunt Annie on the hill tonight. Gave her some apples and cucumbers.

Sat 29: Did Sat. work today. Dad and Ruby went to town this afternoon. Awful hot in there. It's been terrible hot today.

Sun 30: Ma & Ruby went to church. Only ones there besides Mr. & Mrs. Haines. Didn't have any services. We all went up to Aunt Annie's this after. Dad & I rode up the hill with John & Alta Combellick. John Tresidders were up there to. Uncle George, Aunt Lizzie, Wesley & Naomi took Mr & Mrs Johnnie Weis to Galena today. Called at Uncle's toward evening. Had supper. Dad & Ma rode down with them. Dad had a ride up to Temperly's hill with Bert Weis this afternoon.

Mon 31: I got a letter from Vada today. It has been cooler today. An awful nice breeze. Ma & I picked blackberries today. I picked the cucumbers to. My I wish it would rain.

August

Tue 1: Ruby ironed last weeks ironing today. Dad went down to Tresidder's to help shock grain today. Wanted to help John back for helping us with fodder and other things. Ma hemmed up her black silk skirt.

Wed 2: Last day of Chautauqua on Galena. We didn't get to go once. Ma & I picked blackberries this forenoon. Put up six qts. And made some jelly. Ruby & I finished picking this after, didn't do anything with them. I picked cucumbers. Put up two half-gallons.

Thu 3: We washed this afternoon. Dad cut the weeds in the road with Della & Fannie. Old Fannie balked again. We got a card from Anna T. today. From Chicago. Said she may see us in a week or more all depends on how they feel. Are going to take the trip on Great Lakes.

Fri 4: We picked about a milk pail of berries this forenoon. Ma & I put up nine quarts. Got twenty-four qts now. And a ton of jelly. Didn't pick all the berries today. I picked the cucumbers. We also ironed.

Sat 5: Dad & Ruby went to Galena today. It rained a little last night but not enough.

Sun 6: No services at Union today. Haines to lazy I guess. Home all day. But took a walk down to John's this eve. Uncle Edd & Aunt Annie were there to. A few auto went along. Uncle George, Aunt Lizzie, Wesley & Edward took Mr & Mrs Johnnie Hammer over to Alvin Hammer's today. Wesley and Edward were over to Aunt Annie's awhile.

Mon 7: Papa took our lambs over the Station this morning. Seven of them. Got forty-nine dollars. Average about eighty pounds apiece. Ruby & I picked blackberries this morning. This afternoon Aunt Annie came down and she, Ruby & I picked. Didn't get them all picked. Then from this morning's batch Ma put up six qts without sugar and 1 ½ qts jam. One qt. Jar busted and wasted it all. Got the rest to put up tomorrow. Ma put six half-gallon bottles of cucumber pickles up today.

Tue 8: Papa went down to John's to help stack today. Ruby & I picked berries this forenoon. Got forty-five and ½ qts of blackberries put up including two & one half qts jam. We washed this afternoon.

Wed 9: Been awfully busy today. Dad helped stack down at John's again today. We ironed, baked bread bake a batch of cookies and a cake. Ma & Ruby picked berries this forenoon. And made jelly and jam out of them. And other things. We expected to her from Uncle Thomas or Anna today, but didn't. Been thinking Uncle T's would be coming back for the Fair. And Anna to maybe. First day of Fair today.

Thu 10:   Well we got a letter from Uncle Thomas. Didn't say anything about coming back. He thought Anna would be in Galena by Fri for the Fair. Thought she might come out here. Dad hitched to the hack this forenoon to go to fair. We wouldn't go so unhitched started out walking got a ride part way. It stormed. This afternoon showery. Dad walked home. Called at Win Tippet's while it stormed. Quite a few autos going along today. It rained awfully hard. Uncle Herman and Miss Martha Fiedler went to the fair. Came out here at eight tonight. We got some supper for them. They staid until ten oclock. I feel just terribly disappointed couldn't go to the fair. There was a balloon ascension at the fair. Saw the balloon out here.

Fri 11:   I'm just terribly disappointed I couldn't go to the fair today. But didn't expect to go for a long time. A lovely day. We didn't hear anything from Anna. Last day of fair.

Sat 12:   Got a card from Uncle Thomas. He said Anna is home. Got home Thu. At midnight. Tired out. The girl she was with didn't want to stop and Anna didn't want her to go home alone. Ruby is sick today. Has an awful sore throat.

Sun 13: Awfully cool today. Ruby's throat is awful bad yet. Ma & I took a walk up as far as the school house this afternoon. Otherwise we all staid home. Uncle Edd & Aunt Annie came down this eve, Roads are just fine. Not too many autos today but quite a few tonight.

Mon 14: Cloudy most all day. Ma picked and put up three qts blackberries. I picked cucumbers. Nigger cut his foot in wire I guess. Bled terrible. Don't know when or where he did it.

Tue 15: Uncle Ben called up Aunt Annie tonight. Will Dittmar, wife and two children from Kansas and Grandpa & Aunt Tillie are down there. Are coming to Galena tomorrow and want to come out. Uncle Edd has to go thrashing tomorrow.

Wed 16: Dad and Ruby went to Galena. Got some hog feed. John Tippet went in and got the folks in the auto. Ma made a cake didn't get anything.

Thu 17: They all walked down this forenoon. Aunt Annie. The boy's name is Glen and the girl's is Lucille. They are going to stay all night.

Fri 18: Dad hitched up took the women & kids up to Aunt Annie's this forenoon. Will & Grandpa walked and Ruby & I walked. This afternoon Uncle Edd took them all in to Gesselbracht's. Today quite hot.

Sat 19: Ruby is complaining with the ear ache today. I made two angel cakes today. One for us, one for Aunt Annie. Busy as usual.

Sun 20: Ruby quite sick with her ear. Didn't sleep any last night. It seems it breaks and runs some bloody matter. Don't know whether to call a Dr. or not. Quite hot. Aunt Annie walked down this after noon. Agnes, Milton, & Blanche came up this afternoon. A great lot of autos going along today.

Mon 21: Ruby didn't sleep much last night. Some times her ear pains her terrible and some times its easier. I pick all the duchess apples this forenoon. Helped Dad with a fence and picked the cucumbers this afternoon.

Tue 22: Ruby feeling about the same, maybe some better. Slept more last night. I picked our first watermelon today. Ma & I washed a large washing today. Dad helped clean the cemetery this afternoon.

Wed 23: Ruby is about the same today. We ironed today.

Thu 24: We had our first muskmelon today. Ruby isn't much if any better yet. We don't know if we should call a doctor or not. Mama took some apples down to Agnes T. this evening.

Fri 25: A nice day. Ruby is about the same. Ida & Della Bastian came back from Montana today.

Sat 26: Ruby don't seem to get any better. Such a time to know is should get doctor or not. Pa went to Galena today.

Sun 27: There is two services at Union today. But didn't go. Well, we had Dr. Logan come out this afternoon. He lanced some in her throat and some was in to deep. Aid should apply ground flax seed poultice. That the rest might break tonight or tomorrow morning. Maybe longer. She felt a little easier. Nobody else came near.

Mon 28: Well Ruby's throat is more gathered again. The doctor called out this morning and this afternoon. Said he was going away tomorrow. If we wanted another doctor he would send one out. Fiedler's kids were down this afternoon. Had to threaten to give them thrashings several times. Harold Monnier hearing, or what ever it is, is today. My the autos and teams. More than for the fair.

Tue 29:   Its my birthday today. Such a time. Nearly drive a person crazy. Ruby throat is about all shut. Don't know whether to have a dr. out or not. But didn't. Uncle Edds are thrashing this afternoon. Mattie & Mary are out helping.

Wed 30:   Ruby was awfully bad all night last night. We called Dr. Dolamore before six oclock this morning. He didn't come out for several hours. He couldn't do much, it is in to deep to lance. He did lance several points. Dad had to go to town for medicine. He ought to be kicked for not bringing it. But Dad had to go to town anyway. Uncle Edds got through thrashing this forenoon. Ruby is feeling some better today. Aunt Annie came down late this afternoon.

Thu 31:   I got two birthday cards today. Well today is the Schapville picnic. Not a great many people went past here. Aunt Annie went out with Winters. she is coming back with Martha J. tomorrow. Ruby feels quite a little better today. Cloudy all day. Late this afternoon it started to rain.

September

Fri 1: Well we had a nice rain last night. John Tresidder came up this forenoon. Just came home from Des Moines this morning. Stopped at Waterloo Tuesday. He said Uncle Thomas were coming back in their car tomorrow. He doesn't know if they will come now it rained. Wilbur can't come. To busy in packing house.

Sat 2: We were just awfully busy all day. Dad went to Galena this afternoon. Came home at about five. Didn't see anything of Uncle Thomas. Ruby helped us some today. At half past six Aunt Annie called up said Uncle Thomas were coming. That is Al & Nancy and Wilbur, Olive & Wayne came down here. Uncle Thomas and Aunt Rachel staid up to Aunt Annie's. They had their supper at Kloth's. Got to Galena about five oclock. They started at half-past five this morning. Had four blow outs. Mr. Young died this morning. At seven oclock. He had been out door and came in and lay down and died.

Sun 3: They said they wanted to go up and get Uncle Nick & Aunt Lizzie this morning. Coaxed me to go along. Wilbur, Wayne, Al, Dad & I went. They came along down. Uncle Thomas came down this forenoon.

Aunt Rachel went to church with Uncle Edds. Then they came down too. This afternoon John, Agnes, Milton, Blanche & Ida came up. Also Josie & Helen Weis. Quite a house full. Helen is going to start to school again Tuesday. After supper they would have Anna & I go along with them to take Uncle Nicks back. Al run the car. Uncle Thomas went to. Uncle Thomas & Aunt Rachel went down to John's to stay all night. They want to start home at half-past five tomorrow morning.

Mon 4:   Well it rained last night and this morning. They couldn't go home. Wilbur & Al declared they had to be home to go to work tomorrow. So they started out walking to Galena. Hear they got a ride part way. They are going on the one oclock train. O. & N. didn't like to see them go. Don't like to ride with Uncle Thomas. Dad went up church helped to clean up for the funeral. Pa & Ma went up to the church this afternoon. It was about half-past three when the funeral got there. They think the church was about full. Green of Galena preached. Ma went to cemetery with Win Tippet. Uncle Thomas & Aunt Rachel are going to stay here all night.

Tue 5:   Looked quite rainy again this morning. They didn't know what to do. It looked better and they started about eight oclock. It rained just awful hard this afternoon. I suppose they got in to it somewhere.

Wed 6: We didn't hear anything of Uncle Thomas this morning. We washed just an awful big washing today. Ruby works around a little but feel awfully weak.

Thu 7: It rained again last night. Thought sure we would hear from Waterloo today but didn't. We ironed today.

Fri 8: Heard from Uncle Thomas today. They got home Wed. at noon. They had a time of it. Olive and Nancy went home on the train from Dubuque.

Sat 9: The picnic at Apple River today. Ruby & I wanted to go. But Ruby isn't well enough. Uncle Edd & Aunt Annie went.

Sun 10: Home all day. Uncle Edd & Aunt Annie came home from A. R. today. Came down here this evening. A lovely day.

Mon 11: Papa took a calf over the Station this forenoon. Ma went up to the melon patch this forenoon. And all the melons are gone but two little watermelons. and several small muskmelons. Some people took them last night. An awful lot of rinds up there also cut some corn off. Dad & Ruby took a ride up the road this afternoon. Took the insurance card for the school along. It came here. Gave it to Walter Werner. He looked quite pale. They gave Milton, Willie & Mary a ride home. They questioned Milton. He & Willie & Ray Werner had been up in the patch in the afternoon. Took several. We guess who took the rest. We went up to Uncle Edd's this evening. Took up some cucumbers. It rained so Ruby stayed all night. Mrs. John Weis came over a little while this afternoon.

Tue 12:   Cloudy & rainy today so Ruby didn't come home.

Wed 13:   I rode horse back up to Aunt Annie's this forenoon. Thought Ruby could ride the horse home, but I met her down by Weis'. We washed today. Thinking to go to Warren Fair or mission feast at Scales Mound tomorrow.

Thu 14:   We got up early. And Dad took us over the Station. And we went to the Warren Fair. It was just awful cold all day Nearly froze. Ate dinner with Grandpa. Went to Baumgartner's for supper. Came back to Apple River to stay all night at Grandpa's. a big crowd at the fair. Lots of nice things. Uncle Joes were there & Uncle Dan. Sadie was down. Lots of people we knew.

Fri 15:   We didn't know if we should come home or not but decided to stay until tomorrow morning. Tillie went to the fair today with Jake Stauss. Uncle Georges came down to Grandpa's for the evening.

Sat 16: We came home this morning. We went in to Uncle George's store to say goodbye. Aunt Lizzie asked us to go up stairs to say good bye to Pearl. That she had her trunk packed. Mr. Bunker was up stairs. She said come and see _us_ so I guess they are going to be married very soon. We sent for bread with Uncle Edd. (Ruby made a sponge but a mouse got drown in it.) I went up there this afternoon. Dad come up in the evening.

Sun 17: Ma went up to Aunt Annie's this forenoon. Pa & Ruby & I went up this afternoon. A nice day.

Mon 18: I made some chilli sauce this afternoon. Ruby has something the matter with her legs. They have big red spots on them and are quite painful.

Tue 19: Pa Ma, & Ruby went to Galena today. I staid at Aunt Annie's The Dr. said Ruby had something with a long name. On the rhumatic order.

Wed 20: We washed today. We picked off wild grapes today. J Tresidder thrashed today. Dad helped.

Thu 21: We put up peaches today. Nine quarts and a half. Dad cutting corn. Weis thrashed today.

Fri 22: We put up pears and ironed today. Ruby legs are awful bad. Cant walk at all. Just hobble around a little. Fiedlers thrashed last night & this morning. Dad helped this morning for John Tresidder.

Sat 23:   Lots & Lots of work today. Awful tired tonight. A nice day.

Sun 24:   We were home all day. Uncle Edd & Aunt Annie were to church and came down to dinner. John, Agnes, Milton, & Blanche came up this afternoon. Last Sunday for Haines He is going away this week. Ruby's one leg is awfully swelled today. It is just a lovely day.

Mon 25:   I helped cut a little corn this forenoon. I made chilli sauce this afternoon. Ma dug potatoes. Ruby staid in bed nearly all day. One of her legs looks to be quite a little better.

Tue 26:   Mamma went to Aunt Annie's this afternoon to get some crabs. I helped cut a little corn this afternoon.

Wed 27:   Rainy today. We put up a half gallon & a quart of pickled crabs today. We got the National Cloak & Suit Co's catalog today. I picked out my dress, a navy blue silk taffeta and a petticoat and Ruby a serge skirt. Got the order ready tonight. Dress is $7.95 Petticoat 1.69. Skirt 2.98.

Thu 28:   We washed today. Ma churned. I put up three quarts tomatoes. Awfully rainy all day.

Fri 29:   Papa and Ruby went to Galena today. Ruby went to
the Dr. He said she has an ulcer on her eye. Ma and
I husked four sacks of corn for the hogs today.

Sat 30:   Busy as usual. Baking and cleaning. Papa busy
cutting corn.

October

Sun 1: Nice day only windy. We were at home all day. Lottie Hocking came here awhile this afternoon. Ruby's legs are much better. Her eye about the same.

Mon 2: Had lot of men here looking at the calves and steers. Some travelers past here today. Lots of autos on road.

Tue 3: Finished cutting corn. Got three hundred ninety shocks. Papa & I went up to Uncle Edd's tonight. We picked some apples.

Wed 4: We saw something new today. Four big auto loads of dirty ragged gypsies went by here. One lady came in to Papa. Wanted to wish him good luck and tell his fortune. They certainly were a show. The way it looked they had the back of auto all piled full and the woman sitting & lying on that. Some had their legs hanging out. We washed today. Papa busy picking apples.

Thu 5: We ironed today. Thought we might get the stuff from National Co. today but didn't. A beautiful day.

Fri 6: Papa and Ruby took the calves and two steers down to Weis' to weigh this forenoon.

Sat 7: Busy as usual on Sat. Papa husked some corn. It has been just a grand day. We got Ruby's skirt and my petticoat from the National today. Didn't have my dress in stock will send it soon as possible. Ruby skirt is to big. We sent for 28 waist 38 hip + 41 length. It is 30 waist, 40 hip + 43 long. I sent for 40 $\frac{1}{2}$ in for my petticoat it is 45. It makes me mad.

Sun 8: Nearly hot today. This afternoon Papa hitched Della in the buggy and drove off down the road. Didn't tell us where he was going. He went to Galena. He called on Old Mr. Ford. About a quarter after two, Uncle George came in and four fellows from Apple River in a Ford. Left it here and Wesley & they went in Uncle G.'s car and went to Galena. I looked the Ford over good. Sadie & Edward explained some things about it. They staid to supper. We wanted them to stay and spend the evening but I guess Wesley wanted to go home. An awful lot of cars on the road today. Uncle Edd & Aunt Annie came down this evening.

Mon 9: Colder today. Pa & Ma husked corn this forenoon. Ma fixed Ruby skirt this afternoon. Papa & Ruby picked some apples. We picked lots of tomatoes for preserves today.

Tue 10: Well we all went to town today. I bought a new hat. It is black velvet faced in Copenhagen blue with floppy brim. With yellow ornaments. Paid four dollars for it. I also got a new corset and new rubbers. A lovely day.

Wed 11: We picked some apples this afternoon. We had pasty for dinner & supper today. Grandpa & Uncle Dan are up to Aunt Annie's. They started out from A. R. yesterday morning. Went to New Diggings, Benton, Shullsburg and Hazel Green. Staid all night at H. G. Then stopped at Galena. They are coming down here sometime tomorrow.

Thu 12: Grandpa & Dan were here to dinner. They started for home right after dinner. Papa picked some apples today. Ma & I dug some potatoes. I thought surely that my dress would come by this time.

Fri 13: We washed today. Papa picking apples.

Sat 14: Busy as usual with Sat. work and ironing. Well Win Tippet got a new seven passenger Studebaker car today from L Durrstein. Saw them go along here. Charlie Zarndt runs it. the hired man.

Sun 15: Cloudy and rainy this forenoon, cleared up this afternoon. We went up to Aunt Annie's for dinner. Tresidders were up there to in the afternoon. We were thinking something of going to Mt. Morley school house to services today but didn't go because it was raining.

Mon 16: Pa, Ma & Ruby husked corn this forenoon. I have an awful sore front tooth. It aches sometimes. This evening. Win, Martha Tippet and Charlie Zarndt made a short visit here in their new car. Charlie Zarndt has to run it.

Tue 17: This is Mamma's fiftieth birthday today. She got a card from the folks at Apple River. I got my dress today. Not a bit satisfied with it. Its about like cobweb and two short waisted and to big around the waist. Don't know if I should send it back or not.

Wed 18: Papa Ruby & I husked corn this forenoon. Mamma got a broach and handkerchief from Aunts Margaret & Tillie and a post card from Aunt Annie. We washed this afternoon.

Thu 19: We husked ten shock this morning. Papa & Ruby went to town this afternoon. Aunt Annie came down this afternoon. They took three bu. Apples to town got $1.25 per bu.

Fri 20: It rained all last night. And nearly all day. I fixed my dress today also made a batch of cookies. Ma fixed my petticoat.

Sat 21:   We husked some corn this afternoon. It cleared up this afternoon.

Sun 22:   The roads are muddy yet. Not an auto over the road today. We all went for a walk this afternoon up Bastian's pasture. Called in at the school house. Saw the new furnace. Walked out Guilford road and came back on Joe Weis' hill. This evening we all went down to John's. They haven't their car yet. Heard Werner's have a _____

Mon 23:   We all husked corn today. Husked forty shocks tied up up. Shocked it up and hauled in the corn. Nice for husking today.

Tue 24:   We husked this forenoon. Raining all afternoon so we couldn't husk. Getting order ready this afternoon to send for magazines.

Wed 25:   Cold & windy today. Ruby & I husked five shocks of corn this afternoon. It cleared up this evening. We baked bread today.

Thu 26:   Pa, Ma & Ruby husked this forenoon. Took two bushels apples for Tippets at a dollar quarter a bu. Ma & I washed this afternoon.

Fri 27:   Husking corn again today. And hauled it in this evening. A beautiful day. Tonight Uncle Edd, Aunt

Annie and Johnnie & Ethel came down. Uncle Edd & Aunt Annie are going to Galena tomorrow and they are going to stay all night.

Sat 28: We ironed & churned. and baked bread with out salt (I forgot it) coffee cake cinnamon rolls. Apple coffee cake & patty cakes. And cleaned up. And Pa and Ruby husked & hauled in corn this afternoon. Heard over the telephone a lady was run into by a Ford car and terribly hurt. She died soon afterward.

Sun 29: Rainy nearly all day. Quite a lonesome. It wasn't such a bad evening so we all went up to Fiedler's. One visit made.

Mon 30: We all husked today. We have twenty-two shocks left. We got the Montgomery Ward catalog today. that I sent for.

Tue 31: Papa and Ruby husked all and hauled in one load of corn. Glad we are through but would like to have more corn. A very beautiful day. It is Halloween today.

❧

November

Wed 1: Mamma washed bed blankets, comforters today. Papa & Ruby finished hauling in the corn. Ruby & I doing the carrots today. We got two bushel. We got a letter from Uncle Thomas today.

Thu 2: We washed today. Today thirty-one autos went by. A Republican parade. The candidates. We went out and saw them go by. We put out the flag. Some waved some shouted Hurrah, for Hughes. The roads were awful rough but they wore them down nicely.

Fri 3: We ironed and hauled three loads of fodder this afternoon. This evening we all went up to Uncle Edd's.

Sat 4: Papa, Ruby & I went to Galena today. An awful lot of people in town. Ruby had her hat made over. Aunt Margaret came today on the noon train. Lot of autos out today. Aunt Mag rode out with Win Tippets.

Sun 5: Aunts Annie & Margaret came down to dinner today. A lovely day. Ma & I went part way up with Aunts tonight. Lots of car going along.

Mon 6: Pa, Ma & Ruby hauled some fodder this forenoon. It was awful windy all day and quite warm. Tomorrow is election day.

Tue 7: Pa, Ma & Ruby hauled fodder this forenoon. They finished up the one stack. It has been showery all day. Pa & Ruby went to vote this afternoon. The first time she ever voted. Women could only vote for President & Vice President electors and for surveyor and trustees of Ill. University. There were lots of women over there to vote.

Wed 8: We heard today that the election went straight Republican. Awful rainy all day. I started to make myself a night gown with the crochet yoke.

Thu 9: A lovely day. This afternoon Papa & Mamma took Win Tippets apples over. Aunts Annie & Margaret were there too. So Mamma staid to supper then went up to Uncle Edd with them. This evening we went up to Johnnie's. Mamma and Aunts Annie & Margaret came over there to. It is full moon tonight. We washed today. It isn't decided wether Hughes or Wilson won. It seems to be running very close.

Fri 10: Cloudy and clear today. It didn't rain much. We finished with the fodder today. Uncle Edd came down and helped. We ironed today. I baked a batch of cookies. Ma also churned. I finished making my night gown tonight. Will have to make some edging for sleeves yet.

Sat 11:   Papa chanced it to Galena today. He sold the two steers to John Tresidder. Cloudy all day. Started to snow this evening. Rev Paul Palmer our new minister came over to Uncle Edd's to stay all night this eve.

Sun 12:   Well a very stormy day. Pa, Ruby & I went to church this morning. There were seven others there with the minister. The minister seems to be a nicer man than the last man. Aunts Annie & Margaret was not to church. Thought Aunt Mag. would try to come down today. But she didn't.

Mon 13:   Snowing about all day. It cleared up tonight. It is very cold. John Tresidder got our two steers today. We got one hundred four and one half dollars for the two. or seven cents per pound. John T's New Ford car is in Galena. It was in there Sat. Papa saw it.

Tue 14:   A lovely day but awfully cold. It was down to zero this morning. I have an awful cold. Aunt Margaret came down this evening.

Wed 15:   Well today was Mrs. Popp's sale. Papa and Ruby & I wanted to go but Papa has such an awful cold he couldn't go. It is quite cold yet. We sent a big grocery order to Montgomery Ward yesterday.

Thu 16:   Well we washed today. Aunt Annie came down this forenoon. This evening Aunt Annie, Aunt Margaret,

Mamma & I went down to J Tresidder's. Uncle Edd came down there.

Fri 17:   A very nice day. We ironed and churned today. This evening we all went with Aunt Margaret up to Aunt Annie's. She is going home tomorrow.

Sat 18:   Papa & Ruby went to town today. A nice day but muddy. There is going to be a basket social at Ford School next Fri. eve. Ruby bought some pink crepe paper and some white and some pink ribbon. We are going to just tie up some boxes.

Sun 19:   Just a lovely day. But it is muddy. This afternoon we all went to church. There were thirty-three there with the minister.

Mon 20: Cleaned out the stables this forenoon. Cleaned out the chicken house this afternoon. Papa went over the Station this afternoon after the goods from Montgomery Ward & Co. Lots of the things didn't come. And nearly all the rest are not just what we ordered. Two different kinds of flour - all different from what we ordered. We sent for three pks of ice cream powder. Got nine. Well this is Papa's birthday. He is sixty years old.

Tue 21:   We washed today. Papa got a birthday card from Aunt Tillie today. We made ice cream today with ice cream powder.

Wed 22: Rainy today. Didn't do much. Papa took chickens over the Station this afternoon. Got sixteen cents per pound for young roasters.

Thu 23: Cloudy all day. It is awfully dark tonight. Hope it will be nicer weather tomorrow night for the social.

Fri 24: It was just terribly windy last night and today. and cold. But it is nice tonight. Clear. Agnes & Milton came up here and Ruby & I went with them to the social. There wasn't a very big crowd there. There were fifteen or sixteen baskets. They made between twenty-one and twenty-two dollars, Some folks came out from near Galena. Mr. Sanders was auctioneer. The baskets brought from about sixty cents to nearly three dollars. Ruby's basket brought one dollar ten cents. Charles Tobin bought it. My basket didn't bring so much as Ruby's. Albert Schultz bought my basket. Milton bought Mary Fiedler's basket. We had quite a nice time. My basket was a shoe box tied up with pink tissue paper tied with a white ribbon. Ruby had a square box tied up with pink tissue paper and pink ribbon.

Sat 25: Cloudy today. Papa chanced it to Galena and out again today. It is Alvin & Nancy's first wedding anniversary today. It will be Nancy's nineteenth birthday tomorrow.

Sun 26:   Well we all went to church this forenoon. Quite a nice crowd there. Twenty-one with the minister. We all went up to Uncle Edd's this evening to supper. Mrs. Young & Ben were up there this afternoon for dinner.

Mon 27:   Ma & Ruby started to clean the dining room today.

Tue 28:   Dad went up to Scales Mound to buy some roosters. Hicks was buying. He got four. He went up to Uncle Nick's. John Trudgian is married been married several weeks now. The girl own three hundred twenty acres land so they own a section now.

Wed 29:   We are getting a little ready for tomorrow. Ma made a roaster this evening. Ruby & I each made some candy tonight. A very nice day. The roads were dragged today.

Thu 30:   Thanksgiving Day. Uncle Edd & Aunt Annie came down for dinner. We had a can of asparagus. We made chocolate ice cream this afternoon. Lots of cars going along. roads look just lovely along here. Its just a beautiful day warm and not a cloud on the sky. John & Mr Westaby called here to get two bushels of apples this afternoon.

December

Fri 1: Another lovely day. Papa was out working on the telephone line today. We washed. Are ironing this evening. Ma is churning.

Sat 2: We all went to town this afternoon. A very beautiful day. Lot of people in town.

Sun 3: Uncle Edd & Aunt Annie went out to Westaby's with Win & Martha & Charlie Zarndt in car today. John Tresidders all went for a ride this afternoon. Bert Weis went along to run the car. We all went to church this afternoon. Not many there.

Mon 4: Papa took the old sows over the Station this forenoon. We got nine cents per lb. Awful lot of stock over the Station.

Tue 5: We washed this forenoon. Papa and John Tresidder took ten of our hogs over the Station today. We got eight fourty per lb. I went up to Aunt Annie's this afternoon. Ma & Ruby ironed most of the things this evening.

Wed 6: Uncle Edd went over the Station today and ordered two stock cars to take the stock tomorrow. Our poor calves will have to go along. Ma & Ruby did some sewing today.

Thu 7: Well they took the stock over the Station this forenoon. Cloudy all day and very warm this afternoon it thundered and lighteninged and rained. Papa didn't get home till quite late this afternoon. Uncle Edd & Johnnie both went to Chicago. Fiedler hulled clover today. John Weis hulled some but had to stop on account of the rain. Aunt Annie went down to Martha's to stay all night.

Fri 8: About eleven oclock Aunt Annie came down. Rev. Palmer came. We had to hurry and get dinner. Had to make biscuits. Rev Palmer staid until about 2 thirty. Aunt Annie went up to stay at Ethel's about half-past four. She thinks Uncle Edd will come home tonight.

Sat 9: Uncle Edd came home last night. He received the returns by mail this morning. Papa went up, anxious to know what we got. We got two hundred fifty-eight dollars for the calves. We are fairly satisfied. Got seven sixty per lb. And only six cents per lb. For the bull. All did well with cattle. But they didn't do well with hogs. All of the stocker were sold to packers but our bull. Probably he was sold to a farmer. John Tippet and Eustice are going to stay until tonight.

Sun 10:   We all went to church this forenoon. Uncle Edd & Aunt Annie came down to dinner. John Tresidders came up this afternoon.

Mon 11:   Mamma cut out Ruby's green waist today. Papa hauling manure.

Tue 12:   Pa hauling manure. Uncle Edd & Aunt Annie went to Scales Mound today.

Wed 13:   We got up quite early this morning. Didn't know if we should try to get ready to go to Dubuque or not. But didn't go. A very beautiful day but very cold.

Thu 14:   We had thought last night that we would go to Dubuque today. If it wasn't to cold. But it was awful cold. Ruby & I went up to Aunt Annie's this afternoon.

Fri 15:   It has been just awful cold. We ironed today. It was awful windy to. Hope it will get warmer.

Sat 16:   Papa and Ruby went to Galena today. Some warmer today.

Sun 17:   We all went to church this afternoon. Mrs W. Combellick said they are going to have a surprised pound social on the minister Monday night. The people over here are invited. Some said they couldn't go. Lottie, Ruby & I thought we might walk over. Ma went up to Uncle Edd's from church. Then we went up to supper.

Mon 18: We had the terriblest time to make up our mind to know if we should go to the pound social. Didn't hear of anybody else going so we didn't like to be the only ones from over here. We didn't go but feel very disappointed. It is pretty cold. Snowing a little tonight.

Tue 19: Quite cold today. We washed today. I made some fondant last night made it into chocolates and bon-bons today.

Wed 20: I made two batches of candy today. Brown sugar fudge and chocolate fudge. I ironed some this evening. Mamma churned today.

Thu 21: Quite cold. Nice and clear. I baked a batch of cookies. Mamma went down to Agnes' and then called at Weis' and got a dressed duck. John Tresidder went up to Wilbur Tresidder's sale.

Fri 22: We all went to Galena today. It was awful cold. Had to hurry to get our shopping done.

Sat 23: We sent a parcel for Uncle Thomas today. Quite busy today.

Sun 24: Snowing today. Ruby & I went to church. thought there wouldn't be any body else there. but the minister and Mrs W Combellick was there. We sung several songs. And prayed. Then we came home again. This afternoon Anna Trudgian phoned out from Galena she came today at noon. Wants to come out here tomorrow then she wants to go home tomorrow night.

Mon 25: Papa went to meet Anna this forenoon. Got here a quarter of twelve. And left again a quarter of six. Papa and Ruby took her to Galena. Got home about nine oclock. John, Agnes, Milton & Blanche came up this afternoon. We had a nice dinner asparagus, and lettuce, celery. And they had duck.

Tue 26: A bad day, Snowing, raining and warm. We got a card from Raymond said they might come in this week.

Wed 27: Lovely day but cold. We washed today. Aunt Annie came down this afternoon. Uncle Edd came down to supper. I made a green auto cap this evening.

Thu 28: Clear and nice again today. I ironed some today. Poor little Tabby died today. I think she must have froze to death. Poor Kitty.

Mon 25: I forgot to say what we got for Christmas. I got a cap and scarf set. A pair of leggings, and a little tie. A pink and white kimona from Uncle Thomas A nice warm pair of mittens from Aunt Annie. Ruby got a pair of house slippers. A budour cap. A kimona. A pair of gloves from Aunt Annie. Mamma got a table runner from Uncle Thomas a pair of slippers a pocket book. A scissor Ruby & I bought. A woven pillow from Aunt Annie. Papa got a pair of gloves. A light shirt from Uncle Thomas a pair suspenders from Aunt Annie.

Fri 29: Been expecting Uncle Henry's boys in today but they didn't come. Nice day only cold.

Sat 30: A nice day. Lots of teams going along, sleighs and wheels. The boys didn't come today. Don't suppose they will come now.

Sun 31: It was quarterly meeting over the Station today. services afternoon and evening. We would like to have gone but the roads are so icy. We went up to Aunt Annie's this afternoon. We staid to supper. We all went down to John T. tonight. Uncle Edd & Aunt Annie were down to. Snowing this evening.

Well this is the last of nineteen sixteen. And the
last day of leap year.
I left it slip by. Will have to wait
four more year now.

1917

Charles and Amelia [Dittmar] Trudgian. Lillian's parents

January

Mon 1:   It has been an ideal day. Not to cold nor to warm.
         And such beautiful blue sky. And such a beautiful
         evening. We had a good dinner but nothing extra.
         White beans This afternoon Mother and I got ready
         and went over to see Mrs. John Weis. We were just
         there a few minutes when Ruby called up said Gus and
         Ella Dittmar and Lennis and Donald were here. So
         we came home. They just come down for a ride. They
         staid to supper. We had ice cream for supper. Ruby

and I went down to Weis' this evening. Helen has a week more vacation.

Tue 2: Ruby and I cleaned out the stable today. Uncle Edd & Aunt Annie went to Galena yesterday. And Aunt Annie went to Apple River and came back again today. She said Uncle Herman & Aunt Tillie are going to drive in soon.

Wed 3: We all took a sleigh ride to town today. Ruby got a pair of high tan shoes. There isn't any sleighing left near town.

Thu 4: We washed today. Cloudy and quite warm today. Reading day.

Fri 5: We ironed today. At just about six o'clock this evening Raymond, Leon, and Helmer came in. We were surprised. We thought first it was Uncle Herman and Aunt Tillie. They then called in here about half past seven. They staid up to Scales Mound for supper. They went up to Aunt Annie's because the boys were here.

Sat 6: Warm today. The boys went up to Aunt Annie's this forenoon. They went to town this afternoon. Quite busy today.

Sun 7: We all went to church this forenoon. Uncle Edd & Aunt Annie, Aunt Tillie and Uncle Herman came down to dinner. The boys called in about four o'clock just long enough to eat a lunch. Uncle H, Aunts A. & T. staid to spend the eve.

Mon 8: We washed today. Also cleaned the stables. About noon Aunt Tillie called up wanted to know if Ma wanted to go with Herman to Scales Mound. She went didn't get home until about half past nine. About half past five, Rev Palmer came. Quite surprised. He staid til nine o'clock then went up to Aunt Annie's to stay all night.

Tue 9: We ironed today. Uncle Herman here. Papa went to the telephone meeting tonight at J. A. Weis'.

Wed 10: We are busy today. Uncle Herman went up to Uncle Edd's this afternoon. brought Aunts Annie & Tillie down to Tresidder's. This eve. Herman and Tillie came up here. Rev. Mr. Palmer came from Spensley's to stay all night. We had lots of playing and singing. We served brown sugar fudge and apples. Council Hill gave the minister a reception last night. about forty there.

Thu 11: Awfully cold today. Mr. Palmer was going to cut wood for Spensleys again today. Uncle Herman and Aunt Tillie went up to Aunt Annie again this evening.

Fri 12: We got a letter from Uncle Thomas and Anna today. It has been snowing all day today. There is to be a sociable up to Council Hill this evening Mr. Palmer wanted us to try to go up. but it was to stormy.

Sat 13:   Awfully cold. Papa, Ruby & I went to Galena in the sleigh. Nearly froze to death. Quite a few people in town.

Sun 14:   Very cold again today. We all went to church this afternoon. Only nine there. Mother went up to Uncle Edd's from church. Pa, Ruby & I went up for supper.

Mon 15:   Didn't get much accomplished today. Getting more lazy every day. We did get the cow house cleaned out.

Tue 16:   Ruby went up to Aunt Annie's this afternoon to get the large Sears & Roebuck catalogue. She wants to send for a spring coat and a dress.

Wed 17:   We washed today. I wrote a letter to Anna this evening. It's quite windy this evening.

Thu 18:   We ironed today. Reading day. So many people sick with the grip.

Fri 19:   Well Papa, Ruby & I went up to Scales Mound this afternoon. We went up to Uncle Nick's. Uncle Nick is better but quite poorly yet. We did not go up to Uncle Erhard D's. Aunt Tillie came down this evening.

Sat 20: Aunt Tillie went up to Aunt Annie's again this forenoon. She didn't know if she would go home today or not. They went to town. Aunt Tillie came out again. She said this eve she heard Aunt Lizzie D. of Scales Mound is very sick. Had all the children come home yesterday. She said Mrs. John Combellick is very sick to. She had a stroke.

Sun 21: Very, very stormy all day today. It snowed last night and rained this morning. to stormy to go to church. Just awful windy all day. We went to bed at eight o'clock.

Mon 22: A lovely day, but cold. We heard this evening that Mrs. John Combellick is dead. She died this forenoon. Has been unconscious since she had the stroke.

Tue 23: Another lovely day. The services for Mrs. Combellick is to be tomorrow at ten o'clock. She's going to be buried in Galena. Aunt Tillie went home today. Aunt Annie is taking treatments with Dr. Hardy nearly every day. We have a pretty little calf today.

Wed 24: We had to hurry to get ready for the funeral. We all went in the sleigh. Mr. Elvin Palmer preached the sermon. Mr. & Mrs. S. Lupton, Mrs. Benda and John Spencer sang. Minnie Merrifield played the piano. Mrs. Combellick had quite a lot of flowers.

The spray the Ladies Aid gave were very pretty. It was pink rosebuds and little white flowers. They did not have any carriages or hearse. Took the corpse on a long hack with runners. The mourners all went in sleighs. We got home again before twelve o'clock. Ruby's coat and dress came today. They are very nice. Mother's waist is quite nice.

Thu 25:   Papa went to town and to the sale today. Didn't buy anything. A nice day but quite cold.

Fri 26:   Snowing a little today. We had a pasty for dinner. Washed a little this afternoon. Another little calf by this morning. Flossie Ford was married this evening.

Sat 27:   Didn't know what to do all day. Wether I should go to Apple River or not. Ruby isn't able. At last this afternoon I did make up my mind to go. Papa took me over the Station in the cutter. Aunt Annie and Uncle Herman were on the train too.

Sun 28:   We all staid at Grandpa's last night. We all went to the dedication this morning. Aunt Tillie sings in the choir. The church was about full this forenoon. Rev. Warren of Galena preached this morning. Read Liston read and prayed. Grandpa didn't have anybody extra for dinner. They were expecting lots of people. We all went to church this afternoon. the real dedication was this afternoon. They announced it dedicated without dept. The church was full this afternoon. Uncle Herman, Aunt Annie and I were up to Uncle George's to supper this evening. Just about six o'clock as we were eating supper the building just shook. the windows and doors all rattled. We heard afterward that a powder house at the Birkbeck mine exploded. I telephoned home. They felt it terrible at home. It made a terrible noise. Went to church again tonight. The church was crowded to the utmost. The church class room, mothers' room and entry. Uncle Henry & Raymond were up this evening.

Mon 29: Aunt Tillie got a letter from Hattie Taylor said she was coming for a short visit. She and her husband were up to Lindon Wis. Holding meetings. Aunt Annie and I were just ready to go to the depot to come home (12 o'clock) when Mr. & Mrs. Taylor came. They just ate a lunch and then went on the same train up to Scales Mound. Aunt Tillie & Uncle Herman went along up. Uncle Edd came to Galena after us in the cutter. Sleighing is very poor. Very watery. Aunt Lizzie Dittmar of Scales Mound is dead. She died last night at two oclock. will be buried Thu. Morning at eleven o'clock at the Pres. Church.

Tue 30: We got a letter from Uncle Thomas today. He said Anna had a operation yesterday morning for appendicitis. at the Pres. Hospital. Mamma went over to see Mrs. John Weis a little while this afternoon. She is sick. Then she called at John Tresidder's awhile. They butchered today.

Wed 31: We baked bread today. Not a very nice day. Quite windy.

෨෩

February

Thu 1: Uncle Edd and Aunt Annie drove up to Scales Mound to the funeral in the sleigh and took Mother, Ruby & I along. (Papa had to help saw wood at Fiedler's) The funeral was at eleven o'clock at the church. The church was full. She had lots of flowers. She looked very natural I think. Rev Noeding preached both in German & English. They went down to Schapville in sleighs. We and lots of others had dinner at Durrstein's. Uncle Herman came along down with us. Is going to stay here all night. It was terribly cold all day.

Fri 2: Wesley Dittmar went to Kansas C. to study automobiling today. Didn't hear from Anna since Tue. Was expecting to hear today. It has been just terrible cold today. It was eighteen below here this morning. At some places it was twenty-five. Could hardly stand to go outside the house. Uncle Herman went up to Aunt Annie's this eve.

Sat 3: A little bit warmer than yesterday. Uncle Herman went down to Woodbine today. We got a card from Uncle Thomas. He said Anna had a swollen face. Dr. said it was swollen glands. It pained her so awful. Said her side pained her some. And that she was quite weak.

Sun 4:   A very very stormy day. It snowed just a little last night and a terrible wind blew it so all day. Didn't have much fire. We wore coat most all day. And it is just terrible cold. Didn't go to church. Weather to awful.

Mon 5:   Better weather today. Papa and Ruby went to town in the cutter today. Traded at the Sandlin's. Mamma Ruby & I went up to Uncle Edd's this evening to ask Uncle Edd to help butcher. John & Ethel were there too. But Aunt Annie was not at home she staid in Galena today.

Tue 6:   Uncle Edd came down and helped Dad butcher two hogs. Quite a nice day. Got a card from Aunt Rachel today. Anna's face is very painful. Old Fannie has been sick with the colic I guess all evening. Don't seem much better yet.

Wed 7:   Well Fannie was dead this morning. Lying in the front stall. Papa thought when he went to bed last night that she was a little easier. Pulled her up on the hill with Violet and Della. Don't know what we shall do now. We drenched her twice once this soda and then with salt water. Don't know what caused her to be ill unless she ate to much hay seeds. We washed an awful big washing today and baked bread.

Thu 8:   Papa went over to Wallace Ford's sale today. It was a large sale and most things brought good prices especially the cattle. Aunt Annie came along down here when the men went to the sale. We ironed today. I have an awful cold.

Fri 9:   Mamma & Ruby cleaned the stable today.

Sat 10:   Papa drove to town and out several miles south of Galena to a sale. With Della in the cutter. Didn't buy anything. We want to buy a horse. I have a terrible cold.

Sun 11:   A lovely day but cold. Pa. Ma & Ruby went to church this afternoon. I staid at home alone. Had to bad a cold to go. Mamma staid at Tresidder's after church then Papa went down this evening. There is two little lambs this eve. First of the season.

Mon 12:   Quite cold today. One poor rooster froze his feet & legs just solid last night. staid out I guess. Had to keep him in the house for a long time.

Tue 13:   Aunt Annie came down today. The men went to Broderick's sale. Papa didn't go. Mamma ground the sausage today.

Wed 14:   Mamma frying sausage today.

Thu 15:   We got a card from Anna today. She said she was at home. Could go around the house but wouldn't go out on account of her ear. Had it lanced again.

Fri 16:   Mabel Tresidder talked to Agnes today. Said Uncle Nick is quite poorly. Another little lamb today. Papa hauling some wood for stakes down from the woods today. Adam Virtue's sale today. We all have very bad colds. I am some better.

Sat 17:   Nearly all the snow is gone. It is awfully icy. Papa was chopping this afternoon.

Sun 18:   Ruby & I went to church this forenoon. Papa and Mamma had to bad a colds to go. Ruby went up to Aunt Annie's this afternoon. Tresidders were up there too.

Mon 19:   Snowy this forenoon. With thunder and lightning. Nicer this afternoon. Papa went up to Scales Mound this afternoon with Della in the cutter. Brought home a hundred flour and a few other things. Uncle Nick is quite poorly. It is hard for him to breathe. Stella was up there to today.

Tue 20:   We washed an awful big washing today. Papa had an awful ear ache this evening.

Wed 21:   Mamma went up to Scales Mound with John, Agnes & Blanche in the sleigh today. To see Uncle

Nick, Milton stayed here. He has been having a cold. Agnes wouldn't let him go to school. He was a good boy. Uncle Nick thought he was feeling a little better today.

Thu 22: Washington's birthday today. Ma went up to help Aunt Annie with the butchering business. We went up this evening. There is two more lambs today.

Fri 23: Lots of mail today. Gazette, magazines, and a letter from Uncle Thomas. Anna has still been having a time with her face. Papa hauled some wood and some manure today.

Sat 24: A very nice day. Ruby walked over the station to go to Apple River on the five o'clock train. Papa went to town today with Della in the buggy. Brought home some flour and sugar and things.

Sun 25: A very lonesome day. No services at Union today. Rev. Palmer has gone to Apple River and Rev. Liston preaches at Council Hill and Station today. I went down to Tresidder's awhile this afternoon.

Mon 26: Ma & I cleaned stables today. Pa cutting wood. I had an awful scare tonight. We were all sitting here reading. When I heard the telephone wire make a little noise. I was scared. The was nothing out to shake the poles. My first thought was, some one is cutting the wires. I went to the telephone and rang it. It didn't make a sound. I nearly fell over. I had a hard time to make Pa & Ma understand. I had them blow out the lights. I grabbed the gun down. Gave Dad one kept the old one myself. Dad loaded one. Went out on porch and shot it off. After a while we all went out to look at the line. It was wrapped tight out in the cow yard. A bird must have flown against it. Don't see what else it was.

Tue 27: Didn't do much today. It is very icy can hardly walk around.

Wed 28: Ma & I went over to meet Ruby this forenoon. Aunt Maggie & Grandpa isn't very well. Bessie Weis came over this afternoon. Will went to Scales Mound and she rode over.

March

Thu 1: March came in like a lamb this year. A beautiful day. Ma went up to Aunt Annie's this afternoon. Two more lambs today making seven. We had strawberry ice cream today.

Fri 2: Mamma called up Uncle George this morning to find out how Grandpa was. He thought he was a little better. But about noon Uncle George called up and said that Grandpa has pneumonia. Mama & Aunt Annie went out to Apple River on this evening train. We were just in the midst of washing. Ruby & I had to finish that. Ruby & Dad had to look after a sheep that is sick. Ma called up tonight but couldn't hear well.

Sat 3: A lovely day. Ma called up this forenoon. Said thought Grandpa about the same but couldn't tell much for a few days. He can't lie down. Has to sit up in bed. The nurse came last night (Miss Murthey). I went up to Ethel's after some grocerys Ma sent out yesterday. I got a card from Anna, she started to work Mon. wanted to know if I would sell that tatted yoke for $4.00. Said a girl said she would pay that much for one. Think I shall send it out there Monday. Got seven eggs today most yet.

Sun 4:   Ruby & I went to church this forenoon. Only three men, and the minister & Mr. Meyer the YCA man of Galena. He talked about this old preacher friend. Didn't get any subscriptions. Uncle Edd was out to Apple River last night. Grandpa is very sick. Uncle Edd came down here this evening.

Mon 5:   Talked with Mama today. She said Grandpa was quite delirious yesterday. His fever was higher to. But that it wasn't so high this morning. Uncle Henry's Marvin is sick to. Has Bronchitis. Papa hitched up and knocked down the fodder stocks. Ruby called over to Mrs. John Weis' this afternoon.

Tue 6:   Well Aunt Annie came to Galena today. She called out. Said Grandpa isn't any better. Only knows them for a few minutes at a time. Mr. Charlton died this morning. Papa went up to Scales Mound with Della today. We needed some kerosene. He called at Uncle Nick's. He is pretty poorly. He was feeling a trifle better today. This evening Rev. Palmer came. While we were doing chores. He staid all night. He is calling around about old members.

Wed 7:   Haven't heard from Apple River today. So we called for Apple River, said it was out of order. Then we called again some one was talking with Dittmars.

Now, our phone is out of order. Everything that can be. Ruby & I have awful bad colds.

Thu 8: Mother called up today. Grandfather isn't any better. Mr. Charlton was buried this afternoon at two-oclock. Ruby & I cleaned out the cow stable today.

Fri 9: Quite warm today and clear. And very muddy. Aunt Annie called out today from Galena. Today Grandpa is about the same. I guess tomorrow will be the ninth day. The nurse's very nice. Uncle Edd went out to Apple River this evening. I baked oatmeal drops today.

Sat 10: Mother called up this evening when we were out. Ethel told me said Grandfather is better. She said Mother talked like she was coming home tomorrow. I baked bread and coffee cake and a sponge cake today.

Sun 11: Mother came home on the noon train. Ruby & I met her when we went to church. Only John Tresidder, William Bastian and Ruby & I were the only ones there besides Rev. Palmer. Grandfather is quite a bit better. His fever is one degree below normal. Uncle Edd, John & Ethel came down this evening.

Mon 12: Ma & Ruby sewing some today. I tatted some. Getting colder tonight. Very windy.

Tue 13:   Very stormy today. Raining and freezing. Had a terrible time getting the water out of the cow shed.

Wed 14:   We washed today. Just terribly windy. I got a card from Mary Tippet from New Mexico. She said she was sending me some tatting patterns She found in some magazines.

Thu 15:   We ironed today. Got a card from Aunt Annie today. Grandpa is doing nicely. I have been tatting on a yoke today.

Fri 16:   Aunt Annie came home from Apple River today. Quite stormy.

Sat 17:   Awful windy today.

Sun 18:   Mother and Ruby went to church this forenoon. Uncle Edd and Aunt Annie came here to dinner. Fiedlers came down this afternoon and Tresidders came up so we had quite a crowd here.

Mon 19:   Quite a nice day. Dad hauled manure this forenoon. Mother is making herself a dress. I've been tatting. We heard today that Uncle Joe Dittmars have little girl. Mary, born 16 March 1917.

Tue 20:   I've been busy tatting. Mother sewing on her dress.

Wed 21:   We washed this forenoon. This afternoon Mother and I went up to Aunt Annie's. Ethel was there too. I finished the tatted yoke today.

Thu 22:   I sent the yoke and three handkerchiefs out to Waterloo today.

Fri 23:   We baked bread and coffee cake today. Dad walked over the Station took over six dozen eggs and got a few grocery and nails. For the smoke house.

Sat 24:   A lovely day. Ruby & I walked over the Station and went up to Scales Mound on the six train. We staid all night at Uncle Nick's. We went to the school play. We also went to the movies before the play.

Sun 25:   Ruby & I went to church this forenoon. To the Methodist church. We came home on the noon train. And walked home. Then we walked up to Union church this afternoon. A nice day.

Mon 26:   This morning we all went up to Uncle Edd's. Victor Engel is dead. He died Sat. evening. He's going to be buried tomorrow at nine o'clock.

Tue 27:   Dad went to Galena. With Della in the buggy this afternoon. He says the roads are fine. We washed today.

Wed 28:   We ironed today. Papa & Ruby hauled manure. Lots of people going along to the trial.

Thu 29:   We got a card from Aunt Rachel this morning. Said Anna is going through on the five train. Ruby & I wanted to go in to hear the trial. Didn't know if we should drive Della or not. We started out to walk. Mr. Spensley gave us a ride in. We went to the trial awhile this forenoon. We had our dinner at the Merchant's cafe. We were in the courtroom all afternoon until a little after four. We heard August Shultz, John & Charlie Tobin, Leo Werner and Mr. Werner the former sheriff testify. Quite exciting. The courtroom was just full. Anna went through on the flier. She came out on the platform a few minutes. She gave me four Dollars and seventy-five cents. Four dollars for the tatted yoke and seventy-five cents for one handkerchief. She is going to stop at Rockford over night. We started to walk home. Mr. Spensley came along again when we were out by the railroad track and gave us a ride. We are quite tired tonight.

Fri 30: Busy as usual today. I sewed this afternoon and raked some leaves. I heard some one say there was more people than ever at the trial today. Harold Monnier had to testify today.

Sat 31: I guess it was quite an exciting day at the trial today. A good many people went along. This evening Mother went to Apple River. She walked over the Station.

April

Sun 1: Dad, Ruby & I went to church this forenoon. Quite a few there. We went up to Aunt Annie's to dinner. Cloudy all day. This afternoon it snowed. The roads won't be quite as nice as they were.

Mon 2: Well Papa & I went up to Scales Mound with Della in the buggy. It took us over two hours to go. Both had to walk now and then. I ordered my grocerys. Dad bought a grass seeder and horse collar. Papa went down to the garage. Then Mr. Anton Grube took us riding in a Ford car. Went towards Apple River on the south road, then we went out north of town. I got in behind the wheel. And Dad sat in the back seat. My first trial at running a car. I went very crooked at first. We went out about two and one half miles or so. He had to help me a lot. Dad would say look out for that ditch, turn it this way and so on all the time. We came back to Uncle Nick's. When we went down town again Dad ordered the car. Don't know when it will come. Then we came home.

Tue 3: Mother came home this forenoon. Walked home from the Station. She says she saw on this mornings paper that war is declared. Oh its terrible. Aunt Tillie is nearly worn out. I've been raking lawn today.

Wed 4: Well Aunt Annie came down this forenoon. Cloudy today. I raked some lawn. We got a letter from Uncle Thomas & Aunt Rachel today.

Thu 5: We washed today. Papa started to disc today. Well in the Gazette in the Scales Mound item it say Mr. Grube sold sixteen Ford cars this season. Then it said Charles Trudgian was in town Monday and ordered one of them.

Fri 6: A Beautiful Grand day. I nearly finished raking the lawn today. Mother & Ruby went up and swept out the church today. We ironed today. There were numerous number of cars on the road today. roads are in very good condition.

Sat 7: Mother went to Galena today with Tresidders. Took some eggs and got some supplies. Snowy this afternoon.

Sun 8: Easter Sunday. A beautiful day but quite cool. We all went to church this afternoon. Rev. Matlock preached and administered the sacrament. Rev. Palmer didn't come to church today. He went down to Apple River. They are holding meetings near there some where. Quite a few at church. The roads are just lovely.

Mon 9: A very nice day. Papa Ruby & I cut down the evergreen tree today. It was struck by lightning and it died. Mrs.

Will Studier is very sick. Got appendicitis. Had a operation today. Had three doctors and a nurse.

Tue 10: Papa was discing today. We washed today. Mamma, Ruby & I went up to Aunt Annie's tonight.

Wed 11: Dad sowed oats this afternoon. I baked bread and a cake. Ruby ironed. Mrs. Studier is very sick. I don't know how it will go with her. This evening Josie and Helen came up. They didn't stay very late. Helen has to go back to Madison Sat.

Thu 12: Mrs. Will Studier died today at twelve fourty-five. Its so sad. She wouldn't have been twenty-one until next June. The baby is just a week old today. Its name is Pauline Bertha. She wanted to take the baby along with her. She was conscious. Mother and Mrs. Fiedler went over this afternoon. Mrs. Joe Weis and Bessie were there to. They were washing. There seemed to be no one there that knew what to do.

Fri 13: Yesterday & today we cleaned my room. And baked bread, coffee cake, patty cakes and two cakes. Ruby and I were over to the wake tonight. We went with Mrs. Fiedler. Bertha's sister Rosie Dininger was there. She takes it very hard. I think Mrs. Studier looks quite natural. She has lots of beautiful flowers already.

Sat 14: Papa and Mamma went over the house to the funeral. Mother, Mrs. Weis & Mrs. Wachter staid at the house. And Mrs. Weis took care of the baby and Mother the Fiedler's kids. Father was to drive Fiedler's team then there wasn't nobody to go but Mrs. So they had Dad unhitch the team again. So he couldn't go to town either. The funeral was at eleven o'clock from the house and one at the Lutheran church in Galena. The pall bearers were Mr. Fiedler, Sigerman & Herman Studier, Leo Bohnsack, Will Weis & Henry Zarndt. I wanted to go to the funeral so badly. A very nice day. Autos went by here in great numbers today.

Sun 15: Mother and Ruby went to church this forenoon. Uncle Edd & Aunt Annie came down to dinner. This afternoon Tresidders came up this far in their car. Uncle Georges also came in this afternoon. Had quite a crowd here. They staid to supper, all but Tresidders.

Mon 16: Dad plowed the garden today. I made an auto cap. I wish our car would come soon. It rained a little today.

Tue 17: We made garden this afternoon. Made nearly all. A few things yet and some we won't plant till later. Dad hauled manure today. Galena votes on the wet and dry question today.

Wed 18: We planted all the early potatoes today in the garden. It stormed tonight. It rained quite hard and hailed. Heard that Galena went wet again.

Thu 19: We washed today. Threatening rain.

Fri 20: I ironed today. Ruby cleaned her room today.

Sat 21: Dad went to Galena today. Took in twenty-four dozen eggs. They are thirty cents per dozen. Everything is so high now on account of the war. Dad bought a bu. Potatoes for three-seventy-five. They aren't so very good. They are selling for four dollars per bushel sugar at ten dollars per hundred. Flour is awful high to. Uncle Edd & Aunt Annie went out to Apple River today on the noon train. Are coming back to Galena tonight.

Sun 22: A nice day. But the flies nearly eat a person alive. This forenoon John came up with his Ford. Milton too. Pa, Ruby & I rode up and down the bottom with him. He doesn't like to run only on the level. This afternoon we all went to church. Quite a few there. The anemones are out. This evening we all went down to Tresidder's.

Mon 23: Ruby cleaned the rag room today. Mamma, Ruby & I went up to Aunt Annie's tonight. Quite cold.

Tue 24: Cleaned Pa's and Ma's room today. I made a cake but it was a total failure. Cold today. Some garden stuff coming up.

Wed 25: We washed today. We got a letter from Anna today. She is in the diet kitchen.

Thu 26: We ironed today. Quite cold all day. Mother and Ruby washed carpets.

Fri 27: Well this is Grant's birthday. John Tresidder asked us to go to town with them if we wanted to. So Ruby & I went with them this afternoon. Papa drove Old Della in. A great crowd in there. A great parade. All children in town marched and more I guess. We went up the hall. A Mr. Lee, General Lee's son talked quite a nice speech. And a former Secretary of War spoke a short time. They had nice singing. Had quite a nice time. Hope our car will come soon. A sheep had a little lamb today.

Sat 28: Cloudy and cold today. Just doing our Sat. work today.

Sun 29: I got the tooth ache today. I didn't go to church. Pa & Ma & Ruby went this forenoon. Only they and Agnes & Milton & the minister there. Dark cloudy & cold as usual again. It rained last night. We all went up to Uncle Edd's to supper.

Mon 30: Cold and rainy. And this afternoon and evening it snowed. Almost enough if it was cold for sleighing. Everything is white. evergreen limbs hanging to the ground.

May

Tue 1:   Ruby painted the bedroom today. Mr. Spensley came and got some setting eggs today.

Wed 2:   We washed today.

Thu 3:   We ironed today. Tore up the parlor today and took down the dining room stove.

Fri 4:   We churned today. I went up to Aunt Annie's this afternoon. But they had gone to town. So I called at Ethel's for a while. I called in at Agnes' and borrowed to yeast cakes.

Sat 5:   Dad went up to Scales Mound today. Wanted to ask about the car. Mr. Grube thinks we may not get it till the first of August. I'm so disappointed. There is nine orders in ahead of ours. Mother chanced it to Galena today. Rode with Blums in a Ford. Rode home with Tresidders. She purchased a new hat.

Sun 6:   This afternoon we all went to church. Aunt Annie came down from church. Uncle Edd came down to supper. John, Ethel & Mrs. Bauer came down this evening. Full moon tonight.

Mon 7:   A lovely day. Quite warm. I sent for some pumps, a waist and a house dress today to National Cloak &

Suit Co. We washed. Ruby cleaned hall. Planted out some cabbage and tomatoe plants. Also planted some beans & sweet corn.

Tue 8: We ironed today. Also baked bread and a cake. Tore up the dining room today.

Wed 9: Ruby cleaned the kitchen. Ma whitewashed the ceiling of the dining room. Mr. Rob Gill bought two cows with calves from us today. Sold them both for one-hundred-fifty-five dollars. One a heifer and the other a four year old. Uncle Edd & Aunt Annie went out to Uncle Joe's & Henry's today.

Thu 10: Gill got the cows today. Tied the cows together poor things. He was here to dinner. Papa helped drive them up to the crossroads. We got a letter from Uncle Thomas today. Says he had a letter from Alice Trudgian. Uncle Joe T. is quite sick had an attack of gall stones. Now he has paralysis. Mary Fiedler called up this evening inviting us to the school picnic.

Fri 11: We planted our late potatoes today. And Pa & Ruby planted some of the corn. Baked bread and coffee cake today.

Sat 12: Worked hard this forenoon. Ruby & I went to the school picnic. Rode up with John Tresidders in their car. He took them up. Had a nice time. I think about fourty there. Mary Fiedler got a necklace for going to school, not missing a day or being tardy. This evening Rev. Palmer came to stay all night. He was going to stay at Fritz's but they weren't at home. He was feeling kind of sick tonight. His twin brother is going to preach tomorrow.

Sun 13: Papa, Ruby & Mr. Palmer went to church. Ruby thinks he & his brother look quite a little alike. I was sick all day. Ruby went with Tresidders out for a ride this afternoon. They went up to _____ys. Cars went by in great numbers today. Roads lovely. Uncle Edds & Youngs went out to Apple River this forenoon.

Mon 14: Dad went to Galena today. Got fifty pounds flour for four dollars ten cents. We stretched parlor curtains today.

Tue 15: Ma & Ruby whitewashed both cellars today. I made bread. Dad & I went up on Tresidder's hill and got asparagus roots this evening. Had Della in the buggy.

Wed 16: Quite warm today. We washed today. Dad and I planted the asparagus roots today. Dad also planted melons. Aunt Annie came down today. She was here for dinner and supper.

Thu 17: We ironed today. This afternoon John, Ethel & Aunt Annie came along in the car going up to Scales Mound. Said one of us could go along if we could get ready quick. So I went along. We visited at Uncle Eheart's first. Then we called up at Uncle Nick's. They had just returned from Warren. Quite warm today. Had a nice ride.

Fri 18: Baked a batch cookies this forenoon. Baked bread and coffee cake also. I went up to Aunt Annie's this afternoon. Got some strawberry plants.

Sat 19: We got a letter from Aunt Rachel today. Also one from Anna. Papa & Ruby went to Galena today.

Sun 20: We were ready to go to church this afternoon when Agnes called up. Said some of us could go to with them to Apple River. Didn't know what to do. Ruby & I went along. Had a fine ride. Only it was quite cold. First time I ever went to Apple River by road. We called at Grandpa's awhile. Aunt Tillie had gone down to Uncle Henry's with Uncle Georges. We got home at half-past five. Pa & Ma didn't get home until about seven o'clock. They went in to Wilbur B. after church and stayed to supper.

Mon 21: A band of gypsies went along here today. Very, very cold today. I went down to Tresidder's and picked some asparagus today. Ma & Ruby made curtains for dining room.

Tue 22: I sent back the slippers today. Want to get a pair of shoes in exchange. I also sent for shoes and slippers to Montgomery Ward and Co. Mother went up to Aunt Annie's this afternoon. She was feeling quite sick this afternoon. Very cold.

Wed 23: It froze last night. I hope it won't harm the blossoms. We put in some more garden today. I started to cut the lawn today.

Thu 24: Papa went to Galena today. Looked for a horse. Saw a nice one only it is smaller than Della. We washed today.

Fri 25: Papa got a chance to Galena again this morning. He expects to go to Elizabeth & maybe Woodbine today. Horse hunting. He will stay overnight I guess. We ironed today. Ruby cleaned the summer kitchen.

Sat 26: Dad got home this afternoon. Got a chance out. He didn't find anything at Elizabeth. Was down to Uncle Ben's all night. Slattery has one to sell. May get that.

Sun 27: We all went to church this forenoon. I had to play the organ. We all went up to Aunt Annie's to dinner.

She was sick in bed all day. Ruby & I came home and did the chores.

Mon 28: We washed today. All doing other odd jobs. Hope our car will come soon.

Tue 29: We ironed today. Ruby put out the geraniums and other plants today. Mother went up to Aunt Annie's. She washed up there. Rainy this evening.

Wed 30: This is decoration or Memorial day. I made a big collar for my white dress. Aunt Annie is feeling very poorly.

Thu 31: Well Papa and Ruby went to Galena today. Brought home a horse. Bought it of Slattery for seventy-five dollars.

June

Fri 1: Hitched up the new horse with Della today. Papa & Ruby drove up to Uncle Edd's. Then this afternoon they went to Scales Mound. Mother went up to Aunt Annie's and I called at Tresidder's. Then I picked the asparagus. Well Papa & Ruby didn't like the horse at all. Awfully afraid of autos and isn't a bit quiet. Dad said he wouldn't hitch it up again for any thing. Dad called up Slattery told him he wasn't satisfied with the bargain. They are going to take it back tomorrow

Sat 2: Rained nearly all night and nearly all day. Dad started off walking leading the horse. Got a ride part way. But cold mean Slattery wouldn't take it back. I don't know what we are going to do with it. Ruby went up to Aunt Annie's this afternoon.

Sun 3: Dad, Ruby & I went to church this afternoon. Mother went up to Aunt Annie's. Only six to church with the preacher. I had to play the organ today.

Mon 4: Rainy again today. Pa, Ma & Ruby replanted corn. I worked a little in the garden and cut some lawn. All of Jesse Fords are back in their car. Saw them go by today.

Tue 5:   We washed today. Pa & Ruby hauled around stakes.

Wed 6:   It stormed last night. It rained all day. And just terribly windy. Uncle Edd came down for some plants this afternoon.

Thu 7:   Reading day. It say in Scales Mound items that Mr. Grube received a car load of Fords and expects to receive another car load in a few days.

Fri 8:   Dad & Ruby went to Galena today. Drove the new horse again. She wasn't afraid of autos in town but they didn't meet any in the country. My slippers came today.

Sat 9:   We received a graduation card from Helen today. She is going to graduate next Thursday June fourteenth at nine o'clock a.m. A nice day today.

Sun 10:   We all went to church this forenoon. I had to play the organ again! Uncle Edd & Aunt Annie came down to dinner. John Tresidder came up this afternoon awhile. A lovely day.

Mon 11:   Dad took a calf over the Station with Nellie the new horse and Della was awfully worried but he got along alright. This afternoon he and Ruby went over to Hacker's to see if they could get some little pigs. They would sell two sows with 9 pigs each for eighty-five dollars. And one sow with seven pigs for seventy-five. They didn't buy any. I cut lawn.

Tue 12:   We washed today. It rained last night.

Wed 13:   We ironed today. Quite a nice day but had a shower again this evening. Agnes called up today saying they are going to Dubuque tomorrow and some of us could go along.

Thu 14:   Well we got up early and Ruby & I went to Dubuque. Aunt Annie went to Galena and went along to Dubuque with us. I bought a skirt. Navy blue for 4.98. Ruby bought a white waist and skirt 1.98 each. The time seemed so short. We had dinner at the Y.W.C.A. Very cold all day.

Fri 15:   A nice day. Dad & Ruby went to Galena today. Heard today that Mrs. Pearson committed suicide. By cutting her throat. I don't know if she's living now or not. Uncle Edd sheared our sheep today. Got nearly sixty pounds from eight sheep.

Sat 16:   Busy today as usual on Saturday. Dad started to plow corn today.

Sun 17:   We all went to church this afternoon. Tresidders were up with their car. Ruby & I rode down with them.

Tresidders all came up here this evening. They say our car is up to Scales Mound. I believe Mr. Durrstein told Fiedler. Fiedlers have a new interstate car, they say. They all rode to town in it Saturday.

Mon 18: We were very busy all day. Dad plowing corn. Ma & Ruby replanting. I hoed potatoes. Expected to hear or see something of the car today. But didn't. A nice day. Mrs. Pearson is still living. A Keister boy twenty-eight years old committed suicide by hanging himself. In his brother's barn in Guilford.

Tue 19: We washed, churned and baked bread today. Also ironed some. Haven't heard anything about the car yet.

Wed 20: Mother walked over the Station and went to Apple River this afternoon, to take in the reunion tomorrow. We went up to Fiedler's this evening. Saw their car.

Thu 21: I wanted to go to the reunion so bad but didn't get there. Dad talked to Mr. Durrstein today. He says our car is up there. One that came several weeks ago in the car load.

Fri 22: Mother called up from the Station this forenoon. Said she may go up and call on the Palmers. Later it came to a storm. Didn't last long. Papa & Ruby went up to Scales Mound this afternoon. They saw the car. His brother said he would bring it down when the roads got a little better. Ma didn't get home until about half-past three. I was very worried. I called up Mrs. Palmer. She didn't start out from there until after the storm. The minister came over with her as far as Wilbur Bastian's. Mrs. Popp had her baby baptized.

Sat 23: Busy with Saturday work. We got a card from Uncle Thomas yesterday. They moved to a house on Lafayette St.

Sun 24: We all went to church this forenoon. Uncle Edd & Aunt Annie Tillie came down to dinner. Tillie came with Aunt Annie yesterday. Aunt Tillie staid down. Dad & Ruby went over to the Station to children's exercises. Drove Della in the buggy. The church was full. Had the church wonderfully decorated.

Mon 25: It sprinkled rain this forenoon. Aunt Tillie went up to Aunt Annie's. This afternoon Mr. Grube called up wanted to know if it would be alright if one of them would bring down the car this afternoon. We said yes. So his kid brother brought it down. He gave me a lesson. Dad or Ruby could have gone but it seems we went off before they were ready. Went up to the cross roads went down as far as Mt. Zion and came back & went up to the next crossroads. Went down the sand. Came up around by Keanan's went past the Lutheran church went west a long way. And then came home. We went over some terrible roads. I think I did quite well for a beginner.

Tue 26: Young Grube came again this morning. Papa and Ruby went along. We went to Scales Mound. Took the eggs and wool along. Got sixty-two cents per pound. $34.41 all together. We went out north of Scales Mound quite away towards Shullsburg. We bought some gasoline at S. M. also paid for the car. $373.40. Also got an inner tube.

Wed 27: Grube came down again this morning to help me turn and back around. He, Ruby & I were turning around down above John's mail box and as we neared the ditch I tried to stop. As it didn't seem to stop I was going to shut the throttle. Instead I opened it as far as it would go. It just jumped in the ditch. Broke down trees also went through the fence. But a tree stopped the car. Nothing harmed that we could see of but the fender bent and a few scratches. It was a very lucky accident. Tried to pull it out with our big team but they couldn't pull it. He run it through the creek and down Weis' bottom and got out their gate. Then I drove it up the road and back again.

Thu 28: We washed today. Can't get much done and their is so much to do. We didn't try the car today.

Fri 29: We ironed today. Also baked bread & coffee cake. We washed the car today.

Sat 30: Very, very busy all day. Picked and put up some cherries today. Aunt Tillie came down this afternoon to stay all night. Dad cut alfalfa today.

July

Sun 1: We all went up to Aunt Annie's to dinner. We didn't have any services at Union today. Mr. Liston preached at Council Hill. Mr. Palmer at Apple River. About five oclock Mr. Liston and Uncle George came. They came from Council Hill. Had terrible roads over. They tried to fix their tire. After supper they started out had a blow out, came back took our car. Dad & I went along. Mr. Liston drove it. We went up by Scales Mound way. It got quite late before we got into Council Hill. He preached a patriot sermon. Mrs. Palmer came home with us. Then went to Apple River with them. It was nearly twelve oclock before they left here. Mr. Liston ran into our gate post and bent in our fender again this evening.

Mon 2: About eight oclock Grube came down. He wanted to go to Galena, which suited us alright. We got along alright. He drove through town. Dad & Ruby went along. We applied for a license today. We were home at eleven oclock. Well I guess I will have to drive it alone after this. We picked and put up cherries this afternoon.

Tue 3: Picking and putting up cherries again today. We have nineteen and one-half quarts up now. We hauled three loads of alfalfa towards evening. This evening Win & Martha , Mr. Zarndt, Aunt Tillie , Uncle Edd & Aunt Annie called here. They went out for a ride and called here on their way back.

Wed 4: Well we didn't go any where to celebrate the fourth. We celebrated by picking and putting up cherries and making hay. We finished the alfalfa hauled four loads today. A great many cars went along today. There were celebrations at Elizabeth, Schullsburg, Cuba City and Stockton. None near by. A very nice day.

Thu 5: Picking and putting up cherries again. Finished today. Put up thirty-six and one half quarts. We ate the half. Ma is going to give Aunt Tillie some. Aunt Tillie came down this afternoon. She is going to stay all night This afternoon Milton broke his arm just above his wrist by falling off a load of hay. They called Mother down. Dr. Bench came out and set it.

Fri 6: Mother went to Galena with John & Milton in the car this morning. Milton had to go in to the Dr. Tillie went up to Aunt Annie's this morning. We washed today.

Sat 7: As busy as usual. Ironing, baking and cleaning. Dad, Ruby & I went up to Uncle Edd's this evening to eat ice cream.

Sun 8: We all went to church this forenoon. All of Uncle Georges came in to church. Pearl is home now from Wis. We all went up to Aunt Annie's to dinner. Win & Martha came up too in the afternoon. All of Fiedlers were down this evening. Didn't get to take out our car today.

Mon 9: Well after dinner we took out the car. The first time alone. We rode up and down the bottom for quite awhile. Then we went down to Tresidder's and turned around and came back and went up the road as far as where the ridge road turned off. Turned around came home. Got along alright. Killed the engine a few times. Ma and Ruby banked all the late potatoes today. Dad finished plowing corn. I and Ruby fixed a road up back of shed. I also cut some lawn.

Tue 10: Well this forenoon Dad, Ruby & I went to Scales mound. Took two cans cream, two cases eggs and a can & bucket to mend. Had a load. We got along alright. We called at Uncle Nick's a few minutes. I cut some lawn this afternoon.

Wed 11: We washed today. Ruby & I picked a milk pail and a gallon pail of gooseberries this afternoon. Baked bread today. We got our license number plates today. The number is 287081

Thu 12: We ironed today. Put up eight quarts gooseberries. I cut some lawn. Ma hoed some corn. A lovely day.

Fri 13: Ruby and I picked a few raspberries today. Enough for one quart.

Sat 14: Doing Sat. work all day. Before supper we took the car out. We went up to the crossroads and back again. It didn't go right at first but went fairly well afterwards.

Sun 15: A beautiful looking morning. We all got ready and went up to Scales mound this morning. The car went better. There was too much oil in the crank case. The _____ wouldn't run. We were going to the Pres. Church but they minister had got home yet. So we went to the Methodist church. Lucille T was there. She asked us to go out to their place. And I guess we would. But the clouds were gathering and we were afraid it would rain so we came home again. We thought we go up to Union then this afternoon but it looked to much like a storm. It didn't ever rain a drop here. Well it was Mother's first ride in the car today. We were going down to Tresidder's this evening but they weren't home so we went up to Uncle Edd's

Mon 16:   This is Ruby's twenty-fourth birthday. It rained today. We picked a few strawberries before the rain and some after.

Tue 17:   We washed and baked bread & a cake today. Also hauled in two loads of hay towards evening.

Wed 18:   We hauled in one load of hay this forenoon. Dad cut some hay. This afternoon Dad, Ruby & I autoed to Scales Mound. Took two cans cream and twenty dozen eggs. Got thirty cents for eggs. We got along nicely with the car.

Thu 19:   Ruby & I picked raspberries this forenoon. This afternoon we hauled four loads of hay. Making fourteen all together.

Fri 20:   We hauled hay this afternoon. Later Ruby & I picked some berries again. We heard this evening that some of the fellows are drafted for the army.

Sat 21:   Busy as usual. We hauled some hay in afternoon. We have eighteen loads in now. It rained this afternoon. I hope it won't rain tonight and that tomorrow will be a nice day. We want to go to Apple River. We hear by rubbering that the names of the fellows that are drafted are in the daily Gazette. Then again we heard that all the men that are registered have to go and they will pick out what they want. Don't know what kind of a mess it is any way. Hope they don't have to go yet.

Sun 22: Ma, Ruby & I went to church this morning. But we had to come right home for it looked very much like a storm. Nobody there. Only the minister came. After we got home it rained nearly all afternoon. I am so disappointed we could not go to Apple River. Only glad we didn't go this morning and get caught. Ma, Ruby & I went down to Tresidder's tonight.

Mon 23: This afternoon Ma & I picked some raspberries. Ruby picked some gooseberries. Dad took two calves over the Station this morning. He got fifty dollars and five cents for them.

Tue 24: We put up three quarts of raspberries and two quarts of gooseberries this morning. We washed this afternoon. We baked bread and a cake. We also hauled one load of hay. Dad cut some hay this morning.

Wed 25: We hauled two loads of hay this afternoon. Quite hot today.

Thu 26: Awfully hot today. This forenoon Dad, Ruby & I went to Scales Mound took up the cream and eggs. We went in the car. All of the names of the young men that are drafted are in the Gazette. We hauled two loads of hay this afternoon. It makes twenty-three loads all together.

Fri 27: Rev. Palmer came this morning to help us hay. We hauled four loads today. Had to break Della in, in the hay fork this morning. She goes very nicely.

Sat 28: We finished with the hay by eleven oclock today. Hauled two loads, makes twenty-nine all together. We can't decide whether we will cut the oats for hay or not. This afternoon Mr. Palmer, Dad, Ruby & I went for a ride. We might have gone to Galena but Mr. Palmer thought his clothes hardly good enough to go there. So we drove over to Guilford and came out the ridge road and then went to Scales Mound. Mr. Palmer went home after supper.

Sun 29: Well this morning we autoed to Apple River. We went the north road. First time I ever was on that road. We expected to go to the Pres. Church but they didn't have any services there so we went to Methodist. We were a little late. Grandpas were quite surprised to see us. Uncles Dan & Herman & a Evans' boy came there for dinner. After dinner Uncle George's came down. Mr. Siefert took our picture with Sadie's camera. We had supper then came home. Got along quite nicely. This evening Tresidders and Uncle Edd

& Aunt Annie came down but we didn't get through with our chores until a quarter of nine so didn't have much time to visit. A lovely day.

Mon 30: We cut some oats for hay today. Was going to cut with the binder but the horse cut up so had to unhitch before could get in a field. Then he cut with mower again.

Tue 31: We hauled four loads of oats today. At half past five Dad & I went to Scales Mound. took up the eggs and cream and got five gallons of gasoline. I wanted to go to the garage to but saw a storm coming up so came right home. It has nearly cleared up again with out raining.

August

Wed 1: A beautiful day. It rained a little last night so couldn't do much with the oats this forenoon. We hauled four loads this afternoon. Finished one stack started another. Uncle Edd came down and helped us.

Thu 2: Uncle Edd came down to help again today. Aunt Annie also came down this forenoon. A very nice day. Joe Weis are cutting their oats with the tractor today.

Fri 3: We finished with the oats this afternoon. Got twenty-one loads. Two big and one small stacks. Very glad its all put up. We have the alfalfa to cut again soon. We got a letter from Uncle T & Aunt R They said Al thought he would spend his vacation back in Ill.

Sat 4: Doing Sat. work. Lots of cars going along.

Sun 5: Dad, Ma & Ruby went to church this morning. Late this afternoon we took a ride. Went over past Ehrler's and turned around and came back. We called at Win Tippett's awhile. Ma wanted to see Mrs. Westaby.

Mon 6: Ma & Ruby picked a few blackberries. The first picking. Also salted down a half gallon beans.

Tue 7: We washed an awful, awful big washing today. Had quite a rain this morning. Dandy for the corn and garden stuff. We needed it badly.

Wed 8: Dad, Ruby & I went to Scales Mound this afternoon. We saw Uncle Casper Dittmar and his daughter Pearl, from Kansas. We didn't know they were here. They are going to Michigan then coming back this way again. We thought Aunt Maggie would come to the Mound and come down with us, but I guess there was something she couldn't come.

Thu 9: Ruby & I picked some blackberries this forenoon. We finished the ironing today. I cut some lawn.

Fri 10: We hauled three loads of alfalfa this afternoon. Quite cool today.

Sat 11: Well we hauled one load of alfalfa this morning. I guess it finishes the haying for us now, making thirty-nine loads of hay, or fifty-four with the oats. This afternoon Dad, Ruby & I went to Galena. Didn't drive downtown. The first time I drove in alone. Aunt Annie rode in and out of town with us.

Sun 12: Uncle Edd & Aunt Annie came down this forenoon. Kind of rainy. It didn't look so bad this afternoon at church time. So we went but nobody else there. Ma called at Tresidder's awhile.

Mon 13: We finished blackberries this forenoon. Ma put up eleven quarts and have a kettle full for jelly. Ruby & I made a little new garden this afternoon. This evening a dog and pony show came along and wanted to go in the pasture to stay over night. We left them go in the bottom. They had two wagons, four ponies, dogs monkeys and a bear. They wanted us to go down to see the things before dark but had no time. So they promised us free tickets to the show at the fair.

Tue 14: Dad, Ruby & I went to Scales Mound this forenoon. The roads were quite nice. We washed this afternoon. I cut a little lawn.

Wed 15: We picked berries this forenoon and put then up. Fourteen quarts. Don't know how we will get to the fair tomorrow.

Thu 16: Well Papa, Ruby & I were getting ready to go to the fair when Aunt Lizzie, Mayme, Wesley, Sadie, Naomi and Willie Siefert came along. They had been trying to get us but couldn't. thought Siefert could run our car if we wanted to. It was the very thing I had wished - for someone to run the car. Dad went with Wesley and the rest and Sadie and Siefert went with us. Ma got ready then to and went with us. We had a lunch before we went. Had quite a nice time. We came home before the balloon went up. The rest didn't come home till half past seven. We milked so late. They went home about half past nine.

Fri 17: A lovely day. Aunt Annie [Tippett] came down then she, Dad & I picked blackberries. Got quite a lot. This afternoon Mr. Palmer and brother came. He had to go again in a short time because he is going back again tonight. We took them part way to the Station in the car. When we came back we took Aunt Annie home.

Sat 18: Quite a nice day. This afternoon Dad, Ruby & I went to Galena in the car. Al and Nancy came on the five oclock train. We got home alright. Quite dusty.

Sun 19: We all went to church this forenoon. After dinner Mayme Dittmar called up Aunt Annie that they were coming in there. Alvin, Nancy, Dad, Ruby & I started to go to Scales Mound. When we got up on the ridge, they were up there. Had a blow out and didn't have any extra tire. So we came home again. The Ma had gone up to Uncle Edd's. Dad & I went up there and got Ma and Aunt Annie. Then Wesley, Al, Dad & I went to Galena to get a tire. On the way home Wesley was driving. He killed the engine and pulled the emergency. Then it stuck. Couldn't get it forward any more had an awful time.

Got it forward but can't get it back. Aunt Lena was along with them.

Mon 20:   We washed this forenoon. Dad, Al, Nancy, Ruby & I picked the blackberries this afternoon. This forenoon Dad & Al took seven lambs over the station. Got seventy-two dollars and eighty cents for them.

Tue 21:   This afternoon we took Al & Nancy to Scales Mound. They were going to Apple River on the evening train. From there they are going down to Schlichting's. Ma staid at home putting up blackberries. Put up fifty-one quarts or fifty-three I believe.

Wed 22:   Quite warm today. We brought in the onions today. Got quite a lot. Got about four market baskets of multipliers.

Thu 23:   This afternoon Dad & I went up to Scales Mound after Al & Nancy. Harry, Stella & Myrtle Graham were up there. Took Uncle Nick & Aunt Lizzie home with them. The roads are just grand!

Fri 24:   This forenoon, Al, Nancy, & Mamma went up to Aunt Annie's This evening they went down to Tresidder's. So Dad, Ruby & I went down after we got through with the chores.

Sat 25: This afternoon all but Ma went to Galena. Just a lovely day. Uncle Edds went down to Woodbine today.

Sun 26: We had a early dinner then Dad, Ruby & I took Al and Nancy in to take the one-two train home. Then we drove out to Greenwood cemetery. We saw Warren's grave. From there we went out on the turnpike about three miles then we came home.

Mon 27: I canned three pints of corn today. Ma pickled cucumbers and a quart of cauliflower. Ruby picked a few more blackberries and cooked them.

Tue 28: Well today has been a lovely day. We got ready this morning and autoed out to Schapville. We stopped at the cemetery. Saw Grandma's grave. Then we went to Uncle Joe's had dinner there. In the afternoon we went up to Uncle Henry's. Staid there to supper. Then we came home by Mt. Sumner. Got along fine. First time Ma had been out there for four or five years. Uncle Edd's came home from Woodbine today.

Wed 29: Well today is my twentieth birthday. Farewell teens. Now for the twenties. A nice day. We washed and baked bread today. I baked a cake also but its all gone. I got a card from Aunt Tillie, one from Loretta Dittmar and we got a letter from Nancy and one from Mayme Dittmar.

Thu 30: This forenoon Dad & Ruby went up to Roy Tresidder's to see about getting some pigs. They drove the team. Then Roys took them up to Schullsburg in their car. They didn't come home till nearly dark. Was quite worried about them.

Fri 31: Another lovely day. Well about half past twelve we started for Apple River. Aunt Annie went along with us. I guess they were surprised to see us. Saw Mrs. Taylor and two boys. Also Uncle Casper & Pearl. Mayme is going away tomorrow morning. We had supper at Grandpa's. Got home at about dark.

September

Sat 1:   Ma churned today. Got lots of work to do.

Sun 2:   Dad, Ma & Ruby went to church this morning. Sadie Bastian and Evelyn came down to dinner. Wilbur came over after them towards evening. They staid to supper

Mon 3:   Had a lovely rain this morning. It cleared up by noon. Didn't get much done. Just doing a few odd jobs. Labor day today.

Tue 4:   Ella called up today. Wanted to know if we could go up after Uncle Casper and Pearl tomorrow morning. We washed and baked bread today.

Wed 5:   Dad and I went up to Scales Mound after Uncle Casper and Pearl this morning. We got home again about quarter after ten. After dinner Ruby, Pearl & I took a walk up on the hill. This afternoon we went up to Aunt Annie's but we wasn't there long when it looked like a storm so we came home. It stormed and rained till after dark. So they have to stay here all night. they wanted to go back again this evening. Seven of the drafted men had to go to Rockford training camp this morning. Billy Siefert was one that had to go. They are the first from this county that had to go.

Thu 6: Dad & Ruby took Uncle Casper and Pearl up to Scales Mound this forenoon. Came home at half past twelve. This afternoon we all went to Galena. Took the car. A few muddy places.

Fri 7: Rainy today. We ironed today.

Sat 8: Busy as usual today. Don't know any news.

Sun 9: Cloudy all day. Raining this afternoon. We did not go to church this afternoon. It is so cold we nearly froze.

Mon 10: A lovely day only cool. We washed a big washing today. Dad took the old sow over to the Station this forenoon. Got forty-six dollars for her.

Tue 11: Well there was quite a frost last night. froze some things. Ma went down to Tresidder's to get ready for the thrashers this afternoon. They thrashed late this afternoon. Dad had to go down to help to. I washed the car today. Ruby ironed.

Wed 12: This afternoon we all went up to Scales Mound. Had an awful time to get the car cranked. We worked for over an hour. Then a car came along and a man got it cranked for us. I got a new hat at Scales Mound today-a small black velvet one. Paid four-seventy-five for it. We wanted to go to the Warren Fair tomorrow.

But there's no show for going because it is raining. I want to go so bad.

Thu 13: Well it rained last night. cloudy all day today. So we couldn't go to the Warren Fair. Quite disappointed. We put up eight quarts of peaches and two quarts of tomatoes and four of pickles today. Will Weis are thrashing today.

Fri 14: Well we didn't know if we should try to go to the Warren Fair today. The roads were quite slippery yet. We didn't go but Uncle Edd & Aunt Annie went on the noon train. A nice day.

Sat 15: We all went to Galena this afternoon in the car. Dad purchased a new suit of navy blue.

Sun 16: We all went to church this morning. We went down to Tresidder's to dinner. Mr. and Mrs. R. Virtue and Vera and Grandma Virtue were there, also Uncle Edd & Aunt Annie. Uncle Edds were on their way to church when they met a car. Old Bat got scared and run away tipping over the buggy. Aunt Annie got hurt a little but nothing serious I don't think. This evening we all went down to Joe Weis'. Heard Helen play on her violin.

Mon 17: A lovely day. We washed today. I put up three quarts of tomatoes. Dad pulled down the roof of the old porch

today. I don't know what we are going to do now. I
don't see no show of any new one. It looks so different
now. It doesn't look like home.

Tue 18:   We ironed today. Tonight we all went up to Uncle
Edd's It's Uncle Edd's birthday. We took up a
banana muskmelon. The second ripe one. John &
Ethel and Joe were there too.

Wed 19:   Nothing new. Only a lot of the drafted men have to
go to Grant Camp. Next Saturday morning Jack
Combellick and Henry Zarndt have to go.

Thu 20:   Well cloudy and it rained a little this morning. Didn't
think we could go to the mission feast. But got ready
and went yet this afternoon. The church wasn't full. I
guess the weather was to bad. We staid to supper up at
Uncle Eheart's. Aunt Tillie was there. Also Uncle
Casper & Pearl, Mr. Simons, Mrs. Baumgardner,
Mrs. Grebner. It cleared up this evening.

Fri 21:   A lovely day. Tonight is the big doings in Galena
for the Soldier Boys To Be. My the cars have gone
along. I counted fifty-nine and some more. Dad
wanted to go. But Ruby & I would rather go in the
morning to see them go. So we won't be the only ones.
Poor fellows.

Sat 22: Well we got up early this morning, all but Ma. And went in to see the boys go away. My I shall never forget it. We started away from here about a quarter of seven. The band was playing when we got in there at the court house. Quite a parade. My but there was a crowd at the depot. Nearly everybody had tears in their eyes. A very sad affair. Jack Combellick and Henry Zarndt had to go. The train was pulling out and whistles blew and bells rang and the people cheered. And the hands waved and the handkerchiefs fluttered. Rev. Mr. Palmer rode out home with us. We got home about eleven. This afternoon we had to take the minister over nearly to the Station. He took a basket of apples. A lovely morning day.

Sun 23: A lovely day. We all went to church this afternoon. Uncle Edd & Aunt Annie came down to supper.

Mon 24: Another nice day. Put up tomatoes and plums. Tonight we took a ride up to Scales mound. Took up a bushel of plums to W. Berryman. Then we called at Uncle Nick's. We wanted to try the dimmers. First time I ever had it out at night.

Tue 25: Ma went to Dubuque today with Agnes & Blanche and Aunt Annie. John took them in. Ma bought a suit of black serge. Late this afternoon we took a bu.

Of plums to Galena to send to Uncle Thomas and a bu. to send to Mary Potter. Ma came out with us. I drove down and up Main street for the first time today.

Wed 26: We put up plums. Canned tomatoes. Very busy. Rainy today.

Thu 27: A lovely day. We washed today. And baked bread. As busy as usual.

Fri 28: A lovely day. We got a letter from Uncle Thomas today. They got the plums alright.

Sat 29: Very busy with cleaning, baking and canning. A nice day.

Sun 30: This morning we all went to church. Then hurried home and went out to Apple River to John William's funeral. It was held from the Methodist church at two oclock. A very large funeral. Uncle Edd & Aunt Annie went out with Win and Martha this morning. All of Ma's brothers and sisters were there. So many people at Grandpa's. The house was just alive with children. We got home just before dark.

October

Mon 1:   This afternoon Dad and I took in Galena a bu. of plums for Tippetts and a bu, to send to Stella Graham and a peach box to send to uncle Thomas yet. Had an awful load going and coming. Put up tomatoes and plums today.

Tue 2:   Made chilli sauce today. I cut some lawn. This evening at about half past seven Uncle Joe, Aunt Rachel, Harlan, and the baby came. Were quite surprised.

Wed 3:   Made plum jam today. After dinner Uncle Joe's went to Galena. They are going to stay at Uncle Edd's tonight. Ruby & I & Dad cut several shocks of corn.

Thu 4:   Uncle Joes went home after dinner. Just drove in here. We washed today. Twenty-nine more young men have to go to Camp Grant Saturday morning.

Fri 5:   We ironed today. Dad and Ruby cut some corn. Didn't know if we should go to Galena tonight or not. But didn't go. Rather disappointed. Had a doings in there for the soldier boys. Some auto went along but nothing like two weeks ago.

Sat 6:   The corn is all frozen this morning. Had a hard frost last night. Tried to do up our work so we could go to Galena this after but Dad raked the alfalfa. Made it nearly to late so Dad, Ruby & I went to Scales mound. Took some plums to send to Ida Barnum. Got a letter this morning wanting some.

Sun 7:   Quite a nice day only very cold and windy. This morning we all autoed to Galena and went to the first Pres. Church. After church we went out through Hazel Green and Cuba City. Went a mile or so the other side. Then came back again. We ate our dinner this side of Cuba. When we got back to Galena we called at Mr. & Mrs. H. Bastian's. Laura wasn't at home. Ma staid up to Aunt Annie's We came home did up the chores and went up a while this evening. Win & Martha went out to Westaby's today. Took Uncle Edd & Aunt Annie along. Then went to Uncle Henry's Aunt Maggie was there so she came along in. Zarndts and Fiedlers went to Rockford to Camp Grant today. It was eighty miles one way.

Mon 8:   We cut corn this morning. I got a quick in my back so I couldn't work this afternoon. The others made the alfalfa hay. Quite cold today.

Tue 9:   Ruby and I picked some apples today. Also brought in some carrots. Then cut a few shocks of corn. A little sleet or snow or rain coming down this afternoon.

Wed 10:   Ruby & I cut corn today. I cut twenty shocks or thirty-five all together for me. Mother churned this afternoon. Thought probably Aunt Maggie would come down but didn't see anything of her.

Thu 11:   Rainy & snowy and cold today. Cut a little corn this afternoon. Didn't get much doing because the weather is so bad.

Fri 12:   I cut twenty-two shocks of corn. Cut fifty-seven all together. Aunts Annie and Margaret came down this forenoon. Aunt Mag staid here. Still cloudy & cold.

Sat 13:   Wanted to go to town today but the potatoes had to be dug. It froze awfully hard last night but I don't think

Sun 14:   Warm today. We all went to church this morning. We thought maybe Ella and Mr. Simon would come. And maybe Uncle Bens but didn't see anything of them. The roads are just grand. It rained this evening.

Mon 15:   A nice day today. We finished digging potatoes this afternoon. Got thirty-nine and one half bushels but guess will call it fourty. This evening we put new oil in the crank case of the car. Also gave the car a shine.

Tue 16:   We took Aunt Margaret home to Apple River today. Got out there a quarter of twelve, got home at half past six. A very lovely day. Had a little trouble with the car. It would stop when we turned on the light, it was short circuited.

Wed 17:   It snowed last night. also rainy today. We picked some apples this afternoon. Ben Colin called here last night and borrowed on of the spark plugs off the car. Is going to send it back by mail.

Thu 18:   Cloudy all day. We washed today. It has turned cold this evening. We baked bread.

Fri 19:   Mother churned. We ironed. I baked oatmeal cookies.

Sat 20:   Cloudy all day. We went to Galena this afternoon. Had an awful hard time to get the car started. But it started easy in town. Lots of people in town. I got a new pair of shoes and rubbers.

Sun 21:   A lovely morning but it clouded up again this afternoon. We all went to church this afternoon. The minister's mother was there. First time. Sadie Bastian invited us to go over to Young's Wednesday afternoon to surprise Mrs. Young. She wanted to have the Aid Society but wasn't able so they are getting up a little surprise on her. It rained a little this evening.

Mon 22: Had quite a snow storm this afternoon. Cleared up toward evening. Cleaned out stable and chicken houses and pig pen.

Tue 23: We washed today also baked bread.

Wed 24: Well Ma, Ruby & I went over to Young's this afternoon. We walked across. Agnes & Blanche went with us. Quite a few there. Mrs. Young was quite surprised. Had a lap supper with lots to eat. We took sandwiches. Young's new house is a very nice house. Every thing fixed up very fine. It was dark before we got home. Uncle Edd went to Chicago with cattle today. With his, John Tippet's, Win's, John Tresidder's, Joe Weis' and Jim Ivey's cattle. Three car loads. Aunt Annie came down here to stay till Uncle Edd comes home.

Thu 25: Mamma churned today. Quite a nice day but it was raining hard tonight.

Fri 26: A very rainy day. It rained all night last night. it has cleared up this evening. Uncle Edd got home. Came down for Aunt Annie. Came for dinner. I believe they struck quite a good market at Chicago for the cattle.

Sat 27:   Busy as usual on Sat. Dad and I husked some corn this afternoon.

Sun 28:   We all went to church this morning. Then we went up to Aunt Annie's to dinner. After noon Tresidders came up there to. Raining a little this evening.

Mon 29:   It snowed last night and all day today. Would be enough snow for sleighing. If it wasn't so muddy. I made some ice cream this afternoon with snow. I hope we will have some nice weather soon.

Tues 30:   Weather is about as usual. Not very nice. No news.

Wed 31:   Dad and Ruby was going to go up to the Mound, but Nellie balked and cut up so. Had to unhitch her. Dad then went with Della in the buggy. Had eight gallons cream to take. We washed this afternoon. Dad bought us two gent's neck ties. If we should want to go to the Miner's social Friday night. Halloween tonight.

November

Thu 1: Cleaned the dining room today. Reading day. Didn't get much accomplished.

Fri 2: I was very busy baking today. I made a batch of cookies and two cakes. Well Ruby & I went to the social with Josie, Helen & Bert. A very large crowd there. Made sixty-nine dollars on the sale of the neckties. I think thats wonderful. None sold for less than a dollar. One brought nine dollars and a half several at three seventy-five. Ruby's brought two seventy-five. Don't know what mine brought but Ruby thinks two and a quarter. Herman Studier bought Ruby's. A Mr. Virtue, the teacher's cousin bought mine. A very tall man. Charlie Zarndt got Helen's. A Muchow got Josie's. They had a very nice program. We got home about one oclock or a little before. Had quite a nice time. Helen Weis is going to have a pie social at Independence school Thanksgiving evening Nov. 27.

Sat 3: Nothing new. We ironed today. Dad started to walk to town today but got some rides. The roads are terrible.

Sun 4: We all went to church this afternoon. Its just a lovely day. Quite warm

Mon 5: We husked corn this forenoon. Ma churned this afternoon. The roads are all dry along here now. Quite warm today.

Tue 6: We husked corn this forenoon. This afternoon we cleaned the church. Us three, Lottie, Sadie and Mrs. W. Combellick. Quite a job. Quite warm today. Indian summer I guess.

Wed 7: We husked some corn this forenoon. This afternoon we went to Galena in the car. The roads wasn't very good. Ehrler's hill was awful. Had to put chains on coming home so we could get up the hill. Took the car to the garage today. They cleaned out the commutator. Charged a quarter but it would hardly go at all on big gear coming home. Jumped and jerked. I don't know what's wrong. Couldn't get but fifty cents worth of sugar at a time now days. Some say a quarters worth but we got fifty cents worth.

Thu 8: Aunt Annie came down this afternoon. Uncle Edd came down this evening. We washed today. Quite a nice day.

Fri 9: We ironed today. We husked some corn.

Sat 10: Wanted to go to Scales Mound or Galena today but it looked so much like rain and had so much work to do, we didn't go. Lots of cars going by today.

Sun 11: This morning we all went to church. Came home ate a lunch, got out the car drove to Scales Mound. From there called up Will Tresidder's to ask if they were at home. They were so we went out. They had company, Minnie's sister and husband and son. Her brother and wife and another brother. The first time we were up there since I was a child I guess. Got home a little after dark. A very nice day.

Mon 12: Cloudy all day today. Didn't go to town again today. We husked corn today. Mamma churned today.

Tue 13: We autoed to Scales Mound this forenoon, all but Ma. Went called at Uncle Nick's . Brought home some flour and other provisions. The roads aren't very good in some places. Cloudy all day. Kind of misty at times.

Wed 14: Cloudy all day today. We took some of the corn out of the crib again. It was going poor. So much of it is so soft we don't know what to do with it.

Thu 15: We husked corn this morning. We washed this afternoon. This evening we went up to Uncle Edd's. A very beautiful day. Warm and nice.

Fri. 16: Another ideal day. We husked corn and hauled it in today. This evening Josie and Helen came up. Wanted us to sing and act a little song behind the curtains at the social at Independence. Think we'll try.

Sat 17: Another day quite warm. We all went to town in the car today. A very large crowd of people in town. Lots of cars. Didn't get all we wanted in town. Guess we'll have to go again soon.

Sun 18: Nice day only kind of chilly. Uncle Edds went out to Uncle Joe's this morning with Wins . Uncle George called up this forenoon. Said they were going to Galena to see Listons and they would come back here to supper. We all went to church this afternoon. Took the car. First time we ever had it up church. Only Tresidders and us at church. Uncle Georges were here when we got home. They started home again about six oclock. They took Corporal Siefert to Galena to go to Rockford.

Mon 19: We husked eighteen shocks of corn today. Also hauled in a load but didn't unload it. This evening Ruby & I went down to Weis' then Josie & Helen went with us over to Bessie's. We practiced our song or topsy-turvy piece.

Tue 20: Dad's birthday today. He is sixty-one years old. We washed today. baked bread, oatmeal cookies. Also husked some corn.

Wed. 21: We husked some corn today. And hauled in a load. Aunt Annie came down today.

Thu 22: Quite windy today. Dad and Ruby husked some corn. Reading day.

Fri 23: A lovely day only cold. Dad & Ruby husked and brought in a load today. We baked bread and coffee cake. A cake, drop cakes and corn bread today.

Sat 24: Well this afternoon we all autoed to Galena. There was so many folks and cars in town today. It was a little cold. Ma went up to Miss Read's about glasses. She didn't get through testing her eyes. Will have to go again.

Sun 25: Dad, Ma & Ruby went to church. I staid at home. A anti saloon man spoke. Uncle Edd & Aunt Annie came down to dinner. Aunt Annie and Mamma went up to Uncle Nick's with Tresidders this afternoon. Grahams and Monniers were there too. This evening we all went up to Fiedler's.

Mon 26: We husked twenty shocks of corn today. There is fourty-four left. It started to snow this afternoon and is still snowing tonight. Am very sorry.

Tue 27:   Dad went to town today with Della hitched in the buggy. Mamma churned today. This evening Josie & Helen and Bessie came here to practice.

Wed 28:   Baked bread, saffron cake and a batch of cookies today. Cloudy all day. This evening we went over to Independence School house with Weis. Bessie and Will, Josie, Bert and Helen to practice our piece and help get ready. Putting up the curtains, wrapping articles for the grab bag or fishing pond. Will & Bert went to Galena in their cars to get the pop, peanuts, candy gum etc. The roads are rather slippery for the car

Thu 29:   This is Thanksgiving day. Cloudy all day. We had a can of asparagus for dinner and squash pie. Ma baked our pies to take tonight two very cute squash pies. I made a cake this afternoon. We went to the sociable with Weis in their car. Went about half past six. The school house was jammed full there were thirty eight pies or lunches. Helen had a very good program. Our big piece (of standing on our heads) came off fairly well. The crowd just hooted. My pie sold for a dollar so did Ruby's. Archie Virtue bought Ruby's. he also had a Maybank's girl's pie. Charlie Virtue bought mine, also Cathrine Weis' and Ruth Falancer's pies. He certainly ought to have had enough to eat. After supper they fished. I fished twice got a horn once (Ruby did to) and a box of hair pins the second time. We got home twenty minutes to two. Had quite a nice time. They made fifty-three dollars and a quarter from the sale of the pies.

Fri 30: We hauled in a load of corn and unloaded it. Also husked a few shocks of corn. We have twenty-five shocks left yet. Lucille Tresidder is to have a social at the Center school tonight.

⁂

December

Sat 1: We husked corn today. Also hauled in a load. We have twenty-five shocks left. Uncle Edd and Aunt Annie came home from Apple River today.

Sun 2: Cloudy today. Mama, Ruby & I went to church this afternoon. We cam home did our chores and went up to Aunt Annie's to supper. Quite a few cars going by today.

Mon 3: We finished husking corn today. Also hauled in and unloaded a load. Have another load to haul in. A lovely day today. And the roads look swell. We oughtn't to have had any thing to do but go Auto riding. Agnes and Blanche came up this afternoon to get some lard.

Tue 4: Brought in the last of the corn today. Two small loads. Dad & Ruby hauled brush this afternoon to put in the bottom of the fodder stack. Ma churned this afternoon.

Wed 5: Cold today. Snowing a little this afternoon and evening. Wish it wouldn't snow anymore for a week or more. Would have hauled fodder today if Uncle Edd could have helped. Guess we won't haul it any more this week now. We washed today. Dad sold a pink man a load of old iron for five dollars today. Mostly an old reaper. Some of the iron was quite old.

Thu 6: Cold and clear today. Reading day. Cleaned the stalls this afternoon.

Fri 7: Quite cold today. We went to Galena with the car today. The roads were fine. Most of the snow worn off the roads. Had quite a time to crank the car before we came home. A man cranked it for us. We couldn't get it cranked. Helen rode part way home with us.

Sat 8: Very cold today. Mother isn't feeling very well.. Has pains in her stomach. Uncle Herman came in this evening from Woodbine. We were quite surprised. I should think he would have frozen on the way.

Sun 9: The weather was very cold today. But the autos are still arunning. Dad and Uncle Herman went up church this forenoon but there was no fire and nobody there. Uncle Edd and Aunt Annie came down this afternoon.

Mon 10: Clear and cold today. Uncle Herman and Dad hitched up Old Pet and Nellie together. Uncle Herman wanted to do it. Nellie didn't go very good. Uncle Herman would sell us Pet for fifty dollars. I wish we could buy her and get rid of Nellie. Uncle Herman went up to Uncle Edd's this evening. Ma isn't feeling very well yet.

Tue 11: Not quite as cold today. About ten oclock this morning Central called up John Tippetts. Said Alvin Hammers house was on fire. Wanted them to tell the neighbors. Quite an excitement. Dad went over. Rode over with John Tresidder. The house was nearly burnt down when they got there. There was lots of men there. But wasn't there in time to save anything much. They didn't save anything up stairs. Only some of the down stairs. There was a double floor in the room over the cellar. That saved the things in the cellar of course they had to work to save it. Mrs. And the children went down to Henry Huilman's. Ruby & I thought we would go over. We went across the field in Weis but it looked so far we came back again.

Wed 12: It is snowing this afternoon. Bessie Weis came over this afternoon. She came to get two roosters. Ruby carried one down as far as Weis for her.

Thu 13: Enough snow this morning for sleighing. Uncle Herman called here this afternoon. He was going out to Uncle Joe's today. Tomorrow he was going up to Apple River to try to sell Old Pet. There is going to be a horse buyer there. We wanted to buy Old Pet but not while we got Nellie. Didn't know what to do. So at last Dad said we would take her. For fifty dollars. We want to sell Nellie so badly. I guess Uncle Herman won't go up to Apple River now. Suppose he will go down to Woodbine and get his single harness and sho_____ and bring Pet back again.

Fri 14: We baked bread and coffee cake and oatmeal cookies today. Quite cold today

Sat 15: Uncle Herman came back about dinner time today and brought us Pet. This afternoon he and Dad went to Galena with Uncle Herman's horse. Busy with Sat. work today.

Sun 16: Uncle Herman and I went to Galena to church this morning. We went to the Methodist church. Got home ate dinner then went up to Union to church. Uncle Herman drove his horse in the buggy. Dad and Ruby went in the cutter with Pet. Jesse Williams was there. Came with Rev. Palmer.

Mon 17: Not quite as cold today. This afternoon Uncle Herman and Dad hitched up Violet and Pet and hauled fodder. They go quite nicely together. Toward evening Uncle Edd went up to Fiedler's. Aunt Annie rode along to here but only had a short time to stay. Ma and Ruby got their shoes and Dad his socks today that they sent for.

Tue 18: We washed today. Uncle Herman and Dad hauled fodder all day. Have a load to unload and another load to get yet.

Wed 19: Uncle Herman went up to John Tippet's to saw wood today for us. They sawed this afternoon at Uncle Edd's Dad and Ruby took twenty chickens over the Station today. Twelve roosters and eight hens. Got twenty-four dollars and fourty-nine cents. They drove Della and Pet. The first time they were hitched together. They went nicely.

Thu 20: Uncle Edd's finished sawing wood this forenoon and Tresidders sawed this afternoon. Uncle Herman helped for us. Dad and Ruby finished hauling fodder.

Fri 21: The snow is all gone now. A very nice warm clear day. I baked a cake this afternoon. We churned tonight. Uncle Herman started this forenoon for Apple River. He was expecting to stop at Scales Mound for dinner.

Sat 22: Dad, Ruby & I went to Galena today. Drove Pet and Della. Quite a crowd in town today. Folks running every which way. Lots of soldier boys from Camp Grant came home today for Xmas.

Sun 23: Quite cloudy today. Dad went to church this forenoon. The minister was there and another young man. But there was no fire and nobody else didn't come so Dad came home. Afterward Uncle Edd & Aunt Annie & John Tresidder came. It seems they couldn't get together so we didn't have any church. Uncle Edd and Aunt Annie came down here to dinner. We are invited up to Uncle Edd's for Christmas.

Mon 24: We got a letter and box from Uncle Thomas cards and a picture of Wayne from Wilbur and Olive. Dad got a shirt. Mother a crochet centerpiece or doily. Ruby a pr. Silk stockings and I a box of writing paper from Uncle Thomas. Mama went up to Aunt Annie's this forenoon to help Aunt Annie get ready. She is going to stay all night.

Tue 25: Christmas day. We went up to Aunt Annie's this forenoon. Win and Martha were there to. Had lots of good things to eat. Tresidders had been to Herbert's when they came home. Agnes, Milton and Blanche staid up there. John, Win and Dad went home did the chores and came back for supper. John and Ethel came over. Quite a crowd. For Christmas I got five dollars from Mama. Fifty cents from Grandpa. Perfume from Dad. Mittens from Uncle Edds. Writing paper from Uncle Thomas. A very clear bright Xmas. No snow. Quite a few cars on the road.

Wed 26:   We washed today. Cloudy today. Made out an order for a auto tire tonight. Rear anti skid 14.75.

Thu 27:   About nine oclock Helen called up. Wanted to know if we wanted to go along up to Davis'. Josie went up to Engel's. So Helen and I went up to Davis' this forenoon. Ruby was going to town with Papa. But before I left Uncle Herman came. He walked over from the Station. He said that there is horse buyer up at Scales Mound today. He came to help take Nellie up. So Dad and he drove Pet in the buggy and led Nellie. But he [horse buyer] wouldn't give but fifteen dollars so they brought her home again. Then they hitched Della and Pet in the hack and went to Galena to get the roosters that came by express from Hazel Green. Uncle Herman went back to Apple River from Galena. Helen and I had a very nice time at Davis'. we had dinner and supper there. Fannie Trevethan came there too in the afternoon. She Bernetta and Thelma came as far as the school house with us when we came home. It was getting quite dark. They have a very nice new house.

Fri 28:   A very cold day. Baked Graham bread today. Didn't get much done today.

Sat 29: Very cold today. Ten degrees or more below zero this morning. Busy with Saturday work. Aunt Annie went out to Apple River today.

Sun 30: Snowy today. We didn't go to church today. Ollie Popp was buried this afternoon at Galena. He died at the asylum. Agnes called up this afternoon. Wanted us to come down to supper. Didn't know if we should or not. We went. The kids had their Xmas tree lit up awhile.

Mon 31: Dad took Mother up to Scales Mound today. She was going to Apple River on the five train. Dad got home about six oclock. Well nineteen seventeen is nearly over. I hope this war will end before another year is over. Tomorrow I will start a new book for the year nineteen eighteen.

Goodbye 1917

1918

January

Tue 1: Not a very nice day for the beginning of a New Year. Cloudy and snowy. Not as cold today as it has been. Mother called up from Apple River this afternoon.

Wed 2: Quite a nice day. Didn't much done but chores. Our new tire came today by mail. It is a black and red justice anti skid. It came to fifteen dollars. Mamma called up tonight.

Thu 3: Reading day. Aunt Annie and Mamma came home today. They came to Galena and Uncle Edd got them from town.

Fri 4: Mother baked a batch of cookies today. We didn't do much else but chores today.

Sat 5: Dad, Ruby and I went to town today. Dad applied for the auto license today. Lots of cars in town today.

Sun 6: And awful blizzard today. Just awful windy and snowed all last night and today. But it cleared up tonight. No church today. A very lonesome day for a great many people I guess.

Mon 7:   A nice day. My but the snow banks some places and then some places there isn't any snow at all. The roads were all drifted shut. Mail man didn't get out this far till eleven oclock. Dad hauled down some wood from the woods this afternoon.

Tue 8:   We washed today. Also baked bread. Quite a nice day. We had asparagus for dinner today.

Wed 9:   Dad took twenty chickens over the station today. Got twenty-two dollars eighty cents for them. Doing a little sewing today. Callahan's sale today but Dad didn't go.

Thu 10:   Dad started out to go up to Scales Mound to a sale. When he was near Trevarthen's gate the runner of the cutter broke. So he came home again. Dad went to the telephone meeting at J.A. Weis' tonight. Started to snow again tonight.

Fri 11:   We baked bread and coffee cake today. It snowed today.

Sat 12:   It has been an awful blizzard. The wind blew all day so hard and it is worse than ever tonight. It is drifting so. Some awful drifts I guess. No mail today. Couldn't have hardly any fire today.

Sun 13: It wasn't windy today. It is all cleared up. But it is awful cold. Fiedlers came down this afternoon. The roads are all blockaded.

Mon 14: Lovly day today. But quite cold. Well the mail man went today. Had to go through fields. We didn't get any mail today. The trains are not running. Had to shovel some snow down by the mail box.

Tue 15: Mamma went to town with Tresidders today. Aunt Annie did too. In the sleigh. Mother say there were lots of people in town today. Mother bought a new ringer but didn't bring it out. We baked bread today. We got a letter from Uncle Thomas today.

Wed 16: Quite a nice day today. Sewing a little this afternoon.

Thu 17: Reading day. Quite cold again today. Not much news.

Fri 18: Baked bread and coffee cake also a cake today. Ruby went up to Aunt Annie's this afternoon. Heard through Martha having a letter from Westabys that Uncle Joe's little boy Harlan fell of the couch and broke his collar bone. John Westaby is married.

Sat 19: Papa went to town this forenoon with Pet hitched in the cutter. He took Nellie in to the horse buyers. John Tresidder went in with Papa. The buyer didn't want horses like Nellie. Said he would buy her the next time he came to town. Thought she ought to be worth fifty dollars. Lots of sleighs and cutters going by today.

Sun 20: Dad and Ruby drove Pet to church this forenoon. Not many up church. Uncle Edd and Aunt Annie came down to dinner and spent the afternoon.

Mon 21: Dad went to Galena this morning to get a sow. The stores and factories are all closed up today. The government ordered it to save coal. Some kicks coming I guess. A lovly moonlight evening.

Tue 22: We washed today. Pat McDonnell called here for dinner today. A lovly evening.

Wed 23: Snowy at times today. We baked bread and did a little sewing today. Dad cut a little wood this afternoon.

Thu 24: We ironed and baked a batch of cookies today. Gazette day today.

Fri 25: Quite a nice day today. Don't get much done only chores. Dad hauled down some wood this afternoon. Baked bread and coffee cake today.

Sat 26: Had another blizzard today. Lots of snow. Roads all full again I guess nobody ventured out to go to town. The mail man didn't go.

Sun 27: It wasn't such a bad day today between clear and cloudy. Ruby and I up to Aunt Annie's this afternoon. Didn't come home till after supper. Waded in snow above our knees.

Mon 28: A nice clear day today. The mail carrier went today. Hardly expected he would. Had to go thro fields mostly. Didn't get much accomplished today.

Tue 29: Papa went down to Tresidder's to help butcher today. Polly the dog has six puppies three black ones, one yellow one, one brown and one white one.

Wed 30: Ma went down to help Agnes with the pork this afternoon. We baked bread today.

Thu 31: Awful cold today. Clear. Reading day. Milton called in tonight to see the pups. Making aprons and caps today.

February

Fri 1: Thirty degrees below zero this morning. But it was only eighteen below here. Very clear. There was a little calf this morning. Dad and Ruby went to town today. Got a hundred of flour a barrel of salt and lots of groceries.

Sat 2: Baked bread, saffron cake, a cake and oatmeal cookies today. Cold as usual today.

Sun 3: Clear and cold today. Rather windy. Mamma and I started to go to church walking. When we got up past John Weis' we met John Tresidder coming back said it was all drifted up on the level could hardly walk through it. Said there was no fire there. I guess he didn't see any smoke. Tresidders all came up this afternoon. They staid to supper Blanche liked the little puppies.

Mon 4: Very cold again today sixteen below here. Didn't do much but chores. Combellick's sale tomorrow. Would like to go.

Tue 5: An awful stormy day today. So awfully windy and drifting. An awful day for Combellick's sale. Thought surely they wouldn't have it. But by noon it got better the wind went down. A few teams went along. Dad and Ruby went in the cutter. They say there wasn't but a handfull of men there. But I guess thing all went fairly well.

Wed 6: A lovly day all clear and quite warm. The snow settled a lot today. Uncle Edd brought Aunt Annie down this forenoon. Had dinner here. This evening Uncle Edd, John and Ethel came down. They think the dogs are awfully cute.

Thu 7: The sow we bought had seven little pigs last night. Three were dead and the others nearly. Had them in the house warming nearly all day. A terrible time. We washed this afternoon. Also baked bread today. Worked awfully hard today. It was awfully windy this afternoon.

Fri 8: Had the little pigs in all last night. Fed them on the bottle. Ma didn't go to bed last night till three oclock so as to keep them warm. Got them in again tonight. One is nearly dead. Ironed today. An awful stormy day. Quite warm. Then it rained very icy. It thundered and lightened this afternoon and this evening. It is colder this evening and snowing.

Sat 10: Dad and Ruby went to town today. Took Old Nellie in again. But to our dissapointment they brought her home again. One fellow said he would give fourty dollars. But said to wait till the other fellow came. Then they nearly got in a fight and went off and hadn't come back yet when they came home. Lots of horses in there to sell. The little pigs are quite lively now another calf today.

Sun 10:   Quite warm today. Ma, Ruby and I went to church this afternoon. Eleven there.

Mon 11:   Another warm day. Don't get any thing done but chores. Willie, Mary and Raymond Fiedler came down from school to see the puppies. Dad drowned four this forenoon. So there was only two for them to see.

Tue 12:   Well today is the Studier-Meusel wedding. Fiedlers went along this morning. The roads are just terrible. So much water. Heard that Studier's horses got down and broke the tongue this morning. Fiedlers came home just before dark. And Herman and Ester Studier didn't get home till after dark. They went on a wedding trip. It's just been months today that the other Mrs. Studier died. Also Ella Dittmar's wedding day.

Wed 13:   Warm again today. Snow going fast. Dad chopped wood. Heard it took Studiers about four hours to go to town yesterday. They got in at nine oclock.

Thu 14:   A piece in the Gazette about the wedding. It says they took a wedding trip to St. Louis and several towns in

Illinois. Ella and Charlie Siemen went to Parkusburgh, Iowa to get married Tuesday. A dark rainy day.

Fri 15: Baked bread and saffron bread and cookies today. Dad cutting wood.

Sat 16: Doing Sat. work today. Rev. Mr. Palmer came this evening to stay all night. Didn't have any room in the stable but had to make room.

Sun 17: Dad and Ruby went to church with the preacher this forenoon. Dad and Ma went up to Uncle Edd's this evening. A nice day.

Mon 18: Joe and John Weis sent a car load of hogs today. Chas. Berryman's sale at the station today. Dad chopping wood today.

Tue 19: One little pig dead this morning. Had a little lamb last night. First one. It rained last night. This evening it has turned cold and its awful icy. Got a letter from Uncle Thomas today. Anna is home yet. Said he didn't know when she would go back.

Wed 20: A very cold day. We washed a very big washing today also baked bread.

Thu 21: Dad went to Barney Mahan's sale today. Aunt Annie came down today. It is just terrible icy. Man or beast can hardly stand on their feet.

Fri 22: Ruby went up to Aunt Annie's this forenoon to get Mother's glasses. Aunt Annie took them by mistake. Aunt Annie is going to Apple River today. Busy ironing. Mrs. Weis and Josie and Helen came up this evening. Washington's Birthday today.

Sat 23: Busy with Sat. work today. Just a lovly day. Quite warm. Quite a few folks went to town today. One sleigh had a mud ride I guess.

Sun 24: Dad, Ruby & I went to church this afternoon. Not many there. Uncle Edd was out to Apple River since yesterday. Walked up church with the preacher. Fielders were down to Tresidder's this afternoon. Coming home he came in to invite us to some kind of a "time" at Studier's tomorrow night. They are in town now. This evening Herman told them that they had gone to Chicago. So Mrs. Fiedler called up everybody saying it was off for the time. Dad Ruby and I went to Tresidder's today.

Mon 25: Bessie Weis called up Mrs. Fiedler saying it wasn't so that Studiers had gone to Chicago. Herman was just fooling. Herman had gone in after them. Mr. and Mrs. Fiedler got quite mad. Said they wasn't going to have anything more to do with it. So this afternoon Bessie Weis said she was going over tonight. So Will asked John Tippet and told Weis' over here to tell Edd W. and John Tresidder. I heard the other Studiers came over. A very queer thing I think. I'm awfully disappointed. Fiedlers wouldn't go over. Uncle Edd was down today. Helped Dad kill a pig. Uncle Edd say Will Siefert has to go to North Carolina this week. Henry Zarndt has to go to. Don't know if Jack Combellick has to go to or not.

Tue 26: Ma and Dad busy about the pork. I baked graham bread today. Aunt Annie came home from A.R. today.

Wed 27: I hear that some of the Guilford boys had another sheveri on the Studiers last night. I went up to Aunt Annie's this afternoon to get some things she brought us from town yesterday also a frying pan. Aunt Annie wasn't at home she was down to Martha's. Dad hauling wood down today. Twenty-three young men left for camp Grant at noon today.

Thu 28: Had quite a lot of snow again last night. Reading day again today. Had a little lamb in the house now. It is so very little and weak. If it lives I guess we will have to feed it on the bottle.

March

Fri ~~29~~ 1:   Dad went to town today with Pet in the buggy. Got fifty pounds of flour. Had to get 25 lb of others stuff with it such as oatmeal, rice, corn meal, etc. Took seven and one-half dozen eggs to town only got thirty five cents a dozen. Said they came down ten cents a dozen since yesterday. A dirty shame I call that.

Sat 2:   Ma went to town with Tresidder's today. The roads are awful muddy.

Sun 3:   Ma and Ruby went to church this forenoon. Uncle Edd and Aunt Annie came down to dinner. We has asparagus (canned) for dinner. Tresidders came up this afternoon. Blanche liked the little pupps and lamb and pig.

Mon 4:   One sheep is sick. Hope she will get better. The little pig is sick to. It is so awfully muddy now. The roads must be terrible. Took some calves down to Tresidder's for J.A. Weis to dehorn.

Tue 5:   We washed an awful big washing today. The little pig was dead this morning. Feel so bad about it. After we bothered so much with it.

Wed 6:   Mamma, Ruby and I went up to Aunt Annie's tonight. Uncle Dan is up there came out from Galena last night.

Thu 7:   Reading day. Uncle Dan came down this afternoon. A lovly evening tonight. There is northern lights tonight. The sky was all colors red also. I never saw such northern lights before. Extended almost all over the sky. Another sheep had two large lambs tonight. Making twelve lambs from seven ewes. The sick sheep seems to be getting some better.

Fri 8:   Made bread and saffron cake today. Uncle Dan went up to Aunt Annie's this afternoon. He's going to Woodbine tomorrow. He is going to work for Uncle Ben again this year. Tige and Buster the puppies are getting so cute now.

Sat 9:   Just an awful day. So windy. And it snowed just a little and quite cold. Nobody much going to town. Didn't do much baking.

Sun 10: No services at Union today. Rev. Mumford is going to preach at Council Hill this afternoon and evening. Rev. Palmer to preach at White Oak and Scales Mound tonight. This afternoon Ruby and I went over to Sadie Bastian's. J. Tresidders and Mary Westaby were there too. Mary W. was on her way to church. She didn't know that there wasn't any church.

Mon 11: Our little lamb died this morning. Dad chopping wood. Ma and Ruby did some sewing. Don't know anything new.

Tue 12: Just a lovly day today. So warm. I helped Dad chop wood this afternoon.

Wed 13: An awfully bad day today. It rained nearly all forenoon and just awfully windy all day. It was so dark this forenoon we lit a light. We baked bread today. The mail carrier didn't go today.

Thu 14: A nicer day than yesterday because it isn't so windy. It snowed today.

Fri 15: Dad and Ruby hauled down wood with the sleigh today. I made out an order for some seeds today. To Salzer's in Lacrosse.

Sat 16: A very nice day. Dad went over to Guilford with Fiedler. J. Weis and Studier to the Bap. Caucus. Mr. Brickner running against Werner for Road Comissioner. They thought if Brickner got it there wouldn't be much done to our road. Werner got put on.

Sun 17: Another lovly day. So warm. Mother and Ruby went to church this forenoon. Then from church they went up to Aunt Annie's. Dad and I went up there to dinner to. Agnes, Milton, & Blanche came up there to. Johnnie & Win were there awhile in the afternoon. The roads dried quite a little today. The snow bank up by Uncle Edd's is quite high yet.

Mon 18: We washed today. Just a lovly day quite windy and very warm nearly summer heat. The road is about all dry along here. I sent for a white waist today for one-ninety-eight to Sears.

Tue 19: Another very nice day. So warm. Dad went to Galena today with Old Pet to get gasoline for wood sawing and to get some other things.

Wed 20: Another lovly day. Awfully warm. The roads are most dried up. I guess only where there is snow banks yet. Werners dragged the road today. Guess I will have to get the car fixed up.

Thu 21: We sawed wood today. Will Weis brought up the saw with the tractor. They sawed about an hour after dinner. Nick Weis came along looking at nigger this forenoon. They were over to Weis'. They came along this evening. We gave them Buster the little puppy. We gave him the choice of the two. I'm sorry now that I didn't keep that one myself now. I guess Nick almost bought nigger for a hundred-fifty dollars.

He is coming over tomorrow morning. Aunt Annie came down with Uncle Edd this morning. This evening Uncle Edd went out to Apple River. Mrs. Mary Reed is to be buried tomorrow forenoon. Aunt Annie came down again this evening to stay all night.

Fri 22:   Well Poor Nigger is gone. I believe Nick took him kind of on trial. Don't know for sure if he will keep him or not. Nick said Rawland named the little pup Tanner.

Sat 23:   Quite a nice day. Ruby and I walked over the station this afternoon and went to Apple River in the five-fifteen train. Had a nice walk called at the store awhile. Paul Merrifield tried to sell us all kinds of things. Mary Gesselbracht was on the train going to Scales Mound. She said her brother Will had died at Scales Mound today. Grandpas and Uncle Georges didn't know it until we told them. He had been visiting out to Apple River and had just gone up to Scales Mound on the morning train (eight-thirty) had staid all night at Grandpa's and ate a hearty breakfast. It shocked them so when we told them. He hadn't been feeling very well. Said his heart bothered him. He died at Paul Stadel's. He went there because he didn't feel well. He died while Mrs. S. had gone to fix a bed for him. We had supper at Grandpa's then went up the store this evening. Lots of cars in town.

Sun 24: We went to Pres. Church this morning. Had dinner at Grandpa's. Went up to Uncle George's this afternoon. Had supper there. Went with them to the Methodist church. They are having meetings there. The town is just alive with cars.

Mon 25: We came home this morning. Teachers institute at Galena this week and all the school teachers went from the stations along the way. I've been working at the automobile all afternoon. More to do yet. Wanted to try it this after. But the pump won't work anymore. Got one and a half pumped up. Was thinking something of going to the funeral. But I guess we can't go. It is cloudy. Rained a little tonight.

Tue 26: We didn't go to the funeral today. The car wasn't hardly ready. And didn't hardly like to go so far for the first time. Mother didn't feel well enough to go. Uncle Edd & Aunt Annie didn't go either. We took the car out this afternoon. It didn't go good so we took it down to Bert. He run it up the hill and back. He said it was all right. I found out a few things of him I wanted to know.

Wed 27: We washed today. Clayton Combellick bought two cows and a calf of us today. One for eighty-five and the other for ninety-five dollars. One is what we call mother's cow. The other is the spotted one. Dad,

Ruby & I went to Scales Mound in the car today. The roads are all fairly good only in one place it was quite bad. Afraid we would get stuck. Got the car muddy. Was up to see Uncle Nick & Aunt Lizzie.

Thu 28:   Ma and Ruby ironed today. I washed and shined up the car.

Fri 29:   Dad and Ruby went to town today to take in Old Nellie to the horse buyers again. But he wasn't there. I believe he had been there but there wasn't any horses so he went away. It beat everything. This makes the fourth time she was taken to the horse buyer. A very nice day. Lots of cars on the road today. This evening Herman came. He was out to Schapville to church this morning. This is Good Friday.

Sat 30:   Quite a nice day. Uncle Herman went up to Aunt Annie's this forenoon and he is going to Galena today. Baked bread, coffee cake, cake and oatmeal cookies today. I raked some lawn today. A good many card going along today. We heard that Freda Kloth and Squire Chetlain are to be married tonight. Tomorrow is Easter. Tonight at two oclock all the clocks are supposed to be put ahead an hour. I believe next fall it is to be set back again. Some body is gone crazy I guess.

Sun 31: Easter Sunday today. Ma, Ruby & I went to church this forenoon. Uncle Edd and Aunt Annie and Blanche came here to dinner. John, Agnes & Milton came up this afternoon. Just terribly windy today. March going out like a lion I guess. Lots of cars on the road today. A lovly evening tonight.

April

Mon 1: A very nice day. Nearly to warm. Dad hauled manure. I raked some lawn.

Tue 2: Dad, Ruby and I autoed over to Guilford to the election this forenoon. Of course I couldn't vote so didn't go in. The roads are so nice. This afternoon we all autoed to Galena. Didn't know if we should go or not. It started to rain and thunder. We stopped down at John's for awhile. It hailed some. But it looked brighter so we went on. It didn't rain much. Ruby went to the dentist.

Wed 3: Much cooler today. I finished raking lawn. Lots of cars on the road this afternoon. Dad hauling manure.

Thu 4: We washed this afternoon. Quite a nice day. I sent to Sears Roebuck this morning for a spring coat of wool velour, pekin blue. I hope I will like it and that it will fit alright.

Fri 5: We ironed today. Ruby has an awful toothache or neuralagia.

Sat 6: It rained nearly all day today. A lovly rain only rather cold. They were going to have a parade in town today to celebrate it is a year ago today that U.S. declared war.

Sun 7: Very windy today. Dad, Ruby & I went to church this afternoon. Quite a few there. We are invited over to Young's next Sun. to dinner.

Mon 8: Quite cool but clear today. Dad hauling manure. I got my coat. Quite satisfactory every way but the color is quite a prominent green (pekin). Don't know if I should send it back and get medium blue or not. It's rather pretty.

Tue 9: Well we all went to Galena this afternoon. The roads were quite rough. Ruby had a tooth fixed. Uncle Edd and Aunt Annie went out to Apple River last night came back to Galena this morning. Aunt Tillie is quite poorly. Uncle Edds are staying over in Tippet's house getting ready for them to come home. They started this morning. They went over there and called awhile.

Wed 10: This morning Dad shot poor Polly. Our little black dog. It nearly killed him to do it. But the assersor would be around soon and it is such a high tax on female dogs. He shot her while she was sleeping. We took her up on the hill side near the woods and buried her near Bounce's grave and Buster's. I'm afraid poor little Tige will be lonesome now. We washed this afternoon.

Thu 11: We ironed today. A piece on the Gazette today about Annie Kloth's wedding to Mr. Zimmerman.

Fri 12:   Ma and Ruby drove Pet to Galena for the first time. They got along alright. Ruby had to go in to the dentist. They called on Uncle Edd and Aunt Annie in town.

Sat 13:   Quite a nice day. Don't know what to do about going over to Youngs. Ma thinks we can hardly stay away all day. Mr & Mrs. Tippet and Mattie & Mary came home tonight.

Sun 14:   A very nice day. Well we all autoed to church this morning. Then went over to Young's. The road wasn't very good. Ben and Ehmer was up church with their car. Then Sadie and Evelyn rode over with them. And Wilbur drove over. Mr. Polchow was over there. We staid for dinner and supper. Saw their new player piano. Had to play some on it. We had playing and singing. We came home the other way. The roads were much better that way. Only hilly.

Mon 15:   I transplanted asparagus today. It is raining tonight. Hope it will make the grass grow. We got a letter for Al today. Also a picture of Alvin & Nancy on a postal card.

Tue 16:   We washed this afternoon. Dad started to plow the garden but didn't get it all plowed.

Wed 17:   Rained all day today. We wanted to make garden today but couldn't. We ironed.

Thu 18: We got a letter from Uncle Thomas today Anna is at home yet. Dad, Ruby & I burned brush this afternoon. Mr. Baus the assessor was around this afternoon. He left a plate to go on the dog's collar. The number is 2488. So Tige will have to wear a collar soon.

Fri 19: We burned brush again this afternoon. Have some more to burn yet. Ruby & I also cut down three haw trees. Ma baked bread and coffee cakes.

Sat 20: Well Dad & Ruby took Nellie in to the horse buyer again. Awfully ashamed to take her again. This time they saw the buyer. Wouldn't give but fifteen dollars for her. So Dad didn't sell her. Brought her back again. Wish he would have sold her for fifteen dollars. It has snowed almost all afternoon. Very nasty and cold.

Sun 21: Snowy and rainy all day. Didn't have any services at Union on account of the weather. Ma, Ruby & I prodded up to Aunt Annie's this afternoon. Staid to supper.

Mon 22: This morning Dad took two hogs over the Station. He got one-hundred four dollars for the two. One weighed three hundred and the other three hundred fourty. Dad drove Violet and Pet. We were rather worried.

The first time for a long time that Violet was taken anywhere. But he got along alright. Planted thirty-strawberry plants today. Bought of Vandervatt.

Tue 23: Quite a snow storm this morning. Came down thick and fast but it cleared up so we washed this afternoon. Ruby started to clean rag room.

Wed 24: I went up to Aunt Annie's and got some strawberry plants and horse radish. Also got some everbearing strawberry plants from Agnes. I planted them this evening.

Thu 25: Well Ma and Ruby went to town again with Pet. Poor Pet she is all blind now. I planted onion sets today and finished the ironing. This evening at half-past eight or nine Rev. Elwin and Ehmer Palmer and their mother came to stay all night. I guess they had intended to stay at Combellick's or Bastian's but some of Combellicks had gone to town. They all came in a buggy with one little horse.

Fri 26: The Palmers went over to Combellick's this forenoon. We have been very busy today. Mama and I put in quite a little garden. But have some more to put in yet. Ruby's coat came this morning. It is quite nice. I think it is more of a Copenhagen blue than a military blue. It has a tan collar. Ma & Ruby brought home the wall paper and auto tire pump yesterday. It came by express. We couldn't get it to work. So this evening Dad, Ruby & I drove up to John Tippet's. He put in a little oil and it works but not nearly so good as Johnnie's.

Sat 27: Well this morning it was so cloudy and looked very much like rain. It misted a little. But we got ready and went about eleven oclock. Ma wouldn't go. Well we put our car in Gundry's Yard had a fine place for it. Then I went and bought a hat. It is burndt straw and has daisies on it. Paid five-seventy-five for it at least three dollars too much. Then we went down to the depot to see the Boys go away to Camp Grant. A terrible crowd and the train come in from the east that brought the soldier boys from Camp Grant. Also a band. Then we saw the parade. Quite a parade. Then went over the park. Heard Judge Landis speak. A very funny looking man. Then a officer that had been over in the war for several years. And a officer from Camp Grant. Then when we went over town it was nearly time to go home. Dad said he saw Wesley. He said he had an accident on the way down between Weis' and Tresidder's. The car (his Ford) had gone in the ditch went over the bridge. It seems as though he couldn't steer it. He was near there fixing a puncture when we went to town. We stopped on the way home to see it as everybody else did. My it's a terrible sight. You would think it hardly possible that he went in with it without getting hurt. Half of the windshield is broken and steering rod broken or bent and some other things.

Sun 28: It rained nearly all night last night. A cloudy today. Ma, Ruby & I went to church but there wasn't anybody else there. Uncle Edd and Aunt Annie came down this afternoon. About five oclock a automobile went by then after awhile it came back. It was Wesley, a Barrett and another fellow. They came in to take off the tire. For fear they would get stolen. They were here to supper. I guess the roads were worse than they expected. They went down again took off the tires. He left them here. We asked them to stay over night and get the car out tomorrow. Wesley and one fellow was willing, but I guess Barrett didn't want to. So they went home. Guess it was pretty late before they got home.

Mon 29: Awful windy last night. Cloudy all day today. I bake oatmeal drop cookies this afternoon. Took the things out of my room.

Tue 30: Well Ruby & I papered my room today. Ma pasted some of it. It went on quite fast. It is rather blue. The border is of blue crysanthums. It cleared off today.

May

Wed 1: A very beautiful day. Ma & Ruby went to Galena again today. Drove Pet. We got a card from Aunt Tillie today. Dad hauling manure. I baked bread and a cake.

Thu 2: This forenoon Uncle George, Wesley, and Edward came in. They were here to dinner. After dinner they went to work to get the car out of the ditch. About three oclock I went down to watch them. Agnes & Blanche came there too. Mr. Weis and Bert and John Tresidder and Uncle Edd and Dad were helping. We had to help pull it out of the ditch too. Took it out through the creek into Weis' bottom. It wasn't working right so they couldn't take it home. Wesley is going to come in again tomorrow to fix it.

Fri 3: Edward staid all night up to Aunt Annie's. Wesley and Mr. White came in to for the car. Edward came down here this afternoon. They didn't come to supper. After we had waited for hours. After dark they came up with both cars. They started out but the Ford wouldn't climb the school house hill. At ten oclock they came back for a rope to tow it if they could.

Sat 4: Dad drove Pet to town this morning. He wanted to go in with the car but I didn't want to go till afternoon. Ruby & I wanted to take the car this afternoon but Ma wouldn't let us. So I asked if I could go with John. So I did. Lots of people in town. Thirty boys left for Jefferson Barracks this afternoon. Poor fellows. Mr. & Mrs. Tippet had a small celebration for their sixtieth wedding anniversary today. Hot weather today.

Sun 5: We all went to church this morning. This afternoon we autoed out to Apple River. Had a little visit. Uncle Herman was there and Uncle George awhile after supper. Aunt Maggie, Aunt Tillie, Uncle George, Dad and I drove out to West Ella Cemetery and back to give them a little ride. Aunt Tillie is so poorly. Then we came back to Scales Mound. We called at Uncle Nick's. We were quite shocked. Uncle Nick tried to cut his throat with a razor yesterday afternoon. As Aunt Lizzie was upstairs taking a bath. He didn't cut it so very deep tho, didn't cut any veins or arteries. The doctor sewed it up again. He was sitting up on the bed. His mind wanders. Stellas & Maymes were up there today. Ehmer Palmer was going to preach up to Scales Mound this evening. Ruby wanted to go. The weather didn't look so very good. Didn't know if we should go to church or not. We went out before he was through preaching. We could look out the top part of the window and it looked so black. I just couldn't stand to stay any longer. But I didn't look so very bad. It was a quarter to ten when we got home.

Mon 6: Well it didn't rain last night. But I did rain nearly all afternoon. Ma went up to Aunt Annie's this forenoon. And staid till after dinner. Ruby and Ma cleaned Ma's room today. Dad plowed a little. John Weis told Ma that Henrys and Will Ehlers were to Cuba City in Henry's car yesterday. Two girls were driving a Ford and knocked over a man that was stopping fixing his auto. He didn't see the Ford and stepped before it. Henry Weis saw it and stopped the girls became excited and ran into Weis and broke up their car quite badly. And Will Ehler's little boy got cut on the face quite badly.

Tue 7: Cleaned the bed room today. But didn't get the carpet down or things in. Helen called up this evening. She said Miss Virtue told her to ask us to her picnic at Miner's School next Saturday. Helen said we should come to her picnic to the twenty-second of May.

Wed 8: We started to wash today. But it rained nearly all afternoon so we didn't hang any out. I baked bread and patty cakes.

Thu 9: Mother washed today. Ruby finished cleaning the parlor. Awfully windy today. We got a card from Uncle Thomas today. He said Olive has the inflammatory rhumatism. Has to be fed. She and Wilbur are staying at Uncle Thomas'. Wayne is at Al.

Fri 10: Quite a nice day today. We baked bread coffee cake and a cake today. Ruby cleaned the hall but didn't get the stair carpet down. I hear that they are tearing up Burton's bridge and we can't cross it anymore. I believe folks have to go through Marsden's and out to the Elizabeth road. Guess we'll have to trade at Scales Mound now.

Sat 11: Well Ruby & I and Agnes, Blanche and Milton went over to Miners School to the picnic. About thirty-five there. Sadie & Evelyn B. and Lottie and Mrs. Young were there. Had a nice dinner. Quite cool and it looked quite rainy so it broke up quite early. Got home again about half past three. There is going to be a picnic up at our school next Saturday. Dad went up to Scales Mound this afternoon. Got home after nine.

Sun 12: We all went to church this morning. Mother went along up with Uncle Edd & Aunt Annie. Dad, Ruby & I came home then went up with the car.

About four oclock it started to rain and we hurried home. It didn't rain very much. This evening Ruby & I went down to 'Weis'. Will & Bessie were there too. They brought us home in their car. Pa & Ma wasn't home yet. They went down to John's. Uncle Edd and Aunt Annie was there also. Mrs. Young and Ben and Elmer. Elmer thinks he will be one of the boys that have to go away soon. I guess in several weeks.

Mon 13: Nice day only cold. We put in more garden today and stretched two pair curtains. I went up to Aunt Annie's. Took up several thinks and got more strawberry plants but planted them this evening.

Tue 14: Well today is a nice day. We washed and ironed today. Milton got two settings of eggs this evening.

Wed 15: Took the things out of the dining room today. Mamma white washed the ceiling. I went up on Tresidder's hill and picked asparagus late this afternoon.

Thu 16: Dad and Ruby planted corn today. They finished it but it got rather late. John Tippet came down this evening to get some seed corn. Mother and started to paper late this afternoon. Got some on. A very nice day. A week from Saturday seventy-four boys have to leave again. I guess Ehmer Young and Herman

Studier will have to go soon but don't know if they will have to go then or not. I guess all of the first class will have to go very soon.

Fri 17: We papered this forenoon. We wanted to go to the Ford's school picnic but just as we was about to get ready it came up to a storm so we didn't go. My it looked like it was going to be a terrible storm. It rained quite a lot. Agnes, Blanche and Milton went to the picnic before the storm. John had to go after them. Ruby & I finished papering today. Autumn leaf border. It looks quite a little like the old paper.

Sat 18: Busy as usual on Saturday. Not much travel on the road now days. On account of the bridge being gone I guess.

Sun 19: We all went to church this afternoon. Dad & Ma rode. Ruby & I walked. Rather cloudy all day. This evening it came up to a storm again. My but it looked awfully bad. It rained just awfully hard. It cleared off again before the sun went down.

Mon 20: We washed today. Quite a nice day. Milton and Blanche came up for two dozen eggs this afternoon. The first time Blanche ever came up alone with Milton. She is awfully cute. Says such funny things. Quite smart.

Tue 21: We ironed today. Got a letter from Sears Roebuck saying that they didn't have the linoleum in twelve feet lengths. They sent the money back. Quite disappointed. Don't know what we will do now. Dad and Ruby went over the Station. Took eggs over and got some things. They thought the rocking chair might be there but it wasn't. I went up on Tresidder's hill to pick asparagus this afternoon. Blanche & Milton went to. Had quite a storm tonight. Water got quite high.

Wed 22: Ruby & I went over to Independence to Helen's picnic today. We bought five chances on a cow to be given away for Red Cross one dollar a chance. We drove Pet took Blanche along and Milton rode home with us to. Quite a crowd over there. Had a nice time and lots to eat. It is Helen's first year. It was cloudy but turned out to be nice in the afternoon. I cut some lawn this evening. About the first I cut this year.

Thu 23: I cut lawn today. Ma & Ruby cleaned the pantry. It says in the Gazette that twenty-five young men have to leave for Jefferson Barracks tomorrow and seventy-four Saturday to Georgia. Not many I know only Tony Grube is to go.

Fri 24: It rained again nearly all forenoon. It cleared off this afternoon. We baked bread, coffee cake and a cake today. I want to go to Galena tomorrow. Don't know how to get there.

Sat 25: Well all forenoon it looked so much like a storm but by about one oclock it passed off so Dad & I got ready hitched up Pet. But it was so hot we couldn't drive very fast. Left Pet at Marsden's walked over the bridge. My it was a terrible thing to walk over. One of the men helped me over. Just walked on a few irons and hold on the railing. As we were walking down the ~~Ill Centr~~ North Western track the whistles blew. The boys were leaving (seventy-four). My I am so disappointed. I heard some say it was so sad. The boys cried pitifully they said. The town was full of people today. Had a sale on the street for the red cross today. Had for sale calves, a pony, poultry, rabbits, pigeons, an owl, several dogs, one wee puppy, furniture, corn, potatoes, canned fruit, and just everything. We walked up the I.C. track.

Sun 26: Mr. & Mrs. John Tippet have a son born today. Ma, Ruby & I went to church this morning. Mrs. Young & Ben & Elmer and Uncle Edd & Aunt Annie came down from church. They were here to dinner and supper. Elmer expects to enlist in the navy soon. Uncle Edd and Aunt Annie are Grandpa and Grandma now. Quite proud I guess. John Tresidders came up in their car this evening.

Mon 27: It rained and stormed this forenoon again. The mail didn't come today.

Tue 28: We washed today. Dad and Ruby went over the Station this afternoon. To get a rocking chair that came by freight. Took over twenty-four dozen eggs.

Wed 29: Rained this forenoon again. People can't get their corn in. We ironed today. Hope it will clear up soon.

Thu 30: No mail today. It is declaration day today. Uncle Edd and Aunt Annie came down this forenoon. Uncle Edd sheared the sheep for us. We got sixty-pounds of wool. We all went out late this afternoon and replanted corn. We got all over the place awfully tired.

Fri 31: Ma, Ruby & I went up to Aunt Annie's this forenoon to help paper the dining room. We didn't get started to paper till after dinner. We worked awfully hard but got about half of the sides paper yet. I came home after supper. Ma staid all night. It stormed and rained again tonight. I sent for a white skirt today.

June

Sat 1: I canned three pints of asparagus this forenoon. This afternoon Ruby & I drove Pet up to Scales Mound. Took up twelve dozen eggs and got some bread, cookies and so on. Had a nice ride. Quite a nice day. Dad plowing today.

Sun 2: A very nice day. We all went to church this afternoon. After church we did the chores and ate supper and went up to Uncle Nick's in the car. The first time for a long time that we had a auto ride. The roads were quite good. Got home by half past nine. The minister and his mother rode around this way on their way home from church. Elmer Young is going to Chicago this evening to enlist in the Navy. He thinks he will be back again.

Mon 3: Raining again all day. Can't get any thing don. I baked cookies this afternoon. The strawberries are just starting to ripen.

Tue 4: Ma and Ruby washed today. Quite a nice day.

Wed 5: Ironed today. Helen called up this afternoon said there is going to be a red cross sale over to Guilford at the Taylor School or in Tobin's pasture next Sunday. The worst thing I heard yet. They are going to serve or sell ice cream and cake and pop and such things. Just like Guilford.

Thu 6:   Agnes, Blanche & Milton came up this afternoon to get some eggs. Mary, Raymond & Edith were down this morning. We planted some potatoes this evening.

Fri 7:   A very nice day. Finished planting potatoes today. Also planted a little sorghum. I also went up to Aunt Annie's this forenoon and picked the asparagus on the hill.

Sat 8:   A nice day. This afternoon Mamma went out to Uncle Joe's & Henry's with Martha Tippet. They drove one horse in a buggy. Martha wanted to go home and wanted company that why mother got to go. Dad, Ruby & I autoed to Scales Mound. Burton's bridge isn't fixed yet. We called at Uncle Nick's. When we got home we saw the eclipse of the sun. I guess it was before but we didn't notice it. The sun was shining all the while. Yet it got quite a little darker it looked queer like the moon at times.

Sun 9:   Dad, Ruby & I went to church this forenoon not very many there. Elmer Young has joined the Navy and gone to Seattle Wash. He went Fri. He went to Chicago last Sun night to enlist there. He thought he could stay at the Great Lakes camp. But they sent him to Wash. Well today was the great Red Cross sale at Guilford. We didn't go. But most of the folks from around here went. It looked stormy this after but didn't rain much. Just scared some of the folks I guess. This evening we autoed up to Aunt Annie's. Took Aunt Annie out for a ride up as far as Singer ~~Grave~~ Cemetery. Then we went down to John's. It come to rain. We came home quick but it got the car all wet. And had quite a time getting up back of the shed. It was slippery. John & Milton was over to the sale. Had two auctioneers. Had all kind of refreshments for sale also a gambling wheel or whatever you call it. Siegel had a load of fish to sell.

Mon 10: Mother got home about half past eleven today. Dad started to plow corn today. They are grading the road with Weis' tractor today. Above and below Fiedler's. Haven't got down this far yet.

Tue 11: They were grading the road by here this afternoon. Aunt Annie is out to Apple River to the Sunday school convention. Went yesterday so she said we could pick her strawberries. Mother and I went up and picked them. Didn't get very many. Ruby finished cleaning the cellar today.

Wed 12: We washed today. Also picked some cherries. Also put up strawberries.

Thu 13:   I got a card today from the Great Lakes Training station. Surprise. Reading day. Put up

~~Thu 13~~   cherries today. Quite a number of boys have to go away again tomorrow to Kansas City to several auto schools. Some are enlisted boys and some drafted. Clifford Tresidder has to go tomorrow. Also Frank Allen, Bessie's brother.

Fri 14:   Well Dad, Ruby & I went to Galena today to see the boys go away. We took the car as far as Marsden's. Then walked. The bridge isn't done and don't know when it will. They don't work on it anymore. Quite a few boys went. Minnie, Lucille & I guess Clifford's girl was in to see him off. Poor fellows.

Sat 15:   Just killed with work. Then just at dinner time. Rev. Palmer came. Then it took so much longer about dinner and that. Dad cut the alfalfa today. We baked bread, coffee cake, oatmeal drop cakes, a cake, and stoned and put up three quarts cherries, picked strawberries and cleaned up, pumped auto tires, oiled and greased the car and etc and etc.

Sun 16:   This forenoon Uncle George, Aunt Lizzie, Wesley, Edward, and Grandpa, Aunt Maggie and Aunt Tillie autoed in to Aunt Annie's. This afternoon we all went to church. Uncle George, Aunt Lizzie,

Maggie, & Edward were up there. Uncle George drove Uncle Edd's team after church we came home. Did the chores ate supper. Then autoed up to Uncle Edd's. Grandpa, Maggie, & Tillie stayed in. Just terrible hot today.

Mon 17: Cooler today. Dad took two calves, the buck sheep and the largest lamb to Scales Mound this forenoon. Got seventeen dollars, eighty-five cents for the lamb weighing one hundred five pounds. Got seventeen dollars fifty-five cents I believe for the buck. At nine cents and over twenty——seven dollar a piece for the calves. Ma and Ruby cleaned the summer kitchen today. We also banked some potatoes and other things.

Tue 18: Well we got up early this morning went out in the alfalfa field and cocked hay but it came to a storm and it rained ~~nearly~~ all ~~day~~ forenoon. To bad for the alfalfa. We washed this afternoon.

Wed 19: We ironed some today. Hauled three loads of alfalfa this afternoon. Ma churned this morning. The folks were coming down this evening but it rained so they didn't.

Thu 20: Grandpa, Aunts Tillie, Maggie & Annie came down this forenoon. Rather cloudy again today. Dad and Ruby took the eggs over the station this afternoon.

Fri 21:   Aunt Maggie, Ruby & I picked gooseberries this forenoon. We picked two milk pails full. We finished hauling the alfalfa this afternoon. Four loads making seven small loads. Grandpa helped a little. Aunt Tillie & Maggie picked off gooseberries.

Sat 22:   A very beautiful day. So clear quite cool. Dad & I took Grandpa, Aunt Maggie and Tillie up to Scales Mound to go home on the one oclock train. Took our first can of cream up. I believe folks can cross the bridge now, fixed temporarly. I believe. Lots of cars going by today.

Sun 23:   We all went to church this morning. Uncle Edd & Aunt Annie came down to dinner. A little cloudy. Ruby wanted to go over the station to children's day exercises tonight. But I didn't want to take the car. So Dad, Ruby & I went out for a ride. We went over to Nick Weis' to see the little dog. A very lively little fellow. John Weis and Henry Weis came there too.

Mon 24:   Raining today. Ruby & I picked a few gooseberries this afternoon. Uncle Edd fell off of a load of hay and hurt himself today when the trip rope broke. He can't move much.

Tue 25:   Heard today that Herbert Bastian is dead. I guess he died at Rochester or some wheres along the way.

Uncle Edd is some better today. Got a letter from Great Lakes today. First letter. Ruby & I picked gooseberries today. Our car is just a year old today.

Wed 26: We washed an awful big washing today. Ma went down to Agnes' a little while this afternoon. Herbert is going to be buried at two oclock Fri. afternoon. Ruby had her head set on going to Scales Mound to Chantaqua this evening. Thought we couldn't get ready in time. But we hurried around. Didn't get started until about ten minutes after eight. It starts a half past. When we got up there it was just starting. Ma staid at home and Dad up to Uncle Nick's. We heard Jack Rose talk. It was just twelve when we got home. We did our trading at Gless after the Chantaqua.

Thu 27: We ironed today. And put up six quarts of gooseberries. Making twelve with the sugar and three without. Can't have but twenty five pounds of sugar to put up fruit with. We used some white molasses (Karo) It is a year today that we went in the ditch with the car.

Fri 28: Well this morning one hundred more boys went to Camp Grant. I would have like to have gone in to see them go. But they went so early and the roads are slippery. Will Zarndt had to go. I guess it is as nearly all of class one. Dad and Ma went in to Herbert B. funeral this afternoon. They took the hack. Dell Fred

& Tom Bastian is back to the funeral. Ma had to take care of Blanche. Dad & Ma brought home a linoleum for the dining room. Got it a Berger's. Paid thirty two dollars for it.

Sat 29: Busy with Saturdays work today. Auto going by all the time today very thick. Dad plowing corn.

Sun 30: It stormed last night and rained this morning. Not much traffic on the road today. No services at Union today supposed to be quarterly meeting services at the station. This evening we went up to Uncle Edd's.

July

Mon 1:   Very cool today. Ma and Ruby went around to look for raspberries this forenoon but didn't find many yet. We washed this afternoon. Didn't start till three oclock.

Tue 2:   We ironed today. Ma and Ruby worked in the garden today. Quite a nice day.

Wed 3:   It stormed and rained this forenoon. This afternoon Dad and Ruby went to town. Ruby bought herself a new white hat. Ma and I picked some raspberries this afternoon. Dad bought new telephone batteries today.

Thu 4:   We didn't go anywhere today. Quite a number of cars going along. Put down part of the linoleum this afternoon. Quite a nice day. Looks some like rain this evening.

Fri 5:   It rained nearly all night. It cleared off today. Ma and Ruby picked raspberries this afternoon. I sent a letter away today.

Sat 6:   Put up the raspberries today. Very busy with Saturday's work. Just lots of folks going to town today. We kind of expected Uncle Georges and Pearl & husband to come in tomorrow but it came to a storm tonight and rained so much.

Sun 7:   Rainy yet this morning so we didn't go to church. Ruby & I went down to John's a little while this afternoon.

Mon 8:   A very nice day. Dad cut some hay. Ma & I picked a few raspberries this morning. Thought we would get a big picking but got only enough for two quarts. Ma banked late potatoes ~~this af.~~ Ruby hoed corn and I hoed strawberries and asparagus. John Tresidder went down to Elizabeth today to the mill took a sack of wheat along for us, brought us flour, graham and bran. So we don't have so much substitute.

Tue 9:   Rainy this morning also showers now and then all day long. We washed today.

Wed 10:   A nice day today. Well Ma and I picked raspberries this morning and a few gooseberries. Put up two quarts of raspberries. We ironed and got in two loads of hay this afternoon the first except alfalfa. We didn't come in till eight-twenty it was half past ten when we got through separating. Mr. Fiedler called up today said there is going to be a meeting at the school house tomorrow night about these thrift stamps. Have to raise over three thousand dollars in this school district. Terrible I think. And a person has to go or be handed I guess.

Thu 11:   This forenoon we all went to Scales Mound with two cans cream and a egg case and some in a basket.

Quite a little load. Got home at half past twelve. This we hauled two loads of hay and Dad cut some. Dad, Ruby & I ~~went~~ autoed up to the school house. Tobin explained it a little. Then he left most all the men folks were there. Sadie Bastian and Evelyn and Clara Engle and four children, Ruby & I were the only ones but the men. They didn't raise as much as it was supposed to be. The bigger part took twenty. That will make one hundred dollars worth by 1923. Ruby & I took two stamps each. Dad twenty.

Fri 12: Another very nice day. We hauled three loads of hay this afternoon. Making seven loads or fourteen with alfalfa.

Sat 13: We hauled three loads of hay this afternoon and Dad cut some. Have ten and the seven loads of alfalfa making seventeen loads. Wanted to go to town this evening but it looked quite a little like rain afraid to go but it didn't rain. Very disappointed.

Sun 14: A very nice day. Wanted to drive off somewhere but I didn't want to go alone. Of course had to drive up to Union this afternoon. The road was just terrible all wore out by the time I got there. After church we drove up to Uncle Edd's. They wasn't to church. Uncle Edd didn't feel very well. Johnnie & Ethel's baby is quite sick. Have a nurse since yesterday.

Mon 15: A very rainy day. Ma churned. I baked a batch of cookies. Ethel's baby is worse today. They have given up hopes for it now. Got a parcel post package from Sears Roebuck and Co.

Tue 16: Well we washed today. Towards evening Ruby & I went up in the woods. I found enough raspberries for supper. Ruby picked some gooseberries. This evening Agnes Milton and Blanche came up awhile. This is Ruby's twenty-fifth birthday. Got a card today going east.

Wed 17: We hauled in one load of hay today. We ironed today. Ma ~~hoed~~ banked some late potatoes.

Thu 18: Hauled in two loads of hay this afternoon making twenty all together now. Dad cut hay this forenoon. The minister called this forenoon asking for money for missions. About half past five we all autoed to Scales Mound. Got home about eight. Looked like gypsies with such a lot of truck piled up to the top. A lovly day.

Fri 19: We hauled hay today. I got a card from New York today. Johnnie's baby is getting better now they think.

Sat 20: The minister came over and helped us hay today. Have nineteen and seven loads in now. Aunt Annie came down this afternoon. Uncle Edd went up to Scales

Mound. There is three cases of infertile paralysis in Galena now. No children allowed on the street or to leave town. Have a lot of it over in Dubuque. We did chores but milking then Dad, Ruby & I autoed to town. Came home about half past nine. Did the milking then. Didn't go to be till after twelve.

Sun 21: Ma, Ruby & I went to church this morning. Didn't go anywhere this afternoon. An awful hot day. This evening we went for a little ride and called on Joe Engels awhile.

Mon 22: Dad took a calf over the station this morning got thirty dollars for it. He cut hay this afternoon. I cut some lawn. Ma put up half gallon cucumbers and salted down two half gallons beans.

Tue 23: I cut some lawn. Ma and Ruby hoed some potatoes. Couldn't haul any hay today. Mrs. Werner called up this evening for Fiedlers said they were going to have a postal shower for Jeannette at the hospital. Are to send them Thu.

Wed 24: Rainy but we washed. Can't haul no hay again today. Dad and Ruby went up to Scales Mound this afternoon.

Thu 25: I put up three pints of peas today. We also ironed and hauled in one load of hay this evening. Have a very hard rain and storm this morning.

Fri 26: Baked a cake today. Also picked about a gallon blackberries. Didn't haul any hay today.

Sat 27: A very busy day. We hauled four loads of hay today. One of alfalfa. Making thirty-one all together. Eleven oclock tonight when we got through separating. Got a card from Raymond D. said he thought the folks would come in Sun. with Uncle Herman in his car. Ruby wanted to go to Camp Meeting tomorrow and Ma wanted to go down to Apple River. Baked bread and coffee cake today.

Sun 28: Well the folks didn't come today. It came to a storm about noon. It probably kept them home or else Uncle Herman didn't get the car. It didn't rain much. Ruby & I went up church this afternoon but there was no one there so we called at Lottie's awhile.

Mon 29: We washed today. Ruby and I picked blackberries this afternoon. Got a milk pail and half gallon bucket full. Mr. Palmer and mother called here this evening and had supper. Mr. Palmer is coming over to help us hay tomorrow.

Tue 30: Mr. Palmer Dad & Ruby hauled in four loads today. A very beautiful day very cool.

Wed 31: Hauling hay today. Dad finished cutting today. Hope we shall finish haying tomorrow. Another very beautiful day.

August

Thu 1:　We finished haying today. Have fourty three loads all together. The shed isn't full. Ma & I picked some blackberries today. Also baked bread. This evening the minister, Dad, Ruby & I went up to Scales Mound. Took cream up. We bought a quart of ice cream and ate it after we got home. Then had to milk and separate yet. It was after eleven when we got through. Sent a letter from Scales Mound.

Fri 2:　Mr. Palmer went away this forenoon. We ironed, baked a cake, put up berries and cucumbers today. Feels good to be through haying.

Sat 3:　Quite a nice day. We all went to town this afternoon. Dad went over to Pearson's to see about a buck sheep this evening.

Sun 4:　We were ready to go to church this forenoon when it looked like ~~rain~~ a storm and it rained a little. We didn't go. Wanted to go to Apple River today. But weather prevented. About twelve oclock Mr. Palmer & Mother came here but wouldn't come in to dinner as we didn't have it ready yet. Tresidders and Uncle Edds were here this afternoon. I don't feel very good today. Have such pains in my stomach and headache.

Mon 5: I feel bum today. Yet awful pains in my stomach now and then. I picked a big basket of cucumbers this forenoon. Ma and Ruby picked blackberries and put some up. Very hot over ninety.

Tue 6: Very hot again today. Put up more blackberries and the cucumbers have twenty-four and one-half quarts blackberries now. I picked some white beans today. Dad helped John stack grain awhile this afternoon.

Wed 7: We washed and baked bread today. Also all but Ma went up to the Mound late this afternoon with the cream. The roads are very nice now. Ruby drove the car part way up and part way down.

Thu 8: Ruby and I picked blackberries this forenoon and this afternoon. Ma put up five quarts without sugar making twenty-nine and one-half quarts. I picked the cucumbers to and cut some lawn.

Fri 9: Ironed and churned today. Also made some jelly and put up cucumbers. A casuality list of three hundred fourty five names today. My but the list are getting so long. Poor fellows.

Sat 10: Dad, Ruby & I went to Galena late this afternoon. Was almost to busy to go. About midnight before we get to bed. I bought goods for a silk skirt today. Black with green stripes. Irish. Paid a dollar seventy-five a yard.

Sun 11:   Had quite a rain this morning. This afternoon we all went to church sixteen besides the minister there.

Mon 12:   A very nice day but quite warm. Ma & Ruby picked blackberries this morning. I picked cucumbers. Had corn for dinner. Ma put up the berries and fixed the cucumbers. I tried to make my skirt. Two widths was to narrow and three widths too wide. Guess I will have to take out some yet as it seems too wide. Nearly crazy with work.

Tue 13:   Well we all went to Galena this afternoon. Martha Tippet rode along in with us. She and Ruby went to the Chantaqua. I went to the doctor. I went to Rice. Had an examination. He said I will have to have an operation could have it at home. Thinks I should have it in a few days. Had to hurry home for a storm was coming up. Just got home in time. Had quite a storm and rain. They are getting ready for the fair today.

Wed 14:   We washed today. And picked a few berries. Dad went up to Scales Mound with the buggy this afternoon. Hope it will be a nice day tomorrow for the Fair.

Thu 15:   The weather didn't look at all favorable this morning. Sprinkling. But it got to look some better. We all went to the fair left here about one oclock. We left our car outside the fair grounds. Lots of cars in the fair grounds. But there didn't seem to be as many people there as other years. I guess it was the weather. Nobody from off much. I wore my new flesh color crepe de chine waist and my new skirt of black or dark green with green stripes. We came home a little earlier than we would if it hadn't started to rain but didn't amount to much.

Fri 16: A very rainy day. It stormed this morning nearly eleven oclock before we got through milking and separating. We can four pints sweet corn today also two pints tomatoes. I guess the fair wasn't much today.

Sat 17: It stormed last night. Thought the lightning must have struck the house. Dad drove Pet to town today.

Sun 18: Ma, Ruby & I went nearly up church this forenoon. Didn't see anybody but the minister so came home again. We went up to Aunt Annie's this afternoon. About supper time Uncle Herman came with his car. He had been up on the ridge to the mission feast. After supper Ruby & I came home did the chores. Dad & Ma rode home with Uncle Herman. He called here a little while. Mrs. Young had a stroke at P. Dower's this evening.

Mon 19: I picked cucumbers and white beans today. We washed. Mrs. Young is pretty bad can only move one hand and one foot a little can't talk.

Tue 20: We autoed to Apple River today. Ate our dinner on the way. Had our supper at Uncle George's. Saw Mayme. She is on a case but came home awhile this afternoon. We called at Will Tresidder's coming home. Just as we got to Uncle Nick's we had a blow out. Made a noise like a cannon. It blew the casing part way off the rim and took an awful hole in the inner tube. No good anymore. Then we found a big nail run straight in the tire. I guess that's what caused it. Our first tire trouble. Tom Pooley helped us with it. It was twelve oclock before we got through with our chores. I guess Mrs. Young is ~~quite bad~~ about the same.

Wed 21: We ironed today. Made corn salad. Put up a quart and pint of tomatoes and a qt ground cherries. Ruby took up more onions. We cut a little lawn. Aunt Annie came down awhile this afternoon.

Thu 22: Tresidders and Uncle Edds went to Apple River this forenoon. They were going to Darlington fair then found out it isn't until next week. We autoed to Shullsburg, this afternoon. Left here about one oclock. Got home again about five. Got along fine. Dr. Peebles said the same as Dr. Rive. It looked like a storm this evening but believe it passed off again.

Fri 23: Very busy cutting lawn, digging potatoes, picking cucumbers and baking bread and coffee cake. Heard by cross talk that Mrs. Young is about the same. I guess she is in a very bad state though.

Sat 24: Busy with Saturdays work. This forenoon Dad and Ruby took Nellie in to the horsebuyers. Then that old Levi was in there again. They sold her for twenty dollars. She is going to _____. Late this afternoon Ma and Ruby went up and swept the church and cut some weeds. Ma went over to Bastian's to see how Mrs. Young is. She seems to be quite a little better today.

Sun 25: A nice day. Dad, Ma & Ruby went to church this afternoon. While they were gone. All of Uncle Georges came. Mayme got off this afternoon. Aunt Annie & Uncle Edd came down for supper. Mrs. Young was quite a little better again today. Wilbur Bastian asked Mama if one of us girls could go over and help Sadie tomorrow.

Mon 26: Well Ruby went over to Bastian's this forenoon. She helped wash and peeled peaches and other things. They had a letter from Ehmer. He wasn't quite so well.

Tue 27: Dad went over to help clean the cemetery this forenoon. At almost twelve oclock Aunt Annie called up. Said Mr. Palmer and his mother were coming here. Then we had to scurry around. Came to get their butter.

Staid till about five oclock. Put up three and one-half quarts tomatoes today. Also started Ruby's silk skirt. Navy blue striped.

Wed 28: This afternoon Dad, Ruby & I went to Scales Mound. But it come to look like rain. So had to hurry home. Called at Uncle Nick's. They have had several letters from Charles since he been in France. It rained some on the way home. But not enough to make it slippery. Ma went over to Bastian's this afternoon took over some cucumbers. Edd Young and his wife were there. They just came back today. Ma saw Mrs. Young. I guess she is getting along pretty well. She can talk but is hard to understand.

Thu 29: Well this is my twenty-first birthday. Didn't celebrate it much. We washed today. Also put up some tomatoes and one quart ground cherries. I got a card from Aunt Tillie today.

Fri 30: Rather cloudy today. We ironed today. Cooked tomatoe preserve. Sewed on Ruby's skirt. Pa hauling manure.

Sat 31: A very beautiful day. This afternoon we all went to town. Aunt Annie rode home with us. Well tomorrow folks are supposed not to run cars for pleasure. Or on other Sundays. The roads are dandy. Forgot the best news. Got a letter from Al said they had a young daughter born the 30th.

September

Sun 1: A lovly day Dad, Ma, and Ruby went to church this forenoon. We were home all afternoon. Not so many cars on the road today as usual. Aunt Annie expected Uncle Georges and probably Uncle Herman and Henrys but didn't see any of them. This evening we went down to Tresidder's. Uncle Edd & Aunt Annie were down there to. They had been up to Wilbur's today. The first time for many years.

Mon 2: Busy as usual. Picked cucumbers, beans, ground cherries. Put up a quart. Ma went down to helped Agnes get supper for the thrashers.

Tue 3: We washed today. Dad, Ruby & I went to Scales Mound this afternoon. Bought a box of peaches. Ma went up to Aunt Annie's this afternoon got a market basket tomatoes.

Wed 4: It rained last night. Today has been cloudy and cold. Cold enough for a winter coat. Dad and Ruby drove to town this afternoon to hear Bryan speak. He spoke on the dry question. Gave Galena quite a hard knock. He spoke on Main street. Ma and I put up some tomatoes and made some chilli sauce today.

Thu 5:   A very nice day but cool. We ironed put up nine quarts peaches and made a little jelly. Dad cut some clover. Also cut off some rag weeds.

Fri 6:   Dad cut some more clover today.

Sat 7:   Cloudy most of day. Our hay didn't dry very well but as we wanted to do it up yet today. We put one load in the shed and made a stack of three loads as it cleared up so nice. I wanted to go to town tonight but didn't get done till so late.

Sun 8:   A very nice day. Roads very nice but folks aren't supposed to run cars on Sundays. Only a few going by. We all went to church this afternoon. Twenty-one there with the minister. This evening somebody called up wanted to know if ~~we~~ Ruby & I wanted to go to a picnic out at Norris' Tuesday. Given by the Barraca class. Well I didn't know what to say. But said at last thought we could go. Said he would be here at one oclock. Uncle Edd and Aunt Annie & Blanche came down here from church. John, Agnes & Milton came up this evening.

Mon 9:   We washed today. Dad cut some alfalfa today. Cloudy today.

Tue 10: Aunt Annie got a card today saying Uncle Bens have a little boy. Well we went this afternoon. Had quite a nice little time. Knew some of the folks. Didn't get home till nearly eight I guess. I set in the back seat. Awfully cloudy and cold today. Raining like everything tonight.

Wed 11: We ironed today. Dad went over to Guilford to the primaries. Just doing odd jobs today. Cloudy.

Thu 12: Another cold day. Rather cloudy. Wanted to go to the Warren Fair but on account of muddy roads and the weather we did not go. Dad took the team to Scales Mound this afternoon. He took up cream also eggs. Eggs are thirty-seven cents.

Fri 13: I cut lawn today. Also made a cake without baking powder forgot it. Ma made bread & coffee cake.

Sat 14: Well about half-past twelve Mrs. Morris Robert came along brought Elma and Loretta along. Much surprised to see them. Well this afternoon we all went to town but the weather didn't look good so came home quite early. Ma and the girls got off up at Aunt Annie's and walked over to Alvin Hammer's. Then came back to Aunt Annie's about dark. Ruby & I walked up there to get Ma. The girls stayed up there all night.

Sun 15: We all went to church this morning. Mr. Bray talked and Miss Smart from Scales Mound on tithing. Mrs. Bray & daughter was there too. This afternoon Aunt Annie & the girls came down. They went home this afternoon.

Mon 16: Well today we washed. Quite a nice day. We hauled one load of alfalfa hay.

Tue 17: We hauled three small loads of alfalfa today. Ruby & I each cut four shocks corn after supper. I got a letter from N.Y. today.

Wed 18: Quite cool today. Ruby cut twenty-five and I six shocks of corn today. Ma churned, I ironed a little.

Thu 19: Well about noon we started out for Scales Mound with cream and eggs. The creamery man said he was paying fifty-eight or one half don't know which now. Eggs thirty eight cents. Ma bought a hat at Mrs. Prohmershenkel's. Then we went up to Uncle Nick's. Uncle Nick is very poorly has been in bed for several days seems to sleep. Aunt Lizzie tried to wake him but couldn't rouse him enough to know who we were. Then we took a ride out through White Oak and up to New Diggings. My but it is quite a sight to see the dump piles of rock and gravel from the mines. We stopped in New Diggings bought a watermelon for thirty five cents. Saw what I guess is a big government works up there from there we came thro Council Hill and Station and home. We were going to call on the Palmers but they weren't at home. Quite a nice day but chilly.

Fri 20:   Cloudy and cool today. We cut corn today. Dad and I run to the Mound to get the wagon wheel. Towards evening. We went up to see how Uncle Nick was. He seemed about the same. Harry and Stella were up there.

Sat 21:   Ruby went over to help Sadie's get meals for the thrashers this morning. Just a lovly day. Ruby came home again about three oclock. Mr. Palmer and his mother drove over tonight for the butter. But didn't stop long.

Sun 22:   A very beautiful day. And the roads are in very good condition. But folks can't go. A few went to church. All went to church this afternoon but me. I staid at home. This evening we all went up to Aunt Annie's to supper. Tresidder were up there to this evening. Had melon this evening.

Mon 23:   Another lovly day. This evening Milton came in said the teacher sent to that we were to go up to the school house tomorrow evening to register I believe it is for the women that didn't register before. About six oclock

Stella Graham called up said Uncle Nick was very low. Didn't know if he would live out the night. So Dad drove up in the buggy this eve, Guess he will stay all night. If they want him to. We washed today. Dad and Ruby picked some apples.

Tue 24: Dad came home this morning. Uncle Nick is quite bad. Stella, Harry & Charlie were up there. The three men sat up all night. Well about two oclock this afternoon Stella called up said Uncle Nick is dead. He died about noon. Well then we got read and went up to Scales Mound this afternoon. Took the cream and eggs along. They don't know yet when the funeral will be till they hear from the boys. After we did the chores we all autoed up to the school house for us women folks to register. Quite a few there. They make a person go to register and then charge them ten cents for doing it. I said I wasn't going to pay anything. But Ma paid it. I'm mad about it.

Wed 25: Dad and Ruby cut corn today. Ma baked bread. Ma called up Mrs. Pooley this afternoon she said the boys were coming back and that the funeral is going to be Fri. afternoon. She thought probably at two oclock.

Thu 26: Well this afternoon Dad Ruby & I went to Galena went out the Green house to get some flowers for Uncle

Nick. It took quite a while. Dad and Ruby each got a new hat today. After we got home we hurried and did the chores. Then we all went up to Scales Mound. The funeral is tomorrow at one oclock. Uncle Thomas was up there he came last night. Aunt Rachel didn't come back. John and his wife came to while we were up there. They hired several autos to bring them over from Dubuque. Had quite a time of it.

Fri 27: A very nice day we all went to Uncle Nick's funeral. Rev. Mumford preached the sermon. We didn't have to take our car to the church and cemetery. Neither any of them did. Ruby walked with Mrs. Smart Lucille & I walked together. Quite a long funeral I think. Uncle Thomas rode down with John's. Aunt Tillie came along down with us. Aunt Maggie, Uncle George & Grandpa were up there too.

Sat 28: Another nice day. Had to go over to Guilford about this fourth Liberty loan business today. So this after noon Uncle Thomas, Aunt Tillie, Dad, Ruby & I drove over there. This evening Dad, Ruby & I took Uncle Thomas to Galena to go home on the nine thirty train. We called on Mr. & Mrs. Zimmerman.

Sun 29: We all went to church this forenoon. This was Mr. Palmer's last Sunday. His brother was up there too. There was twenty to church today. Uncle Edd &

Aunt Annie came down to dinner. Agnes, Milton, & Blanche came up after dinner.

Mon 30: We cut corn this forenoon and some this afternoon. Ma & Aunt Tillie put up six quarts pears. Dad Ruby & I took cream to Scales Mound this afternoon.

October

Tue 1:　We finished cutting corn today. Have two hundred fourty one shocks I believe. It rained a little this afternoon. Made chilli sauce. Cooked ground cherries etc.

[The following recipe was clipped from a newspaper and pasted every which way with several other recipes on a page of a small booklet. Most of the other recipes were written in German.]

"Chili Sauce"

"Peel and chop fine 1 peck ripe tomatoes. Chop fine 4 large peppers and 6 large onions. Stir together, add 2 tablespoons salt, 1 tablespoon cinnamon, ½ teaspoon ginger, ½ teaspoon cloves. 4 cups brown sugar and 8 cups vinegar. Boil until quite thick and seal in glass jars. If more sugar and vinegar is needed let there be just half as much sugar as vinegar. If not wanted so hot put in less of the peppers.- Mrs. Marion Graves, Inola, Okla."

Wed 2:　We washed an awful big wash today. Uncle Ben called up Aunt Annie saying they are coming up tomorrow. Dad started to strip the sugar cane today.

Thu 3:　Uncle Ben's came about nine oclock. But they went right up to Aunt Annie's had dinner up there. After dinner they came down also Aunts Annie, Tillie & Uncle Ed all here to supper. A very lovly day. Aunt

Lizzie called up today wanted us to come up to get them. So Dad & I went this evening. Aunt Tillie went along up to go to the Pres. Church tonight. They are going to install their minister. Thinks she might get a chance down again tomorrow. Well Aunt Lizzie, John and his wife Leona came down with us.

Fri 4: Rather cloudy and windy today. This afternoon Dad & I took the folks to Galena they then went to Scales Mound on the train. Leona took our picture several times. Took us four in the car.

Sat 5: Made bread, coffee cake and cake. Busy as usual. I guess Clayton Combellick is very sick at Camp Grant of Spanish influenza. Heard by cross talk. That Alta wanted Mr. Combellick to come down there this evening. Dad took the sugar cane over to Shultz to be ground.

Sun 6: Heard this morning that Clayton is dead. Died last night I guess. Feel so sorry for Alta and Mr. Combellick. Poor Jack when he gets to hear it. He's over in France. This morning Tillie Ruby & I drove Pet to Galena. We went to the South Pres. Church. Then after church we walked out the Elizabeth road and ate our dinner. Came back went up to see Bessie Weis'. Then came back. Sat in the Park awhile. Then called on H. Bastians. Then we came home. Dad & Ma were up to Aunt Annie's today.

Mon 7:   Well about noon, Dad, Ruby & I autoed over to Schultz's to get the sorghum. Got two gallons paid a dollar to have it made. Haven't tasted it yet. This afternoon we all went to Scales Mound took cream up. Called at Aunt Lizzie's. John & wife are going home Wed. Haven't heard when the funeral is yet. The body hasn't arrived yet.

Tue 8:   Rainy today. Had pasty for dinner and supper today. About noon Edd Pulco called wanted to borrow our tire chains. Didn't like to but did. This evening he brought us back a new pair. Clayton's body hadn't come to Galena yet today. But heard its coming tonight.

Wed 9:   A very nice day. Well Dad, Ruby & I went in to the funeral today. It was this afternoon at two oclock. Am very dissappointed we did not get here to see him. We were a little late. Thought that he wouldn't be opened at all but Agnes said folks saw him. Rev. McGlade of the South Pres and Rev. Funston conducted the services. Quite a large funeral. A quartet of four men sang. Two Winzilsky boys. George Trevarthan Jr. Jackson, Edgerton and Krachmer were the pallbearers. Clayton had a cream or gray coffin. We drove the car in the funeral procession. And went to the cemetery. The band played as they past out of town. And at the grave they sounded taps. Agnes

& Blanche rode home with us. Heard today that Clarence Rouse was killed "over there". I guess his folks just got word. Got a letter today.

Thu 10: About noon today Uncle Joes came along. But they went along up to Aunt Annie's. They went to Galena this afternoon. We washed an awful big wash today.

Fri 11: Rainy today. Uncle Joes and Aunt Annie and Tillie came down this forenoon. Uncle Joes went home a little after four. Ma churned today also baked bread and coffee cake. I ironed a little.

Sat 12: Finished the ironing and doing the Sat. work. Husked several shocks of corn.

Sun 13: No services at Union on account of this Spanish influenza. Most churches and schools are closed. Lots of cases in Galena. Ma went up to Fiedler's a little while this afternoon to see the baby. It's name is Loretta I believe. Today Aunt Lizzie Trudgian called up said that Willie Trudgian and family were up there wanted us to come up after them this evening or tomorrow morning. We decided not to go till morning.

Mon 14: Well Dad and I went up after them this morning. The first time I have seen Willie. They have two children. A girl seven and a boy four. Dorothy & Billy. We got home about eleven after dinner we took

them down to see Johns. They have been down to
Chicago for several months. They are going to leave
there for Virginia next Sat. They seemed to be tickled
to get out on the farm. They have all been sick with
influenza. We had to take them back to Scales Mound
again at four oclock. They called in to Fiedler's to get
a drink at the spring and take a picture of the house
because Willie was born there. They and Aunt Lizzie
went down to Warren on the five train. We took them
down to the depot. The roads a rough. Aunt Tillie
and Annie came down and staid all night. Uncle Edd
went to Galena to stay along.

Tue 15: Quite warm today. We dug potatoes today. Not much
of a crop. Aunts went home this afternoon. By the
papers there seems to be some peace talk. Hope peace
will be soon.

Wed 16: This morning I had an awful headache and sick
stomache thought I was getting influenza but was able
to get up to eat dinner again. Uncle Edd & Aunts
Annie and Tillie drove out to Apple River today.
Uncle Edds came back again by nine oclock. Had
Win's team and theirs or Johnnie's surry. Said they
had a fine ride a very nice day.

Thu 17:   We washed today. Also dug some potatoes have a few to dig yet. This influenza seems to be very bad all over the country.

Fri 18:   Ironed some today. Dad finished digging the potatoes. And hauled them in. Haven't enough to do us I don't think. Dad & Ruby cleaned out the chicken house. Ehmer Young went along today. Talked to Dad. He is home on a furlow.

Sat 19:   Cloudy today. Dad, Ma & I autoed to Scales Mound today this forenoon. It is raining this evening.

Sun 20:   Mrs. Hammer called up this forenoon said if we would be home they would come over this afternoon. But they didn't come. Uncle Georges came in to Aunt Annie's this afternoon. Ma called up Hammer's to see if they were coming. They wasn't so we went up to Aunt Annie's to. Today Will & Charlie Ehler and the children were up in John Weis' pasture looking for nuts. He left the car on top the hill without the brake on. The wind must have started it and it run down the hill. Smashed it some. We had supper at Aunt Annie's. Our new minister called up there this evening.

Mon 21: This morning we took two steers up to Scales Mound we sold them to Wright for nine and one half to ten cents. We took the cattle most of the way. Uncle Edd helped drive. Ma, Ruby & I rode in the car. A very lovly day. Got one hundred fifty-three dollars for the steers.

Tue 22: We washed today. Also husked and hauled in a little corn. Cloudy today.

Wed 23: Quite a nice day. I shelled beans this afternoon. Ma ironed some also baked bread. This evening Ben and Elmer came. Elmer has a thirty day furlow. It started to rain about ten oclock.

Thu 24: Cloudy all day. Reading day. This influenza seems to be terrible. See in the Gazette that so many folks are dying. Its bad in Galena, Shullsburg and so many places. This afternoon we husked corn.

Fri 25: Husked corn this forenoon. This afternoon Ruby took the cream to Scales Mound with Pet. Aunt Annie came down this afternoon.

Sat 26: Misty today. A dandy day to husk shock corn. But had to do the Sat work. We husked eight shocks and hauled in some corn. Sold the bull and what is called my cow or the three titted cow to C. Berryman this evening. Bull for one hundred and twenty and the cow for eighty dollar. Hate to see the cow go.

Sun 27: Very rainy this forenoon. Turned out nicer this afternoon. But just stayed at home all day. John Tresidder came up awhile this afternoon.

Mon 28: Dad, Ma & Ruby took the bull and cow over the station this forenoon. Took all the cattle nearly all the way. Aunt Annie came down this eve to stay all night. Uncle Edd went to Galena.

Tue 29: Rained a little this forenoon. We husked twelve shocks corn this after. Ma churned got over two gallons butter.

Wed 30: Husked and hauled in corn today. Ma made bread. Hear that a Miss Bernice Bray died of influenza. Grandpa Tippet has to have an eye taken out tomorrow.

Thu 31: Well its Halloween. Dad went to Galena today with John about his questioneers. Blanche came up here. Washed today.

❧❧

November

Fri 1:   Husked twenty-one shocks corn, ironed and blackened and put up stoves today.

Sat 2:   A lovly day but raining tonight. Heard today that Jim Spencers received word yesterday I believe that Byron died in England Sept 28. He had just landed. Now only one left out of six children. Uncle Edd saw the Spencers in town. They came to Galena today. Mr. Tippet came home from Dubuque today after having his eye taken out.

Sun 3:   We all went to church to hear our new minister (Cavanaugh) this afternoon. E asked if he could come this evening so he and Bruere here this evening.

Mon 4:   We husked twenty-four shocks corn today. Also churned a very nice day.

Tue 5:   Well I cast my first vote today. Such as it was. Could only vote for three trustees of the University of Ill. There was a patriot meeting to over to Guilford this afternoon. So Dad, Ruby & I and Helen Weis went over. Also took Mr. Fiedler along. Quite a few there. Mr. Birkbeck, Mr. Dillon and a Sargent of the Canadian Army spoke. He had been in the war three years. Had his gas mask and tin hat along.

Wed 6: Helen called up said Miss Virtue is to have a weeny roast tomorrow night. Asked us to come. She said they might go if we go. We all went to Galena today. A nice day.

Thu 7: Husked some corn today. Rainy this after and tonight. So we didn't go to the weeney roast at Miner's School. Heard this afternoon and tonight that the was is over. Haven't heard particulars.

Fri 8: It was a false report about Germany signing that armitice. But there is some hopes that they may yet. Husked corn today. Got 39 shocks yet.

Sat 9: Hauled corn and churned today. E called up this eve. I wasn't here. Ma told him wanted to know if I would be home tomorrow. Said she didn't know. Heard this evening that Willie Zarndt is dead. His folks heard today. Died in England of pneumonia.

Sun 10: We autoed to Apple River this forenoon. Went to Pres. Church. Had dinner at Grandpa's. Uncle Georges came down there this afternoon. Wesley has to go to some camp. Thu. got home about six thirty. Well Ruby and I were asked to take a ride to Galena. But we didn't get far before we had a break down. Wanted to take someone to the train so we took our car. He is going away tomorrow.

Mon 11: This morning about three thirty I was awakened by whistles blowing. At Galena and it kept up till after day light a continues noise. I supposed it a peace report. Heard later that Germany surrenderd nearly all. The Keiser and the Crown Prince fled to Holland. The palace is for rent. Galena began celebrating at two thirty am. Even had a parade. Quite a doings. Oh, I so hope all countrys will have peace now. There is quite a celebration at Galena tonight we didn't go. So much influenza in there. 29 new cases I believe. Dad went over to Guilford to give to this drive for different organizations this afternoon.

Tue 12: We husked 12 shocks today. They aren't going to take anymore boys to train at least for awhile. Paper gave the terms of the armitice. We all went up to S.M. this evening. Lovly day and evening.

Wed 13: Husked some corn this forenoon. Washed this afternoon. Another lovly day, influenza is just awful bad in Galena again.

Thu 14: Ruby's coat came today. Husked corn and haul some in this afternoon. Ironed this afternoon.

Fri 15: We finished husking corn today. Sixteen shocks. Ma churned and baked bread and coffee cake. Had cucumber slaw for dinner. Found the cucumbers in the garden yet.

Sat 16: Doing our Sat. work. Hauled in the corn. Nothing much doing in Galena on account of influenza. Rainy. Got a card today.

Sun 17: Rainy all day. Nobody went to church. B. didn't come tonight.

Mon 18: Cloudy & colder today. It says in today's paper that they are going to send 1,790,000 of the soldiers in U.S. home. Expect to send a good many home before Thanksgiving.

Tue 19: Cloudy today. Mamma went over to see Mrs. Young today. She had a very bad spell yesterday. She is in bed now. Her mind is wandering. She didn't want Ma to go in to see her. So she didn't go.

Wed 20: Dad's birthday sixty-two years old. Cloudy again today. We washed today. This influenza is terrible in Galena and other places I guess. Quite a few deaths in Galena.

Thu 21: I ironed and ma churned. Dad & Ruby drove to Scales Mound. Drove Violet and Pet. First time drove Violet on the road for long time. Especially when there was cars. Got a letter.

Fri 22: Saw the sun today. First time for a long time. We started to haul fodder today. Ma baked bread and coffee cake.

Sat 23: Hauled fodder again today. A nice day.

Sun 24: Cold but clear. Ma, Ruby & I went to church this morning. Only Wilbur and Evelyn and the minister besides us there. A Thanksgiving sermon. Tresidders come up this afternoon. This eve we went up to Uncle Edd's first time since he was sick.

Mon 25: A lovly day. Hauled fodder again today. Heard of several deaths from influenza again today.

Tue 26: We finished stacking fodder today. Ma washed curtains and blankets and also churned. Nice day.

Wed 27: Another beautiful day. We washed today. Ironed some this evening. Tomorrow is Thanksgiving day.

Thu 28: Thanksgiving Day. But a very stormy day. It rained nearly all night last night. This morning it turned into snow. It snowed till sometime this afternoon. It has cleared up this eve. Well we staid at home all day as I guess most people did. Didn't have much extra. Had a pint of asparagus. And squash pie and etc.

Fri 29: Aunt Annie came down this afternoon. Uncle Edd came down for supper. We had pink ice cream for supper.

Sat 30: A very nice day. Busy with our Sat. work.

December

Sun 1: Rather stormy today. Snowing. Didn't have no services at Union on account of the weather. Home all day. Nobody come to see us either.

Mon 2: Cloudy today. Heard today that Mr. Fiedler's brother died (Willie) his brother in law died last week of flu I guess. Made at every day peticoat for myself tonight.

Tue 3: We washed today. Yesterday the first shipload of returning soldiers arrived at New York. Most of them had only been in England.

Wed 4: Nice day. Dad & Ruby took twenty rooster to Scales Mound today. Got thirty dollar eighty-six cents at twenty-one cents. Eggs were sixty-six cents up three today. Wish we had some to take.

Thu 5: Reading day. A nice day. Ma churned today. Pres. Wilson sailed for France yesterday.

Fri 6: Ma, Ruby & I went up to Aunt Annie's this afternoon. Dad went to Scales Mound to have Pet shod. Then went out to Wright's and got some roosters.

Sat 7: Busy with Sat. work. Days are so short now.

Sun 8: Ma, Ruby & I went to church this morning. Uncle and Aunt Tippet came down to dinner. Uncle, Dad, Ruby & I took a walk on the hill this afternoon. This evening we all went down to Tresidder's.

Mon 9: A very damp day. Gloomy. Saw wheel track going in the yard this morning. Guess someone was here last night. I guess who. I got another card today.

Tue 10: We washed today. Dad went to Galena today. The roads are in bad condition. I guess the flu is some better.

Wed 11: We baked bread and ironed some. Windy and cloudy most of the day. But it is just a lovly evening.

Thu 12: Reading day. See by the paper a good number of boys from camps are returning to their homes. There is a letter in the A.R. items that Mrs. Siefert received from a lady of N.Y. She said she had met her boy in New York. He had just come back two days before. He said he was just going to walk in on the folks at home.

Fri 13: Very cloudy and muddy. I am starting a crochet yoke for Ruby today. Ma baked bread and coffee cake and churned today.

Sat 14: The roads are still awfully muddy. So not many folks on the road today.

Sun 15: We all went to church this afternoon. A very nice day. Had company this evening. Guess who?

Mon 16: Another nice day. Ma went down to Agnes' to help pack geese. This eve. Josie & Helen came up. Nick Weis has appointed Helen & I to go around about this Red Cross business. I have to go to Fiedlers, Bastians, and Whites.

Tue 17: Washed today. We all went up to Fiedler's this eve. Got a dollar up there.

Wed 18: Dad took two hogs over the Station today. The old one weighed four hundred eighty-five pounds at sixteen and a quarter. The young one weighed 280 lbs. / This afternoon I went over to Orland Bastian's, White's and Wilbur Bastian's about this Red Cross business. I have thirteen dollars now.

Thu 19: A very nice day. Rev. Cavanaugh came this forenoon. Had dinner here. I washed up the car this afternoon. This evening Ruby & I went down to Weis to take down the red cross money. Will & Bessie there. I got another letter today.

Fri 20: Today Ruby & I drove Pet to Scales Mound. Took two hours each way. Dark when we got home. Very foddy and damp. Dad bought a young bull of Amos Ford for fifty dollars today.

Sat 21: Very foggy again today. Busy with Sat. work. Dad went to town with John today. Roads very bad.

Sun 22: We all went to church this morning. I had to play the organ. This eve we all went up to Uncle Edd's. Don't hardy know if we had company or not.

Mon 23: Sent some post cards and a package this morn. Two pounds butter to Uncle Thomas and Aunt Rachel and a dollar bill a piece for Wayne and Geraldine. Cloudy and colder today. Ma expects to go to A.R. tomorrow. We are invited down to Tresidder's for X-mas.

Tue 24: Well the day before Christmas such a day an awful blizzard all day. Driving snow into every crack. Ma nor Aunt Annie didn't go to A.R. Got a package from Uncle Thomas' today. Mitts for Pa, aprons and a bag for me.

Wed 25: Well a nicer day than yesterday. Lots of snow and drifts. We all went down to Tresidder's to dinner. Had a nice time. Aunt Annie rode in Galena with Studiers. Went to A.R. on 5 train. Ruby and I gave Dad a pocket knife and Ma a pair of slippers. Dad and Ma gave us ten dollars a piece or get us a wrist watch each.

Thu 26: I crochet some today. Doing odd jobs. Have a Christmas cactus out with four or five flowers. Very pretty.

Fri 27: Ironed some today. Ma went up to Fiedlers and ordered a goose for New Year's today. We moved the cubboard out in the dining room today.

Sat 28: Pa and Ma went to Galena in the cutter today. Snowed a little today. I got a box of six lovly handkerchiefs thro the mail.

Sun 29: Pa, Ma and I went to church this after. No others there but Tresidders and the pastor. Rode up and down with Tresidders. Well we or she had company tonight. Hardly expected it. Ruby got a pound of chocolates.

Mon 30: Dad hauled manure. I baked a cake for New Year's. Will have to get busy tomorrow for the New Year's dinner.

Tue 31: Dad & Ruby took twenty roosters and eight hens to S.M. today. Got 24 per lb. Or fourty-three dollars fourty-four cents. Mr Ford and Mr Trevethan brought over the Bull calf today. Baking up for New Year dinner.

1919

Ruby and Lillian Trudgian, circa 1919

January

Wed 1:   Happy New Year. Well we had a big dinner today. Goose, dressing, gravy, asparagus, cabbage slaw, pickles, mashed potatoes, celery, apricots, squash pie, pie plant pie, bread, butter, cream, saffron buns, white date cake, fruit cake, as tidbits candy, oranges, bananas, cigars. Uncle Edd, Aunt Annie, John, Agnes, Milton, and Blanche were up here. Quite a little snow fell last night and this morning. But the sun shined part of the day. Tonight clear and cold.

Thu 2: Very cold today. Clear and bright. This afternoon Dad went over the Station. Sold the hogs for Mon. at seventeen cents. Dad bought a little pig of Amos Ford for two dollars. Only little one he had.

Fri 3: Very cold again today. Ma washed out a few things. To cold to wash much. About eight below this evening.

Sat 4: Another very cold day. To cold to go to town.

Sun 5: It got almost to late to go to church this morning and some of us got colds. Home all day and had no company. No not even tonight. Not quite so cold today.

Mon 6: Dad took four hogs over the Station today. They weighed just three hundred each at seventeen dollars a hundred making two hundred four dollars all together.

Tue 7: Well today Dad and I took a cutter ride to town. Quite cold today. But not as cold as it has been I guess. We bought two wristwatches today. Ruby's and my Christmas presents. They are very plain. Gold filled bracelet and watch case warranted for ten years and works for fifteen. Have swiss movement. Fifteen dollar watches two for twenty-eight. Got our auto license today no. 22887.

Wed 8: We washed today. Clear and cold.

Thu 9: Reading day. We ironed today. A very beautiful day and evening. Beautiful sleighing and lots of teams on the road. Dad helped saw wood for Fiedler today.

Fri 10: A very beautiful day. Baked bread and coffee cake today. Didn't do much else in particular.

Sat 11: A great many teams and sleighs going by today to town. A nice day. Aunt Annie told Ma tonight that Elmer came home this morning from Brooklyn. Uncle Edd and Aunt Annie were to town.

Sun 12: Quite warm today. The sleighing is getting poor. We all went up to Aunt Annie's to supper. In the eve they had other company. There were here first although they didn't say so.

Mon 13: Another warm day. Dad some sewing today. Dad hauled some manure. Quite a celebration at Chicago today for the Black Hawks that have just returned from oversees.

Tue 14: Leroy Tresidders came down to John's today. And Aunt Lizzie came down here with them. She said Charles had been in the hospital six weeks wounded. A nice day. Clifford Tresidder is home for good now. Came home Sat. eve.

Wed 15:   Another lovly day. Dad helped saw wood down to Tresidder's today. We baked bread a cake and sewed a little.

Thu 16:   Ma and Ruby went to Galena in the buggy this afternoon. Sleighing is done for. They got home at seven thirty. Dad hauled manure. Well in today's paper it says that thirty-four states have ratified the National prohibition amendment. And thirty-six to ratify will make the U.S. bone dry. More states are voting on it.

Fri 17:   Well thirty-eight states have ratified. Hurrah, a dry nation. A year from yesterday Jan.16,1920. Sooner I guess for from next July 1 all the salloon were to be close anyway until the army was completely demobilized. We washed today. Very warm. We used the wash machine out in the kitchen.

Sat 18:   Very warm today. Busy with Sat. work.

Sun 19:   Dad, Ma, and Ruby went to church this forenoon. Uncle Edd and Aunt Annie came down to dinner. Tresidders came up this afternoon. We had company this evening. Ruby or both of us are asked to go to Galena to a chicken pie supper in the Methodist Church Thu. evening. Suppose we'll go but don't want to.

Mon 20:   Foggy today. Very warm. Ironed a little.

Tue 21: Finished ironing today. Also did some sewing. Foggy and warm. Aunt Annie got a letter from Aunt Tillie. She is sick now. Has the flu. Aunt Maggie is sick yet.

Wed 22: Another warm foggy day. Aunt Annie came down today. The roads are getting very muddy. Think the roads will be bad for tomorrow night. Also will be awful dark if it is like tonight.

Thu 23: A little cloudy today. Well we went tonight started here about half past five. By the time we got to town all the chicken pie was gone (we didn't mind that) and everything else I guess. So we had supper at a restaurant. The went to Dreamland. After that came home. Had a box of candy to eat. The roads are very muddy. About eleven when we got home. Quite a time.

Fri 24: Clear and warm. A spring day. Didn't get much done today.

Sat 25: Just a lovly day. It would be lovly automobiling today if it wasn't muddy. Baking today. Dad splitting wood.

Sun 26: Another lovly day. Had company this afternoon. Bernetta and Thelma quite a surprise. They walked down. Had a nice visit. They had supper with us.

Then walked home. Dad and I was about ready to go to church when they came. Dad went to church. We didn't have any company tonight. Hardly knew weather to expect it or not.

Mon 27: Warm again today. Ma cut out a dress for herself.

Tue 28: Cooler today. We all went up to Uncle Edd's tonight. We washed today.

Wed 29: We ironed today. Another lovly day. Today Ruby & I got an invitation over to Mrs. Win Tippet's for Fri. afternoon to a sewing club for girls. Were to take our sewing.

Thu 30: Ruby & I drove to Scales Mound today. We called at Aunt Lizzie's. The Red Cross met there this afternoon to work.

Fri 31: My but I've got the toothache in front tooth. Had in about all last night and all day. I couldn't go over the doings. Disappointed. Ruby got a ride home with Davis. Poor old Della lay down today and couldn't get up again. Poor thing has to stay out all night.

❧❧

February

Sat 1: Della died today. This forenoon of old age. She has so poor lately. Dad went to town today. He had to pull Della away yet when he got home. Dragged the road by here today. Dad said there was lots of cars in town today.

Sun 2: Ground hog day. Cloudy. Dad & Ruby went to church this morning. Didn't have any company today. It rained a little this eve. Ma & Ruby laughing at me today. Look funny because my face is swelled but don't think I look so funny as I did yesterday.

Mon 3: Dad and Ruby buried Poor Old Della today. Up near Nellie, Della's colt and a steer. All kinds of weather today. Windy and cold tonight.

Tue 4: Sewing some today. Dad went over to John Combellick's and got a load of oats today.

Wed 5: A very nice day. We washed today. Ruby and I went up to Aunt Annie's today. We got a letter from Aunt Tillie. She is getting better slowly. Aunt Maggie is still in bed. Aunt Annie expects to go out to Apple River tomorrow.

Thu 6: Today there is a cattle show in Galena. Reading day.

Fri 7: A lovly day. Dad had to go to Galena today with John to help him bring home a through bred cow. Ruby baked a cake. Ma bread & coffee cake.

Sat 8: Didn't know if we should try to take the car to town today or not. Didn't have the tires pumped up. So Ma and Ruby went with Pet. A very nice day.

Sun 9: Another lovly day. Uncle Edd came down to dinner. We all went to church this afternoon. I had to play the organ. Well Ma went in to Agnes' from church and Blanche came up here. So this evening we took her down. When we were nearly there we met Ben. So he went in there too. Don't know how he liked it. Uncle Edd was down there to.

Mon 10: Well we took the car out today for the first time this eve. We went as far as Tresidder's then up the road past the school house and back. Afraid the weather is going to change. John Tresidder came up and helped Dad butcher a hog. Quite a few cars on the road.

Tue 11: I got a Valentine today. I know who its from if it doesn't say. Found the little pig "Jane" dead this morning. Late this afternoon we thought we would try to auto to Scales Mound but up on the ridge it was muddy and bad in a place so we came home again. The car runs junk anyway. Very warm.

Wed 12: Another warm day. Ruby and I washed this afternoon. Ma busy with the sausage, lard, & etc.

Thu 13: It rained last night and this morning. Its very muddy now. It was terribly windy. Rainy again this evening. Ironed today.

Fri 14: Had very sad news this forenoon about half past ten. Uncle George called up said Uncle Herman was killed. Yesterday afternoon by a tree falling on him. He was living yet but died soon after. Aunt Annie answered the telephone it was an awful shock for her. I had to tell Ma but told her first that he was awfully hurt. He was down at Fred Horsch's near Uncle Ben's. Of course we don't know much particulars. Aunt Annie and Ma went out to Apple River this afternoon. Uncle Edd took them to town. Uncle Edd came down this evening. If John will do our chores we are going to drive out tomorrow toward evening. Ma called up this evening. Said he and Mr. Horsch was cutting down a tree near the house and the tree fell the wrong way. And hit Uncle Herman on the side of the head. The funeral will be Sun. morning at half past tem from Uncle Joe's.

Sat 15: Had to work hard to get ready. We started from here at twenty-minutes to five with Pet and Uncle Edd's Prince in the hack. My but the roads were terrible. Partly frozen and brake thro and some drifts op on the ridge but it was a beautiful moonlight night. We got out at Uncle Joe's at ten after nine four hours and a half. Ma came down there too today. Uncle Herman looks real nice. But they have his head turned so one side of his head couldn't be seen. One eye was all black. I guess the brain was pressed outward. Uncle Ben said it was an awful sight. He did not regain consciouness. An awful hole on the side of head. He has a very nice coffin. His shoulder was broke also a thumb. It is bluish gray brocaded. We had a supper at midnight then went to bed.

Sun 16: The funeral was quite a large one. Grandpa and Aunt Annie, Maggie and Tillie did not come to the funeral. None able unless Aunt Annie. Maybe she wasn't. Uncle George, Aunt Lizzie, Mayme and Wesley hired a team and rig to come. Uncle Dan came down with Hammers this morning. Mrs. and Miss Wilson and Ehrdt & John D and Mr. Shapp sang at the house and church also at the grave. It was about half past twelve when we got to the church. Wesley, Raymond, John Westaby, Walter Schlichting, Herbert Brickner, and Adam Dittmar's son were pallbearers. He had three spray of flowers all of carnations but one had some different flower along with them white and pink carnations. One from the family, one from Apple River Sunday School and one from the Woodbine Sunday School and another from the Young People's Society of Schapville Church. Uncle Dan took two spray up to Apple River for the folks. The minister preached a sermon in German and one in English. We staid around the church and got warmed up a little before we started for home. We started at two oclock got home four thirty.

Mon 17: Mother called up from Apple River this afternoon. Just wanted to know how we got home. Didn't do much but chores today.

Tue 18: I baked bread today. One sheep had a lamb today. But lay on it and killed it.

Wed 19: I baked pies, (squash pies) and biscuits today. Ma called up today. Said she is coming home in the morning.

Thu 20: Ruby and I went to meet Ma this forenoon. It snowed this afternoon, an awful storm. Aunt Annie isn't coming home for a few days yet.

Fri 21: Cloudy today. Dad got a load of straw down at John's today.

Sat 22: Snowy today. Dad has the toothache. Uncle Edd went out to Apple River today.

Sun 23: A nice day but very muddy. And what do you suppose. Who came at about half past one S.S (guess) very very much surprised. Ruby and I were just getting ready to go to church. We run up stairs got ready and climbed out the parlor window and went to church. Dad and Ma had to entertain. The mystery is which one? (no one). ~~Ethel~~ Ruby & I called into Tresidder's awhile after church. Uncle Edd came down tonight. He came home today. But did not have any other company.

Mon 24: Ruby & I drove Pet to Galena today. Took back to Coatsworth the second watch Ruby had. It wouldn't run at all. Ruby paid five dollars more and got another watch. It was marked twenty-five dollars. He claims it's a better one. I hope so. This one is ingraved a little. The case is warranted for twenty years and the works for three years against defects. It rained about all the way home from town. Roads very muddy.

Tue 25: Clear and cold today. Bessie Weis invited us over to her place to the club for Friday afternoon.

Wed 26: We washed today. Quite a big wash. It snowed some.

Thu 27: We ironed today. Reading day of coarse.

Fri 28: Blanche came up today. While John and Agnes went to Galena. Snowing and windy. Uncle Edd also came down tot dinner. This afternoon didn't know if we should go over to Bessie Weis' or not. Quite stormy. Nobody else was going so we didn't either. Glad we didn't for it got to be a terrible blizzard.

March

Sat 1: Colder today. Will make nice sleighing. Dad hauling straw from up at Landos Bastian's. John bought it for $25.00. We're to have half. Late this afternoon Uncle Henrys came in the sleigh. Uncle Henry, Aunt Lue, Olive, Clifford, Marvin, Alverna and Dorothy. Had lots of noise tonight.

Sun 2: Uncle Henry, Aunt Lue, Dorothy, Dad, Ruby & I went to church this forenoon. The minister didn't show up. Don't know what the trouble was. Only William B. John and Milton there besides us. The folks went over to Alvin Hammer's this afternoon. Pa and Ma went up to Aunt Annie's. Didn't see anything of S.S. today. But had company this evening. B. Ruby is asked to go to a show (movie) Tue eve.

Mon 3: Ma went up to Aunt Annie's to help keep the children while Uncle Henry and Aunt Lue went to Galena. They staid up to Aunt Annie's again tonight. Ma came home tonight.

Tue 4: Uncle Henrys came down this forenoon. They expected to go home today but it snowed all day so they didn't go. Of course because it was stormy Ruby didn't go to the show.

Wed 5: Clear and colder today. Uncle Henrys expected to go home this morning. But as Aunt Lue wasn't feeling well they didn't go till this afternoon.

Thu 6: Dad went to Galena in the cutter today. Paid the taxes. ~~fifty~~ It was sixty-two dollars. Ruby & I got awfully bad colds. We washed today.

Fri 7: We ironed, baked bread, coffee cake and a cake today. Had a calf dehorned and a ring put in the bulls nose. Had to drive them down to Tresidder's.

Sat 8: I baked a batch of cookies today. Snow is going fast today.

Sun 9: Dad & Ma went to church this afternoon. Ruby & I didn't go because our colds were to bad. Aunt Annie came down a staid with us while Uncle Edd went to church. They spent the evening here. Didn't have any more company tonight.

Mon 10: A lovly day. Doing a little sewing. Dad hauling manure.

Tue 11: Another nice day. Snow about all gone. Sewing some today. Heard today that there is going to be a social at Independence School Fri. night. I guess Bernetta is going to try her luck. Ruby & I also got a card inviting us to a novelty shower at Mr. and Mrs. J. L. Tippet in honor of Irma Falancer Saturday afternoon.

Wed 12:   Nice day. We washed and ironed and baked bread today. Quite good I think.

Thu 13:   Milton brought us up a box of honey for our colds I guess. Cloudy and windy today. Ruby & I walked went over to the Station this afternoon to get some things. But couldn't get no fruit for our basket very troubled about it. And we haven't anything yet for the shower yet. Don't know how we shall make out yet.

Fri 14:   Was called up this morning to tell us the Independence Social is put off. Some of the children are sick. Dad went to town today with Johns. The roads are terrible. Dad bought us several dishes to take to the shower tomorrow. Uncle Edd went to town this after. Aunt Annie came down to stay all night. Raining tonight.

Sat 15:   Rainy today. Didn't know if we should go to the shower or not. Sometimes it looked brighter. Josie said if we could go she thought she could to. It started to rain when we got down there. It rained awfully hard. So when it stopped a little we came home. Don't think there was many to the shower. Bernetta didn't come. She thought she would come and go with us. Uncle

Edd didn't come home so Aunt Annie is going to stay with us again tonight.

Sun 16: The weather wasn't very good this morning so we didn't go to church. Aunt Annie went home this afternoon. Didn't have any company this eve. A nice eve but muddy of coarse.

Mon 17: A lovly spring day. Ma fried down pork. I made a petticoat for myself. Dad chopping posts and stakes. Got thirty eggs tonight most for the season. St. Patrick's day but didn't celebrate in no way.

Tue 18: Another spring day. Saw the first robin today. Ruby & I dressed in pantaloons went up the woods to chop this afternoon. Chopped off a haw tree and piled brush.

Wed 19: We washed today. A nice day.

Thu 20: We ironed baked bread and filled cookies. Ruby also cleaned out the chicken house. We all went up to Aunt Annie's this eve. Uncle Edd offered to go with us to the social if we wanted to.

Fri 21: Busy getting ready for the social but didn't know how to go. Thought probably B. would say something but didn't. We didn't know if we should ask Weis or not. Ma went with us up to Uncle Edd's then he had to get ready yet. I was quite late but not to late when we got there. A fairly good crowd. Good program. Twenty-nine baskets I believe. Charlie Virtue bought mine for two dollar and five cents. Ruby's was sold first for a dollar five. Charlie Zarndt the buyer. B & E were there bought two baskets a piece about half past twelve when we got home. Weis didn't go.

Sat 22: Ruby & I drove up to Scales Mound in the buggy today. Had a sale up there so there was a big crowd there. Roads are quite good till the foot of Temperly hill till up the Mound they are bad. Ruby & I each got a new spring bonnet. Each of shiny black straw mine is green in under and some on top. Ruby's was five fifty mine four fifty.

Sun 23: A very nice spring day. Dad & Ruby walked over the Station to quarterly meeting services. John T did also. He came back with them. Had dinner here. Agnes Milton & Blanche came up this afternoon. Didn't have any company. Don't have anybody to expect now I'm sure.

Mon 24: Dad, Ruby & I burned a brush pile up in the orchard this afternoon. Also cleaned up lots more trees and limbs. Started to rake lawn.

Tue 25: We washed today. Also baked bread and raked some lawn.

Wed 26: Cooler today. Ironed today. Baked patty cakes. Pumped tires and etc. Neighbors are plowing with tractors.

Thu 27: Fiddled away some time looking over car and raked some lawn today. Uncle Edd & Aunt Annie came down this evening.

Fri 28: Raked lawn again today. We also baked bread and coffee cake. Just as we were thro eating supper Raymond Leon and Helmer came. They staid here tonight.

Sat 29: Well the boys went up to Aunt Annie's this forenoon. We didn't know who are how to go to town today. We got out the car and tried it. First time since Feb. It seemed to go pretty good so Dad, Ruby & I went to town this afternoon. Quite a crowd in town. The boys are going to go over to Hammer's awhile this eve. Then are going to stay all night at Aunt Annie's.

Sun 30: Well the time was supposed to be set ahead an hour sometime this morning. Crazyness. Dad, Ma, & Ruby went to church. Dad & Ma went up to Aunt Annie's to dinner. Well B was here tonight. Didn't expect it. Ruby is asked to go to Dubuque by auto some Sunday.

Mon 31: Cooler today. Dad hauling manure. Ma sewing a little.

April

Tue 1:   Ma cut out my blue plaid gingham dress today. Ruby made some curtains for my room. Ma, Ruby & I went up to Uncle Edd's tonight to get some sugar they brought for us. Aunt Annie was out to Apple River from yesterday noon till noon today.

Wed 2:   We washed today. Cloudy today. Two years ago today we ordered the Ford.

Thu 3:   Ironed today. Ma cut out my blue plaid gingham dress today.

Fri 4:   We baked bread, coffee cake, cake and doughnuts today. Dad & Ruby made a fence to keep the sheep in.

Sat 5:   We wanted to go to town today. But it rained this morning so we didn't go. Showery late this afternoon. Aunt Annie came down today. It is warmer today.

Sun 6:   Very warm today. To warm to wear a coat. Lots of cars on the road today. We all went to church this afternoon. This evening Agnes, Blanche, and Milton came up. No other company.

Mon 7:   It stormed several times last night and again this afternoon. Had lots of rain grass very nice and green. Hope it clears now.

Tue 8: Ruby & I intended to go to town today but Aunt Annie said Uncle Edd was going in and we could go and would take the eggs. So I went in with Uncle Edd. We had thirty five dozen. Took to Sheean. Got thirty-five and a half cents. I went to the dentist made an appointment for next Tue. Aunt Annie was down here today.

Wed 9: We started to wash today but it was so rainy we didn't hang any out. Ma sewed on my dress.

Thu 10: Reading day and rainy all day so we didn't get our wash out again today.

Fri 11: Finished washing today. Also ironed. Cloudy yet today.

Sat 12: Dad went to town today. Got thirty six cents a dozen for eggs at Stauss'. Weather cleared off today. Do hope it will keep clear for awhile.

Sun 13: We all went to church this morning. Then we went down to John's for dinner. Uncle Edd & Aunt Annie were there too. Had two guineas for dinner. This afternoon Milton, Blanche, Ruby & I took a walk away down to the Old Bartell house. Thought we would find some flowers but only found one crocus. Had company this evening. Also a little excitement.

Mon 14: Rainy, cold, very windy all day. Ma cut out and sewed on Ruby's green gingham dress. I finished a crochet yoke.

Tue 15: Still rainy and cold an awful day. I did not go to town to the dentist today. Wasn't fit for a dog to be out. Ma sewing I making up a corset cover with crochet yoke.

Wed 16: Still chilly and rainy. Ruby & I drove up to Aunt Annie's this afternoon to get some potatoes. Dad fixing fence. Had pie plant sauce today.

Thu 17: A nice day. Cleared off for once. We washed today. Sent for paper for the parlor today. Cost $6.66.

Fri 18: Baked bread and coffee cake. Also ironed.

Sat 19: Dad, Ruby & I went to town today in the car. The roads wasn't so bad as I thought they might be but the car didn't go very good. We brought home a big load. 100 oyster shells, plow, groceries, & etc. Got thirty-seven cents per dozen for thirty-one dozen. I made an appointment with the dentist for next Mon. at two.

Sun 20: A Beautiful Easter day. Warm. Ma, Ruby & I went to church this afternoon. Picked some flowers to put in church. Agnes, Milton & Blanche walked home with us to pick some flowers. Our sow had four little pigs today.

Tue 21   Uncle Edd, Aunt Annie & John were here this
          evening. But didn't have any other company.

Mon 21:   Another nice day. Ruby & I drove Pet to town
          today. Had a xray picture taken of my two front teeth
          and two teeth pulled upper jaw left side. Awful hard
          getting out broke off a good many times. In a way it
          didn't hurt but wasn't very pleasant. In a little while
          it started to ache and ached till I went to bed. Ruby
          bought a pair of brown shoes for five dollar and I a
          brown pair oxfords for four dollars.

Tue 22:   Well my jaw or whatever it is doesn't ache any more.
          Another lovly day. Washed today. Also ironed all
          but the starched clothes. I baked a batch of cookies this
          afternoon. Also made rhubard sauce. Ma & Ruby
          cleaned some weeds out of the strawberry patch. Dad
          hauled manure on garden also started to plow it.

Wed 23:   Finished ironing also baked bread. Had an awful
          storm and heavy rain early this morning. Can't plow
          the garden now for a long time. I wanted to go to
          Scales Mound too today awfully bad to get the car
          fixed up. I painted three chairs this afternoon.

Thu 24:   Ma and Ruby cleaned Ruby's room today. Also
          went up to Aunt Annie's and got three bu. potatoes
          also went over to Hammer's and got one bu. early

potatoes. Quite cold today. We got our parlor paper today. From Montgomery Ward.

Fri 25:   Cold again today. Had an awful hard frost last night think ice on a tub of water. Made bread and coffee cake and a cake. Well this evening Ruby and I went over to the Miner's Social with Josie, Helen & Bert. We walked. Quite a crowd there. Had a very good program. Tresidders were over. Blanche had to sit on the platform holding a doll while Mrs. Wingler sang. Baskets sold well none below a dollar. Ruby's brought a dollar. Joe Dower had hers he had two others. Archie Virtue bought mine for a dollar and a half. Also Miss Reddington's. Fourth time I got a Virtue. First time a cousin of theirs, second and third time Charlie Virtue and now Archie Virtue. Had a very nice time. Very interesting. Got home at half past twelve.

Sat 26:   Very nice day. A great celebration at Galena today. One hundredth anniversary of the odd fellows. We didn't go. Ma & Ruby made some garden today. The first we made.

Sun 27:   Rainy this morning. Ma & Ruby went up on the hill this morning but didn't see anybody at church so came home again. Uncle Edd and Aunt Annie came down to dinner today. Rainy this afternoon and eve.

Mon 28:   Well cloudy this morning and road muddy. Dad & Ruby went to town to the big celebration this forenoon with Old Pet in the buggy. I had a chance to go with Uncle Edd but didn't know what to do. Just awfully dissappointed. In spite of the muddy roads just an awful lot of cars went by also teams. They saw Charles Trudgian in town. He has been home since Wednesday. He's working roads now driving tractor. It wasn't such a bad day after all (the weather).

Tue 29: Cleaned the rag room today. At noon John Tresidder asked to borrow our grass seeder. After dinner he came up to get it. Came up in the car. I was looking out the window to see him crank it. It back fired and hurt his arm or wrist. We bathed it in hot water thought probably it was only a sprain also put linament on it. It began to swell. Couldn't use his hand so I drove him home. He had the spark to far advanced that why he broke his arm. Also the car was missing one cylinder. Then Agnes thought he'd better got to the doctor so I said I would take him in. I had to have other clothes on so we drove back up. His car went so bad that we took our car. The doctor said the both bones in his arm were broken. Said it would be four weeks before it could be taken out of the cask. Ruby went to town to. Then when we got home I had to drive John's car down again.

Wed 30: Raining all day today. Ruby cleaned Dad's & Ma's room today.

May

Thu 1:   Rained a little today. Cleared up this afternoon. Ma washed today or finished she started yesterday.

Fri 2:   Clouded up and started to rain again this eve. Ironed today. Also baked bread and coffee cake. Ruby cleaned my room. Rec'd from Sears Roebuck wall paper for the kitchen. Brown varnished paper. I trimmed most of it today.

Sat 3:   Very rainy again. Baked a cake and cookies today.

Sun 4:   Cloudy and looked like it might rain any minute. Mr. Cavanaugh called up to know if he should come up to Union. Uncle Edd thought not. But later on it started to clear off. Dad, Ma and I went up to Aunt Annie's this afternoon. Ruby staid at home to do up the chores early. She thought she might have company. And she did. Parlor was used tonight. Milton came down with the 'flu' today. Had the doctor this eve. Nearly all of Fiedlers sick.

Mon 5:   Cloudy again today. Tore up the parlor today. Tore off the paper. Tomorrow the woodwork had to be painted. Ruby has to decide a question soon.

Tue 6:   Rainy all day. Three or four storms today. A little sunshine between several times. I painted three chair and Ruby and I painted the woodwork of the parlor.

Wed 7:   Aunt Annie came down this forenoon and this afternoon we papered the parlor ceiling. Ma also churned. Ruby baked bread about the first time. Getting interested. Milton and Fiedlers are getting better. A nice day for once.

Thu 8:   Pete McDonald was here for breakfast. But it was before I got up. Always likes to get a meal here. I painted this morning. Ruby & I went to town this afternoon in the old buggy. Got thirty-nine cents for eggs today. Couldn't get an appointment with the dentist till a week from Tue.

Fri 9:   Finished painting the parlor this forenoon. Ruby and I papered the parlor this afternoon Aunt Annie came down this evening. The paper looks quite dark. It has a rose applique border.

Sat 10:   Had to straighten up the parlor today. Very busy. We all autoed to Galena early this evening. Bought Ma a hat. About half past ten when we got home. An awful big crowd in town tonight. Something new for us to go to town Sat. night. Well Ruby isn't going to Dubuque tomorrow.

Sun 11: A lovly day. We all went to church this morning. This afternoon we autoed to Scales Mound. Thought we would see Charles. But he has gone out to Washington. Has a girl out there. Saw a German helmet and belt and a cap taken off a dead hun. Graham were up to Aunt Lizzie's too. Ben was here this evening. Elmer is going away to be operated on again Tue.

Mon 12: I cut some lawn today. We also planted early potatoes and Ma & Ruby planted more garden stuff. Received a dress today from Philkipsborn today. I didn't like it very well but Ma thinks its nice.

Tue 13: Ruby cleaning the bedroom. After dinner Ruby & I went to Scales Mound. Our first trip alone with the car at least for that far. I wanted o see if I could get the car fixed. But Mr. Bird was too busy. He opened the spark plugs for me anyway. Got fourty-two cents for eggs at Tippet's. We also bought a hundred bran. On our way home on Kane hill a ford was coming we going up. I got to far to the side in the ditch one wheel went down. The man in the other ford backed it out for me after awhile. A Kane boy an old man & Ruby & I pushed.

Wed 14: We washed, churned, baked bread. Cut lawn also straightened up the bedroom and set two hens. Bernetta invited us over the telephone last night to go to her picnic tomorrow. Would like to go.

Thu 15: Threatened rain this morning. We did not think much of going to the picnic but about eleven it looked better we hitched up Old Pet and went. Twelve before we started but was over there a long time before we had dinner. Not a very big crowd there. Had dinner outdoors. Had lots of good things. Had a big basket of oranges and bananas. Lots of ice cream and candy besides other dinner. Lots of cake. Bernetta must have spent a lot. Josie Helen & Bessie were over there. Bessie rode part way home with us. Had a nice time. But hardly had time to go.

Fri 16: Ruby cleaning the hall. Ma finished ironing I cut lawn. Dad plowing.

Sat 18: Busy all day. This eve, we all went to town again. Getting quite sporty. Well Ruby is going to Dub. tomorrow. An awful crowd in town. There is quite an excitement about some of the neighbors. The sherrif has been out after one. Uncle Georges are coming in to Aunt Annie's tomorrow.

Sun 19: Well Ben & Ruby started at nine for Dubuque intends to go to church in Dub. After dinner all of Uncle Georges and Mr. Sam Hanson and Clifford

Price came in to Aunt Annie's with the Buick and the Ford. Had to sell Wesley some gas thought the carbruater leaked. First time we met Mr. Hanson. It came to look like rain toward evening. Uncle Georges started for home then we. It rained a little on the way home and was rainy all evening but not enough to make the roads slippery. As it started to rain at seven I thought sure Ruby & Ben would have started for home early. But it was after ten when they got home. Thought surely something happened to them. They say from Dub. to Hazel Green the roads were awful muddy. Had quite a time getting up one hill.

Mon 20: Washed today. Started to plant corn. I went with Agnes & Blanche to cut asparagus. The sheriff was out to the neighbors again today and took him along.

Tue 21: Dad & Ruby finished planting that piece of corn today. I had an appointment with the dentist today so Ma and I drove Pet to town. I had a wisdom tooth filled and two more teeth pulled. It hurt a little and it aches this evening. Two big fellow heads about all teeth.

Wed 22: We ironed today. Also did some sewing or mending. Raining a little today. And raining quite a lot tonight.

Thu 23: Made bread today. Also planted late potatoes. Made a spice cake. And fixed a little on the car. Raining tonight. Hear this eve that Henry Zarndt came home from across Sun. eve.

Fri 23: Ruby & I went to Galena today in the buggy as the roads are rather muddy. The dentist didn't work much on my teeth just put some stuff in two front teeth to treat them. One aches tonight. Ruby bought herself new white skirt for four ninety-five.

Sat 24: My face is all swelled up and achy. Baked bread & coffee cake & cake. Ruby did. getting to be quite a cook.

Sun 25: Mom and Ruby went to church this morning. I'm an awful funny looking human. Face all swelled up. No company this afternoon. But this eve. Uncle Edd & Aunt Annie John, Agnes, Milton, and Blanche were up. Also Ben Y. staid till late.

Mon 26: A beautiful day. Well I guess Ruby gave B her promise last night. Dad, Ruby & I autoed to Galena this morning. The Dentist stuck in a needle or somethink away up at the root of the tooth where it was so swollen. Left out pus. It feels lots better now. Bought a roll of bard wire. Had a puncture in front tire on the way home from a tack. Put in a new tube. Our neighbors had to appear before the jury this afternoon. But were out in the field again late this afternoon. Coming quite an excitement in the neighborhood.

Tue 27: Ma ironed today. Dad & Ruby finished planting corn this afternoon.

Wed 28: Ruby & I got an graduation invitation to the Galena commencement exercises June 5. from Thelma Davis. A warm day. The picnic at Ford School today. But I didn't feel hardly able to go. And Ruby didn't feel like walking up either. Wanted to go badly. Weis girls & Agnes & Blanche went.

Thu 29: Ruby went over to Sadie Bastian's this afternoon. I went up on John's hill to pick asparagus. Called in to John Tippet's as Aunt Annie was staying with the baby while Ethel, Mary and Grandpa Tippet and Uncle Edd went over the grave yard. Ascension day today. And so many many cars on the road. Warm day.

Fri 30: About ten oclock we started out for Apple River. Roads good. Took an hour and fifteen minutes stopped in Scales Mound awhile. Had dinner at Grandpa's after dinner we went up the hall head the priest speak. Also had supper at Grandpa's. the weather didn't look good. Afraid we'd get wet yet. But got home without. Then the clouds scattered. Mother staid out to Apple River and Aunt Maggie came in. Myrtle Graham graduates tonight. Uncle Edd and Aunt Annie started out for Schapville this forenoon.

Sat 31: A very hot day. After dinner it came to quite a storm. Rained quite hard. After the rain a Ford stopped and it was Uncle Ben & Mr. William. They were to Galena and when it looked like rain started out here. But got caught on the road. Some were wet. We were very much surprised. It rained again tonight. Had quite a time to get them all put away for the night.

June

Sun 1:   Had quite a storm and lots of rain in the night. I got up at six oclock new time this morning. They were here to breakfast and dinner. Started from here at one. Afraid it might come to rain again. Dad went over the Station at noon today to get Ma. Before they got home Uncle Edd & Aunt Annie came along. Aunt Annie staid here. Aunt Maggie went up after supper with Aunt Annie. Looked stormy this eve. Also rain later on. Ben didn't come.

Mon 2:   Tore off the paper in the kitchen today. And washed woodwork. Wanted to paper ceiling but didn't get it done.

Tue 3:   The weather brightened up a little so Ma & I drove to Galena. The roads awful bad. Then the dentist only treated my two front teeth. Took out the stuff and put in new. Looked like a storm on the way home but it didn't rain till tonight when it rain awful hard. And stormed so. The lightning was terrible. About ten oclock saw a reflection on the sky of a fire over towards Werner's or Spensley's. It looked as though it might be nearby. We thought we would go up on the hill to see but thought the grass to wet.

Wed 4: Heard that the fire was up on Tom Pooley's farm. Two barns burned. Also hay, oats and machinery. Uncle Edd & Aunt Annie took Aunt Maggie to town today to go home. Cleared off today. This eve the sky was just pink up north I suppose Northern lights. We papered the kitchen today, a tan paper.

Thu 5: Straightened up the kitchen this forenoon. Uncle Edd came down to shear the sheep this forenoon. Aunt Annie came along. Had ten sheep to shear. After dinner Uncle Edd went down to Weis' and Tresidder's to shear their sheep. Found several ripe strawberries yesterday and today.

Fri 6: Rainy again this morning. Ruby & I went to town again today. The dentist just treated the two teeth again. Roads awful muddy.

Sat 7: Busy with Sat. work. We got so much work to do. Had some strawberries for supper tonight. First mess. A lovly evening tonight. Would like to have went to town the roads were good.

Sun 8: We all went to church this morning. The minister has resigned. Will be his last Sun. next Sun. Uncle Edd & Aunt Annie came down to dinner. Mr. And Mrs. Fiedler, Mary, Ida & Loretta came down this afternoon. And Ben was here this evening. It gets quite late till he goes home lately.

Mon 9: A very nice day. But warm. Hoed and weeded in the garden and cut lawn today. Had a big dish of strawberries for supper. Um Um.

Tue 10: We washed today. Also ironed some clothes from last week. Had an awful hard rain and storm last night.

Wed 11: We ironed today. Ruby baked bread and a batch of cookies. Also made pie plant sauce. Had a storm at noon also a shower this afternoon. I cut some lawn. We worked in garden.

Thu 12: Dad & I went to Galena this afternoon with the car. Took in the wool. Had seventy nine and one half pounds and got fifty-five cents per pound. Sold to Hathaway. Well finished with my teeth today. Filled those front teeth but they don't look as nice as I wanted them too. Also filled a wisdom tooth. Don't know the bill yet. When we got home Rev. Elvin Palmer was here. He came last Monday. This eve we all rode up to Uncle Edd's. Mr. Palmer is going to stay here all night.

Fri 13: Mr. Palmer went away this morning. Hot day today. We wanted to go to Scales Mound to Sunday School convention tonight. The weather wasn't looking good when we started when we got up there it lightened so came right back. Just got home before it rain. Didn't rain much. But I guess they got it some places maybe Scales Mound.

Sat 14: Very busy. Stormy looking all day but it cleared off a little better towards eve. So we got ready and went to Galena didn't get there till after nine oclock. The town was crowded. Got home alright.

Sun 15: We all went to church this afternoon. Mr. Cavanaugh is going to stay. The Elder wouldn't accept his resignation. Ben said at church we wouldn't be over this evening. Has a little business in Galena. So we all went down to Tresidder's this eve.

Mon 16: Ruby & I picked cherries this forenoon till a storm came up. Rained the rest of the day. We put up seven quarts of cherries have a few more to pick yet. I picked two soup bowls of strawberries. Have some more to pick yet.

Tue 17: I picked another bowl of strawberries today also picked more cherries. We washed today.

Wed 18: We ironed today and baked bread. Made cherry cream pies. Ma worked some in garden. Dad cut some alfalfa. Had another hard storm and rain tonight.

Thu 19:   Ma & Ruby cleaned the cellar today. A shooting occurred in Galena today. Frank Willy shot Earl Fitch at noon. I suppose they had some trouble. Mr. Fitch was a cashier in a bank. Aunt Tillie came in to Aunt Annie's today.

Fri 20:   Hauled two loads of alfalfa this afternoon. I went up to Aunt Annie's to pick strawberries. We picked quite a lot. But there was so many rotten ones. It's a shame. I got quite a few. We picked them off tonight.

Sat 21:   Hauled three loads of alfalfa this forenoon. This eve Dad, Ruby & I autoed to Galena. Came home rather early for fear of rain. Mother had company Agnes, Milton & Blanche.

Sun 22:   No services at Union today. We all went up to Aunt Annie's to dinner. This afternoon Ben came along so Ruby came on home with him. He had horse & buggy as usual. They drove up as far as Singer Cemetery. Ben was here for supper. I guess its his last visit.

Mon 23:   Hauled in three more loads of hay today. Have some out yet. And its coming to a storm. Wish it wouldn't rain on it.

Tue 24:   Had an awful electrical storm last night. The folks hauled in one load of hay towards evening.

Wed 25: Aunt Tillie came down this afternoon. We picked a few strawberries yet for supper. Ma & Ruby washed an awful big washing and hauled another load alfalfa. Finished. Found the little calf dead this evening. It was weak and it got in the creek and couldn't get out. Dad skinned it.

Thu 26: Got up early this morn. Dad, Ma & I went to Galena early. Took in the calf hide and had a little other important business. A Odd Fellows Steam boat excursion today. Would like to have gone very badly. And really would have if I had known something before. A beautiful day but warm. We bought and brought home a new perfection oil stove. Equipped with back and oven for thirty one dollars. Brought it home in the Ford. Dad, Ma, & I had to ride in the front seat. Aunt Annie rode down with us. Dad stood on running board. Ruby & Tillie picked some gooseberries this after. We took Aunt Annie home this eve.

Fri 27: Finished ironing. Ma & Ruby worked in garden. Tillie picked more gooseberries.

Sat 28: Baked a cake on the new oil stove. We have Aunt Annie oven. Aunt Tillie made it. She went up to Aunt Annie's this afternoon. We all went to town again this eve. Well the Germans signed today.

Peace. An awful crowd in Galena. Sort of celebrating I guess. The saloons all over the U.S. is suppose to close Mon. night at twelve. My won't that be grand. Hope its so. I guess Ruby feels a little better since going to town. Passed some folks on the road this eve. I bought a white wash skirt looks like satin. Paid eight dollars for it. Too much but very pretty.

Sun 29: A lovly day. All but Ruby went to church this after. Only Uncle Edds & Aunt Tillie there besides us and the minister we went for a little ride this eve. So Ruby wouldn't feel so lonesome. Will Tresidders came down to John's today.

Mon 30: Another nice day. Ruby & I each sent for a white silk Georgette waist today. Five ninety-five each. We washed and ironed today. I cut some lawn. Dad cut hay.

July

Tue 1: We hauled two loads of hay late this afternoon. Ruby picked some gooseberries. I cut some lawn.

Wed 2: We ~~all went July to Galena this forenoon~~ hauled hay today four loads. We all took a ride up to Aunt Annie's this eve.

Thu 3: We all went to Galena this forenoon. Ma bought a white skirt also shoes and a pair for me. Also paid my dentist bill twenty one dollars. Well tomorrow is the fourth. Big celebration at Scales Mound but Ruby & I didn't get our waists today.

Fri 4: Dad, Ruby & I went to Galena this morning went in to see if our waists were in the Post Office. But no. No waist. I was awful sore. Well we got ready to go to Scales Mound the weather didn't look very favorable but we went. A very big crowd there. Uncle Bens from Woodbine and Uncle Dan, Uncle Henrys, Uncle Joes, Uncle Georges, Irish Virtues and lots more were there. It rained several showers but not enough to settle the dust. Made a person rather nervous. About half after four we started for home as the weather didn't look good. It rained a little on the way home. After we were home awhile it rain very hard. And rain so hard about all night.

Sat 5: We didn't go anywhere today. Didn't know if we should go tonight or not. Wanted to go awful bad. Would like to know something awful bad.

Sun 6: Dad, Ma, & I went to church this morning. Lottie was there. I found out some things I wanted to know about B. Lottie came over this afternoon. Had supper. We thought we would go to Galena to the Methodist church this eve. But when we got in there church looked to be shut up so we call on Tippets awhile.

Mon 7: We hauled two loads of hay this afternoon.

Tue 8: Hauled a load of hay this morning but it came to rain so couldn't haul anymore. We washed today.

Wed 9: My waist came today. My first Georgette waist white with blue embroidery and collar. We got a letter from Uncle Thomas today. It stormed nearly all afternoon. A very heavy rain. And hard storm. We baked bread in cookies on the oil stove. Mrs. Seck was buried today.

Thu 10: Didn't haul any hay today. To wet. I cut a little lawn. Ruby & I cleaned out the carbon from the combustion chamber of the car this forenoon. We all rode down to Tresidder's today.

Fri 11: We hauled five loads of hay. Making twenty-six loads of hay in now.

Sat 12: Hauled in five loads of hay again today. Nearly killing ourselves. Got all in we had cut and all of that field. We baked bread. We all went to town again tonight. Nearly all the farmers around in. We saw somebody riding around in the Old Ford roadster and the girl with the yellow waist.

Sun 13: Ma & I went to church this afternoon. Looked a little rainy. The minister Sadie Bastian and Evelyn & Elmer Y. were there. Small crowd. When we got home Aunt Annie was here and Uncle Edd came down for supper. We took them home this eve.

Mon 14: Rained several showers today. We washed and ironed a good part of them also cut some lawn. Put on the car a new radiator hose. And filled up the new tire cuts.

Tue 15: Finished ironing. Baked a cake and bread. We hauled three loads hay this after.

Wed 16: Ruby's twenty-sixth birthday. Spent the day haying. A very beautiful day. Such beautiful blue sky. We hauled four loads hay in this afternoon. Making thirty-eight loads now. Shed nearly full.

Thu 17: Mother sent Mrs. Young a birthday card. Had a postal shower for her. Well this afternoon Uncle Edd came down to help us hay. Aunt Annie came down also. We put up seven loads in a stack. Making fourty-five loads. We took Uncle Edd & Aunt Annie home this eve. About a dozen young folks had a picnic supper down in our bottom. Don't know who they were.

Fri 18: Put on load of hay in the shed. It's full now. And put a load on the stack fourty seven loads.

Sat 19: Put up three loads hay today. One on the stack and two for a new stack fifty loads. We all went to Galena this eve. An airplane was to make a flight over the Fairground this afternoon. But as there was only five tickets sold he would fly. We shook hands with Jack Combellick this eve. He has been home since July 2.

Sun 20: Da, Ma, & I went to church this morning. This afternoon we took a ride up as far as Mt. Morley school house where Ma use to go to school and back through Guilford around by Heer's and stopped at Aunt Annie's for supper.

Mon 21: Had a shower rain this forenoon. Dad & Ruby put up two loads hay today.

Tue 22: John Tresidder came up this afternoon to help hay. Finished now except the alfalfa. Have fifty-eight loads.

Wed 23: We washed, baked bread. Dad took five lambs and an old sheep over to the Station this forenoon. Got sixty-five dollars fourty-five cents for them. Fourteen cents a pound for the lambs and seven for the sheep. Ruby & I picked a few blackberries afraid we won't get many.

Thu 24: We (all but Ma) went to Scales Mound this forenoon. We bought a new firestone 30x3 tire from Birds. 6000 mile guarantee. Had the car looked over. Called on Aunt Lizzie. This afternoon we ironed I put new oil in crankcase of car also greased it. Dad raked alfalfa.

Fri 25: We put up three loads of alfalfa hay today. Finished haying. Sixty-one loads. Aunt Annie came down today. Uncle Edd went down near Hanover. We went up there last night to ask them if they wanted to go with us to Waterloo by car. Uncle Edd has backed out now.

Sat 26: Well we didn't go to Waterloo today. But has been quite a nice day but hot. We all went to Galena tonight. Saw somebody going around alone.

Sun 27: We all started out for Apple River at nine this morning. Uncle Edd was going with us but he got a ride with Haydens. Got to Apple River by ten. Waited for Mayme to get ready then we went to Lena. Made that in a hour fifteen minutes. Ate dinner. Attended Sunday School and services. Mr. Liston preached. Some folks down there we knew. We started for home twenty to five. Went quite fast as it looked like a bad storm. Wanted us to stay for supper at A.R. but we came home. Was awful dusty. It looked much brighter when we got nearly home and then it cleared off without a drop of rain. Uncle Edd stayed to supper. Johns were up this eve. Tomorrow is Grandpa's seventy-fifth birthday. Had a beautiful birthday cake. Uncle Georges and Louise Sutton and children were to be there to supper to.

Mon 28: A nice day. Ma churned Ruby & I picked a gallon and a half of blackberries today. Josie Weis called up said she would go with us on the excursion Fri if we were going. Wish Helen could go to.

Tue 29: We washed today. Dad, Ruby & I went to Galena late this afternoon. Bought three excursion tickets for sixty-cents each. Brought home our oil stove oven today. We all went down to Tresidder's after a can of soft water. Heard in Galena today that Leroy Tresidders had a child but it died.

Wed 30: We ironed today also picked some blackberries and put up two and one half quarts and made jelly. I washed my white skirt. Its threatening rain tonight. Hope we will get a good shower.

Thu 31: Weather partly cloudy today. But hope tomorrow will be nice. We baked bread, cake and cream puffs today.

August

Fri 1: Well we got up this morning quite early. Weather not looking bad. It cleared off so at eight we started for Galena. Josie, Ruby & I put the car in Edgerton's Garage. An awful crowd at the depot and the train was crowded. Had to stand. Portage we had to walk away to get to the boat landing. Our first boat ride. My it was swell. The boat had four decks lots of dancing. It was ten or after when the boat started. It was one oclock when we got to Dubuque and five when we got to Cassville. The boat started again at twenty-five to six. We walked up and down the main street of Cassville. Got back to the landing and ~~started~~ on the train by ten oclock. Eleven when we got to Galena. Hurried to garage to get car. And was charge seventy-five cents for storing the car. I asked last Tue and ~~they~~ he said fifty cents. I got mad at the old fellow. Got home quarter to twelve. Dad and Ma was quite worried. Some folks didn't go we thought might go. Bernetta & Thelma were on.

Sat 2: Quite bummy today. Ma & I picked blackberries this forenoon. This evening we all went to town.

Sun 3: Got nearly ready to go to church this forenoon. It came to rain. Uncle Edd & Aunt Annie came down to dinner. Ruby & I went down to Weis' this eve. Took Josephine's veil that she left in the car.

Mon 4: Ruby & I picked a gallon and half blackberries this forenoon. Ma made jelly out of them.

Tue 5: We washed today. I also washed and ironed our Georgette waists.

Wed 6: Saw first airplane go over this eve about a quarter after eight. Ruby and I were out on the lawn we heard a noise thought it an automobile. Ruby went in the house. I looked up and down the road. Didn't see anything. The noise seemed to come from over towards Studier's. Then up in the air. I looked. And behold I saw a airplane. Quite high. My one glance and knocked on the window for Mother and Ruby. Then watched it a while. Telephoned Aunt Annie then rang the bell for Dad. He was up in the corn field. It went nearly straight west then turned northward. Watched until it went down over the horizon. Causes some little excitement in the neighborhood. We ironed today. Also picked berries and put them up. Baked bread, cake and tarts and pie. If its nice tomorrow we expect to go to the Schapville picnic or Soldiers' doings. Asked Helen to go along.

Thu 7: A lovly day. We started at a quarter to one for the picnic. Helen went along. A very large crowd there. Mostly relatives. Had our supper along. Started for home about a quarter to eight. Came home thro Schapville. Stopped at the cemetery to see Uncle Herman's monument. A good many folks out there from around here.

Fri 8: Very cool. Ruby & I picked and put up blackberries today. Mother went up to the church and cleaned a little cut off some weed. Then called in at Sadie's awhile.

Sat 9: Picked and put up some berries also pickled a half gallon yellow beans. Baked bread, coffee cake and cake. Dad, Ma & I went to Galena this evening. Ruby staid up to Aunt Annie's. Not so many in town as usual.

Sun 10: All but Ruby went to church this afternoon. Uncle Edds, Lottie, Jack, Alta, Sadie, & Evelyn there. This evening we went over to Win Tippet's. Took Uncle Edds along.

Mon 11: We put up ten quarts peaches, cooked 4 pints corn. Picked blackberries made jelly and cut some lawn. Fiedlers thrashed. Weis did the job.

Tue 12: We washed. Put up four pints sweet corn. Cut some lawn. Always busy.

Wed 13: Ironed. Ruby & I picked a few blackberries. Enough for supper and breakfast. Put up four pints field corn. Cut some lawn. Had a heavy rain last night and early this morning. Then cleared a beautiful day.

Thu 14: A beautiful day. We all went to the Fair. Started at twelve thirty. Drove the car in the Fairgrounds. A large crowd there. The grounds were just full of chance games or playing for dolls (especially). And most everything imagineable. One race horse broke its leg another ran away. We staid for evening. An awful crowd in the eve. The fireworks were just fine. Had singing. Band music. Acting. A girl wire walker. Very good. We started for home at ten. Very much worn out. But not completely satisfied. Saw somebody early in the eve. alone.

Fri 15: Didn't get up till late this morning. Late this afternoon we all went to Scales Mound to get flour, kerosene & some gas. Didn't know if we should go to the Fair this eve or not. But did not go. Cut some lawn.

Sat 16: Doing Sat. work. Lawn cutting. Staid at home all day.

Sun 17: Dad, Ma, & Ruby went to church. A lovly day. Ma & Ruby went down to Tresidder's this eve.

Mon 18: A very nice day. Quite cool.

Tue 19: We washed put up two quarts tomatoes and two pints big cucumber slice pickles. Aunt Annie came down this afternoon and Uncle Edd came down to supper.

Wed 20: We ironed, baked bread. Ma churned. Dad, Ruby & I went in Galena this after. Took in a wagon wheel to be set. Ruby & I looked around a little on ~~the~~ Cemenery hills. William Sincock was buried this afternoon. A returned soldier died of tubercolosis. We bought a box of peaches and a watermelon.

Thu 21: A beautiful day. Put up ten quarts peaches. Thought we would like to go down to Uncle Ben's but we had such bad colds.

Fri 22: We auto to Scales Mound to Chantaqua this eve. Ruby & I, Dad & Ma didn't go. Called at Aunt Lizzie's a little while after Chantaqua.

Sat 23: Busy with Sat. work. This eve. we all autoed to Galena. Didn't see a great deal tonight.

Sun 24: We all went to church this afternoon. Came home did the chores. Went up to Aunt Annie's to supper. After supper Aunt Annie, Ma, Ruby & I took a ride to Galena and back.

Mon 25: We washed, Ma plum (wild) preserves. Canned tomatoes. Dad took the saw over to the Station this morning. Got seventy-three dollars. Got a card from Al saying they are coming soon.

Tue 26: Decided to go to Woodbine this morning. Aunt Annie went with us. We started at nine oclock. Stopped at Schapville for to telephone to Uncle Bens and get gas. Got down to Uncle Ben's ~~for~~ at eleven. Went down from Salem church. Some roads. Uncle Ben, Lester and Wardie weren't at home but came home soon. Uncle Dan was thrashing but came home this afternoon. We went riding several times around Woodbine, etc. A beautiful day. Started six thirty got home at eight. A shorter way.

Wed 27: We ironed. Made tomatoe preserves. Cooked ground cherries. Cut some lawn. Uncle Edd went to Iowa today. Aunt Annie came down this evening.

Thu 28: Dad & I went to Galena this afternoon. Brought home box peaches, 100 salt, 100 oyster shell, roll roofing, paper, etz. We put up six quarts of peaches yet today.

Fri 29: Put up four quarts more peaches. Two and half quarts tomatoes. Two pints sweet sliced cucumber pickles. Baked bread and coffee cake and cookies. This is my twenty second birthday. Got a card from Aunt Tillie.

Sat 30: Didn't know what to do today. So we decided to do our work. Go to Galena this afternoon, got a late started Aunt Annie went along. Had sort of a blow out or something on the way. Had to put in another inner tube and inner shoe. Thought probably Als would come today but didn't. Waited for the train. Came home. Dad, Ruby & I went to Scales Mound this evening. To the soldiers welcome. A big crowd. Fireworks and dance. Got home quarter to twelve.

Sun 31: We all went to church this forenoon. Late this afternoon we went to Galena to Greenwood cemetery. Then drove out in the country away and ate our supper. Back to town. Drove around up in the hill came down Franklin. Talked with Scotts and Barters. Had nearly a flat tire. Cause screw. Change inner tubes. Came home. Met someone and his girl when we were nearly home.

September

Mon 1: Labor Day. So many cars on the road today. Uncle Edd came home from Iowa today so we went up there this eve. Uncle Edd seems to think Als are coming next week.

Tue 2: John Weis thrashed today. Tresidder thrashed wheat late this afternoon. Ma went down to help. Also Dad. We took him down in the car. Ida Bastian came back last night.

Wed 3: Canned tomatoes. Made a little tomatoe preserve. Made five pints chilli sauce. Dad helped thrash at Tresidder's again this forenoon. Got a letter from Al today saying they would come here next week. Are coming back to Schlichtings this next Sat. Just coming. The worst of all times. Its terrible.

Thu 4: Ma dug some potatoes. Ruby & I looked for wild grapes. Found a few. The Platteville fair today. Had nearly a notion to go this forenoon. Weis went.

Fri 5: We all went to Apple River this afternoon. Took Aunt Annie along. Also lots of fruit put up for Aunt Tillie and brought back empty bottles for Aunt Annie. Had a blow out on Kane's hill. A bad one. Put on the new Sears Roebuck tire. Had a terrible time. Staid at

Grandpa's to supper. Called at Uncle George's store. Came home in an hour. Dad staid up the school house to the big telephone meeting all the lines that are on our poles about getting on the bell line.

Sat 6:   Busy all day. This eve we all went to town. Quite a crowd in town.

Sun 7:   We all but Ruby went to church this afternoon. Sadie asked Ma to ask Agnes to help her thrash tomorrow. At last she asked if Ruby or I could come to. We went down to Tresidder's this eve.

Mon 8:   Agnes said she could go very well to help Sadie. So Ruby went early and I at ~~eight~~ ten oclock. Got thro it alright but didn't hear much. A bit embarrassing at times.

~~Tue 9:~~   Aunt Tillie called up today. Said Grandpa has pneumonia. Aunt Annie went out today.

Tue 9:   Washed. Put up ground cherries and tomatoes. Aunt Annie called up this forenoon. Said Grandpa is quite sick. Have a nurse for him. Schlichtings brought Al, Nancy & Geraldine in late this afternoon. Nancy's sister and Arthur and Laura Schlichting went on to Galena to a dance. But came back again at about dark. Just called. Then went home. Nancy's sister went along back till Thu. or Fri. But made a cake and cookies.

Wed 10: We ironed. Put up some tomatoes. Dad and Al cutting corn. Had quite a storm and rain last night.

Thu 11: Mother got a ride to Apple River this forenoon with John Glicks. She came back to Scales Mound on the nine oclock train. Dad, Uncle Edd & I went up after her. John Tippets & John Tresidders & Ida were up here this evening. Grandpa is quite sick. Have a nurse. Mother hardly knows if he knew her or not.

Fri 12: Al, Nancy, Dad and Ruby hauled a load of alfalfa hay this after. This eve all but Ma took a ride to Scales Mound. Aunt Lizzie wasn't home. After we got home Lena Hanson and Arthur Schlichting came. He brought her in. Staid till twelve.

Sat 13: The folks hauled the hay today. This eve Ruby, Dad, Al, Nancy, Geraldine & Lena went to Galena. Al drove the car. Got along fairly well.

Sun 14: Dad & I took the folks in to Zimmerman's to dinner then they were going home on the one oclock train. We all went through Grant's old home. Uncle Edd & Tresidders went to Apple River this after. Uncle Edd here to supper. Think Grandpa just a little better.

Mon 15: Washed an awful wash. Put up four quarts ground cherries. Didn't hear from Grandpa today. Big Soldiers Welcome home at Apple River today.

Tue 16: We all went to Apple River this afternoon. Uncle Edd went with us. Beautiful day. Mother staid out. Aunt Annie came along back. Grandfather a little better. Quite a crowd at Apple River. Mostly cars. Expected to stay for evening. But Uncle Edd & Ma wanted us to go home so home we came. But terribly disappointed and could just as well did the chores several hours late. Mad clear though.

Wed 17: Ironed and churned today. Rainy today. Ma called up this eve. Grandpa better but Aunt Tillie not very well.

Thu 18: Rainy today. Ruby & I picked some grapes and picked them off for jelly. Baked bread & a cake. Aunt Annie got a card from Aunt Tillie today. She has pleurisy now.

Fri 19: A hard rain last night. It cleared off nicely today. We baked a cake made jelly. Put up seven quarts tomatoes picked up and hulled ground cherries and cooked them a little.

Sat 20: We went to Galena late this afternoon. Quite a good many in. Saw Miss somebody today. Somebody we didn't know before. I looked at hats but didn't buy any. We came home with out our flour. Thought we would go back again this eve but the weather didn't look very good. We didn't for it rain this eve.

Sun 21: We went to church this afternoon. Uncle Edds and John Tresidder there but no minister. I guess it was too wet for him but it didn't rain till this eve.

Mon 22: Cleared off fine this morning. Ruby churned today. I working on auto tires. Mother called up said she is coming home tomorrow.

Tue 23: We went up to Scales Mound this afternoon to get Mother. Took a coop of ten old roosters along. Got only twelve cents a pound or eight dollar seventy six cents. Nearly gave them away. Called at Aunt Lizzie's. She wants to come down Fri. We all went up to Aunt Annie's this eve.

Wed 24: Another lovly day. Washed today. Dad & I husked a load of corn this afternoon.

Thu 25: Ironed today. We all went to Galena this afternoon. I bought a pair brown shoes for six dollars and a hat for five. I wanted the one I liked last Sat. but it was sold. Very disappointed.

Fri 26:   Late this afternoon Dad & I went to Scales Mound to get Aunt Lizzie. Werners graded the road from the school house down to Tresidder's this week.

Sat 27:   Busy all day. We all went to Galena this eve. Saw somebody alone tonight. We had a puncture on the way home. Winsicker helped us. Saw a areoplane go over today at three thirty. Going west second I ever saw.

Sun 28:   Rainy this morning and this eve. Uncle Edds came down to dinner. Tresidders came up this afternoon and staid to supper.

Mon 29:   Ruby took Aunt Lizzie home this afternoon with Old Pet. Ma & I washed.

Tue 30:   Rained very heavy last night. Also raining mostly all day and raining hard tonight. Wanted to go to Freeport. Expect we'll have to put it off again and again. Put up six and one half quarts pears. Also churned & baked cookies.

October

Wed 1:   Ma and I went to Apple River this afternoon. Walked over the Station for the five train. Very warm day.

Thu 2:   Ma and I went to Freeport this morning on the eight thirty train. We went to see Dr. Mary Rosenstiel. Lucky to find a lady dr. Aunt Tillie had heard of her. Seemed very nice. She said something on the same order as the other drs. Said there was three ways. An operation. Electric treatment or medicines. She gave me lots of medicines. I'm to go again in 3 weeks. Came back to Apple River at nine oclock. Very tired. Walked around quite a little.

Fri 3:   Intended to go home this morning. But it rained early so didn't prepare to go but it cleared off. Grandpa was down stairs to dinner and supper today. First time since he was sick. Uncle Joes were up. We helped to make sourkraut this after.

Sat 4:   We came home this morning. Walked home. Had a hard rain about noon. And then an awful hard rain about five thirty. The creeks were higher here than I ever saw. The culbert was full and the water run over the top of the bridge and along the road. The awful best thing I ever saw. Took fences.

Sun 5: We all went to church this afternoon. Uncle Edd, Aunt Annie, Tresidders, Wilbur B & Ben Young there. Mr. Kravenberg's last Sun. He says we will have a student from Dubuque Pres. School to preach. We all went up to Uncle Edd's this eve.

Mon 6: A lovly day. Cleared off last night. Dad husked corn. Ma dug potatoes. Ruby picked apples. I picked up ground cherries.

Tue 7: We washed today. Hulled ground cherries. Ruby went down to Agnes's to pick some hopps this afternoon. A lovly day.

Wed 8: Ironed today. Also dug some potatoes. Very poor crop. Mary Tippet was married today at noon to Mr. Snow. They went to Buffalo and Niagara Falls.

Thu 9: A beautiful day. Aunt Annie came down this forenoon. Brought us a sample of the wedding cake. Uncle Edd came down this evening. Hulled beans this eve.

Fri 10: Ma & Ruby dug some potatoes this afternoon. Poor crop. Also baked bread and coffee cake. Quite cold today.

Sat 11: A lovly day. Busy with Sat work. Would like to have gone to town tonight.

Sun 12: Had our first frost last night. Another lovly day with lots of cars going by. I was in bed most of day. Had no company.

Mon 13: Ruby went up to Aunt Annie's this forenoon to get a cauliflower and peppers. Ma & Ruby dug for potatoes this afternoon. Ma did this forenoon also. Dad hauling manure.

Tue 14: Finished digging potatoes today. Got about eleven bushels late potatoes. Awful poor crop. Chopped ingredients for chow chow this evening. This forenoon Dad, Ruby and I went up to Baus'. Dad bought a hog. Then we went to Scales Mound.

[The following recipe was found in a very old newspaper column written by Lula G. Parker, that had been cut, folded and placed loose in a booklet.]

"Chow-Chow"

"Chop in large pieces one peck of green tomatoes, half a peck of ripe tomatoes, six onions, three small heads of cabbage and one-half dozen green or red peppers. Sprinkle with one pint of salt and let set over night. In the morning drain off the liquid, put into a kettle with two pints of brown sugar, half a cupful of grated horseradish and two tablespoonful of black pepper, white mustard, mace and celery seed. Cover with vinegar and boil until tender. Seal while hot."

Wed 15: Cloudy all day. Started to rain late this afternoon and raining steady since. Ma baked bread and a cake. Dad Ruby & I husked a load of corn.

Thu 16: All clear today but cool. We washed and husked a load of shock corn. Sixteen shocks. Mr. Baus brought the hog today.

Fri 17: Lovly day. Ironed, baked bread & coffee cake. Also husked another load of shock corn. And polished the car. Mother's birthday. Fifty-three. Got a card from Aunt Tillie.

Sat 18: We all went to Galena this afternoon. Then came home and then went to town again this eve. Ruby & I went to the movies. Ma and Pa saw B & E and girls.

Sun 19: Cloudy today. We all went to church expected to probably see a new minister. But no minister arrived. Wilbur and Evelyn came out also. She said Mrs. Young was poorly in bed. She said the boys wasn't over yet and that Elmer doesn't come over very often. She said they both have girls. Ruby and I thought we'd go down to Tresidder's but didn't find them home. We all went down this eve. Heard Whites had a shower on Emily Winsicker Fri. night.

Mon 20: Didn't get much corn husked as it was rainy today.

Tue 21: A beautiful day. Busy husking standing corn. We all went up to Aunt Annie's this eve. They heard that John Combellick and Elmer Young had got married today. Had heard before that Jack was going to get married.

Wed 22: Husked a load of corn. Also washed. Dad, Ruby & I went to Galena late this afternoon. Think it must have been a mistake about Elmer getting married. We saw his girl also Ben's. Think they were coming home from work. Ruby sent Ben a letter this morning.

Thu 23: Ironed, churned, baked bread. Also finished husking standing corn. A load this afternoon and some this forenoon. Didn't read much in the Gazette today. Only a piece about the novelty shower at Mrs. Clinton White's in honor of Emily Winsicker who is to be married to John Combellick Oct. 22. That was yesterday. Heard they went to Freeport to get married.

Fri 24: Cloudy today. I baked a batch of cookies this afternoon.

Sat 25: Rather rainy today. Rained last night. To wet for husking corn.

Sun 26: Misting today. Uncle Edds came down this afternoon. And Tresidders came up.

Mon 27: Got up early and took Ma & I and Aunt Annie over the Station to go on the eight-five train for Freeport. Had such a nasty day. Rained all day. Got six and a half dollars of medicine again. Looked in several stores were astonished at the prices. We came back to Apple River this eve. Staid all night at Grandpa's.

Tue 28: We called at Uncle George's this morning before train time. Saw Pearl and Baby Mayme said she couldn't come in anymore as time is to short. Said she is going up north to live soon. Going to get married I guess. Got home this forenoon. Ma & I walked from the Station. We all husked corn this afternoon.

Wed 29: We husked corn this forenoon. This afternoon Ruby and I hauled and unloaded two loads of corn while Dad tied up fodder. Mother Baked and churned.

Thu 30: Rainy all day. Ma blackened and put up the dining room stove. I didn't feel very good today. Sick to my stomach last night.

Fri 31: Halloween tonight. But not much for us. A social at Guilford school tonight. We husked corn this afternoon. Have a hundred twenty three shocks yet.

November

Sat 1: A lovly clear day. Busy with Sat. work. Husked five shocks corn and hauled in two loads today. Would like to be in town tonight.

Sun 2: Father and Mother went up to Aunt Annie's to dinner. Ruby & I went over to Lottie's this afternoon. Staid for supper. Had no company today.

Mon 3: We washed a big wash and husked corn today and hauled in a load. Ninety-seven shocks yet. Our line was connected with the Bell today. Some folks quite tickled.

Tue 4: Windy and cold today. Husked some corn this forenoon. This afternoon we all autoed to Galena. Bought some goods for myself a skirt. Had a flat tire just as we were going to start for home. Had to fix it. Got my feet cold and froze my toes.

Wed 5: Clear today. Husked corn today. I staid in partly made my skirt and dyed my white Georgette waist a pale blue. Also ironed some.

Thu 6: Rainy today. Ma and Ruby churned and finished ironing.

Fri 7: I sewing on my skirt. Also made a cake. Ma & Ruby husked some corn. Well we went to the social at Ford's School tonight. Had nobody to go with so Dad went up with us. And then came home again in a little while. Quite a crowd there for the roads. Had lots of little tots speak. ~~Miss~~ Our boxes both brought a dollar quarter. A Bell boy from Council Hill got Ruby's. Don't know who got mine. A fellow from Galena or Menomonee. He bought a whole bunch of baskets and went out side with some girls and ate it. I didn't get any supper. Very gentlemanly also took Clare Engel's too. Then the poor kids didn't get anything to eat. We had a nice visit with Jeannette. I guess I could have had someone else buy my basket had I wanted to. After twelve when we got home.

Sat 8: Busy with Sat. work and husking corn. Wonder whats going on in town tonight.

Sun 9: Rainy all forenoon. This afternoon Uncle Edd & Aunt Annie came down. It started to rain again late this afternoon and rained hard all evening so Uncle Edds are going to stay all night.

Mon 10: It cleared off this morning. But partly cloudy all day. My but its windy today and tonight. Haven't any fire tonight. Got supper on the oil stove.

Tue 11: A nice day. We washed and husked a load of corn. Josie & Helen came up this evening. I am to go to the Studier's and Fiedler's about the Red Cross business. A year ago today the armistise was signed.

Wed 12: Very, very cold and windy today. Too cold to husk corn. Ironed today.

Thu 13: We husked six shocks today. I was up to Fiedler's this afternoon about the red cross. Studier was there too. But I didn't get anything. Ma and I went up to Aunt Annie's this eve. But didn't find anybody home. So we called at Johnnie's.

Fri 14: We finished husking corn today. Husked twenty shocks today. Very dry husking. Also hauled in two loads of corn. Have a load of unload tomorrow. And lots of fodder to tie up. We have bad colds.

Sat 15: We all went to Galena this afternoon in the car. Quite a nice day. Had the car all closed in. Lots of people in town today. Would like to have been in town again tonight to see whats going on.

Sun 16: We all went to town to church. We went to the Methodist church. A very nice day and good roads. So many cars on the road. Received quite a royal welcome at church. A certain person was singing in the choir. We came back to Aunt Annie's to dinner. And spent the afternoon.

Mon 17: A nice day. Warmer. We didn't wash on account of our bad colds. Mr. Will Swing's funeral today. He died Fri eve of pneumonia.

Tue 18: We washed and ironed and baked bread today. Not so bad.

Wed 19: Uncle Edd and Aunt Annie came down this morning. Uncle Edd helped haul the fodder. They didn't get through so they are going to stay all night. A lovly day.

Thu 20: Got through hauling fodder today. We did a little mending, patching, crocheting and etz. Late this afternoon Dad, Ruby & I went to town. Got a sack of potatoes for five dollars. ~~This is~~ Dad is sixty three years old today.

Fri 21: Tried to rain a little this morning. Dad & Ruby took twenty rooster to Scales Mound today. Got twenty-eight dollars & twenty cents. 20 cents per pound.

Sat 22: A nice day. This eve Dad, Ruby & I went to Galena. Went to the movies. Somebody and his girl also was there.

Sun 23: Well we hurried around and got ready and autoed out to Schapville. A lovly day. Had German services. Uncle Henrys and Uncle Joe was there. Aunt Rachel was down to her mother's so we went out to Uncle Henry's.

Had lots of music on the player piano. Got home at about dark.

Mon 24: Got up early and Ruby & I walked over the Station and went to Freeport on the eight train. Did not of walking down there. The doctor gave me medicine for about five weeks. Came back to Apple River on the nine train. Staid all night at Grandpa's.

Tue 25: We came home on the morning train. Aunt Annie here today. Dad drove John Tippet's team to Scales Mound while others drove the cattle. Started to crochet Ruby a green tam.

Wed 26: Cold and cloudy today. Washed today. I crochet on the tam-o-shanter. Tomorrow is Thanksgiving.

Thu 27: Thanksgiving day. Didn't have much extra for dinner. Ruby wouldn't eat any and Ma couldn't eat much. Ruby & I went down to Tresidder's awhile this afternoon. Snowy all day. First of the season. Blanche trying to sleigh ride.

Fri 28: Snowy today. Rainy this evening. So afraid automobiling has gone up for this year or more. Baked bread coffee cake cookies cake.

Sat 29: A very bad day snowy, cold and very windy.

Sun 30: Very cold today. At home all day.

December

Mon 1:   Snowy a little most all day. Dad went to town this afternoon with Pet in the buggy.

Tue 2:   A nice day but cold. We washed today.

Wed 3:   We baked bread also a spice cake. John Weis, John Tresidder and we were going to send a car of cattle tomorrow, but John T backed out. Wants to take his hogs away tomorrow.

Thu 4:   I am terribly disappointed tonight. Wanted to go so badly over to the social at Independence. But hardly knew if I felt able or not. Got everything to fill a box. Had a notion to go with the car yet and have Dad go along. Heard Weis are going but they didn't say anything to us. Doesn't look very nice. I don't think. Feeling so bad. Lovly evening.

Fri 5:   Heard there wasn't a very big crowd to the social. There was twenty-six baskets but no young men to buy them. Made twenty-seven dollars. Ethel T was over. Also Will & Bessie Weis. Wilbur Bastian came over and bought four roosters. Evelyn came along. Talked like a streak. They brought us eight boxes of honey.

Sat 6: Snowed last night. Also quite heavily this afternoon. Dad & Ruby went to town this afternoon in the cutter.

Sun 7: This afternoon Ruby & I drove Pet in the cutter up to Davis'. They were quite surprised to see us. Mr. Davis had just come back from taking Bernetta down the Station to go to Scales Mound. But the rest were at home. Had a nice visit. Staid to supper. Dark before we got started for home. But it was quite light. Full moon tonight. Didn't have any company today.

Mon 8: Cold today. Just mending and crocheting and so on today.

Tue 9: Very cold again today. Don't get much done but chores. Dad & Ma went down to Tresidder's this evening.

Wed 10: Very cold again. Our thermometers were fourteen and eighteen degrees below zero. It was thirty below in Galena. We made two kitchen aprons this afternoon. Also crochet and etc. Uncle Edd came down this eve. He came out from town today. Don't know when they will come home as Mattie hasn't come back from Mary yet.

Thu 11: Well our cattle went today. Heard first this morning couldn't have a car. Then later on that we could. But didn't know if they could get ready and get them loaded in time or not. All had to rush around. Didn't know if Dad would go along to Chicago or not. John Weis, Tresidder and our cattle went. Sent six calves, two steers, one heifer and one bull. They got them over on time. But didn't have much time to waste. John Weis went along with them and Dad came along back again.

Fri 12: Warmer today. Baked bread, saffron bread and a cake today.

Sat 13: Another cold day. But Dad, Ruby & I went to Galena in the sleigh. My first sleigh ride and the first time we been to Galena with the teams for an awful long time. Had Violet and Pet. Quite a few in town today. Saw Santa Clause today. Uncle

Sun 14: ~~Very cold and clear~~ Edd came down this eve. Dad went over to John Weis'. Got the returns for the cattle. Got twelve seventy-five down there for the calves. Average sixty-eight sixty each. The heifer eight and one half cents or ninety dollars. One bull seven cents or sixty dollar ninety cents. Altogether when the expenses taken out six hundred ninety-eight nineteen cents.

Sun 14: Very cold and clear. Agnes, Milton, & Blanche came up this afternoon. This eve. Mother, sister and

I went up to Fiedler's. Saw the new house. It isn't finished yet. Will have nine rooms.

Mon 15: Cold again. Didn't do anything much in particular. Our line is crossed with several other lines. Heard on cross talk that Elmer Young has gone to Chicago about his arm. We got a letter from Uncle Joe Trudgian also a card from Mary Potter saying Aunt Hattie died Nov. 25 at seven a.m. She was buried at Centralia Wash.

Tue 16: We washed today. Also baked graham bread. Ruby received a note from L.S. asking if he could call next Sun.

Wed 17: Dad & Ma went to Galena today. Snowed a little today. It was predicted that the world would come to an end today or earthquakes and other disturbances. I received a card from Raymond Dittmar said he expected to come in soon.

Thu 18: We ironed today. It snowed some today.

Fri 19: We baked bread and coffee cake also filled cookies and churned. Not quite so cold today. The Zarndt and Young telephone line was connected on the Bell today.

Sat 20: Quite a lot of folks going to town today. Busy getting ready for company tomorrow.

Sun 21: Uncle Edd and Aunt Annie came down to dinner today. This afternoon about three oclock Leonard came. First call. Staid until about eight thirty or nine oclock.

Mon 22: Cloudy and frosty. Washed today. Dad drove over to Guilford to get the horses shod. But couldn't get it done. He got four pounds sugar. Had to take some other groceries with it. We are going to have a dozen men telephone men for dinner tomorrow.

Tue 23: We had eleven telephone men for dinner today. Got fifty-cents for each. But the way we figured it out we didn't make anything and all the work for nothing. Ruby & I went to Galena in the cutter this afternoon. Had Pet shod. Came back as far as Aunt Annie and Dad & Ma came up there this evening. Sent a Christmas booklet today.

Wed 24: Mother and Aunt Annie went to Apple River today. Uncle Edd took them to town. Baked bread and saffron bread today. Got a box from Uncle Thomas. Dad got a pair of gloves. Mother a little white apron. Ruby a box of corospndence cards. I a box of writing paper. I got a handkerchief and fifty cents last night. Five dollars today. Ruby & I gave Dad a razor and Ma a pair gloves. Sent lots of Christmas cards today.

Thu 25: Well Dad, Ruby & I had dinner together. Had mashed potatoes, creamed asparagus, baked sweet potatoes, pickles, celery, saffron cake, bread butter, chocolate pie, cake etc. We went down to Tresidder's for supper. Had a Christmas tree lit.

Fri 26: Busy choring all day. We ironed this eve. Quite warm today. Spoiling the sleighing.

Sat 27: Very busy all day. Ruby & I made doughnuts this afternoon. My first ones. They got very nice. Mother came home today. She rode out with the Tresidders. Ruby got a letter from L today.

Sun 28: Ruby & I went to Galena to church. Went to the Methodist Church. Heard a Christmas sermon. Quite a few there. But no neighbors. Came back to Aunt Annie's to dinner. Dad & Ma were up there to. Sleighing will be gone soon. We drove Pet in the cutter.

Mon 29: Dad and Ruby took chickens to Scales Mound. Twenty-two roosters at twenty-two cents and eight hens for twenty-three. They bought four roosters. Three Plymouth rocks and one black one. They got ten pounds sugar at by going three places at thirteen and fifteen cents per pound. Heard yesterday that the Equity folks were going to get sugar for eleven and one half cents per pound. Now they heard they have to pay nineteen and won't get it very soon. I guess there stung. They had a meeting about it last night.

Tue 30: We churned yesterday afternoon and night till midnight and all day today till about three or four this afternoon. It came at last. A beautiful day. Dad chopping in the woods this afternoon.

Wed 31: Well this is the last day of nineteen-nineteen. We washed today. Colder this evening. This eve Ruby is crocheting a rug. Mother knitting mittens. I crocheting a daisy filet crochet night gown yoke for Sis. Well nineteen-twenty is leap year. Have to get ready and get up courage.

Acknowledgements

A special *thank you* is extended to Barbara Gillam, who, with her husband Claude, moved into the Trudgian house after Lillian's death in 1974. Barbara and her husband restored the home and kindly gave this editor Lillian's diaries, as well as, other written pieces of the Trudgian family history. Most, including the diaries were rescued from the debris left behind in the house after Lillian's death.

A *thank you* also goes to Karlene Nesbitt White who has shared the text of Lillian's 1916 and 1917 diaries. Karlene has obtained these diaries through the Dittmar line rather than the Trudgian line.

Finally, I send my heartfelt *thanks* to my family. First to my husband, Dennis, who has patiently listened to me read passages from Lillian's diaries, even in the middle of a sport's event, as well as supported my search for more information about Lillian, our family and the Galena area. And to our daughters, Heather, Tambi and Melissa, who transcribed the first draft from the dusty, crumbling pages of the actual diaries and who help throughout the process of preparing this book to move their mother into the new age of technology. And, perhaps most of all, thank you to my mother, Dorothy Trudgian, who ignited the flame of searching for one's family's history.

Surnames Found in Lillian's 1913 thru 1919 Diaries

(surnames may appear as a single entry or as multiple entries in the indicated year(s))

Ahler-1915

Anchute -1914,1915

Allan/Allen-1913,1914,1918

Altfilich-1914

Atkinson-1913,1914

Bail-1914

Balbach-1914

Baumgardner-1916.1917

Bardell-1914,1915,1916

Barnes-1914

Barnum-1913,1915

Barrett-1918

Bastian-1913,1914,1915,1916,
1917,1918,1919

Bauer-1917

Baus-1918,1919

Bell-1919

Bench-1914

Benda-1917

Berryman-1914,1915,1918

Bird-1919

Birkbeck-1913,1914,1917,1918

Bixtin/Buxtin-1914

Bohnsack-1917

Bray-1913,1918

Brick-1915

Brickner-1913,1918,1919

Baumgardner/Baumgartner-1916,
1917

Bunker-1913,1915,1916,1917

Burton-1914

Callahan-1918

Carson-1913,1914

Cavanaugh-1918,1919

Charlton-1917

Chetlain-1918

Clark-1913,1915

Cleary-1913

Collins-1913,1914

Collier-1913

Combellicks-1913,1914,1915,
1916,1917,1918,1919

Cording-1914

Corey-1913

Curly-1913,1914,1915

Davis-913,1914,1915,
    1916,1919

Dillon-1918

Dinsdale-1913

Dittmar-1913,1914,1915,
    1916,1917,1918,1919

Drink-1913

Dolamore-1914,1916,1917

Dower-1913,1914,
    1915,1918,1919

Duggan-1914

Dunne-1913

Durrstein-1917

Dwyer-1916

Edgerton-1918

Ehrler-1913,1914,1915,1918

Erby-1913

Eustice-1914,1917

Falancer-1913,1914,1919

Fiedler-1913,1914,1915,
    1916,1917,1918,1919

Fisher-1915

Fitch-1919

Franklin-1915

Freeman-1914,1915

Fritz-1913,1914,1917

Ford-1913,1914,1915,1916,
    1917,1918

Fuller-1914,1915

Funk-1913

Gaber-1916

Garrity-1913,1914,1915

Gesselbrachts-1916,1917,1918

Genshirt-1913

Gill-1913,1917

Ginn-1913

Glasco-1915

Glick-1913,1914,1915,1919

Graham-1913,1915,1918,1919

Grebner-1913,1916

Griswold-1914

Grube-1913,1917,1918

Grundy-1915,1918

Gunnow-1915

Hacker-1915,1917

Hammer-1914,1915,1916,
   1918,1917,1919

Hammon-1913

Hansen/Hanson-1915,1919

Haines-1916,1917

Hardy-1918

Hart-1913,1915

Hathaway-1919

Heer-1913,1914,1915,1916,
   1919

Heuberger-1914

Hick-1914,1915,1916

Hocking-1913,1914,1916,1917

Horsch-1919

Huilman-1914

Isbell-1913

Ivy-1914,1915

Kasner-1913

Keister-1917

Kinsler-1915

Kittoe-1914,1915

Kloth-1914,1915,1916,
   1917,1918

Laird-1913

Lenor/Lennor-1913,1916

Levins-1915

Liston-1917,1919

Lipton/Lupton-1914,1915,1917

Logan-1916.1917

Long-1916

Madlock/Matlock-1915

Madoo-1914

Magret-1916

Mahan-1918

Malloy-1913

Marsden-1914,1918

Machurkin-1914

MacDonald/McDonald-1914,
   1918,1919

Menzemer-1914

Merrifield-1913,1914,1917.1918

Meusel-1918

Miguet-1913

Miller-1914,1915

Milton-1914

Monnier-1913,1914.1915,
   1916,1917

Muller-1914

Mumford-1918

Ortscheid-1914

Palmer-1916,1917,1918,1919

Pearson-1917,1918

Pemperlys-1913

Pooley-1913,1914,1915,
1918,1919

Popp-1913,1914,1915,
1916,1917

Potter-1915,1916

Poundstone-1915

Polchow-1918

Pratt-1916,1917

Price-1919

Pulco-1913,1918

Rawlins-1918

Reddington-1919

Redfern-1913,1914

Reed-1918

Rice-1918

Ritter-1914,1916

Rittwagers-1914

Robert-1914,1918

Robinson-1913

Rouse-1918

Sander-1916,1917

Sanderson-1914

Schlichting-1913,1919

Schoenhard-1913,1914

Seck-1913,1919

Shaneheart-1913

Shapp-1915,1919

Sheean-1913,1916

Shulty-1913

Shultz/Schultz-1913,1914,
1916,1917,1918

Siefert-1918

Siemen-1918

Siegel-1918

Sigerman-1917

Sincox/Sincock-1913,1919

Slattery-1917

Smart-1913,1915,1918

Smith-1913

Snow-1919

Spear-1916

Spencer/Spenser-1913,1914,
1915,1916,1917.1918

Spensley-1913,1917,1919

Stauss-1913,1914,1916, 1917,1919

Stephan/Stephen-1913

Stadel-1915,1918

Studier-1914,1915,1917,1918, 1919

Sutton-1916,1919

Swift-1914

Swing-1919

Taylor-1917

Temperly-1913,1915,1916,1917

Tippet-1913,1914,1915,1916, 1917,1918,1919

Tobin-1913,1914,1915,1916, 1917

Trask-1913

Tresidder-1913,1914,1915,1916, 1917,1918,1919

Tressel-1913

Trevarthen/Trevarthan-1913, 1914,1915,1917,1918

Trudgian-1913,1914,1915,1916, 1917,1918,1919

Tyrell-1914

Vincent-1913

Virtue-1913,1914,1915,1916, 1917,1918,1919

Wachter-1913,1914,1915,1917

Walters-1915

Warren-1913, 1917

Weis-1913,1914,1915,1916, 1917,1918,1919

Weizel-1913

Werner-1913,1914.1915,1916, 1917,1918,1919

Westaby-1913,1914,1916,1917, 1918,1919

White-1918,1919

Williams-1913,1914,1915,1916

Willy-1919

Wilson-1919

Wingler-1919

Winsicker-1919

Winter(s)-1914,1915,1917,1916

Woodside-1913

Young-1913,1914,1915,1916, 1917,1918,1919

Zarndt-1916,1917,1918,1919

Zimmerman-1918,1919

Made in the USA